SNOOKER YEAR

To Chris,

All the best for 1988

Love

Terry Smith

BENSON and HEDGES
SNOOKER YEAR

FOURTH EDITION EDITED BY TERRY SMITH
ASSOCIATE EDITOR DENNIS TAYLOR

PELHAM BOOKS

First published in Great Britain by
Pelham Books Ltd
27 Wrights Lane
Kensington
London W8 5TZ
1987

British Library Cataloguing in Publication Data
Benson and Hedges snooker year. —1987–
1. Snooker—Periodicals
794.7′35′05   GV900.S6
ISBN 0 7207 1797 3

Typeset by Goodfellow & Egan, Cambridge
Printed and bound in Great Britain
by Hazell, Watson & Viney Ltd., Aylesbury

CONTENTS

ACKNOWLEDGEMENTS

My thanks go to my journalistic colleagues in and out of Fleet Street: Alexander Clyde *(London Evening Standard)*, Roy Collins *(Today)*, Ron Gubba, John Hennessy *(Daily Mail)*, Gaye Jones, Jean Rafferty and Karen Smyth. Referees John Street and John Williams have provided valuable assistance, as have Martyn Blake of the WPBSA and David Ford of the B&SCC. Associated editor Dennis Taylor has supplied an informative introduction, while Mark Wildman has given a deep insight into the revival of billiards. Indeed, all players and officials have responded superbly to my constant badgering for information. No book is complete without pictures, and the following photographers have supplied prints of quality: Allsport (on pages 37, 42, 45 *below*, 66 and 103 *below left*); Frank Fennell (on pages 38 *above* and 72); David Muscroft and Trevor Smith (on pages 10, 11, 14, 26, 38 *below*, 43 *above*, 44, 46, 59, 62, 68, 76, 79, 82, 84, 101, 102 *below*, 103 *above right*, 107, 110, 113, 114, 119, 120, 121, 124); the Press Association Ltd (on page 16); Jos Reypens (on pages 125, 126 and 131); M. Ward (on page 30) and Eric Whitehead (on pages 27 *above* and 29). Grateful thanks are due to Benson and Hedges and Pelham Books for giving me the exciting challenge of compiling this yearbook. Finally, I must praise four hard-working ladies – my wife Eileen for checking and re-checking the facts and figures, Pat Mead for hours of typing, Monica Chia for designing the book and Ruth Baldwin who prepared the manuscript for the printer, corrected the proofs and bullied me to keep to impossible deadlines.

WE'RE TAKING OVER THE WORLD

by Dennis Taylor

Snooker is ready to take over the world sporting stage. I'm convinced that the game is going to double in popularity in the next ten years, and I feel sure that those people who say we have reached a peak will be proved wrong. Snooker is the number one sport in these islands and that's where we intend it to stay. There is no sign that it has yet arrived at saturation point here, and now the world is waiting for us. And when we 'explode' world-wide, I'm sure that extra popularity will create even more interest at home.

I can hardly believe what has been achieved in snooker while I have been connected with the game. It's amazing how far we have travelled since I started out back in 1971. Snooker used to have a seedy image of back-street halls and clubs: not any more. Pay a visit to your local club and you are very likely to find top businessmen rolling up their sleeves for a game in their lunch-hour. They might still have their gin-and-tonics but they will be drinking them in one of the many, many high-class snooker clubs that have sprung up all over the UK.

Snooker is now a sport that encompasses all sections of the community. There is no favoured group: everyone can join in – and that's not only in Britain. Just look what is happening overseas. I have been travelling the globe for many years (in fact, I have been going to Australia for thirteen years) and I am thrilled by the recent increase in snooker's popularity.

Let's take Hong Kong: the growth rate over there is phenomenal. If you think we have a lot of tables in British clubs, then nip over to Hong Kong and take a peek behind the scenes. One club I visited must have had forty private rooms. I glanced in and was amazed at what I saw. In each room were whole families who had booked for an afternoon or even a whole day. Snooker was their family day out. Mum would be sitting doing the knitting, the youngsters would be watching the television and dad and eldest son would be playing snooker. They would order refreshments and spend the day together. That seems a great idea.

I have also visited Japan. Tony Meo and I were the first professionals to play a match out there in 1986. The response was quite staggering considering they had never seen snooker. We had to work hard through interpreters to tell them the rules and the object of the game, but they were so keen and loved every minute. That market could be quite a breakthrough.

Then, of course, there is China. We held a tournament in Peking early in 1987. I heard that 170 million – yes, 170 million – people watched the final between Jimmy White and Willie Thorne live on television.

All smiles: Dennis Taylor

Perhaps surprisingly, the really tough market to break into must be the United States. The problem there is that they have played pool for so many years. It's going to be a long hard struggle to establish a foothold in Uncle Sam's country, but we'll keep trying. Steve Davis, our number 1, and Steve Mizerak, one of the all-time great pool players, took part in the Fiat Snooker/Pool Challenge in St Moritz, Switzerland, last summer. It was shown coast to coast in prime time on ESPN, America's sports channel. That was tremendous news.

Yes, the 1990s should see snooker firmly established as a world-wide sport. The possibilities are endless — a World Series circuit, as in tennis, is one exciting opening that is being developed.

For the past couple of years Europe has been the main target area for 'conversion to the cause'. The only really popular table game there at the moment is carom — a type of billiards without pockets. Yet continental audiences already enjoy the televised snooker they pick up from our TV companies and I'm sure they will soon love our game. I have played in Belgium and West Germany and found that the people of those countries took to snooker immediately.

Talking of overseas — I was delighted by the performance of Dene O'Kane in the 1987 World Championship. To beat Cliff Thorburn and take 9 frames in a row was certainly an impressive performance by the young New Zealander. Dene came to the UK a few years ago as a young man to a new country and new environment. To be honest, he didn't have a good start to his career, and he must take a lot of credit for the way he stuck at his task. And now, thanks to Dene, New Zealand could start to take a much bigger interest in snooker. I understand that, during the World Championship, the lines were hot in the press room with, seemingly, every New Zealand television and radio station and all the newspapers trying to get hold of their likeable young countryman.

Going places: Dene O'Kane, the New Zealander who shocked Cliff Thorburn at the World Championship.

Many people ask me if I ever get fed up with talking about the 1985 World Championship final when I potted that last black to beat Steve Davis 18–17. The short answer is 'No': how can I get bored with talking about the greatest sporting moment of my life? And, of course, snooker fans want to chat about that night. I'm still amazed that 18.5 million people stayed up until 12.23am to watch the final frame. It just shows you what a grip this sport has on the country. I'll be upset when they start forgetting. I just hope it's not for a long while.

Looking back: Dennis Taylor after winning the epic 1985 World Championship final.

Rothmans Grand Prix at Reading. That will always be special. I had been on the professional circuit for thirteen years and never won a title. Then in 1987 I finally achieved success at the Benson and Hedges Masters at Wembley. For some reason I had never played well at Wembley, and until 1986 I hadn't even won a match. When I finally broke the duck by beating Doug Mountjoy, I did a lap of honour around the table. The people in the crowd must have thought I had gone mad.

I won the Masters by beating Alex Higgins 9–8 in the final. That was quite a match. I was 8–5 behind and was told later that Alex's champagne was already on ice waiting for him to win. I'm sorry I had to spoil the party.

I have often been asked why I took so many years to start winning tournaments. I reply that I wanted to wait until the prize money was really worthwhile!

Now I hope that the Irish can win the Tuborg World Team Cup for the fourth successive time in 1988. One thing is certain – I will be using the cue that my pet dog, a West Highland Terrier called Chalkie, chewed rather badly at the tip. I stopped using the cue, but that is something I shouldn't have done. I started playing with it again – teethmarks and all – and I won the Masters. Thanks, Chalkie!

The funny thing is that I had the video recording of the final frame at home for a long time but I never watched it. It was only when David Vine, of the BBC, came round to my house a few months later to interview me that I watched the whole frame for the first time since playing it. I hadn't seen it on TV but I could remember every shot in my mind. That's a night – sorry, early morning – that I will never forget.

Of course, there have been other major highlights in my career. My big break-through came in 1984 when I won the

SPONSOR'S MESSAGE

In its first three editions the *Benson and Hedges Snooker Year* proved its popularity as an authoritative report on the sport of snooker.

Now, with a completely new look, even more information is included: profiles of the snooker stars and the sport's characters; the tournaments, the activity behind the scenes, and the game's effect on the world of sport as a whole.

The book takes an in-depth look at the way television has dominated snooker and turned a pastime into the most popular sport on the small screen. Dennis Taylor, our distinguished Associate Editor, looks into the future to predict that snooker is now ready to become even stronger on a world-wide basis. Our photographers have captured some of the best action from the past season – on and off the table. There is also a fascinating comparison between the two main 'camps' of the snooker world – Barry Hearn's Matchroom squad and the team built up by Howard Kruger of Framework. We have even remembered the ladies: their side of the sport is growing all the time. We look in depth at the career of Allison Fisher, the best-known female player on the circuit.

Most important this year is the inclusion, for the first time, of the complete Official Rules of Billiards and Snooker. This will enable *all* snooker players to reach for our book when they wish to sort out those little technical problems that create discussion and controversy in snooker clubs up and down the country.

We feel sure that this edition, published by Pelham Books and edited by one of the top writers on snooker, Terry Smith, will provide an enjoyable reminder of the past season for enthusiasts and all those professionally involved in the game.

John Slade
Marketing Manager – Benson and Hedges,
on behalf of the company.

WIN A SEAT AT THE BENSON AND HEDGES MASTERS 1988

You too can enjoy the spectacle and excitement at Wembley during the final of the Benson and Hedges Masters 1988.

Just answer the following questions correctly and complete the tie-breaker, and you and your guest could be one of three couples to be entertained by Benson and Hedges.

QUESTIONS

1   Whom did Dennis Taylor beat in the 1986 Benson and Hedges Masters final?

2   When was the first Benson and Hedges Masters held?

3   Who made a 147 break during the 1984 Benson and Hedges Masters?

Now complete the tie-breaker below in not more than 15 words:

'I would like to see the 1988 Benson and Hedges Champion pot the winning shot at Wembley because ....

....

Write your entry on a postcard and send to:

BENSON AND HEDGES SNOOKER YEAR
43 KING STREET
LONDON WC2E 8JS

Entries must be received by 1 January 1988.

Do not forget to include your name, address and telephone number.

RULES

1   Entrants must be aged 18 years or over, resident in the United Kingdom and not employees, or their families, of Gallaher Limited, Benson and Hedges Limited, or their advertising agencies.

2   Three winners and their guests will be awarded tickets to the Benson and Hedges Masters 1988. The winners will be the entrants who, in the opinion of the judges, have correctly answered the questions and completed the tie-breaker in the most apt and original manner.

3   The prize must be taken as and when described. There is no cash alternative to the prize. No entrant may win more than one prize.

4   Closing date for receipt of entries for the competition is 1 January 1988. Proof of posting is not accepted as proof of delivery.

5   Any entries that are received after the closing date will not be considered and no responsibility can be accepted for entries that are lost or delayed in the post or otherwise, or which were offered for delivery insuf-ficiently stamped. Entries received incomplete, illegible, mutilated, altered or not complying with the competition rules and instructions exactly will be disqualified.

6   The decision of the panel of judges will be final and legally binding and no correspondence will be entered into. The panel of judges will include at least one member independent of the promoter and its agents.

7   The solution to the competition, the names and counties of the winners and the names of the judges will be available to all applicants who send an s.a.e. to the competition address after the closing date.

8   All entrants will be deemed to have accepted and agreed to be bound by the competition rules and instructions.

9   All entries will automatically become the property of Benson and Hedges Limited, and will not be returned.

10 Promoter: Benson & Hedges Limited,
        13 Old Bond Street,
        London, W1X 4QP.

DRUGS, BUTTS AND BETS – BUT SNOOKER'S A WINNER

by Terry Smith

Listen to some people and you might believe that professional snooker is full of money-grabbing young men who are high on drugs and spend their life gambling. Of course, snooker has skeletons in the cupboard – can you name one other popular sport that doesn't have problems in its ranks? But, for some reason, snooker last season became the sport to knock. It was fashionable.

> #### WHO SAID THAT?
>
> 'I am going away to learn to swim and drive. The last time I drove a car, I went broadside into a corporation van.'
>
> ▲
>
> *– Alex Higgins after being knocked out of the World Championship and beginning his five-tournament ban*

There was the now-infamous Alex Higgins head-butting affair, which justified every column inch it received. Here was a sporting superstar – a man who had done more for one game than possibly any other individual. Suddenly he had 'gone over the top'. The press had forgiven Alex many times in the past and I'm sure we will do the same in the future. But this incident at the Tennents UK Open at Preston was different. He had broken the snooker code before, but this time he had shattered it to smithereens.

Higgins paid the penalty – £250 in a Preston magistrates court and then a £12,000 fine and a five-tournament ban imposed by Gavin Lightman, QC, at an independent inquiry set up by the WPBSA. Higgins was a lucky man: in other sports he might never have been seen again. Time

Together again: Alex Higgins and WPBSA tournament director Paul Hatherell at a press conference during the Embassy World Championship.

Family man: South African star Silvino Francisco, wife Denise and young son Dominic.

is a great healer, however. Let us hope he hasn't stained his character beyond repair.

Then other 'stories' started to emerge, starting with the 'betting coup' reports. One such 'coup' was suggested to have taken place in the Mercantile Credit Classic match between Silvino Francisco and his nephew Peter Francisco. That was followed by reports that the match between Tony Meo and Tony Knowles at the Irish Benson and Hedges Masters at Goffs, County Kildare, was 'fixed'. One Irish journalist, John Martin, later put forward the sound theory that it was the results of one Irish bookmaker laying off a big bet with other bookmakers.

Paul Hatherell, the WPBSA tournament director, reported that details of the alleged betting coup at the Mercantile Credit and at a Benson and Hedges Match in 1985 had been passed over to the Fraud Squad at Scotland Yard, but they found no evidence of any such coup. Surely these top players have far too much to lose to involve themselves in this kind of activity. In Ireland the suggested amount lost by the bookies didn't even top £10,000. What player, who could earn a minimum of £50,000 a year, would risk all for such a miserly amount? 'The bookmakers only scream when they lose,' suggested Willie Thorne, a player who knows more about betting than most. 'They don't shout when they win.'

In Ireland the odds were so generous on some matches that even I might have invested a few pounds of the Smith 'fortune' if a bookmaker had been on site at the venue. 'With odds like that, the bookies deserved to catch a cold,' was one observation from an Irish punter. 'They got the odds all wrong and then blamed the players.'

There was more alleged scandal to come. While Steve Davis was amassing more than £300,000 in one season and Ireland were winning the team trophy for the third successive year, the behind-the-scenes scandal-mongers were hard at work. 'Beta-blockers' emerged as a new word for the sporting dictionary and the press was immediately full of beta-blocker experts. Doctors, MPs, the Sports Council and newspapers all became preoccupied with these drugs. (Beta-blockers are prescribed for people primarily suffering from nervous complaints and minor heart disorders. They have a calming effect which some people feel gives snooker players an advantage.)

'Get out now, Rex,' screamed the headline in the *Star* calling for Rex Williams to quit the Embassy World Championship for taking beta-blockers. 'This sick joke,' said the same paper when young Neal Foulds was prescribed the tablets for a heart complaint. There was even a suggestion in one quarter that the players were 'cheating' by taking this medicine. The 'antis' said it was on the banned list of the International Olympic Committee – but snooker is not yet an Olympic sport!

To be fair, the Sports Council did praise the WPBSA for their drug-testing procedures and said that no other sport tested so many players. The WPBSA stuck to their guns and said that as long as the medicine was properly prescribed, they would allow a player taking it to continue playing. As Foulds said, 'I didn't worry about snooker when they told me I had to take tablets – I just wanted to stay alive.' Williams has been taking the same tablets for seventeen years following a nervous

Money, money, money . . . John Virgo, WPBSA vice-chairman, Neal Foulds, ITV celebrity Dickie Davies and Rex Williams, WPBSA chairman, celebrate after the signing of the ITV contract in London.

breakdown. And John Spencer, one of the game's most respected figures, also admitted having beta-blockers as part of the daily intake of steroid tablets that he needs to help his serious double-vision problems. 'What would happen if I didn't take the tablets?' said Spencer: 'I would die.' Who would want that on their conscience?

Finally we had poor old Ted Lowe, the doyen of snooker commentators, plastered all over the front page of the *Sun* after it was revealed that his wife had left him. And Jimmy White was the subject of a 'Hooked on Drugs' charge in the *Sunday People*.

In the end, however, snooker was the winner. The sport finished the season as strong as ever. ITV recorded record viewing figures of 15.2 million for the Mercantile Credit Classic final between White and Steve Davis. And there was a tremendous Embassy World Championship won su-

> **WHO SAID THAT?**
>
> 'We had 15.2 million watching the final of the Mercantile Credit Classic between Steve Davis and Jimmy White. That's one of the biggest viewing figures we have achieved for any sport.'
>
> ———— ▲ ————
>
> *– Trevor East, an ITV executive sports producer*

perbly by Davis – an 18–14 victor over Joe Johnson. ITV have signed a £1.5 million deal to screen snooker until 1992 while the BBC contract lasts until 1990.

Many people are still writing and broadcasting that snooker has reached its peak – but they were saying that back at the start of the 1980s. John Bromley, head of sport at ITV, summed it all up when he said, 'The talk of snooker being a nine-day wonder is ridiculous – we don't invest £1.5 million in a bubble that is about to burst.'

THE WPBSA AND WHAT IT STANDS FOR

The initials 'WPBSA' stand for 'World Professional Billiards and Snooker Association', which is the controlling body for all professional snooker and billiards. Its main objective is to promote the sport in the UK and throughout the world.

The WPBSA started life in 1968 as the Professional Billiards Players Association with just eight members on the books. It changed its name in 1971 and has grown ever since. The real breakthrough came in 1976 with a lucky meeting at Chester races between Rex Williams, the chairman of the WPBSA, and BBC sports executive Nick Hunter. Hunter told Williams that he wanted to promote snooker on the television screen, and from that moment snooker and the WPBSA have gone from strength to strength.

The Association has over 130 members but only 128 are full tournament status members who are allowed to take in the six ranking tournaments on the professional circuit. Other players are non-tournament status members who can only play in the World Championship. There are also billiards-only members – this once-dying sport is enjoying a revival with tournaments in the UK and abroad.

In charge: WPBSA chairman Rex Williams.

The WPBSA takes control of all policy decisions and looks after the financial affairs of billiards and snooker. That means master-minding all tournament and television contracts and, of course, liaising with the other media. The Association also has a promotions company – WPBSA Promotions Ltd – which runs snooker day by day. The company is responsible to the main board of the Association. The WPBSA is based in Bristol in the charming suburb of Clifton, where its headquarters boast the best in latest office technology – a vital link helping the tremendous growth of this game into the multi-million-pound boom sport of the 1980s.

Professional snooker and billiards are run by the players for the players who vote in the board of directors. Any player who, during the three previous years, has been in

WHO SAID THAT?

'I resent any suggestion that the earlier plan of using the top twenty-four players for the World Cup was made because three members of the board would have benefited. Comments that we would have been guaranteed prize money and television exposure are disgraceful.'

▲

– *Rex Williams on the switch back to the country-style format for the World Cup*

the top twenty is eligible to vote. Any player can stand for the board which is currently made up of ten members – seven players and three non-players. Each director can serve for three years and can offer himself for re-election.

Control point: The WPBSA headquarters in Clifton, Bristol.

WHAT'S ON IN 1987/88:
SNOOKER AND BILLIARDS

PROPOSED SNOOKER TOURNAMENT DATES

DATES	EVENT	VENUE
1987		
Aug 28–31	World Series – British Caledonian Masters	Tokyo
Sept 2–6	World Series – Hong Kong Masters	Hong Kong
Sept 9–12	Fidelity Unit Trusts International (Prelims)	Trentham Gardens, Stoke-on-Trent
Sept 14–16	Carlsberg Challenge	RTE Studios, Dublin
Sept 16–23	Rothmans Grand Prix (Prelims)	Redwood Lodge, Bristol
Sept 17–20	Langs Supreme Scottish Masters	Glasgow
Sept 25–Oct 4	Fidelity Unit Trusts International (Finals)	Trentham Gardens, Stoke-on-Trent
Oct 7–13	Tennents UK Open (Prelims)	Bolton Town Hall, Bolton
Oct 17–25	Rothmans Grand Prix (Finals)	Hexagon Theatre, Reading
Oct 26–28	Hofmeister World Doubles (Prelims)	Crest Hotel, Portsmouth
Oct 28–Nov 1	World Series – Canadian Masters	Toronto
Oct 29–31	MIM Britannia British Open (Prelims)	Bournemouth International Centre, Bournemouth
Nov 7–10	Mercantile Credit Classic (Prelims)	Norbreck Castle, Blackpool
Nov 13–18, 21–29	Tennents UK Open (Finals)	Guild Hall, Preston
Dec 1–13	Hofmeister World Doubles (Finals)	Derngate Centre, Northampton
Dec 12–16	Tolly Ales English Championship (Prelims)	Redwood Lodge, Bristol
Dec 16–20	World Series – US Masters	Las Vegas

All dates and venues are subject to change without notification.

Dates	Event	Venue
1988		
Jan 1–10	Mercantile Credit Classic (Finals)	Norbreck Castle, Blackpool
Jan 24–31	Benson and Hedges Masters	Wembley Conference Centre, London
Feb 4–6, 8–10	Tolly Ales English Championship (Finals)	Corn Exchange, Ipswich
Feb 8–12	Welsh Professional Championship	Newport Leisure Centre
Feb 8–12	Irish Professional Championship	
Feb 11–14	Scottish Professional Championship	Glasgow
Feb 21–24, Feb 26–March 6	British Open (Finals)	Assembly Rooms, Derby
March 16–19	Tuborg World Cup	Bournemouth International Centre, Bournemouth
March 22–27	Benson and Hedges Irish Masters	Goffs, County Kildare
March 22–April 2	Embassy World Championship (Prelims)	Guild Hall, Preston
April 16–May 2	Embassy World Championship (Finals)	Crucible Theatre, Sheffield

PROPOSED BILLIARDS TOURNAMENT DATES

Dates	Event	Venue
1987		
Dec 17–19	Monarflex World Billiards (Prelims)	Redwood Lodge, Bristol
1988		
Jan 16–23	UK Championship	Middlesbrough
Feb 13–20	Professional Players' Tournament	Leeds
March 5–12	Monarflex World Billiards (Finals)	Bolton Town Hall, Bolton
To be arranged:	European Championship	Antwerp

All dates and venues are subject to change without notification.

THE RANKINGS AND HOW THEY WORK

There are six ranking snooker tournaments every season which count towards the world ranking list. This list reflects how many points each player has picked up in those events in the preceding two years – his position is determined on his showings in the previous twelve ranking tournaments.

Once the world list has been drawn up at the start of the season, there is no alteration. In tennis, rankings change tournament by tournament; in snooker, players keep the same ranking all season. It might be a better guide to form to change rankings after each event, but this proves impractical because in some events the early rounds take place months before the final stages of the tournament.

Every player in the lower ranks has one immediate aim – a place in the top sixteen. After he has reached that elite top group, there is less pressure on him in the qualifying

The King and the Young Pretender: Steve Davis, world number 1, and Stephen Hendry, world number 23.

rounds, and then the ultimate dream is to take over the number 1 spot from Steve Davis.

The six ranking tournaments in the 1986/87 season were (in order of playing): BCE International, Rothmans Grand Prix, Tennents UK Open, Mercantile Credit Classic, Dulux British Open and Embassy World Championship. In all ranking tournaments, apart from the World Championship, points are awarded as follows:

Winner	6	points
Runner-up	5	points
Losing semi-finalist	4	points
Losing quarter-finalist	3	points
Fifth-round loser	2	points
Fourth-round loser	1	point
Third-round loser	1	merit point
Second-round loser	1	'A' point
First-round loser	Frames won in match	

The World Championship is the most prestigious tournament of the season and higher points are awarded, as follows:

Winner	10	points
Runner up	8	points
Losing semi-finalist	6	points
Losing quarter-finalist	4	points
Second-round loser	2	points
First-round loser	1	ranking point unless member of top sixteen who receive 2 merit points
Fourth-round prelim-round loser	2	merit points
Third-round prelim-round loser	1	merit point
Second-round prelim-round loser	1	'A' point
First-round prelim-round loser	Frames won in match	

In the event of ties on ranking points, the player who has picked up most ranking points in the most recent season is allocated a higher placing. If there is still a tie, the player with the greatest number of merit points is given the higher placing. If scores are still equal, the number of merit points in the preceding season applies. In the unlikely event that players are still level, their positions are decided on 'A' points followed by frames won. If, by a remote chance, the players still cannot be separated, their performances in the preceding World Championship will determine their ranking order; and, if this method fails, the other ranking tournaments are worked through in reverse order until the players' positions can be established.

THE WORLD PROFESSIONAL BILLIARDS AND SNOOKER ASSOCIATION
OFFICIAL WORLD RANKING LIST 1987/88
(Previous season's position in brackets)

POSITION	NAME	R	M	A	F
1 (1)	S. Davis (Eng)	61	–	–	–
2 (5)	J. White (Eng)	46	2	–	–
3 (13)	N. Foulds (Eng)	38	1	–	–
4 (2)	C. Thorburn CM (Can)	38	3	–	–
5 (8)	J. Johnson (Eng)	33	1	–	–
6 (10)	T. Griffiths (Wales)	30	1	–	–
7 (4)	A. Knowles (Eng)	29	3	–	–
8 (3)	Den. Taylor (NI)	25	4	–	–
9 (6)	A. Higgins (NI)	25	1	–	–
10 (12)	S. Francisco (SA)	22	2	–	–
11 (7)	W. Thorne (Eng)	22	6	–	–
12 (16)	R. Williams (Eng)	20	4	–	–
13 (17)	J. Parrott (Eng)	18	4	–	–
14 (14)	D. Mountjoy (Wales)	17	2	–	–
15 (29)	D. Reynolds (Eng)	16	3	–	–
16 (27)	M. Hallett (Eng)	16	2	–	–
17 (23)	C. Wilson (Wales)	16	5	–	–
18 (26)	P. Francisco (SA)	16	4	1	–
19 (19)	J. Virgo (Eng)	16	1	–	–
20 (11)	A. Meo (Eng)	16	6	–	–
21 (9)	K. Stevens (Can)	16	6	–	–
22 (18)	J. Campbell (Aust)	15	3	–	–
23 (51)	S. Hendry (Scot)	14	1	3	–
24 (20)	E. Hughes (Rep Ire)	13	5	–	6
25 (21)	Dav. Taylor (Eng)	12	6	–	–
26 (25)	E. Charlton AM (Aust)	10	6	–	–
27 (28)	D. Martin (Eng)	10	3	–	–
28 (34)	J. Spencer (Eng)	9	7	–	–
29 (30)	B. West (Eng)	9	6	–	4
30 (22)	M. Macleod (Scot)	9	8	–	–
31 (31)	S. Longworth (Eng)	8	7	1	–
32 (37)	A. Drago (Malta)	8	2	3	–
33 (24)	W. Werbeniuk (Can)	8	8	–	6
34 (56)	W. Jones (Wales)	7	6	2	–
35 (39)	D. O'Kane (NZ)	7	6	3	–
36 (32)	J. Wych (Can)	7	7	1	–
37 (35)	S. Duggan (Eng)	7	5	3	–
38 (15)	R. Reardon MBE (Wales)	6	8	–	–
39 (41)	W. King (Aust)	6	6	2	–
40 (33)	D. Fowler (Eng)	5	7	2	–
41 (53)	R. Chaperon (Can)	4	7	2	–
42 (38)	M. Gauvreau (Can)	4	5	6	–
43 (48)	P. Browne (Rep Ire)	4	2	7	–
44 (57)	T. Murphy (NI)	3	9	3	–
45 (40)	S. Newbury (Wales)	3	9	3	–
46 (55)	A. Jones (Eng)	3	9	1	–
47 (43)	M. Wildman (Eng)	3	8	2	5
48 (50)	G. Cripsey (Eng)	3	6	2	–
49 (45)	R. Harris (Eng)	3	6	3	–
50 (71)	J. McLaughlin (NI)	2	7	3	–
51 (68)	L. Dodd (Eng)	2	6	5	–
52 (–)	K. Owers (Eng)	2	3	1	2
53 (–)	J. Wright (Eng)	2	2	1	2
54 (–)	M. Bennett (Wales)	2	2	–	12
55 (65)	J. O'Boye (Rep Ire)	2	7	2	8
56 (54)	M. Bradley (Eng)	2	7	4	–
57 (66)	R. Bales (Eng)	2	2	6	9
58 (49)	A. Chappel (Wales)	2	7	4	–
59 (46)	R. Edmonds (Eng)	2	5	6	–
60 (44)	G. Scott (Eng)	2	5	5	–
61 (47)	F. Davis OBE (Eng)	2	3	7	–
62 (79)	G. Foulds (Eng)	1	5	5	1
63 (112)	R. Grace (SA)	1	2	2	13
64 (91)	P. Houlihan (Eng)	1	3	3	25
65 (101)	A. Kearney (Rep Ire)	1	–	8	15
66 (–)	S. James (Eng)	1	8	3	7
67 (58)	P. Medati (Eng)	1	9	4	–
68 (52)	G. Miles (Eng)	1	8	3	–
69 (62)	John Rea (Scot)	1	7	4	–
70 (60)	M. Gibson (Scot)	1	7	4	–
71 (59)	J. van Rensburg (SA)	1	6	6	–
72 (63)	V. Harris (Eng)	1	5	6	–
73 (61)	B. Mikkelsen (Can)	1	5	6	–
74 (64)	I. Black (Scot)	1	4	7	–
75 (42)	P. Fagan (Rep Ire)	1	3	7	–
76 (70)	E. Sinclair (Scot)	–	8	4	–
77 (75)	M. Morra (Can)	–	6	6	–
78 (74)	C. Roscoe (Wales)	–	6	5	3
79 (69)	R. Foldvari (Aust)	–	6	7	–
80 (67)	I. Williamson (Eng)	–	4	8	–
81 (77)	M. Watterson (Eng)	–	4	2	8
82 (72)	D. Gilbert (Eng)	–	4	5	17
83 (–)	D. Roe (Eng)	–	3	3	–
84 (84)	B. Oliver (Eng)	–	3	9	4

POSITION		NAME	R	M	A	F
85	(86)	G. Rigitano (Can)	–	3	8	5
86	(82)	J. Bear (Can)	–	3	4	4
87	(73)	J. Donnelly (Scot)	–	3	7	8
88	(76)	J. Fitzmaurice (Eng)	–	3	5	8
89	(78)	M. Darrington (Eng)	–	3	3	13
90	(–)	B. Rowswell (Eng)	–	2	3	1
91	(85)	J. Meadowcroft (Eng)	–	2	8	6
92	(87)	M. Fisher (Eng)	–	2	7	8
93	(95)	G. Jenkins (Aust)	–	2	5	8
94	(81)	D. Sheehan (Rep Ire)	–	2	4	18
95	(98)	F. Jonik (Can)	–	1	7	12
96	(102)	Glen Wilkinson (Aust)	–	1	6	13
97	(104)	P. Burke (Rep Ire)	–	1	5	23
98	(–)	P. Gibson (Eng)	–	1	4	6
99	(–)	N. Gilbert (Eng)	–	1	4	1
100	(116)	I. Anderson (Aust)	–	1	1	–
101	(110)	J. Rempe (USA)	–	1	1	2
102	(88)	B. Kelly (Rep Ire)	–	1	9	11
103	(83)	J. Dunning (Eng)	1	1	4	20
104	(92)	J. Hargreaves (Eng)	1	4	20	17
105	(93)	D. Hughes (Eng)	–	1	4	–
106	(90)	E. McLaughlin (Scot)	–	1	4	29
107	(94)	M. Smith (Eng)	–	1	3	8
108	(96)	G. Watson (Can)	–	1	–	6
109	(97)	P. Thornley (Can)	–	1	9	11
110	(99)	D. Chalmers (Eng)	–	–	9	6
111	(103)	Jack Rea (NI)	–	–	7	7
112	(100)	C. Everton (Wales)	–	–	7	7

POSITION		NAME	R	M	A	F
113	(106)	P. Watchorn (Rep Ire)	–	–	5	26
114	(108)	D. Mienie (SA)	–	–	3	29
115	(–)	T. Whitthread (Eng)	–	–	2	12
116	(–)	F. Ellis (SA)	–	–	2	10
117	(107)	D. Greaves (Eng)	–	–	2	31
118	(105)	J. Caggianello (Can)	–	–	2	7
119	(115)	M. Hines (SA) (NT)	–	–	1	6
120	(109)	B. Demarco (Scot) (NT)	–	–	1	28
121	(111)	P. Morgan (Aust) (NT)	–	–	1	–
122	(113)	M. Parkin (Eng) (NT)	–	–	1	27
123	(114)	B. Bennett (Eng) (NT)	–	–	1	20
124	(117)	J. Giannaros (Aust) (NT)	–	–	–	–
125	(–)	L. Condo (Aust) (NT)	–	–	–	–
126	(–)	M. Francisco (SA) (NT)	–	–	–	–
127	(–)	S. Mizerak (USA) (NT)	–	–	–	–
128	(–)	W. Saunderson (Can) (NT)	–	–	–	–
129	(–)	J. Chambers (Eng)	–	–	–	–
130	(–)	M. Clark (Eng)	–	–	–	–
131	(–)	A. Harris (Eng)	–	–	–	–
132	(–)	D. Heaton (Eng)	–	–	–	–
133	(–)	E. Lawlor (Eng)	–	–	–	–
134	(–)	R. Marshall (Eng)	–	–	–	–
135	(–)	S. Meakin (Eng)	–	–	–	–
136	(–)	J. Smith (Eng)	–	–	–	–
137	(–)	Gary Wilkinson (Eng)	–	–	–	–
138	(–)	A. Robidoux (Can) (NT)	–	–	–	–

Key to table

R – ranking points
M – merit points
A – A points
F – frames
NT – non-tournament status

NATIONALITIES

Aust   – Australia
Can   – Canada
Eng   – England
Malta   – Malta
NI   – Northern Ireland
NZ   – New Zealand
Rep Ire – Republic of Ireland
Scot   – Scotland
SA   – South Africa
Wales   – Wales
USA   – United States of America

UPS AND DOWNS OF THE RANKING LIST

Established professionals have started to slide down the ranking list – an inevitable consequence of the improving younger players making such a big impact. Ray Reardon, six times World Champion, was, perhaps, the biggest name to fall, slipping from 15 to 38. There are also other players

> **WHO SAID THAT?**
> 'There's no use worrying about this game. If you do that, you're dead.'
> ▲
> – *Ray Reardon*

who will be desperate to halt their downward movement: men like Tony Meo, a regular member of the top sixteen, whose indifferent season saw him tumble nine places to number 20. Kirk Stevens, the Canadian who once occupied fourth place in the world, has had more personal problems than most. It obviously affected his snooker and his drop to number 21 was predictable though unfortunate for one of the nicest people on the circuit.

The places of players on the downward path have been taken by others who have battled through the ranks. Dean Reynolds, from Grimsby, enjoyed a tremendous season and his improvement from 29th to

Down swing: Canadian Kirk Stevens, who has slid down the rankings to number 21.

15th position was a reward for his impressive match performances.

Liverpool's John Parrott has struggled to make the big leap into that top sixteen. Two years ago, he was number 18 and he only managed a rise of one place at the start of the 1986/87 season. Now he is in 13th place and obviously has his sights on the top eight.

Scottish teenager Stephen Hendry set himself a target of the top thirty-two. He reached that easily as he went up from 51 to 23. But he was just one frame away from making the top sixteen, losing 13–12 to Joe Johnson in the World Championship when victory would have pushed him higher. That top sixteen place will almost certainly arrive for Hendry at the end of the 1987/88 season.

Many people were predicting that Peter Francisco, nephew of Silvino Francisco (number 10), would also join the elite group at the top. A poor performance in the World Championship put paid to that dream for another twelve months.

Rex Williams, chairman of the WPBSA, continues to prove the best of the 'Golden Oldies'. He reached his first final last season, in the Rothmans Grand Prix, and has moved up four places to number 12.

There were downward moves, however, for Dennis Taylor (to number 8), Tony Knowles (to number 7), Alex Higgins (to number 9) and Willie Thorne (to number 11). Perhaps the most surprising slip was Cliff Thorburn, the Canadian, who after a long stay in 2nd place went down to number 4.

Predictably, Steve Davis stayed at number 1 and he had a 15-point lead over Jimmy White whose two ranking titles last year helped him move up to 2nd position.

The most significant upward movement in the higher reaches of the charts belonged to Londoner Neal Foulds, who started the season at number 13. Foulds was in his first year as a member of the Matchroom stable and the change certainly paid off as he won

Jovial Jim: Jimmy White, up three places to number 2, with wife Maureen and daughter Lauren.

> **WHO SAID THAT?**
> 'Steve Davis is harder to play, but Jimmy White can be more frightening.'
>
> ▲
>
> *– Neal Foulds*

his first title – the BCE International at Stoke-on-Trent. Consistent performances for the rest of the season made sure that Foulds raced up to number 3. At one stage he had even amassed more ranking points than Davis, but that, of course, changed after the World final.

Welshman Cliff Wilson, who says his eyesight verges on blindness, was looking ready for a place in the top sixteen. But he failed to make the first round at Sheffield and had to settle for 17th place.

John Virgo, the 1979 Coral UK Champion, started and finished the season at number 19, while Australian John Campbell must have been disappointed with his drop of four places to number 22.

Eugene Hughes, the Irishman from Dun Laoghaire, is another solid professional who will now be hoping for a better season. He started well, reaching the semi-final of the BCE International, but then faded badly. He will want to go higher than 24th position.

David Taylor (number 25) nearly moved to Spain in 1986 and would have become a snooker commuter. Australian veteran Eddie Charlton is 26th, though the time is coming when 'Steady' Eddie might spend

Maximum man: Ireland's Eugene Hughes, down four places to number 24.

less time in this country. At the age of fifty-six, he became a father again.

Dave Martin, at number 27, is an Englishman who always troubles the top players without making a great impact on the world rankings. He moved up just one place from the previous season.

Rotherham pairing Barry West (number 29) and Steve Duggan (number 37) have impressed senior professionals over the past couple of seasons. They are ready for a move in the right direction. Murdo Macleod, the popular Scot, however, was glad to see the end of last season in which he hardly won a match. His hoped-for move into the top sixteen ended with a fall of eight places to number 30.

Ringing the changes: Scot Murdo Macleod, dropping to number 30.

Tony Drago is the Maltese youngster who was one shot away from knocking Davis out of the Tennents UK Open. He has an exciting brand of snooker and will this season be looking for the big break-through. He moved up five places to number 32. Blackburn's Steve Longworth, so nervous at the World Championship, remained at number 31.

Wayne Jones was delighted with his early-season form and moved up twenty-two places to number 34, while three first-year professionals earned places in the top sixty-four: Fleetwood's Ken Owers (number 52), young Londoner Jon Wright (number 53) and Welshman Mark Bennett (number 54) produced some consistent displays to earn their first ranking points.

Geoff Foulds admits that he has sacrificed his own career while concentrating on that of his son, Neal. Even so, he earned a top sixty-four spot at number 62. One place below Foulds was extrovert South African Robbie Grace who wears the most outrageous waistcoats. He did well at the Tennents UK, picked up his first ranking point and rose dramatically forty-nine places to number 63.

In the lower half of the rankings, players have one objective at the start of the season – to improve their placing. That objective can change for some players towards the end of the campaign when they are desperate to stay out of the danger zone at the foot of the list. The bottom ten on the list (numbers 119–128) have to play for their professional status against ten amateurs: the World Amateur Champion, the English Amateur Champion and the top eight players in the Pro-Ticket tournaments which take place all over the country. These ten amateurs have the right to challenge the lowest ten ranked players for a place in the pro ranks. Victory for an amateur will then allow him to apply for professional status. Professionals who lose have two choices – to apply for reinstatement as an amateur or stay as a professional as a Non-Tournament Status (NTS) member. The NTS player is allowed to play only in the World Championship – the other ranking tournaments are restricted to the 128 ranked professionals.

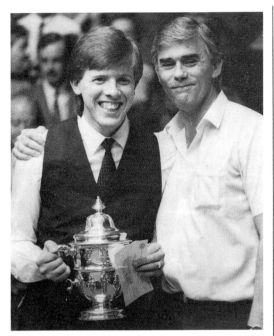

Well done, son! Proud father Geoff with Neal Foulds.

At the end of the 1986/87 season, World Amateur Champion Paul Mifsud of Malta, a former professional, declined the opportunity to become a professional again, leaving the English Amateur Champion, Anthony Harris, and the top eight Pro-Ticket players. There were already vacancies in the pro ranks, while five players – Mike Hines, Bert Demarco, Paddy Morgan, Bernard Bennett and James Giannaros – all opted for NTS. That left Maurice Parkin to face amateur Steve Meakin, who beat him 9–1.

THE NEW FACES

The talk in snooker is all about the young players coming through to challenge the established stars. Even Alex Higgins says, 'The game is getting tougher all the time. These young players have certainly got plenty of talent.' Some new professionals look so young that it seems as though they shouldn't be left alone without a responsible adult. It's a sign of the modern era.

One new 'boy' doesn't quite fit that mould, however. He is Eric Lawlor, who made the big breakthrough into the pro ranks at the age of fifty. Lawlor, from Nuneaton, finished eighth in the pro-ticket matches. He said, 'I would have liked to make the pro ranks earlier but I wasn't sponsored then and money was tight. That meant I couldn't attend all the events that I wanted.'

Last April, Lawlor was due to take part in a play-off match at Preston. 'I didn't feel

Fifty up: Nuneaton's Eric Lawlor, who has turned pro at fifty.

like playing, he recalled. 'I had bronchitis and felt terrible. My fear was that I could lose my professional chance just because I was ill. But just before I left home to go and play, the phone rang telling me I didn't have to compete. I was very relieved.'

One man who did have to engage in a play-off for his place was Blackpool's Steve Meakin, twenty-six, who took on Maurice Parkin and beat him 10–1. Meakin, who finished ninth in the rankings, earned his opportunity because third-placed Anthony Harris had gained his chance by winning the English Amateur title in 1986. Meakin said, 'It was a tough match against Maurice because that one result decided

Just champion: Anthony Harris, a new professional who won the English Amateur title.

whether I turned pro or stayed an amateur.' He also paid tribute to the Commonwealth Sporting Club in Blackpool: 'They gave me a lot of valuable practice time, free of charge.' Meakin is sponsored by two local businessmen.

Harris, from Sutton Coldfield, said, 'I have never been coached. Okay, I have been given some tips and listened to people. When those tips have paid off, then I put them into practice, but basically I am self-taught.' There was disappointment during the Websters Open in 1986 when Harris scored a tremendous 141 break but this new world amateur record was not allowed because one of the pockets was a fraction too big.

Gary Wilkinson, who is twenty-one, finished first in the pro-ticket rankings and is signed up with Peter Mellor of PM Sports who used to look after the interests of Grimsby star Mike Hallett. Wilkinson, from Kirkby-in-Ashfield, has bags of natural talent and is renowned for coming back from seemingly hopeless positions to win. That has earned him the nickname 'Houdini'.

Martin Clark is still a teenager but he is being tipped to make the top thirty-two in his first season. This impressive youngster from Sedgely in the West Midlands has a string of tournament victories under his belt. He is the resident professional at the Dudley Snooker Club and finished second on the list. Graham Morris, manager of the Dudley club, said, 'His safety play is A1 and he seems to pot shots from nowhere.'

At number 4 on the pro-ticket circuit was Pelsall's Jimmy Chambers, who has already been making quite a name for himself. Chambers, thirty, has spent a lot of time playing and coaching for BCE in Belgium. 'It's a different way of gaining experience, but it has been very rewarding,' he said.

He is known as 'The Entertainer' because of his impressive exhibition act. He explained, 'After I have played some

New boy: Martin Clark is being tipped for the top.

frames of snooker, I spend forty-five minutes doing trick shots and telling jokes. I believe in giving value for money.' He would appear to have the right attitude about the game, for he said, 'It's not a life-or-death situation – the best man will win.'

Derek Heaton is another of the 'older brigade' to turn pro — at thirty-nine. He comes from Hastings and has managed the Deluxe Club for the past nine years. He was fifth in the pro-tickets. 'The club is very important to me,' he said. 'It has always come first, but now it will have to take a back seat. I'm proud of this club as we have 200 juniors ranging from eight to seventeen years of age. Even with my busy schedule, I have always found time to coach them.' And, with a boost for the girls, he added, 'We have 100 lady members, which proves just how this side of the sport is building up.'

Peterborough's Jason Smith, in joint sixth spot, already has one major scalp under his belt after beating Alex Higgins 5–0 at the Willie Thorne Club in Newmarket. Now he is delighted that he has made the big breakthrough. He is also a bit of a hustler: 'I played in tournaments that gained me ranking points,' he said. 'Outside that, I just played for money.'

Robert Marshall, of Exeter, joint sixth, has been playing for eight years, since he was fourteen. He will partner South Wales' Mark Bennett in the Hofmeister World Doubles this season. His parents run a newsagent's shop in the West Country.

That completes the list of nine hopefuls for the 1987/88 season. There should have been ten but Paul Mifsud, the World Amateur Champion, turned down his chance of becoming a pro – for the second time.

It's a long hard road to the top. But all nine players know that the rewards of success can be astronomical. If they thought it was tough becoming a professional, the hard work has only just started.

WHO CASHED IN ON SN

	Carlsberg Challenge	Langs Supreme Scottish Masters	Matchroom Trophy	BCE International	Rothmans Grand Prix	BCE Canadian Masters	Tennents UK Open	Hofmeister World Doubles
1 S. Davis	–	–	20,000	5,250	8,250	18,750 3,125 (HB)	60,000	25,000 2,000 (HB)
2 J. White	8,000	4,000	–	765.62	55,000 5,500 (HB)	4,218	4,500 6,000 (HB)	3,750
3 N. Foulds	–	–	5,000	35,000	16,500	–	36,000	3,750
4 Dennis Taylor	12,000 2,000 (HB)	–	10,000	2,625	4,125	4,218	2,906.25	7,500
5 W. Thorne	–	–	50,000	765.62	4,125	11,250	4,500 750 (HB)	1,875
6 C. Thorburn	–	13,000	–	21,000 3,500 (HB)	1,203.12	4,218	9,000	1,875
7 A. Meo	–	–	5,000	765.62	8,250	–	2,906.25	25,000 2,000 (HB)
8 J. Johnson	5,500	2,500	–	1,695.31	1,203.12	4,218	2,906.25	1,875
9 A. Higgins	5,500	8,000 1,000 (HB)	–	1,695.31	4,125	6,250	18,000	3,750
10 T. Griffiths	–	–	10,000	2,625	4,125	–	4,500	7,500
11 S. Francisco	–	–	–	5,250	16,500	–	2,906.25	3,750
12 A. Knowles	–	2,500	–	2,625	8,250	6,250	9,000	1,875
13 S. Hendry	–	2,500	–	1,695.31	8,250	–	1,312.50	12,500
14 R. Williams	–	–	–	2,625	33,000	–	1,312.50	1,875
15 J. Parrott	–	2,500	–	765.62	2,664.06	–	18,000	3,750
16 D. Mountjoy	–	–	–	1,695.31	4,125	–	2,906.25	1,875
17 K. Stevens	–	4,000	–	765.62	1,203.12	–	2,906.25	7,500
18 M. Hallett	–	–	–	765.62	4,125	–	4,500	12,500
19 E. Hughes	–	–	–	10,500	1,203.12	–	4,500	–
20 D. Reynolds	–	–	–	5,250	1,203.12	–	4,500	–
21 J. Virgo	–	–	–	1,695.31	2,664.06	–	2,906.25	7,500
22 P. Francisco	–	–	–	10,500	2,664.06	–	2,906.25	3,750
23 R. Reardon	–	–	–	1,695.31	1,203.12	–	2,906.25	3,750
24 C. Wilson	–	–	–	5,250	2,664.06	–	1,312.50	937.50
25 David Taylor	–	–	–	2,625	1,203.12	–	2,906.25	1,875
26 J. Spencer	–	–	–	765.62 875 (HB)	1,203.12	–	4,500	937.50
27 D. O'Kane	–	–	–	1,695.31	–	–	2,906.25	937.50
28 E. Charlton	–	–	–	1,695.31	1,203.12	–	2,906.25	1,875
29 W. Jones	–	–	–	765.62	2,664.06	–	9,000	1,875
30 W. King	–	–	–	1,695.31	2,664.06	–	1,312.50	937.50
31 A. Drago	–	–	–	1,695.31	2,664.06	–	9,000 750 (HB)	937.50
32 L. Dodd	–	–	–	765.62	2,664.06	–	–	–
33 J. Campbell	–	–	–	765.62	2,664.06	–	1,312.50	937.50
34 D. Martin	–	–	–	765.62	2,664.06	–	2,906.25	1,875
35 W. Werbeniuk	–	–	–	765.62	1,203.12	–	1,312.50	937.50 500 (HB)
36 B. West	–	–	–	1,695.31	1,203.12	–	1,312.50	1,875
37 S. Longworth	–	–	–	765.62	1,203.12	–	4,500	–
38 M. Macleod	–	–	–	765.62	1,203.12	–	1,312.50	1,875
39 J. Wych	–	–	–	1,695.31	2,664.06	–	2,906,25	937.50
40 A. Jones	–	–	–	–	1,203.12	–	2,906.25	3,750
41 S. Newbury	–	–	–	765.62	4,125	–	–	937.50
42 S. Duggan	–	–	–	1,695.31	1,203.12	–	–	1,875
43 J. O'Boye	–	–	–	765.62	2,664.06	–	1,312.50	–
44 T. Murphy	–	–	–	765.62	–	–	1,312.50	937.50
45 R. Chaperon	–	–	–	2,625	2,664.06	–	1,312.50	937.50
46 D. Fowler	–	–	–	–	–	–	1,312.50	937.50 500 (HB)
47 A. Chappel	–	–	–	765.62	1,203.12 1,375 (HB)	–	1,312.50	–
48 G. Cripsey	–	–	–	–	1,203.12	–	1,312.50	–
49 P. Browne	–	–	–	–	4,125	–	–	–
50 K. Owers	–	–	–	2,625	–	–	1,312.50	937.50

KER'S MONEY-GO-ROUND

Mercantile Credit Classic	Benson and Hedges Masters	Dulux British Open	Tuborg World Cup	B & H Irish Masters	Embassy World	National titles	Rothmans Matchroom League	TOTAL
50,000	5,000	2,906.25	3,333.33	22,500	80,000 8,000 (HB)	–	53,600	367,714.58
30,000 5,000 (HB)	5,000 5,000 (HB)	60,000	–	5,400	24,000	1,625	2,700	230,458.62
1,093.75	5,000	36,000 6,000 (HB)	–	–	24,000	750	3,100	172,193.75
1,093.75	51,000	9,000	10,666.66	9,000 2,500 (HB)	6,000	8,500 600 (HB)	2,800	146,534.66
1,093.75	11,000	4,500	–	13,500	3,375	6,500	2,300	115,034.37
2,421.87 1,250 (HB)	16,000	18,000	6,666.66	5,400	3,375	2,829	2,500	112.238.65
3,750	16,000	1,312.50	3,333.33	5,400	3,375	20,000 2,000 (HB)	2,600	101,692.70
2,421.87	11,000	4,500	3,333.33	5,400	48,000	6,500	–	101,052.88
2,421.87	28,000	1,312.50	10,666.66	3,100	6,000	–	–	99,821.34
7,500	5,000	4,500	3,333.33 4,000 (HB)	9,000	12,000	2,000	2,800 2,400 (HB)	81,283.33
7,500	11,000	2,906.25	2,000	–	6,000	5,329.15	–	63,141.65
1,093.75	5,000	18,000	–	3,100	3,375	750	–	61,818.75
15,000	–	–	2,000	–	12,000	4,000 500 (HB)	–	59,757.81
2,421.87	5,000	4,500	–	–	3,375	3,250	–	57,359.37
7,500	–	1,312.50	–	–	6,000	3,250	–	45,742.18
1,093.75	11,000	4,500	3,333.33	–	6,000	8,000 1,000 (HB)	–	45,528.64
2,421.87	5,000	4,500	6,666.66	3,100	3,375	1,157	–	42,595.52
2,421.87	–	2,906.25	–	–	12,000	3,250	–	42,468.74
1,093.75	–	2,906.25	10,666.66	3,100	3,375	2,500	–	39,844.78
15,000	–	2,906.25	–	–	3,375	3,250	–	35,484.37
2,421.87	–	9,000	–	–	3,375	1,625 500 (HB)	–	31,687.49
3,750	–	2,906.25	–	–	2,625	1,567.39	–	30,668.95
1,093.75	5,000	2,906.25	3,333.33	–	6,000	500	–	28,388.01
7,500	–	4,500	–	–	2,625	500	–	25,289.06
1,093.75	–	9,000	–	–	3,375	1,625	–	23,703.12
2,421.87	–	9,000	–	–	2,625	750	–	23,078.11
–	–	–	2,000	–	12,000 2,000 (HB)	–	–	21,539.06
3,750	–	2,906.25	2,000	–	2,625	1,271.18	–	20,232.11
3,750	–	–	–	–	1,375	500	–	19,929.68
1,093.75	–	2,906.25	2,000	–	3,375	3,177.96	–	19,162.33
–	–	1,312.50	2,000	–	–	–	–	18,359.37
–	–	–	–	–	–	12,500	–	18,351.55
2,421.87	–	1,312.50	2,000	–	3,375	1,906.77	–	18,023.95
3,750	–	2,906.25	–	–	2,625	1,625	–	17,789.05
2,421.87	–	1,312.50	6,666.66	–	2,625	–	–	17,744.77
3,750	–	2,906.25	–	–	3,375	1,625	–	17,742.18
2,421.87	–	1,312.50	–	–	6,000	750	–	16,953.11
1,093.75	–	1,312.50	2,000	–	6,000	500	–	16,062.49
1,093.75	–	1,312.50	–	–	3,375	1,672 145 (HB)	–	15,801.37
1,093.75	–	2,906.25	–	–	2,625	750	–	15,234.37
1,093.75	–	–	–	–	2,625	5,000	–	14,546.87
3,750	–	2,906.25	–	–	1,375	750	–	13,554.68
1,093.75	–	1,312.50	–	–	1,375	5,000	–	13,523.43
1,093.75	–	4,500	2,000	–	2,625	150	–	13,384.37
1,093.75	–	1,312.50	–	–	1,375	835	–	12,155.31
3,750	–	1,312.50	–	–	2,625	1,625	–	12,062.50
–	–	1,312.50	–	–	2,625	2,000	–	10,593.74
1,093.75	–	2,906.25	–	–	2,625	750	–	9,890.62
1,093.75	–	–	2,000	–	–	2,500	–	9,718.75
–	–	1,312.50	–	–	1,375	1,625	–	9,187.50

	Carlsberg Challenge	Langs Supreme Scottish Masters	Matchroom Trophy	BCE International	Rothmans Grand Prix	BCE Canadian Masters	Tennents UK Open	Hofmeister World Doubles
51 J. McLaughlin	–	–	–	765.62	2,664.06	–	1,312.50	–
52 R. Harris	–	–	–	–	1,203.12	–	1,312.50	–
53 J. Wright	–	–	–	–	1,203.12	–	1,312.50	–
54 M. Gibson	–	–	–	765.62	1,203.12	–	1,312.50	937.50
55 S. James	–	–	–	–	–	–	–	1,875
56 M. Bennett	–	–	–	765.62	2,664.06	–	–	–
57 M. Bradley	–	–	–	765.62	–	–	1,312.50	–
58 M. Wildman	–	–	–	765.62	2,664.06	–	–	937.50
59 M. Gauvreau	–	–	–	2,625	–	–	–	937.50
60 G. Miles	–	–	–	765.62	1,203.12	–	1,312.50	1,875
61 John Rea	–	–	–	765.62	1,203.12	–	1,312.50	–
62 P. Medati	–	–	–	765.62	1,203.12	–	–	–
63 R. Edmonds	–	–	–	765.62	–	–	1,312.50	937.50
64 G. Foulds	–	–	–	1,695.31	1,203.12	–	–	937.50
65 R. Grace	–	–	–	–	–	–	2,906.25	937.50
66 E. Sinclair	–	–	–	765.62	–	–	–	–
67 D. Roe	–	–	–	–	1,203.12	–	1,312.50	1,875
68 V. Harris	–	–	–	–	1,203.12	–	1,312.50	937.50
69 C. Roscoe	–	–	–	–	–	–	1,312.50	937.50
70 G. Scott	–	–	–	–	–	–	1,312.50	937.50
71 J. van Rensburg	–	–	–	765.62	–	–	–	–
72 P. Fagan	–	–	–	–	1,203.12	–	–	937.50
73 G. Rigitano	–	–	–	–	–	–	–	937.50
74 M. Morra	–	–	–	–	1,203.12	–	–	–
75 I. Williamson	–	–	–	–	–	–	1,312.50	937.50
76 B. Oliver	–	–	–	–	–	–	–	937.50
77 A. Kearney	–	–	–	–	–	–	–	–
78 R. Foldvari	–	–	–	765.62	–	–	–	–
79 B. Mikkelsen	–	–	–	–	–	–	1,312.50	–
80 F. Ellis	–	–	–	–	–	–	–	–
81 J. Donnelly	–	–	–	–	–	–	–	937.50
82 I. Black	–	–	–	765.62	–	–	–	–
83 R. Bales	–	–	–	1,695.31	–	–	–	937.50
84 B. Rowswell	–	–	–	–	–	–	1,312.50	–
85 F. Jonik	–	–	–	–	–	–	–	–
86 G. Wilkinson	–	–	–	–	–	–	–	–
87 I. Anderson	–	–	–	–	1,203.12	–	–	–
88 P. Mans	–	–	–	–	–	–	–	937.50
89 P. Burke	–	–	–	765.62	–	–	–	–
90 J. Bear	–	–	–	–	1,203.12	–	–	–
91 P. Houlihan	–	–	–	1,695.31	–	–	–	–
92 G. Jenkins	–	–	–	–	–	–	–	–
93 J. Rempe	–	–	–	–	–	–	–	–
94 N. Gilbert	–	–	–	–	–	–	–	–
94 P. Gibson	–	–	–	–	–	–	1,312.50	–
94 M. Watterson	–	–	–	–	–	–	1,312.50	–
97 F. Davis	–	–	–	–	1,203.12	–	–	–
97 J. Meadowcroft	–	–	–	–	1,203.12	–	–	–
99 M. Fisher	–	–	–	–	–	–	–	–
100 D. Sheehan	–	–	–	–	–	–	–	–
101 D. Chalmers	–	–	–	–	–	–	–	937.50
101 M. Darrington	–	–	–	–	–	–	–	937.50
101 D. Gilbert	–	–	–	–	–	–	–	937.50
104 L. Condo	–	–	–	–	–	–	–	–
104 P. Morgan	–	–	–	–	–	–	–	–
106 D. Mienie	–	–	–	–	–	–	–	–
107 P. Thornley	–	–	–	–	–	–	–	–
107 G. Watson	–	–	–	–	–	–	–	–
109 J. Fitzmaurice	–	–	–	–	–	–	–	–
110 J. Caggianello	–	–	–	–	–	–	–	–
111 B. Demarco	–	–	–	–	–	–	–	–
112 J. Giannaros	–	–	–	–	–	–	–	–
113 M. Hines	–	–	–	–	–	–	–	–
114 B. Kelly	–	–	–	–	–	–	–	–
114 Jack Rea	–	–	–	–	–	–	–	–
114 P. Watchorn	–	–	–	–	–	–	–	–

HB = high break

Mercantile Credit Classic	Benson and Hedges Masters	Dulux British Open	Tuborg World Cup	B & H Irish Masters	Embassy World	National titles	Rothmans Matchroom League	TOTAL
1,093.75	–	2,906.25	–	–	–	150	–	8,892.18
2,421.87	–	1,312.50	–	–	1,375	750	–	8,374.99
2,421.87	–	–	–	–	3,375	–	–	8,312.49
–	–	–	2,000	–	1,375	500	–	8,093.74
–	–	2,906.25 1,500 (HB)	–	–	–	1,625	–	7,906.25
1,093.75	–	–	–	–	3,375	–	–	7,898.43
2,421.87	–	–	–	–	2,625	750	–	7,874.99
–	–	1,312.50	–	–	1,375	750	–	7,804,68
1,093.75	–	1,312.50	–	–	1,375	–	–	7,343.75
–	–	–	–	–	1,375	750	–	7,281.24
1,093.75	–	1,312.50	–	–	–	1,250	–	6,937.49
–	–	1,312.50	–	–	2,625	750	–	6,656.24
–	–	–	–	–	2,625	750	–	6,390.62
1,093.75	–	1,312.50	–	–	–	–	–	6,242.18
–	–	1,312.50	–	–	–	846.39	–	6,002.64
1,093.75	–	1,312.50	–	–	1,375	1,250	–	5,796.87
–	–	1,312.50	–	–	–	–	–	5,703.12
–	–	1,312.50	–	–	–	750	–	5,515.62
1,093.75	–	1,312.50	–	–	–	500	–	5,156.25
–	–	1,312.50	–	–	1,375	–	–	4,937.50
1,093.75	–	–	–	–	1,375	1,567.39	–	4,801.76
–	–	–	2,000	–	–	150	–	4,290.62
–	–	1,312.50	–	–	1,375	540	–	4,165.00
1,093.75	–	1,312.50	–	–	–	540	–	4,149.37
1,093.75	–	–	–	–	–	750	–	4,093.75
–	–	–	–	–	2,625	–	–	3,562.50
2,421.87	–	–	–	–	–	1,000	–	3,421.87
–	–	1,312.50	–	–	–	1,271.18	–	3,349.30
1,093.75	–	–	–	–	–	835	–	3,241.25
–	–	–	–	–	–	3,134.79	–	3,134.79
–	–	–	–	–	–	2,000	–	2,937.50
–	–	–	–	–	1,375	500	–	2,640.62
–	–	–	–	–	–	–	–	2,632.81
–	–	1,312.50	–	–	–	–	–	2,625.00
1,093.75	–	–	–	–	–	1,157	–	2,250.75
–	–	1,312.50	–	–	–	847.45	–	2,159.95
–	–	–	–	–	–	847.45	–	2,050.57
–	–	–	–	–	–	846.39	–	1,783.89
–	–	–	–	–	–	1,000	–	1,765.62
–	–	–	–	–	–	540	–	1,743.12
–	–	–	–	–	–	–	–	1,695.31
1,093.75	–	–	–	–	–	423.72	–	1,517.47
–	–	–	–	–	1,375	–	–	1,375.00
–	–	1,312.50	–	–	–	–	–	1,312.50
–	–	–	–	–	–	–	–	1,312.50
–	–	–	–	–	–	–	–	1,312.50
–	–	–	–	–	–	–	–	1,203.12
–	–	–	–	–	–	–	–	1,203.12
1,093.75	–	–	–	–	–	–	–	1,093.75
–	–	–	–	–	–	1,000	–	1,000.00
–	–	–	–	–	–	–	–	937.50
–	–	–	–	–	–	–	–	937.50
–	–	–	–	–	–	–	–	937.50
–	–	–	–	–	–	847.45	–	847.45
–	–	–	–	–	–	847.45	–	847.45
–	–	–	–	–	–	846.39	–	846.39
–	–	–	–	–	–	835	–	835.00
–	–	–	–	–	–	835	–	835.00
–	–	–	–	–	–	750	–	750.00
–	–	–	–	–	–	540	–	540.00
–	–	–	–	–	–	500	–	500.00
–	–	–	–	–	–	423.72	–	423.72
–	–	–	–	–	–	407.52	–	407.52
–	–	–	–	–	–	150	–	150.00
–	–	–	–	–	–	150	–	150.00
–	–	–	–	–	–	150	–	150.00

WHO'S WHO IN THE TOP THIRTY-TWO

STEVE DAVIS

World ranking: number 1

Date of birth: 22 August 1957

Star sign: Leo

Steve Davis is, in the opinion of many people, the greatest snooker player the world has seen. He has won every major title and has a yearly income of more than £1 million. Endorsements, advertising contracts and sponsorship make up two thirds of that total, while last season he earned a record £367,714 from tournament play. He relaxes by listening to rhythm and blues records. On tour Steve can be seen scouring the local shops for more records to add to his collection. He has spearheaded the drive to spread snooker world-wide, playing in countries like Brazil, Switzerland, China, Hong Kong and Canada in the past twelve months. He lives at home with his parents in an Essex countryside farmhouse. Davis is the current World Champion after beating Joe Johnson 18–14 to capture the title for the fourth time.

JIMMY WHITE

World ranking: number 2

Date of birth: 2 May 1962

Star sign: Taurus

Jimmy White is arguably the most talented snooker player on the world stage today. Last season was his best as he rose from number 5 to number 2 in the rankings, won two major ranking titles and became only the second player to earn more than £200,000 in one season. White last season joined the Matchroom organization, which immediately increased his world-wide earnings. He was the youngest ever English

Amateur Champion at sixteen and two years later he became the youngest World Amateur Champion. He was also the youngest winner of a professional tournament when, at nineteen, he took the Langs Supreme Scottish Masters crown. Controversy has followed this youngster but he seems to shrug it off. A popular member of the travelling band of professionals, White is accompanied at all major tournaments by his dad, Tom. He is married to Maureen and they have one daughter, Lauren. They live in Wimbledon.

NEAL FOULDS

World ranking: number 3

Date of birth: 13 July 1963

Star sign: Cancer

Neal Foulds was the success story of the 1987/88 season. He lifted himself from number 13 to number 3 in the rankings and, before the World Championship, had collected more ranking points than any other player, including Steve Davis. He won his first major title – the BCE International – and went on to reach two more finals, the Tennents UK Open and the Dulux British Open. Neal is an avid cricket fan and spends his off-duty time in the summer watching Middlesex at Lord's. Foulds also had his share of personal problems, including taking the controversial beta-blockers during the World Cham-

pionship after being prescribed the drug for a heart complaint. Shortly afterwards, to prove his luck was really out, his car was stolen and used in a bank raid!

CLIFF THORBURN

World ranking: number 4

Date of birth: 16 January 1948

Star sign: Capricorn

Cliff Thorburn, after being kept out of the number 1 spot by Steve Davis, took a downward turn on the rankings, slipping from number 2 to number 4. Thorburn moved permanently to Britain last season from his native Toronto. He now lives in North London with wife, Barbara, and two sons. Thorburn had a disappointing season by his normally high standards, though he did retain the Langs Supreme Scottish Masters title and reached the final of the BCE International. He went into the record books in the 1982 World Championship when he scored a 147 – the first person to achieve the maximum in the World event. He is a member of the Robert Winsor stable and a golfing fanatic. He spends much of his spare time on the golf course and is a single-figure handicapper.

JOE JOHNSON

World ranking: number 5

Date of birth: 29 July 1952

Star sign: Leo

Joe Johnson started the 1986/87 campaign as World Champion following his 18–12 victory over Steve Davis. He finished the season losing his World title 18–14 to Davis. But he still remained one of the most popular players on the circuit despite an awful season that finally came good at the World event in Sheffield. Poor Johnson could hardly win a match as the pressure of being World Champion proved too much of a handicap. But even though written off by the bookmakers, Johnson wrote another fairy-tale chapter to his own life story when he came through to face Davis again – only this time with the wrong result. Apart from his family, Johnson's other great love in life is singing and he has made records with his group, Made in Japan. He rose to 5th on the rankings from 8th.

TERRY GRIFFITHS

World ranking: number 6

Date of birth: 16 October 1947

Star sign: Libra

Terry Griffiths ended the 1986/87 season as the only player to reach the televised stage of every ranking tournament. That consistency enabled Griffiths to move up four places, even though he failed to make the last four of any ranking event. Griffiths' name will stay on snooker's Roll of Honour for a remarkable performance at his first World event back in 1979. Then, this Welshman from Llanelli, a former insurance agent, bus conductor and postman, arrived at the Crucible, unseeded and virtually unnoticed. A fortnight later he had collected the World title. Griffiths, a family man with two sons, will be upset that he lost his Welsh title, especially as the Matchroom organization was sponsoring the event. His father, Martin, is a regular viewer on the circuit. Griffiths once frightened his manager Barry Hearn by buying a high-powered motorbike. He also tried to give up smoking but failed.

Bubbling: Terry Griffiths after taking the Matchroom team past £1 million in earnings last season.

TONY KNOWLES

World ranking: number 7

Date of birth: 13 June 1955

Star sign: Gemini

Tony Knowles has started a slow slide down the rankings and reversing that trend will be the main thought of this talented man from Bolton. He even managed to disappoint in the World Championship which had been a happy hunting ground for him in previous years. Three times in the past four years Knowles had reached the semi-final stage, but that impressive performance came to a halt last season when he was beaten by Mike Hallett in the first round. Controversy has surrounded this good-looking young man, though he has the character to shake off problems and concentrate on his snooker. He prepared for the World Championship by relaxing at his idyllic retreat on the banks of Lake Windermere where he can enjoy one of his favourite pastimes – windsurfing. He is a sun-lover and spends a lot of time at his apartment on the island of Tenerife. His best performance last season was to reach the semi-final of the Dulux British Open where he was beaten 9–2 by Neal Foulds. He has been campaigning for a reduction in the size of pockets which he feels is making the game too easy.

DENNIS TAYLOR

World ranking: number 8

Date of birth: 19 January 1949

Star sign: Capricorn

Whatever Dennis Taylor achieves during the rest of his snooker career, he will never forget that day in 1985 when he beat Steve Davis 18–17 on the final black to take the World title in front of an 18.5 million television audience. And Taylor has said: 'People everywhere keep on asking me about that night and that's great. I'll never forget the moment when that black went in.' Taylor waited thirteen years for his first major title when he won the Rothmans Grand Prix in 1984. Now he is a regular member of snooker's top set, though he has slipped badly down the rankings for this season. Taylor's moments of success came outside the ranking events when he won the Benson and Hedges Masters title 9–8 after a magnificent fightback against Alex Higgins, in the Matchroom Irish Championship when he beat Joe O'Boye, and in the Tuborg World Cup when he skippered Ireland to their third successive

title. Taylor has long been a member of snooker's world jet set. He is a devout family man and lives in Blackburn with his wife Pat and three children. He switched cues for a while last season when his pet terrier, Chalkie, chewed the tip of his usual cue, but now he is back using the one that won that now-famous World crown.

ALEX HIGGINS

World ranking: number 9

Date of birth: 18 March 1949

Star sign: Pisces

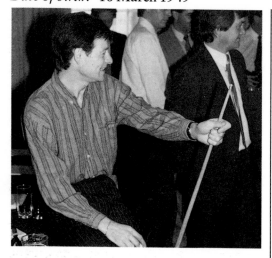

Alex Higgins remained the People's Champion despite the head-butting incident in Preston in 1986 that many observers felt could have ended his career. Higgins was penalized for that offence by a five-tournament ban and also paid a £12,000 fine. He must now look to the future and try to recapture the form that made him the biggest drawing card in the game. Mention the Hurricane and the fans will respond – whatever has happened in his personal life. Higgins will be disappointed by his drop in the rankings, though he didn't enjoy a good season – his best performances bringing him to the semi-final of the Tennents UK Open and the final of the Benson and Hedges Masters. He was banned from competing in the Irish Championship, and not being allowed to play in front of his fervent fans back in his native Northern Ireland would have hurt his pride. He was an impressive member of Ireland's Tuborg World Cup-winning side for the third year in a row. He has been World Champion twice (in 1972 and 1982), but by the end of last season hadn't won a major championship for nearly four years.

SILVINO FRANCISCO

World ranking: number 10

Date of birth: 3 May 1946

Star sign: Taurus

Silvino Francisco is the son of a Portuguese fisherman who was brought up in Cape Town, South Africa. He turned professional in 1978 but it wasn't until the 1982/83 season that he began to play the lucrative British circuit on a regular basis. He is now settled in Chesterfield with his family and is accepted as one of the sport's most consistent performers. He has moved steadily up the rankings and made his mark in the world top ten for the first time – after a rise of two places. He was hoping to end his bad run at the World Championship as he had failed to get past the second round in five attempts. He overcame the first-round hurdle against Australia's John Campbell then fell, yet again, in the second round to Grimsby's Mike Hallett. The highlight of the Francisco career came in 1985 when he won the Dulux British Open with a 12–9 victory over Kirk Stevens. That final was surrounded by controversy when his comment that Stevens took illegal drugs was covered in a national newspaper. Francisco, whose nephew, Peter, also lives in Britain and is ranked number 18, last season reached the semi-final of the Rothmans Grand Prix and the last eight of the Mercantile Credit Classic. He won the South African title for the first time.

WILLIE THORNE

World ranking: number 11

Date of birth: 4 March 1954

Star sign: Pisces

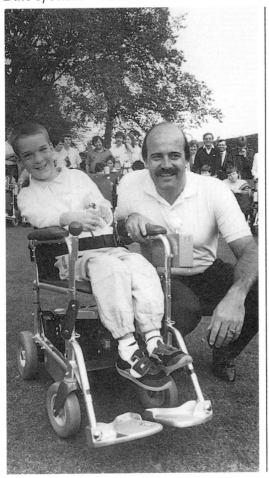

Willie Thorne finished high up on last season's money charts but that will give him little consolation for his drop of four places on the ranking list. Thorne, known in the game as Mr Maximum for his impressive tally of more than seventy 147s, won titles in Hong Kong and China. He also won the first in-house Matchroom title that carried a £50,000 first prize. But his performances in the ranking tournaments were below his usual high standard – he failed to reach the last eight of any event. He was also a first-round casualty in the World Championship, going down to Stephen Hendry. Thorne owns a flourishing snooker centre in Leicester. He is also a virtual teetotaller – a rarity on the circuit – though it is common knowledge that he does enjoy a flutter . . . or two! It was in 1985 that Thorne made his big breakthrough, winning the Mercantile Credit Classic, and shortly afterwards he joined Barry Hearn's Matchroom stable.

Helping hand: Willie Thorne with a young friend at the Snooker Golf Society's day out at Sheffield. The society has provided more than seventy powered wheelchairs for handicapped children.

REX WILLIAMS

World ranking: number 12

Date of birth: 20 July 1933

Star sign: Cancer

Rex Williams nearly retired a few years ago when he suffered a nervous breakdown. But this former World Professional Billiards Champion fought back and is now established in snooker's top sixteen – a remarkable achievement for one of the busiest men in the game. He is in charge of a public company, is chairman of the WPBSA, commentates for ITV and is enjoying a revitalized snooker career. His first snooker success came at the age of just seventeen when he captured the English amateur title. Then, thirty-six years later, he was on the brink of becoming snooker's oldest professional champion but that dream ended when he was beaten in the final of the Rothmans Grand Prix by Jimmy White. Williams is keen for the game to progress world-wide and recently took part in an eight-man tournament in Peking, China. He was under pressure during the World Championship when he was criticized for taking a beta-blocker drug for his nervous problems. Those newspaper articles affected his performance and he was knocked out in the first round. In previous World events he has twice reached the semi-final and lost twice when the competition was organized on a challenge basis.

JOHN PARROTT

World ranking: number 13

Date of birth: 11 May 1964

Star sign: Taurus

John Parrott is one of the most talented young professionals on the circuit but he has had trouble getting into the top sixteeen. He has hovered on the brink – first at number 18, and then at number 17 for the 1986/87 season. As other players have discovered, that final move into the top sixteen is not easy. But Parrott, a Liverpool lad through and through, has made it, being rewarded with the number 13 spot after a consistent season. A football fan, Parrott can be seen regularly at Liverpool and Everton, though he refuses to say which side is his favourite.

DOUG MOUNTJOY

World ranking: number 14

Date of birth: 8 June 1942

Star sign: Gemini

Doug Mountjoy has combined being a snooker professional with running a public house down in Ewyas Harold. Now he is back as a full-time snooker professional. One of the longer-serving members of the top sixteen, Doug saved his place yet again when he edged into the last sixteen of last season's World Championship. A former winner in the Coral UK, Benson and Hedges Masters and Benson and Hedges Irish Masters, Mountjoy is still a force to be reckoned with and scored a superb victory over world number 1 Steve Davis in the last Masters at Wembley.

DEAN REYNOLDS

World ranking: number 15

Date of birth: 11 January 1963

Star sign: Capricorn

Dean Reynolds is a recent member of Howard Kruger's Framework organization and looks set to go even higher up the rankings. Last season was his most significant since he turned professional in 1981 and he looked impressive as he made the semi-final of the Mercantile Credit Classic and the last eight of the BCE International.

MIKE HALLETT

World ranking: number 16

Date of birth: 6 July 1959

Star sign: Cancer

Mike Hallett is another young player who has enjoyed the best season of his career after turning professional in 1979. He has just switched managerial camps from Peter Mellor to Glasgow's Ian Doyle, manager of young sensation Stephen Hendry. Hallett and Hendry teamed up for the Hofmeister World Doubles and surprised many of the top names by reaching the final where they lost to Steve Davis and Tony Meo 12–3. Mike relaxes on the golf course.

CLIFF WILSON

World ranking: number 17

Date of birth: 10 May 1934

Star sign: Taurus

Cliff Wilson is a born joker. Buy him a pint, start him talking and the stories will flow . . . forever. He remembers the early days when he came from the same Welsh town of Tredegar as Ray Reardon. Wilson, at one stage, became bored with the game and that factor, coupled with his failing eyesight, made him 'retire' for fifteen years. But he returned, won the World Amateur title and turned professional. An exciting potter, Wilson delights the crowd by going for the impossible shot. He missed out on a top sixteen place after failing to make the final stages of the World Championship.

PETER FRANCISCO

World ranking: number 18

Date of birth: 14 February 1962

Star sign: Aquarius

South African Peter Francisco is a player to watch. He is one of the most talented and consistent young professionals and was reckoned to have been a certainty to reach the top sixteen. But that hope of glory ended for at least one more year when he was knocked out of the World Championship by New Zealand's Dene O'Kane. Peter is the nephew of Silvino Francisco, who is riding high in the rankings at number 10. Peter is based in the Essex seaside town of Clacton where he is the professional at the Clacton Snooker Centre. Like many other players, he is a very keen golfer.

JOHN VIRGO

World ranking: number 19

Date of birth: 3 April 1946

Star sign: Aries

John Virgo is a snooker all-rounder. As well as being one of the game's top players, he is a television commentator, is vice-chairman of the WPBSA and has one of the most famous exhibition acts with his brilliant impersonations (see left). If a major final ends quickly and Virgo is around, the fans will be treated to a session of mickey-taking in the best possible taste. The highlight of Virgo's season was a victory over Steve Davis in the Dulux British Open, but he is still trying to capture the form that made him Coral UK Champion in 1979 – form that would certainly see him move back up the ranking list.

TONY MEO

World ranking: number 20

Date of birth: 4 October 1959

Star sign: Libra

Tony Meo dropped down the rankings nine places, was beaten in his first match at the World Championship and yet still finished the season with two titles and more than £100,000 in prize money. Meo's biggest career success came in 1986 when he won the Tolly Ales English title – his first major solo success. He retained that title last season and he said afterwards: 'That win gave me tremendous satisfaction. I was desperate to hold on to the trophy.' His other title triumph came, inevitably, in the Hofmeister World Doubles when he partnered Steve Davis to their fourth title in five years. Always a snappy dresser, Meo embarks on periodic keep-fit campaigns, though his liking for good food often conflicts with those worthwhile aims.

KIRK STEVENS

World ranking: number 21

Date of birth: 17 August 1958

Star sign: Leo

Many snooker fans are saddened by Kirk Stevens' dramatic slump down the rankings. At one time he stood proudly at number 4. Then he slipped to number 9 and last season saw him drop out of the top sixteen. Admissions of drug-taking all but ruined this young man's life. Now he is desperate to find a way back to the top. He has moved away from the bright lights of Central London to a place in North London near to manager Robert Winsor, the man who looks after the fortunes of fellow Torontonian Cliff Thorburn. Whatever his problems, Stevens keeps smiling. He has friends throughout the game.

JOHN CAMPBELL

World ranking: number 22

Date of birth: 10 April 1953

Star sign: Aries

John Campbell has been a professional since 1982. He won the Australian title for the first time in 1985 but was pipped in the final a year later by Warren King. This tall gangling Australian looked destined for a place in that coveted top sixteen when he raced thirteen places up the rankings to settle at number 18 for the start of the 1986/87 campaign. But that progress — albeit temporarily — stopped and Campbell's indifferent form saw him slip four places. His last big hope came in the World Championship, but in the first round at Sheffield he was destroyed 10–3 by Silvino Francisco. He is the highest-placed Aussie, taking over from veteran Eddie Charlton.

STEPHEN HENDRY

World ranking: number 23

Date of birth: 13 January 1969

Star sign: Capricorn

Stephen Hendry will probably earn more than £400,000 in the current season from prize money and lucrative endorsement and advertising deals. He has already been featured in a TV campaign by Clydesdale Bank who just happen to look after this young man's investment portfolio. As he drives up and down the country in his £18,000 Mercedes, Hendry knows that all he has to do is play snooker as manager Ian Doyle takes care of everything else. The experts tip him as the man to take Alex Higgins' record as the youngest World Champion. He retained his Scottish title, finished 13th on the money list, and was one match away from the top sixteen. That dream ended when, 12–8 down, he fought back to level at 12–12, only to lose 13–12 to Joe Johnson in the World Championship quarter-final. But he was still delighted with his rise of twenty-eight places and has now set himself a target of the top eight.

EUGENE HUGHES

World ranking: number 24

Date of birth: 4 November 1955

Star sign: Scorpio

Eugene Hughes finished last season with an end-of-term report that read: 'Plenty of ability but could do better.' Hughes, who comes from the Irish port of Dun Laoghaire, the same city as Band Aid hero Bob Geldof, now lives in East London and plays at the Ilford Snooker Centre. He began the season, which promised to be his best ever, at number 20 on the list. He reached the semi-final of the BCE International and an upward move seemed assured. But the rest of the season fell away and he slid down four places – a situation which disappointed this intense family man. One success did come his way as he helped Ireland to their third victory in a row in the Tuborg World Cup in Bournemouth.

DAVID TAYLOR

World ranking: number 25

Date of birth: 29 July 1943

Star sign: Leo

David Taylor nearly moved away from the British snooker scene, considering a move to the Spanish sunshine. But the deal fell through and he has given up the idea – for the time being – of becoming a snooker commuter. Taylor, once a regular member of the elite group of sixteen, again slipped down the rankings – this time a fall of four places. Two years ago he was comfortably placed at number 14. He couldn't have made a better opening to the season with a victory over World Champion Joe Johnson. That came in the BCE International, but despite a brief return to his best in the Dulux British Open, Taylor's form never reached the heights of which he is obviously capable.

EDDIE CHARLTON

World ranking: number 26

Date of birth: 31 October 1929

Star sign: Scorpio

Eddie Charlton's sporting life could come straight from a kid's comic. You name it, Steady Eddie seems to have done it – from snooker to surfing to boxing. He was also a good tennis player and a top athlete. He just happened to carry the Olympic torch during the Games in Melbourne in 1956. He has reached six World semi-finals and two World finals, losing to Ray Reardon on both occasions. Charlton failed to reach the Australian Championship final in 1986 for the first time in more than twenty years. He has hinted that he is becoming tired of all the travelling around the world from his home back in Kangaroo Point, New South Wales.

DAVE MARTIN

World ranking: number 27

Date of birth: 9 May 1948

Star sign: Taurus

Dave Martin is creeping up the rankings – from number 29 to number 28 – and now this season he's slotted in at number 27. Many professionals know what a tough competitor this north-easterner can be, but he has yet to make a major impact on the ranking tournament scene. Martin was desperately upset when he failed to find a place in the TV stages of the World Championship. He was a victim of Scottish teenager Stephen Hendry who went on to reach the last eight. Martin has proved he can live with the best – now he must prove he can beat the best consistently!

JOHN SPENCER

World ranking: number 28

Date of birth: 18 September 1935

Star sign: Virgo

When John Spencer started to fall down the rankings, many people said he was finished. That was mainly due to a serious eyesight problem that can only be controlled by a daily intake of steroid tablets. Spencer has been described as the 'best ever' in snooker. Certainly his three World titles in the 1970s were testimony to his great talent. Now he has moved up six places to number 28 – not a huge jump, but significant considering the health problems he has endured that might have ended the career of a less determined player. Spencer found moments of his old magic last season: in one memorable frame against Jimmy White, he needed six snookers and got the lot to win the frame.

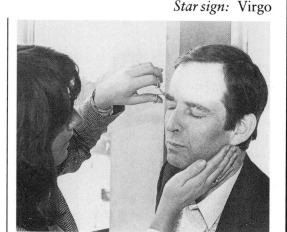

In trim: John Spencer is 'tidied up' before a TV appearance.

BARRY WEST

World ranking: number 29

Date of birth: 24 October 1958

Star sign: Scorpio

Blackburn's Barry West was once a regular member of England's amateur team. Now he is aiming to become a regular member of the top thirty-two and hopes to move into the top sixteen. He has risen one place up the rankings but didn't enjoy the best of fortunes in the ranking tournaments. A solid, dependable performer, West reached the first round of the Embassy World Championship for the first time. There he faced Ray Reardon, but the former World Champion came through a 10–5 winner.

MURDO MACLEOD

World ranking: number 30

Date of birth: 14 January 1947

Star sign: Capricorn

Scotland's Murdo Macleod is another snooker 'nearly man'. But he has so much natural ability that he will be keen to turn around last season's setbacks. He started the campaign as world number 22, but lost his touch completely. In fact, he failed to win a single match all season until the World Championship when he reached the first round proper. His fortunes changed and he recorded a superb 10–5 victory over Rex Williams – incidentally the first time that a Scot had won a round at the Crucible Theatre. But the run was short lived and Macleod went down 13–7 to Joe Johnson in the last sixteen.

STEVE LONGWORTH

World ranking: number 31

Date of birth: 27 July 1948

Star sign: Leo

Steve Longworth captured the coveted English amateur title in 1984 before embarking on his professional career. He has moved slowly but surely up the rankings from number 37 to number 31 and now stays at that position. He admitted he was nervous before his first appearance at Sheffield's Crucible Theatre in the first round of the World Championship last season. But he kept those nerves under control and overwhelmed Kirk Stevens, then the number 9 seed, 10–4. His world glory dream ended abruptly in the next round, however, when he came unstuck 13–7 against Stephen Hendry. Overall, he was disappointed with his performance in the other ranking tournaments.

TONY DRAGO

World ranking: number 32

Date of birth: 22 September 1965

Star sign: Virgo

Tony Drago is Malta's only professional following the departure of Paul Mifsud, the World Amateur Champion, from the pro ranks. Drago is another one of the younger breed of players being tipped for greatness. Certainly, his quickfire style has already earned him a lot of admirers at the venues and on the television screens. He goes for his shots and nearly caused one of the biggest upsets of the season against Steve Davis in the Tennents UK Open. But he failed on a yellow that would have certainly clinched him the match and a relieved Davis went through. At one stage, Drago was very homesick and was a regular traveller on Air Malta to see his family on the George Cross island.

WHO SAID WHAT

'My nerves had gone when I was 11–8 in front. If I had lost, I might never have won another event.'

– *Neal Foulds after his 12–9 victory over Cliff Thorburn in the final of the BCE International*

'I'm amazed by the Chinese viewing figures. That total of over 100 million is nearly twice the population of Britain.'

– *Mark Aitken, chairman and general manager of British American Tobacco, which sponsored the Kent Cup China International Masters in Peking*

'Since we announced the League, the phone hasn't stopped ringing. I have had proposals from Belfast, Dublin, Monte Carlo, Paris, Amsterdam, Brussels, Paris, Marbella, Antwerp and even West Berlin. This is the most exciting development in snooker since colour TV.'

– *Barry Hearn after announcing the Rothmans Matchroom League*

'I can read a book from 1 foot away with my left eye, but I can't see anything with the other eye for 50 yards.'

– *Welshman Cliff Wilson*

'These won't be exhibition matches. I don't like losing anywhere and I don't intend to start in Scotland.'

– *Steve Davis before his Scottish Challenge Tour with Stephen Hendry which he won 6–0*

'I'm very proud to have been the player to have taken the Matchroom team past the £1 million mark for the season. Funnily enough, I'm the one who has earned the least.'

– *Terry Griffiths*

'If you don't get confidence after beating Steve Davis, then you might as well pack the game in.'

– *John Virgo after beating Steve Davis in the Dulux British Open*

'I have never made a penny from the players I have coached. I just love the game. I just look for reasons why people miss shots.'

– *coach Frank Callan who has assisted the careers of Steve Davis and John Parrott, and last season helped Welshman Terry Griffiths*

'We have a £100 side bet every time we play. Last time I beat him, he paid me in dollars – eighteen months later.'

– *Jimmy White joking before his match with John Spencer in the Dulux British Open*

'My hero was John Spencer. I read his book Spencer on Snooker thirty or forty times.'

– *Dene O'Kane*

'He couldn't stop shaking out there.'

– *Dennis Taylor talking about opponent Mark Bennett at the World Championship*

'Players don't want tablets that make them relaxed. They want to play with the adrenalin flowing, keyed up and raring to go.'

– *John Spencer*

'We spent a year researching where to invest sponsorship money. The image was right and our studies showed that many people interested in snooker fitted our market. They were between the ages of thirty-five and sixty-four and in the middle income bracket.'

– *Barry Bateman, managing director of Fidelity Investment Services, who became a new snooker sponsor with the Fidelity Unit Trusts International*

'For one week we can have all these super-stars on our doorstep. We pride ourselves on the personal touch.'

–*Kevin Norton, tournament co-ordinator of the Benson and Hedges Irish Masters*

'Snooker's success has become a target for the snipers. It's easy to knock a sport that has reached the top.'

– *Editorial comment in the WPBSA's* Newsbreak *magazine*

'We are aiming for the top eight this season. That must be our realistic aim after accumulating so many points last season.'

– *Ian Doyle, manager of Stephen Hendry*

'Somebody has got to break Barry Hearn's monopoly of winning all the titles. I would love it to be Stephen Hendry or Mike Hallett.'

– *Ian Doyle*

'I don't know of any drug that will help any player.'

– *John Spencer*

'I feel horrible, terrible. Even if I was playing very well, I would have struggled to win.'

– *Cliff Thorburn after losing 9 frames in a row to go down 10–5 to Dene O'Kane in the first round of the World Championship*

'I couldn't stand the slow play in my previous round against John Campbell. I even started to talk to myself out there.'

– *Silvino Francisco after his 10–3 first-round victory over John Campbell at the World Championship*

'I couldn't stop my legs shaking. I was frightened to death.'

– *Steve Longworth after his 10–4 victory over Rex Williams – his first ever appearance at the Crucible Theatre*

'I got the message. I got ran over. It's scary when you look down your cue and see a nightmare.'

– *Kirk Stevens after losing at the World Championship*

'Perhaps Idi Amin buys more drinks than me.'

– *Steve Davis on Alex Higgins' comment in his autobiography that he would 'rather have a drink with Idi Amin'*

'Sixteen years ago I had a nervous break-down and thought about calling it a day. Now I am sorted out and I can look to the future.'

– *Rex Williams after reaching the final of the Rothmans Grand Prix*

Cheers: Cliff Thorburn receives his trophy after retaining the Langs Supreme Scottish Masters title.

THE SEASON

LANGS SUPREME SCOTTISH MASTERS

The snooker merry-go-round, worth a remarkable £3 million, began turning in Glasgow with the Langs Supreme Scottish Masters. Even this normally quiet pipe-opener to the season was to throw up controversy in later weeks: at an after-match gathering, Alex Higgins was alleged to have said that Canadian Cliff Thorburn takes 'little bags of white stuff'. As a result, Thorburn's manager, Robert Winsor, was to put in a complaint to the WPBSA – one of three serious charges that Higgins faced during the season.

Greg Millard, spokesman for Framework, the company which looks after Higgins' interests, said, 'Words were exchanged at a private party. That is how it should remain.' However, it seems that nothing can remain private for these snooker stars and certainly not for the Hurricane. Winsor, understandably, was upset. 'It is very sad and tragic,' he declared. 'Cliff has just moved to this country with his wife, Barbara, and two young sons. He is a dedicated professional.'

Thorburn was certainly dedicated at the Langs when he retained his title with a 9–8 final victory over Higgins. The Grinder is at his best when he seems to be struggling and that was the case at 5–7 down.

Jimmy White, who had just signed for Barry Hearn's Matchroom stable, provided the highlight of the first round in an eagerly-awaited match with Scottish starlet Stephen Hendry. The sell-out crowd expected fireworks between these two, whom many consider to be the best young players in the game. White, maturing and destined to finish the season as world number 2, needed just sixty-nine minutes to complete 6 frames and go away with a 5–1 victory. But he lost 2–6 against Thorburn in the semi-final, while Higgins, 2–0 down against Kirk Stevens, came back to reach the final by a similar margin.

Langs Supreme Scottish Masters Results

FIRST ROUND:	C. Thorburn (Can)	bt	J. Parrott (Eng)	5–1
	J. White (Eng)	bt	S. Hendry (Scot)	5–1
	K. Stevens (Can)	bt	A. Knowles (Eng)	5–3
	A. Higgins (NI)	bt	J. Johnson (Eng)	5–2
SEMI-FINALS:	C. Thorburn	bt	J. White	6–2
	A. Higgins	bt	K. Stevens	6–2
FINAL:	C. Thorburn	bt	A. Higgins	9–8
PRIZE MONEY:	C. Thorburn £13,000; A. Higgins £8,000; J. White, K. Stevens £4,000; J. Parrott, S. Hendry, A. Knowles, J. Johnson £2,500			
HIGH BREAK:	131 – A. Higgins £1,000			

MATCHROOM TROPHY

While Glasgow was hosting the Langs, Southend-on-Sea, better known for jellied eels and the world's longest pier, was the venue for the Matchroom Trophy. The Matchroom outfit, later to dominate the season, were staging their own tournament with ten sponsors putting up a total of £100,000 in prize money. Matchroom's Hearn said, 'Our sponsors were willing to back our own tournament. There's no television, but I am convinced that the public want to see live snooker.'

Without doubt, they wanted to watch this competition. Even newcomer White was to fly down to the tournament for the first picture of Hearn's seven players together.

Inside the Cliffs Pavilion the action was certainly hot. Willie Thorne, who had just arrived back from winning the Camus Hong Kong Masters, was to take the £50,000 first prize, for which he had to beat Steve Davis in the final. Thorne opened with a 7–5 lead, but when Davis won the 13th on the black, the world number 1 added 3 more frames in succession to move to within 1 frame of success at 9–7. Yet the man from Leicester kept his nerve and shocked Davis' supporters by reeling off 3 frames in succession for a 10–9 victory. Thorne gratefully banked the £50,000 cheque – it was the biggest pay-day of his life. He had scored the highest break as well – a 137 in his opening 6–3 victory over Neal Foulds.

The Hearn boys were virtually encamped at the venue to meet guests, possible sponsors and existing sponsors. Snooker these days is all about money, PR and prestige. Hearn makes sure his lads 'do the business'.

WHO SAID THAT?

'We have only been offered business class flights by the Australian promoter, Eddie Charlton. I asked him to pay us the club class fares and we would make our own arrangements to fly out first class. He turned that down.'

▲

– *Barry Hearn after withdrawing his seven players from the Winfield Masters in Sydney*

Matchroom Trophy Results

FIRST ROUND:	T. Griffiths (Wales)	bt A. Meo (Eng)	6–3
	W. Thorne (Eng)	bt N. Foulds (Eng)	6–3
SEMI-FINALS:	S. Davis (Eng)	bt T. Griffiths	6–2
	W. Thorne	bt Dennis Taylor (NI)	6–5
FINAL:	W. Thorne	bt S. Davis	10–9
PRIZE MONEY:	W. Thorne £50,000; S. Davis £20,000; T. Griffiths, Dennis Taylor £10,000; A. Meo, N. Foulds £5,000		
HIGH BREAK:	137 – W. Thorne (no prize)		

BCE INTERNATIONAL

Neal Foulds races greyhounds as a hobby. This young man from Perivale certainly sprinted away with his first title of the season as he captured the £35,000 first prize in the BCE International at Trentham Gardens, Stoke-on-Trent.

Foulds, then ranked number 13 in the world, swapped frames on the first day of the final with Canadian Cliff Thorburn and they finished all square at 7–7. The second day started badly for Thorburn as he went 7–9 behind and had to call for a fifteen-minute recess to change his cue tip which had been damaged. Thorburn later admitted that he should have made the change a day earlier as Foulds pulled away for a 12–9 success. There were emotional moments after the match when Neal came out to embrace his dad, Geoff, a fellow professional. Geoff has said that he has sacrificed his own career to help Neal get to the top. This was the first step towards that ultimate dream.

In the semi-final Foulds was 4–6 down against Irishman Eugene Hughes, the man who had overcome Steve Davis 5–4 in the quarter-final. But Foulds fought back to go through 9–8.

The second semi-final saw Thorburn with a fight on his hands after looking an easy winner when he led Peter Francisco 6–2. He finally squeezed home 9–7 with the help of a 116 break – the best of the championship – in the 15th frame.

BCE International Results

Fifth Round		Quarter-finals		Semi-finals		Final	
C. Thorburn (Can)	5						
v		Thorburn	5				
T. Griffiths (Wales)	4						
		v		Thorburn	9		
Cliff Wilson	5						
v		Wilson	1				
A. Knowles (Eng)	4			v		Thorburn	9
P. Francisco (SA)	5						
v		P. Francisco	5				
M. Gauvreau (Can)	2			P. Francisco	7		
S. Francisco (SA)	5						
v		S. Francisco	3				
Dennis Taylor (NI)	0					v	
S. Davis (Eng)	5						
v		S. Davis	4				
R. Williams (Eng)	4			Hughes	8		
E. Hughes (Rep Ire)	5						
v		Hughes	5				
R. Chapero (Can)	0			v		N. Foulds	12
K. Owers (Eng)	1						
v		N. Foulds	5				
N. Foulds (Eng)	5			N. Foulds	9		
D. Reynolds (Eng)	5						
v		Reynolds	2				
David Taylor (Eng)	1						
Losers: £2,625		Losers: £5,250		Losers: £10,500		Loser: £21,000	
						Winner: £35,000	

High break: £3,500 – C. Thorburn 116

ROTHMANS GRAND PRIX

Rothmans felt the brunt of the BBC's clampdown on cigarette advertising before a ball was struck in Reading's Hexagon Theatre. Colour changes on the TV set were the result of long negotiations and then, just before the cameras rolled on day one, Rothmans were told that the officials' jackets didn't fit the bill. A trip to Marks and Spencer produced a satisfactory compromise.

The tournament was eventually won by Jimmy White whose 10–6 success denied Rex Williams, at fifty-three, the glory of becoming the oldest professional tournament winner. In fact, Williams looked a likely winner in the first session when he went 5–3 ahead, leaving White a worried young man. But White took the final frame of the afternoon and then allowed Williams to win just one more frame. As well as the £55,000 top prize, there was a £5,000 bonus for a new tournament best break of 138.

White enjoyed a 9–6 semi-final triumph over Silvino Francisco, while a tough

White hot: on-form Jimmy White after his victory in the Rothmans Grand Prix.

encounter saw Williams edge out Neal Foulds 9–8.

In the quarter-final the emergence of Stephen Hendry was a real threat to the game's top players. In a 9-frame battle with White lasting just one hundred minutes, Hendry went down 5–4 – only losing the last frame after a bad miss on the blue into the middle pocket. 'I must be getting too old for this game,' joked White as he finally got through against the seventeen-year-old Scot.

Steve Davis went down in another quarter-final – hammered 5–1 by Williams whose career stretches back nearly thirty-six years. Williams had already proved himself in good form when he trounced Alex Higgins 5–1 in the previous round. He had also beaten Higgins in their last battle in the Mercantile Credit Classic.

WHO SAID THAT?

'I played like a complete amateur – it was a pathetic match. I played awful and didn't deserve to go through.'

▲

– Willie Thorne after going down 5–3 to Neal Foulds in the Rothmans Grand Prix

'That miss on the yellow has cost me £4,000. I'll be back and next time I won't miss.'

▲

– Irishman Paddy Browne after losing 5–3 to Stephen Hendry in the fifth round of the Rothmans Grand Prix

'I'm disappointed, but in that mood Jimmy would have beaten anyone in the world. I couldn't hide the cue ball anywhere.'

▲

– Rex Williams after losing 10–6 to Jimmy White in the final of the Rothmans Grand Prix

Rothmans Grand Prix Results

FOURTH ROUND		FIFTH ROUND		QUARTER-FINALS		SEMI-FINALS		FINAL	
S. Davis (Eng)	5	S. Davis	5						
v				S. Davis	1				
A. Drago (Malta)	1	v							
T. Griffiths (Wales)	5	Griffiths	2	v		Williams	9		
v									
J. Campbell (Aust)	1								
R. Williams (Eng)	5	Williams	5						
v				Williams	5				
M. Wildman (Eng)	1	v						Williams	6
A. Higgins (NI)	5	Higgins	1			v			
v									
D. Martin (Eng)	2								
W. Thorne (Eng)	5	Thorne	3						
v				N. Foulds	5				
W. King (Aust)	2	v							
N. Foulds (Eng)	5	N. Foulds	5						
v						N. Foulds	8		
C. Wilson (Wales)	0			v					
A. Meo (Eng)	5	Meo	5						
v				Meo	3				
J. Parrott (Eng)	3	v				v		v	
Dennis Taylor (NI)	5	Dennis Taylor	2						
v									
J. Virgo (Eng)	3								
S. Newbury (Wales)	5	Newbury	2						
v				S. Francisco	5				
J. O'Boye (Rep Ire)	2	v							
S. Francisco (SA)	5	S. Francisco	5						
v						S. Francisco	6		
W. Jones (Wales)	4			v					
D. Mountjoy (Wales)	5	Mountjoy	1						
v				Knowles	2				
J. Wych (Can)	1	v							
A. Knowles (Eng)	5	Knowles	5						
v						v		White	10
P. Francisco (SA)	3								
J. White (Eng)	5	White	5						
v				White	5				
J. McLaughlin (NI)	2	v							
L. Dodd (Eng)	2	Hallett	3			v			
v						White	9		
M. Hallett (Eng)	5								
R. Chaperon (Can)	2	Hendry	5						
v				Hendry	4				
S. Hendry (Scot)	5	v							
P. Browne (Rep Ire)	5	Browne	3						
v									
M. Bennett (Wales)	0								

Losers: £2,644.06	Losers: £4,125	Losers: £8,250	Losers: £16,500	Loser: £33,000
				Winner: £55,000

High break: £5,500 – J. White 138

BCE CANADIAN MASTERS

The last ball was potted at the Hexagon Theatre, Reading, in the Rothmans Grand Prix, a few celebration drinks were sipped and snooker's travelling circus journeyed to Heathrow to catch a flight to Canada: that is a sample of international snooker 1980s-style.

The venue for the BCE Canadian Masters in Toronto was CBC's Television Studio 7. CBC had been delighted with their coverage

> ### WHO SAID THAT?
> 'I am going to beat the Nugget. It's about time I struck gold again.'
> ▲
> – Alex Higgins before losing to Steve Davis in the BCE Canadian masters

On cue: the eight players line up at a press conference before the Canadian Masters in Toronto.

the year before when the event finished high on the ratings charts – a factor of TV life across the Atlantic that makes or breaks a programme even more decisively than in the UK. The top eight players in the world were lined up for this, an event that the WPBSA hopes will establish the sport even more in Canada.

Steve Davis arrived determined to end an eight-month run without a title. Jimmy White arrived with a cut finger – courtesy of slicing a loaf of bread – and he, Joe Johnson, Cliff Thorburn and Dennis Taylor all departed in the first round. Knowles, after a titanic battle with Willie Thorne, and Alex Higgins went out in the semi-finals. That left Davis and Thorne to battle for the £18,750 top prize, which Davis earned after a convincing 9–3 victory.

Davis also picked up £3,125 for a 134 break against Higgins – the highest of the event and largest break ever seen in a tournament in Canada. The packed house was so delighted that they gave the Englishman a standing ovation. Davis was back in business and he said, 'It is the perfect build-up for the Tennents UK Open back in England.'

The bags were packed, the goodbyes exchanged and the circus was back on another plane across the Atlantic. Thank you, Toronto; hello, Preston.

BCE Canadian Masters Results

QUARTER-FINALS: W. Thorne (Eng) 5, Dennis Taylor (NI) 4; A. Knowles (Eng) 5, C. Thorburn (Can) 1; S. Davis (Eng) 5, J. White (Eng) 2; A. Higgins (NI) 5, J. Johnson (Eng) 3
Losers: £4,218

SEMI-FINALS: Thorne 8, Knowles 7; S. Davis 8, Higgins 2
Losers: £6,250

FINAL: S. Davis 9, Thorne 3
Loser: £11,250   *Winner:* £18,750

HIGH BREAK: £3,225 – S. Davis 143

TENNENTS UK OPEN

Steve Davis soared past the £1 million mark in tournament earnings, since he turned professional, after winning the Tennents Open title for the fifth time at Preston. The tournament will be long remembered, however, for a less savoury incident which occurred in an earlier round when Alex Higgins, after beating Mike Hallett, head-butted tournament director Paul Hatherell.

Snooker, understandably, took second place as the incident was given front-page newspaper coverage up and down the country. News reporters and television crews shuttled between Preston's Guild Hall, the Crest Hotel and Higgins' home in Cheshire. Higgins' return in the next match was greeted with crowd scenes and media interest that would normally be reserved for much more famous personalities. The Hurricane blew over Wayne Jones but then fell to Davis in the semi-final. Davis took the £60,000 top prize for beating Neal Foulds 16–7 in the final.

> **WHO SAID THAT?**
>
> 'I'm disgusted with the game. Snooker has gone far too commercial. It has lost its magic. The game is on a tightrope and just being geared to suit television and sponsors.'
>
> ▲
>
> 'We have got to get snooker back where it was. It is like a game of pool. Anybody can win now. I have been in this game seventeen years as a pro and now anybody can knock in a 100 break.'
>
> ▲
>
> *– Alex Higgins after reaching the last eight of the Tennents UK Open*

Yet Davis was nearly a quarter-final casualty against Tony Drago, the Maltese potter, who had staggered the Guild Hall crowd earlier in the event with a 141 break that took just six minutes. Drago, at 8–8, led 54–1 in that final frame but crucial misses let Davis back in and put Drago out.

There were other debates at the tournament – apart from the Hurricane's. Tony Knowles, with the support of many players, announced his conviction that pockets are too big. 'These days, players don't have to work hard for the breaks,' he claimed. 'Anybody is getting 50s or 60s now.'

Tennents, in the first year of their sponsorship, just sat back and watched the tournament fill up columns of newspaper space and hours of prime television time.

That man again: Steve Davis with the Tennents UK Open trophy.

Tennents UK Open Results

First Round		Second Round	Third Round	Quarter-Finals	Semi-Finals	Final
S. Davis (Eng)	9	S. Davis 9	S. Davis 9	S. Davis 9	S. Davis 9	S. Davis 16
A. Chappel (Wales)	7	v				
E. Charlton (Aust)	9	Charlton 6				
V. Harris (Eng)	2					
S. Francisco (SA)	9	S. Francisco 6				
K. Owers (Eng)	3	v	Reynolds 5			
D. Reynolds (Eng)	9	Reynolds 9				
B. Mikkelsen (Can)	6					
R. Williams (Eng)	7	Drago 9		v		
A. Drago (Malta)	9	v	Drago 9			
J. Virgo (Eng)	9	Virgo 6				
G. Miles (Eng)	7			Drago 8		
W. Thorne (Eng)	9	Thorne 9				
T. Murphy (NI)	4	v	Thorne 5			
M. Macleod (Scot)	6	Grace 1				
R. Grace (SA)	9				v	
A. Higgins (NI)	9	Higgins 9				
S. Hendry (Scot)	8	v	Higgins 9			
D. Martin (Eng)	9	Martin 6				
I. Williamson (Eng)	5			Higgins 9		
A. Meo (Eng)	9	Meo 4				
J. O'Boye (Rep Ire)	3	v	Hallett 7			
M. Hallett (Eng)	9	Hallett 9				
W. King (Aust)	5			v	Higgins 3	
R. Reardon (Wales)	9	Reardon 5				
M. Gibson (Scot)	6	v	Hughes 5			
E. Hughes (Rep Ire)	9	Hughes 9				
C. Roscoe (Wales)	8			W. Jones 5		v
Dennis Taylor (Eng)	9	Dennis Taylor 2				
D. Roe (Eng)	6	v	W. Jones 9			
J. Campbell (Aust)	3	W. Jones 9				
W. Jones (Wales)	9					

Knockout draw (scores shown; winners advance)

Last 32 (Losers: £1,312.50)

C. Thorburn (Can)	9	
D. Fowler (Eng)	7	
David Taylor (Eng)	9	
R. Chaperon (Can)	8	
K. Stevens (Can)	9	
G. Scott (Eng)	2	
C. Wilson (Wales)	5	
J. Spencer (Eng)	9	
N. Foulds (Eng)	9	
G. Cripsey (Eng)	7	
J. Wych (Can)	9	
R. Harris (Eng)	3	
J. White (Eng)	9	
R. Edmonds (Eng)	4	
P. Francisco (SA)	9	
M. Watterson (Eng)	4	
A. Knowles (Eng)	9	
John Rea (Scot)	4	
Barry West (Eng)	4	
A. Jones (Eng)	9	
T. Griffiths (Wales)	9	
P. Gibson (Eng)	3	
W. Werbeniuk (Can)	5	
D. O'Kane (NZ)	9	
D. Mountjoy (Wales)	9	
J. McLaughlin (NI)	6	
S. Longworth (Eng)	9	
B. Rowswell (Eng)	3	
J. Johnson (Eng)	9	
J. Wright (Eng)	1	
J. Parrott (Eng)	9	
M. Bradley (Eng)	4	

Last 16 (Losers: £2,906.25)

Thorburn	9
David Taylor	4
Stevens	4
Spencer	9
N. Foulds	9
Wych	3
White	9
P. Francisco	5
Knowles	9
A. Jones	2
Griffiths	9
O'Kane	0
Mountjoy	1
Longworth	9
Johnson	1
Parrott	9

Quarter-finals (Losers: £4,500)

Thorburn	2
Spencer	9
N. Foulds	9
White	7
Knowles	9
Griffiths	6
Longworth	6
Parrott	9

Semi-finals (Losers: £9,000)

Spencer	2
N. Foulds	9
Knowles	4
Parrott	9

Final stages (Losers: £18,000)

N. Foulds	9
Parrott	3

Final — N. Foulds 7 (Loser: £36,000 / Winner: £60,000)

High break: £6,000 – J. White 144

HOFMEISTER WORLD DOUBLES

Stephen Hendry and Mike Hallett secretly thought they could go all the way to the title in the Hofmeister World Doubles at Northampton. The pair didn't quite make it to victory, but they picked up some famous scalps on the way – the first time either player had appeared in a major tournament final. Unfortunately for them, holders Steve Davis and Tony Meo were waiting in the final. Davis and Meo cantered to a 12–3 victory to earn the £50,000 first prize and take their fourth World Doubles title in five years.

The final was virtually over as a spectacle on day one, when Hendry and Hallett found themselves 11–2 behind. They had scored a magnificent 5–4 victory over Cliff Thorburn and Willie Thorne in the fourth round and then destroyed Neal Foulds and John Parrott 5–1 in the quarter-final.

The quarter-final saw the cue tip of Hendry fly off while he was having a practice during the interval. That might have panicked more experienced pairings, but Hendry brushed it aside and Hallett calmly picked up a tube of superglue and stuck the tip back on.

Crowd pullers Alex Higgins and Jimmy White had seen their chances end with a 5–4 quarter-final defeat by Dennis Taylor and Terry Griffiths, who in turn were beaten 9–6 by Davis and Meo. Kirk Stevens and John Virgo also came through the pack, but were toppled 5–2 by Hendry and Hallett. The final hurdle proved too much for the young pairing, however, and they had to settle for the £25,000 runners-up cheque.

> ### WHO SAID THAT?
> 'I'm convinced that if Stephen can maintain his phenomenal rate of progress, then he will make a million pounds out of the sport. It's there waiting to be made.'
> ———— ▲ ————
> – Ian Doyle, manager of Stephen Hendry, after Hendry reached the final of the Hofmeister World Doubles

Double delight: Steve Davis and Tony Meo, winners of the Hofmeister World Doubles for the fourth time in five years.

Hofmeister World Doubles Results

THIRD ROUND:
S. Davis (Eng) & M. A. Meo (Eng) 5, J. Spencer (Eng) & G. Rigitano (Can) 1; S. Duggan (Eng) & B. West (Eng) 5, C. Wilson (Wales) & W. King (Aust) 4; David Taylor (Eng) & E. Charlton (Aust) 5, M. Gauvreau (Can) & R. Chaperon (Can) 1; S. Francisco (SA) & P. Francisco (SA) 5, V. Harris (Eng) & D. Gilbert (Eng) 4; Dennis Taylor (NI) & T. Griffiths (Wales) 5, M. Darrington (Eng) & B. Oliver (Eng) 1; S. James (Eng) & D. Roe (Eng) 5, J. Campbell (Aust) & P.Mans (SA) 2; R. Williams (Eng) & G. Miles (Eng) 5, I. Williamson (Eng) & R. Grace (SA) 3; J. White (Eng) & A. Higgins (NI) 5, G. Scott (Eng) & G. Foulds (Eng) 2; J. Johnson (Eng) & A. Knowles (Eng) 5, M. Wildman (Eng) & R. Edmonds (Eng) 2; R. Reardon (Wales) & A. Jones (Eng) 5, A. Drago (Malta) & K. Owers (Eng) 3; D. Mountjoy (Wales) & W. Jones (Wales) 5, M. Gibson (Scot) & D. Chalmers (Eng) 1; J. Virgo (Eng) & K. Stevens (Can) 5, P. Fagan (Rep Ire) & T. Murphy (NI) 1; J. Parrott (Eng) & N. Foulds (Eng) 5, S. Newbury (Eng) & R. Bales (Eng) 1; D. Martin (Eng) & M. Macleod (Scot) 5, J. Donnelly (Scot) & C. Roscoe (Wales) 0; M. Hallett (Eng) & S. Hendry (Scot) 5, W. Werbeniuk (Can) & D. Fowler (Eng) 3; W. Thorne (Eng) & C. Thorburn (Can) 5, J. Wych (Can) & D. O'Kane (NZ) 2
Losers: £1,875 (shared)

FOURTH ROUND:
S. Davis & Meo 5, Duggan & West 3; Francisco & Francisco 5, David Taylor & Charlton 1; Dennis Taylor & Griffiths 5, James & Roe 2; White & Higgins 5, Williams & Miles 2; Reardon & A. Jones 5, Johnson & Knowles 4; Virgo & Stevens 5, Mountjoy & W. Jones 4; Parrott & N. Foulds 5, Martin & Macleod 2; Hallett & Hendry 5, Thorne & Thorburn 4
Losers: £3,750 (shared)

QUARTER-FINALS:
S. Davis & Meo 5, Francisco & Francisco 0; Dennis Taylor & Griffiths 5, White & Higgins 4; Virgo & Stevens 5, Reardon & A. Jones 2; Hallett & Hendry 5, Parrott & N. Foulds 1
Losers: £7,500 (shared)

SEMI-FINALS:
S. Davis & Meo 9, Dennis Taylor & Griffiths 6; Hallett & Hendry 9, Virgo & Stevens 2
Losers: £15,000   (shared)

FINAL:
S. Davis & Meo 12, Hallett & Hendry 3
Losers: £25,000   (shared)
Winners: £50,000   (shared)

HIGH BREAK:
£4,000 – S. Davis & A. Meo 217   (shared)

MERCANTILE CREDIT CLASSIC

Steve Davis made it four title wins in a row as he lifted the Mercantile Credit Classic title with a breathtaking 13–12 success over Jimmy White at Blackpool.

There had been some people who had had reservations about Mercantile's move to the Norbreck Hotel on the Blackpool sea-front: it had been suggested that the seaside in January was not the ideal choice. The cynics could not have been more wrong, however, as the crowds delighted in the new venue and the tournament. Mind you, the sponsors and WPBSA were also secretly concerned because eleven of the top sixteen – including Alex Higgins, Dennis Taylor and Cliff Thorburn – had already been eliminated before the final stages got under way.

Those fears also proved unfounded as viewers switched on in their millions, particularly when Scottish teenager Stephen Hendry was in action. Here was a new sporting hero and he was only eighteen! Hendry made it all the way to the semi-final but then he came up against Davis, a player at the top of his form, and went down 9–3. Davis started with breaks of 75

Classic winner: Steve Davis collects his Mercantile Credit trophy.

Reynolds who had produced some of the best snooker of his career.

Davis had enjoyed his moment of good fortune in the quarter-final when John Parrott led the deciding frame 61–0. Davis fought back and, when Parrott missed a brown, the world number 1 cleared up to black to squeeze through.

On to the final that was watched by a peak audience of 15.2 million – the biggest ever for an ITV snooker presentation. ITV insiders could only vaguely remember one bigger sporting audience on their channel from a distant World Cup match. On this occasion those millions of viewers were rewarded with some remarkable snooker. White trailed 7–8 overnight, but then the frames were exchanged before Davis edged into a 12–11 lead. A twenty-eight-shot contest on the pink saw White make it 12–12. White led that final frame 31–0, but then he failed to escape from a fine snooker and Davis came through to win the £50,000 top prize. That made Davis £158,000 richer from a twenty-one-match unbeaten run that stretched back to 24 October.

> ### WHO SAID THAT?
> 'That was an unbelievable time to get a fluke. I have never had a fluke like that in the final frame of a match.'
>
> ▲
>
> *– Jimmy White talking about his 9–8 semi-final victory over Dean Reynolds in the Mercantile Credit Classic*

and 108 and, by the interval, he was ahead 6–1 and Hendry's confidence had been shattered.

White came through his semi-final with a 9–8 win over Grimsby's Dean Reynolds. A fluke in the final frame set up a match-winning break of 74, though White was quick to admit, 'It was an unbelievable time to get a fluke.' It was a sad ending for

Mercantile Credit Classic Results

FIFTH ROUND		QUARTER-FINALS		SEMI-FINALS		FINAL	
J. White (Eng)	5						
v		White	5				
S. Duggan (Eng)	2			White	9		
T. Griffiths (Wales)	5						
v		Griffiths	3			White	12
J. Campbell (Aust)	3						
W. Jones (Wales)	3						
v		Wilson	1				
C. Wilson (Wales)	5			Reynolds	8		
B. West (Eng)	3						
v		Reynolds	5			v	
D. Reynolds (Eng)	5						
S. Davis (Eng)	5						
v		S. Davis	5				
A. Meo (Eng)	2			S. Davis	9		
E. Charlton (Aust)	4						
v		Parrott	4			S. Davis	13
J. Parrott (Eng)	5						
D. Fowler (Eng)	4						
v		Hendry	5				
S. Hendry (Scot)	5			Hendry	3		
S. Francisco (SA)	5						
v		S. Francisco	0				
P. Francisco (SA)	1						
Losers: £3,750		Losers: £7,500		Losers: £15,000		Loser: £30,000	
						Winner: £50,000	

High break: £5,000 – J. White 126

BENSON AND HEDGES MASTERS

Alex Higgins and Dennis Taylor are both Irishmen and excellent snooker players. There the similarity seems to end: Higgins, the nervous, controversial man from Belfast; Taylor, the determined family man from Coalisland, County Tyrone. They met in the final of the Masters at Wembley – the first time their paths had crossed in a major final. An epic was promised but, until the deciding frames, that epic never materialized.

In fact, Higgins' behind-the-scenes management team even had the champagne on ice as Higgins opened an 8–5 lead, needing just one more frame for victory. The Higgins Army of fans were ready to acclaim their hero's first important success for more than three years. When Higgins went well ahead in the next frame, Taylor looked beaten. But Higgins missed a blue, later claiming he got a kick, and Taylor was suddenly back in the match. As his opponent reeled under the pressure, Taylor gritted his teeth and got on with the job. He finally made it 9–8 and collected the £51,000 first prize. Higgins' celebratory champagne had gone warm and flat.

Taylor went away to celebrate his first title triumph since the BCE Canadian Masters nearly fifteen months earlier. He said: 'That was a tremendous victory,' while Higgins looked down at his warped cue – inadvertently left on a hot radiator. The result of that bent cue was, as Higgins explained, 'no chance of going for those power shots'.

Taylor's victory ended a nightmare run for him at the Masters. 'I had been coming to the Masters for nine years and I had only won one match,' he said. 'That was in 1986. Still, winning the title is one way to find my touch.'

Taylor had battled to a fine 6–5 victory over Canada's Cliff Thorburn in the semi-

The Master: Dennis Taylor in jubilant mood after winning the Benson and Hedges Masters at Wembley.

final, ending Thorburn's dream of winning the Masters for a remarkable fourth time in five years. In the other semi-final, Higgins had trounced young Londoner Tony Meo by an emphatic 6–2 margin. Meo had begun the tournament with a tremendous 5–4 victory over Jimmy White – one of the best matches of the championship. That had been a shock in the first round but not as big a surprise as Steve Davis' 5–2 hammering at the hands of Doug Mountjoy. It was so nearly a whitewash as the Welshman at one stage led 4–0.

The Masters said goodbye to Ray Reardon – at least for a year. Reardon lost 5–2 to Joe Johnson and his slide down the rankings means he won't be invited this season. It ended a spell of thirteen consecutive Masters for this six-times World Champion.

There was a moment of snooker history in the quarter-final between Taylor and Foulds when, for the first time, a frame had to be re-racked *twice*.

Benson and Hedges Masters Results

FIFTH ROUND		QUARTER-FINALS		SEMI-FINALS		FINAL	
C. Thorburn (Can)	5	Thorburn	5				
v		v		Thorburn	5		
R. Williams (Eng)	1	Thorne	2				
K. Stevens (Can)	3					Dennis Taylor	9
v				v			
W. Thorne (Eng)	5						
A. Knowles (Eng)	2	S. Francisco	3				
v		v		Dennis Taylor	6		
S. Francisco (SA)	5	Dennis Taylor	5				
N. Foulds (Eng)	2						
v						v	
Dennis Taylor (NI)	5						
S. Davis (Eng)	2	Mountjoy	4				
v		v		Meo	2		
D. Mountjoy (Wales)	5	Meo	5				
A. Meo (Eng)	5					Higgins	8
v				v			
J. White (Eng)	4						
A. Higgins (NI)	5	Higgins	5				
v		v		Higgins	6		
T. Griffiths (Wales)	4	Johnson	1				
R. Reardon (Wales)	2						
v							
J. Johnson (Eng)	5						
Losers: £5,000		Losers: £11,000		Losers: £16,000		Loser: £28,000	
						Winner: £51,000	

High break: £5,000 – J. White 136

DULUX BRITISH OPEN

The third British Open at Derby turned out to be the final occasion on which Dulux were to sponsor the £300,000 event. ICI Paints later decided that Dulux had achieved their market objective. One problem was that snooker is now shown on television in more than twenty countries. Dulux sells in most of those countries but, unfortunately, under different brand names.

Jimmy White made sure that Dulux finished with a flourish, winning the £60,000 first prize with a magnificent display on the second day. A tough opening day had seen opponent Neal Foulds take an 8–7 lead. The stage was set for another nail-biting finish – or so we thought. White was in an unstoppable mood, allowing Foulds just one more frame in ninety-five minutes of extravagant potting that gave him the title by a 13–9 margin.

The Whirlwind: winner Jimmy White.

WHO SAID THAT?

'I made a New Year's resolution – to start playing snooker again.'

▲

– *John Spencer after beating Dave Martin in the fourth round of the Dulux British Open*

'When I see two yellows, I now take the easiest one. Before I used to go for the difficult one.'

▲

– *John Spencer after his fifth-round victory in the Dulux British Open over Joe Johnson. (Spencer has to take daily steroid tablets to combat double vision)*

Foulds summed up White's performance perfectly when he said, 'Steve Davis is certainly harder to play, but Jimmy can be more frightening.' White's comment was simply, 'My game came together and I was buzzing out there.'

The turning point had, perhaps, come in the final frame on the first day, which White took. 'I would have probably lost at

9–6,' he said, 'but 8–7 was a different story.'

Foulds had demolished Tony Knowles 9–2 in the semi-final and Foulds included a superb break of 140 that was to earn him £6,000 for the high break. White took on Cliff Thorburn who had been suffering from a virus, but the Canadian still proved a tough customer before White came home 9–5.

There were some memorable moments in the earlier rounds. On day one John Virgo put out Steve Davis 5–4, and in the quarter-final Thorburn and David Taylor put their names in the record books: the seventh frame of their match went 90–87 to Thorburn – the most points ever scored in one frame of professional snooker.

Dulux British Open Results

FOURTH ROUND		FIFTH ROUND		QUARTER-FINALS		SEMI-FINALS		FINAL
S. Davis (Eng)	4							
J. Virgo (Eng)	5	Virgo	5					
		v		Virgo	3			
S. Francisco (SA)	4	Wilson	2					
C. Wilson (Wales)	5					N. Foulds	9	
N. Foulds (Eng)	5			v				
W. King (Aust)	4	N. Foulds	5					
		v		N. Foulds	5			
W. Thorne (Eng)	5	Thorne	2					
S. Duggan (Eng)	2							N. Foulds	9
A. Knowles (Eng)	5					v		
D. Reynolds (Eng)	0	Knowles	5					
		v		Knowles	5			
R. Reardon (Wales)	4	Murphy	3					
T. Murphy (NI)	5					Knowles	2	
T. Griffiths (Wales)	5			v				
A. Jones (Eng)	3	Griffiths	4					
		v		Dennis Taylor	4			
Dennis Taylor (NI)	5	Dennis Taylor	5					
E. Charlton (Aust)	1							v
C. Thorburn (Can)	5							
G. Cripsey (Eng)	2	Thorburn	5					
		v		Thorburn	5			
D. Mountjoy (Wales)	5	Mountjoy	4					
P. Francisco (SA)	3					Thorburn	5	
K. Stevens (Can)	5			v				
B. West (Eng)	4	Stevens	2					
		v		David Taylor	3			
J. McLaughlin (NI)	2	David Taylor	5					
David Taylor (Eng)	5							White	13
J. White (Eng)	5					v		
M. Hallett (Eng)	2	White	5					
		v		White	5			
R. Williams (Eng)	5	Williams	0					
S. James (Eng)	2					White	9	
J. Spencer (Eng)	5			v				
D. Martin (Eng)	2	Spencer	5					
		v		Spencer	3			
J. Johnson (Eng)	5	Johnson	3					
E. Hughes (Rep Ire)	3							
Losers: £2,906.25		Losers: £4,500		Losers: £9,000		Losers: £18,000		Loser: £36,000 Winner: £60,000

High break: £6,000 – N. Foulds 140

TUBORG WORLD CUP

Tuborg stepped in at the last minute to sponsor the World Cup at Bournemouth, a tournament that was plagued by problems before a ball was struck. The WPBSA wanted to change the system, using the top twenty-four players in the ranking list and eliminating the country-style format. This plan came quickly under fire, however, and world number 1 Steve Davis decided that he didn't want to play. The decision was reversed, Tuborg arrived and the event went ahead with Ireland defending the title they had won for the past two years.

Four days later, Ireland's team of skipper Dennis Taylor, Alex Higgins and Eugene Hughes collected the trophy for a record third time after an easy 9–2 victory over Canada. Taylor commented: 'When we

The toast is victory: skipper Dennis Taylor, Eugene Hughes and Alex Higgins celebrate their Tuborg World Cup win.

first won this title, some people suggested it was a fluke. I hope this will silence them once and for all.'

Canada earned their final place with a superb 5–4 success over England, with Cliff Thorburn beating Joe Johnson in the deciding frame.

England pair Steve Davis and Tony Meo arrived just in time after their helicopter was forced down in a snowstorm on the way to the coast from the racing at Cheltenham.

Ireland had ended Welsh hopes in the semi-final with a 5–2 victory.

WHO SAID THAT?

'We have all had colds and we are going to celebrate by cracking open a bottle of cough medicine.'

▲

– Alex Higgins after Ireland won the Tuborg World Cup title for the third successive year

---

Tuborg World Cup Results

FIRST ROUND: Ireland A (Dennis Taylor, A. Higgins, E. Hughes) 5, Ireland B (P. Fagan, P. Browne, T. Murphy) 1; Wales (T. Griffiths, D. Mountjoy, R. Reardon) 5, Australia (J. Campbell, E. Charlton, W. King) 1; Canada (C. Thorburn, K. Stevens, W. Werbeniuk) 5, Rest of World (S. Francisco, A. Drago, D. O'Kane) 4; England (S. Davis, J. Johnson, A. Meo) 5, Scotland (M. Macleod, S. Hendry, M. Gibson) 1

   Losers: £6,000 (shared)

SEMI-FINALS: Ireland A 5, Wales 2; Canada 5, England 4

   Losers: £10,000 (shared)

FINAL: Ireland A 9, Canada 2

   Losers: £20,000 (shared)

   Winners: £32,000 (shared)

HIGH BREAK: (individual) £4,000 – T. Griffiths 113

BENSON AND HEDGES IRISH MASTERS

The horse sales-ring at Goffs, County Kildare, is used to seeing thoroughbreds go through their paces. Last season there was another thoroughbred in action: Steve Davis, who collected the Benson and Hedges Irish Masters title in magnificent style with a 9–1 hammering of Willie Thorne.

Davis had declined the invitation to take part in the 1986 Irish Masters because it was too close to the World Championship. The dates were changed for 1987, and Davis crossed the Irish Sea and predictably won the title. The final was a walkover for him as Thorne, beaten finalist in 1986, blew hot and cold over the air conditioning and heating. Poor Thorne was hardly in the game from the first frame. Then he led 65–38, went in off green and watched Davis steal the frame on the black. Thorne did level at 1–1, but then the Davis machine

It's mine: Steve Davis after winning the Benson and Hedges Irish Masters.

switched smoothly into gear and snapped up 8 frames in a row.

Davis had come through his semi-final with a comfortable 6–2 defeat of Terry Griffiths, while Thorne had reached the final with a 6–2 success over Dennis Taylor. In the quarter-final Thorne had beaten Jimmy White 5–4 to earn his revenge for his defeat in the final twelve months earlier. 'I should have won 5–1,' said Thorne. 'I have never missed so many shots.' Griffiths, in his 5–0 quarter-final triumph over Joe Johnson, hadn't missed a ball. 'That was almost the ultimate in snooker,' admitted an honest Johnson. 'Terry hardly missed a shot.'

Davis had come through 5–2 in the last eight against Tony Meo, who was justifiably upset by allegations of a betting coup in his first-round victory against Tony Knowles. Irish bookmakers claimed that there was an attempted coup on the match, which Meo won 5–2, though the money involved turned out to be less than £10,000! Meo and Knowles dismissed the claims as 'rubbish', and Matchroom's Barry Hearn stepped in to call for his players voluntarily to stop betting on matches. Davis said, 'I have never had a bet on snooker but I will support Barry. Tony was certainly upset, and with good reason. I know we are all professionals but we are only human beings. It was tough for Tony out there.'

Taylor completed the semi-final line-up with a 5–1 destruction of an out-of-touch Cliff Thorburn.

In the opening match of the tournament, Canada's Kirk Stevens had arrived in the arena waving a white flag on the end of his cue in a mock symbol of surrender for his failure to turn up in 1986. This time he had managed to catch his plane, but he still didn't hang around too long as he went down 5–1 to Thorne.

Alex Higgins was also a first-round loser, 1–5 against Griffiths. Higgins was still

Winning smile: Steve Davis and Terry Griffiths before their Benson and Hedges Irish Masters semi-final which Davis won 6–2.

taking antibiotics for a heavy cold, but he wasn't too pleased, either, with the performance of some of his own supporters. 'Some of that crowd weren't much help to me,' he commented. 'That's probably why there has never been an Irish winner at this event. Even so, I didn't feel like playing and I didn't play well.'

Most crowds want Higgins to win. There is something about his nature that inspires his fans. It's not that they shout against him. It's just that he doesn't like them shouting 'Come on Alex!' as he gets down on a shot.

The Irish Masters is a tournament that everyone enjoys – the players, officials and certainly the travelling band of press who are now regulars at Goffs and the Hotel Keadeen. It might just have something to do with Kevin Norton, the Benson and Hedges man-on-the-spot, and his band of fifty-four helpers.

The last time Davis won the Masters was in 1984. Then he went on to win the World title. That's exactly what happened again last season.

Benson and Hedges Irish Masters Results

FIRST ROUND		QUARTER-FINALS		SEMI-FINALS		FINAL	
J. White (Eng)							
Bye		White	4				
		v		Thorne	6		
W. Thorne (Eng)	5	Thorne	5				
K. Stevens (Can)	1			v		Thorne	1
C. Thorburn (Can)							
Bye		Thorburn	1				
		v		Dennis Taylor	2		
E. Hughes (Rep Ire)	4	Dennis Taylor	5				
Dennis Taylor (NI)	5						
S. Davis (Eng)						v	
Bye		Davis	5				
		v		Davis	6		
A. Knowles (Eng)	2	Meo	2				
A. Meo (Eng)	5			v		Davis	9
J. Johnson (Eng)							
Bye		Johnson	0				
		v		Griffiths	2		
T. Griffiths (Wales)	5	Griffiths	5				
A. Higgins (NI)	1						
Losers: £3,100		Losers: £5,400		Losers: £9,000		Loser: £13,000	
						Winner: £22,500	

High break: £2,500 – Dennis Taylor 117

ROTHMANS MATCHROOM LEAGUE

The snow was falling heavily when Barry Hearn and Rothmans decided to announce their latest venture – a soccer-style league. The venue was audacious: the Royal Albert Hall. The prize money was sizeable: £50,000 to the winner. And the reward for a 147 break was suitably magnificent: a Rolls-Royce Silver Spirit, worth £69,000. Steve Davis and the Matchroom men, plus guest Cliff Thorburn, were photographed cueing snowballs off the bonnet of the Rolls-Royce. The Rothmans Matchroom League was on the way.

The format was simple. The eight players would play each other once at fourteen different venues all over Britain. Cynics, however, were dismissive of the League because there was no television coverage. TV, it seems, in some quarters is the god these days. If there is no TV, the plan will flop. But Hearn did not want TV. He boldly proclaimed: 'I want to get snooker back to the people. I am certain the fans will come out and watch these players in action. The Matchroom has helped pioneer snooker all over the world. A world league is the ultimate aim.'

Many assumed that Rothmans' involvement would mean the end of their Grand Prix competition at Reading. Nothing could have been further from the truth, though pressure was being exerted on the cigarette companies by BBC's clampdown on cigarette advertising. Rothmans not only continued their Grand Prix, but also put up a special 'double' prize for the player who could win the League and the Grand Prix. The ultimate reward for the double would be £150,000 – the highest amount yet offered in snooker. Rothmans' spokesman Brian Roach said, 'Our involvement in the League and the Grand Prix gives us an excellent mix of televised and live snooker of the very highest quality.'

As snow threatened to cause problems for the opening matches at Torbay, Hearn had a fleet of helicopters standing by just in case. Fortunately, the weather eased and the League kicked off with Terry Griffiths meeting Dennis Taylor.

The scoring was based on soccer's with 3 points for a win and 1 point for a draw. The 8-frame format was also revolutionary. Would the fans settle for watching a 4–4 draw and not seeing a result?

Griffiths was the early leader but Steve Davis finally edged in front as the League built to a tremendous climax. The action had switched from Torbay to Hull, from Cardiff to Croydon. Most evening sessions were sell-outs with more than 2,100 turning up at the Brighton International Centre.

Davis arrived at Derby Assembly Rooms – scene of many of his triumphs – needing to beat Jimmy White to take the title. Six days earlier, Davis had regained the World crown after beating White 16–11 in the semi-final. On this occasion, White won 5–3, leaving Davis on 13 points from his 7 completed matches. White went away to work and practise as the League moved on to Cleethorpes the following weekend.

Cleethorpes, rain pouring down, hardly seemed the place to settle a £50,000 first prize. White, like Davis a few days earlier, just required a victory to pick up the cash, while Foulds, troubled by personal problems, was hardly in the best frame of mind. He was still taking beta-blocker tablets for a heart condition, there had been allegations about his marriage in the *Sun*, and his car had been stolen and used in a bank raid! Foulds, Mr Nice Guy, was, understandably, quiet and thoughtful. But he was still a professional and he went out to beat White who was now destined to finish third. The road maps were studied as the League team, led by Ken Upperton, moved camp yet again – this time across England to the Everton Park Sports Centre in Liverpool.

Now it was Foulds who could steal the title with Tony Meo standing in his way.

When Foulds went down 1–3, his father, Geoff, was resigned to failure. The snooker was not of the highest quality but the tension was almost unbearable as Foulds fought back to lead 4–3. Even the rain was beating a tattoo on the roof as Foulds opened a 65–0 lead in the final frame.

At his Essex countryside home, Davis had been relaxing quietly waiting for the telephone call to tell him if he had won yet another title. The phone rang. It was manager Hearn informing Davis he was runner-up as Foulds led 65–0. Davis put on the kettle to make a consolation cup of tea.

While Davis waited for the kettle to boil, the atmosphere was certainly warming up in Liverpool as Meo got down to play with 75 points on the table. Poor Foulds could only sit back and admire Meo's clinical potting. The final black went in to signal a break of 71 to leave Foulds desolate. 'I'm absolutely sick – I thought I had done enough to win,' he said.

The phone rang again in the Davis farm-house, 'You've won,' announced Hearn. 'Meo has cleared up with a break of 71.' He admits that, although he looks after seven players, Davis has been and will always be his number one.

'I couldn't believe it,' said Davis. 'I thought I was the outsider when I lost to Jimmy in Derby. It's not a bad way to earn £50,000 – on a day off. That was the first day's holiday I had had for more than a month. I just lazed around at home and watched a bit of television.'

After the second phone call, the kettle was switched off and something stronger was substituted – a few bottles of his favourite Kronenberg beer. Davis had even found time to tidy up his room. He said, 'I

KO King: Tony Meo, who ended Neal Foulds' hopes of winning the Rothmans Matchroom League.

had clothes all over the place. I even threw a lot of old gear away. Now I will be able to afford some more new ones.'

The League had been a success and Rothmans were delighted. Crowds had, indeed, flocked to see 'live' snooker without television cameras following every move. Riley's packed their table away for the last time. The League was over but plans were already being made for excursions into Europe in 1988. The Rolls-Royce, sponsored by Minolta Copiers, was unclaimed. The Minolta slogan summed up Davis yet again – boringly reliable.

Rothmans Matchroom League Results

Dennis Taylor 4, T. Griffiths 4;   S. Davis 7, W. Thorne 1;   Taylor 7, A. Meo 1; Davis 4, Griffiths 4;   Griffiths 5, Meo 3;   J. White 5, Taylor 3; C. Thorburn 2, N. Foulds 6;   Thorne 4, White 4;   Foulds 4, Griffiths 4;   Davis 7, Meo 1; Thorne 5, Griffiths 3;   Davis 6, Foulds 2;   Thorburn 5, Thorne 3; Davis 6, Taylor 2;   Taylor 3, Foulds 5;   Davis 3, Thorburn 5;   Thorne 4, Foulds 4; White 1, Meo 7;   White 6, Griffiths 2;   Taylor 5, Thorburn 3; Thorne 2, Meo 6;   White 4, Thorburn 4;   Thorburn 2, Griffiths 6;   Davis 3, White 5; Thorburn 4, Meo 4;   White 2, Foulds 6;   Meo 4, Foulds 4;   Taylor 4, Thorne 4.

FINAL TABLE

	P	W	D	L	F	A	Pts
S. Davis (Eng)	7	4	1	2	36	20	13
N. Foulds (Eng)	7	3	3	1	31	25	12
J. White (Eng)	7	3	2	2	27	29	11
T. Griffiths (Wales)	7	2	3	2	28	28	9
D. Taylor (NI)	7	2	2	3	28	28	8
A. Meo (Eng)	7	2	2	3	26	30	8
C. Thorburn (Can)	7	2	2	3	25	31	8
W. Thorne (Eng)	7	1	3	3	23	33	6

PRIZE MONEY: S. Davis £53,600; N. Foulds £3,100; T. Griffiths £2,800; D. Taylor £2,800; J. White £2,700; A. Meo £2,600; C. Thorburn £2,500; W. Thorne £2,300.

HIGH BREAK: £2,400 T. Griffiths – 136

EMBASSY WORLD CHAMPIONSHIP

Steve Davis shed a few tears as he earned his fourth Embassy World Championship title with an 18–14 victory over defending champion Joe Johnson at Sheffield's Crucible Theatre. It was an emotional moment for the Essex millionaire who had been beaten in the previous two world finals. 'It would have been catastrophic if I had lost three finals in a row,' admitted Davis. 'I cried back in the dressing room.' The £80,000 first prize meant little to him; it was this title that he needed. He was assured of being number 1 in the rankings but that wasn't good enough for this snooker perfectionist. He wanted to be number 1 *and* World Champion.

Facing Davis across the other side of the table was Johnson, the likeable pop-singing player from Bradford. As they prepared for the final, recollections of their final meeting twelve months earlier must have flooded their minds. Then Johnson, the 150–1 outsider, had stood with the trophy raised to an adoring audience after his 18–12 defeat of Davis. The loser could only applaud the man who had achieved what many people had believed impossible.

> ### WHO SAID THAT?
> 'I am going back to Canada to practise, practise and practise until I want to eat my cue.'
>
> ▲
>
> – *Jim Wych after losing in the Embassy World Championship*

Would 1987 be any different? Certainly Johnson, whom the bookmakers had written off as a 66–1 no-hoper, had surprised everyone, including himself, by reaching the final. After his 16–9 semifinal victory over Neal Foulds, he said, 'I used to read a lot of comics as a kid. This is the stuff that comics are made of.' He was right.

Davis opened with a break of 127 that was to earn him an £8,000 bonus for the high break of the tournament. Remarkably, it was Davis' only century. Johnson, however, whose courage had never been questioned, captured 3 frames in a row and finally finished the first session 4–3 ahead. In the evening, Davis took just forty-four minutes to move into a 6–4 lead but his opponent did his chances a power of good by taking the final frame of the first day to

Well played! Joe Johnson congratulates Steve Davis after the 1987 Embassy World Championship final.

reduce the deficit to 7–9. Afterwards Johnson returned to his hotel room to watch a video – *Curse of the Living Dead*. Davis, snooker's Mr Cool, had a meal with his dad, Bill, and driver, Robbo, and just waited for the final day.

Davis had won his last World title in 1984. It had been a long wait since then for a young man many people reckoned to be the finest ever exponent of snooker. This match had the added appeal of being the first 'repeat' World Championship final since 1956, when Fred Davis, still playing, had beaten John Pulman, now an ITV commentator, 38–35.

On the second day of the final, Johnson put on the pressure with a break of 40 to reduce the arrears to just 1 frame. But then Davis took control and 4 frames were quickly under his belt to make the score 13–9. Davis – who, Johnson admitted later, was playing the better snooker – stretched that advantage to 14–9. Johnson refused to lie down and 4 frames in a row threw the match and the title wide open yet again. Then Davis switched up a gear and collected 4 more frames to record his fourth World title in seven final attempts.

'That was the most satisfying win of my career,' he declared afterwards as the champagne flowed. 'I know I sound like a Boy Scout, but I have never been so prepared for an event.' The 1987 World Champion was engulfed by his dad, manager Barry Hearn and his wife Susan, and minder Robbo. The celebrations continued long into the night. The following day, however, Davis was back at work fulfilling a Courage exhibition night down in Bournemouth. Even World Champions have to carry on as usual.

Johnson, meanwhile, went back to his club in Morley for a 'good old-fashioned sing-song'. He said, 'Steve is a worthy champion – he deserved to win.' There was the consolation of the £48,000 loser's cheque. And losing that World title was probably, looking back, a weight off Joe's mind. Poor Johnson had hardly won a match after his 1986 win. Headlines just seemed to carry the same sorry tale: 'Johnson loses – *again*.' Now he's established as the number 5 player in the world, and his results will probably improve as well.

In the semi-final, Jimmy White had gone down 11–16 to Davis. White, now the world number 2, was another of the 'let's get out of Sheffield' brigade. The Whirlwind stayed at a hotel in the Peak District National Park and, although not known for his cultural involvements, even ventured down a cave to see the sights.

'Steve just got stronger and stronger. He's the hardest man to beat,' said White after their clash, but then that cheeky little smile crept across his face as he thought of the £200,000 plus in prize money he won last season. 'I've gone up the rankings and this is my best ever season,' he added.

Johnson, meanwhile, had overcome Foulds, the young Londoner who had caused a stir by announcing he was taking beta-blocker tablets for a heart condition discovered just before the tournament started. There had been calls for Foulds to quit the tournament and even professional snooker until he was fit again. Exhausted by the tablets, he didn't do his game justice. The season that had been his best finished on a sour note, though he was full of praise for Johnson.

The quarter-finals saw the exit of Dene O'Kane, the revelation of the tournament, and Stephen Hendry, the young Scot who will only get better. O'Kane, from Auckland, New Zealand, produced one of the most outstanding individual performances in the history of the world event when he met stablemate Cliff Thorburn in the first round. It was known that O'Kane fancied his chances, but Canadian Thorburn, then number 2 in the world, looked like completing the formality of a victory as he went 5–1 in front. The young New Zealander, however, who said he learnt the game playing with ping-pong balls and a broom-handle, had other ideas. He compiled break after break and ran in 9 frames in a row for an amazing 10–5 victory. 'I've lost my fear of the top players,' said O'Kane, who had arrived in Britain four years earlier on the proceeds of snooker and poker.

Thorburn, now settled in this country, didn't have a good season. This was the final straw. He said, 'I felt as good as I have felt in my life out there. If I can find out what went wrong, I'll get back to you.'

O'Kane kept the run going with a 13–5 second-round win over Doug Mountjoy, the Welshman who scrambled into the top sixteen yet again, courtesy of his 10–5 first-round victory over David Taylor. But then O'Kane, known as 'Doctor Death' because of his pallid appearance and matchstick 9-stone frame, came up against White in the last eight. It proved too big a task and White romped home 13–6.

Hendry, at eighteen, would have been the youngest World Champion but he came unstuck in a memorable match against Johnson. Already this fresh-faced Edinburgh youngster is being hailed as the game's greatest potter, and his yearly earnings are estimated at £400,000. That's not bad for a kid who didn't start playing until he was twelve when his dad was stuck for a present and brought him a small snooker table! He had earned his last-eight place in this World Championship by beating Willie Thorne 10–7 in the first round and then Blackburn's Steve Longworth 13–7. Against Johnson now he trailed 12–8 and defeat looked a certainty, but then frame after frame went his way until

Taking it easy: Scottish sensation Stephen Hendry.

the scores were locked at 12–12. The miracle didn't appear, however, and Johnson took the decider to go through.

Johnson said, 'I remembered what happened the previous year against Terry Griffiths in the same round. I was 12–9 down and won 13–9.'

Hendry even kicked the dressing room in disgust during one mid-session interval and bruised his foot! After his defeat he said, 'One more win and I would have been in the top sixteen. I was confident of winning. Before that last frame I went for a walk and told myself: "You've got him now."' It wasn't to be.

Johnson had finished the first day of the quarter-finals by going in off the final black to make his lead just 10–6. 'I was having nightmares about that black ball,' he admitted. 'I had a restless night.'

Another young man making a name for himself was Grimsby's Mike Hallett, now guaranteed a top sixteen ranking. Hallett, who beat defending champion Dennis Taylor in the first round in 1985, picked up the prized scalp of Tony Knowles in the first round this time by a 10–6 margin. Knowles had prepared by relaxing and resting at his home on the banks of Lake Windermere with Ireland's Eugene Hughes who was another first-round casualty – going down 10–9 to Johnson.

Hallett, whose talent has never been properly rewarded, followed his victory over Knowles by beating South Africa's Silvino Francisco 13–9. But he wasn't happy about his 13–9 defeat by Foulds and castigated himself, saying, 'I played like a clown.'

The fourth quarter-final was between Davis and Terry Griffiths, the Welshman whom many people thought an outside hope for his first title since 1979. Davis was too strong, coming home 13–5, though Griffiths did help create a little bit of history in his first-round victory over Jim Wych of Canada. Griffiths won 10–4, and that took the season's earnings of the

Matchroom stable officially past the £1 million mark. 'It's an honour,' he said, 'but, ironically, I have earned the least of the seven Matchroom players.'

In the second round – the last sixteen – one old favourite said goodbye to automatic qualification for the World Championship: six-times winner Ray Reardon. When he went down 13–4 to Davis, he said, 'This is a young man's game these days, but I'll be back in the top sixteen by 1989.' Davis commented, 'Ray was my hero when I was a kid. He was the complete player.'

Alex Higgins also blew out 10–13 at the hands of Griffiths, and the Hurricane departed to start his five-tournament ban for a series of misdemeanours in 1986 culminating in head-butting tournament director Paul Hatherell.

Other second-round casualties were Liverpool's John Parrott (11–13 to White), Dennis Taylor (10–13 to Foulds) and Scot Murdo Macleod (7–13 to Johnson). Macleod had also enjoyed a slice of snooker history in his 10–5 first-round victory over Rex Williams – the first ever win by a Scot in the eleven-year history of the Crucible Theatre. Tony Meo, who now dropped out of the top sixteen, went down 8–10 to Parrott, while Canada's Kirk Stevens was another seeded departure, losing 4–10 to Longworth.

One of the toughest matches in the first round was between White and Grimsby's Dean Reynolds, arguably the most improved player on the circuit. White was losing 7–8 to a man who had beaten him 6–5 in the Tolly Ales English Championship. Reynolds also lost on a fluke to White in a last-frame decider in the semi-final of

On top of the world: Steve Davis with the Embassy World Championship trophy.

the Mercantile Credit Classic. But the Whirlwind, who later agreed that he was only in second gear, won 3 frames in succession to scrape home 10–8.

Even Davis, the eventual champion, had been given a tough ride by Australian Warren King in the first round. Davis won 10–7, but King nearly made it 8–8 before Davis came through. And Davis said, 'Warren got the taste of blood and then went for my throat. I hate the first round.'

Those last five words were echoed by virtually every player in Sheffield and just about summed up the 1987 Crucible cauldron.

Embassy World Championship Results

First Round

J. Johnson (Eng)	10
E. Hughes (Rep Ire)	9
R. Williams (Eng)	5
M. Macleod (Scot)	10
K. Stevens (Can)	4
S. Longworth (Eng)	10
W. Thorne (Eng)	7
S. Hendry (Scot)	10
A. Knowles (Eng)	6
M. Hallett (Eng)	10
S. Francisco (SA)	10
J. Campbell (Aust)	3
N. Foulds (Eng)	10
J. Virgo (Eng)	4
Dennis Taylor (NI)	10
M. Bennett (Wales)	4
C. Thorburn (Can)	5
D. O'Kane (NZ)	10
D. Mountjoy (Wales)	10
David Taylor (Eng)	5
A. Meo (Eng)	8
J. Parrott (Eng)	10
J. White (Eng)	10
D. Reynolds (Eng)	8
A. Higgins (NI)	10
J. Wright (Eng)	6
T. Griffiths (Wales)	10
J. Wych (Can)	4
R. Reardon (Wales)	10
B. West (Eng)	5
S. Davis (Eng)	10
W. King (Aust)	7

Second Round

Johnson	13
Macleod	7
Longworth	7
Hendry	13
Hallett	13
S. Francisco	9
N. Foulds	13
Dennis Taylor	10
O'Kane	13
Mountjoy	5
Parrott	11
White	13
Higgins	10
Griffiths	13
Reardon	4
Davis	13

Quarter-finals

Johnson	13
Hendry	12
Hallett	9
N. Foulds	13
O'Kane	6
White	13
Griffiths	5
Davis	13

Semi-finals

Johnson	16
N. Foulds	9
White	11
Davis	16

Final

Johnson	14
Davis	18

Losers: £3,375

Losers: £6,000

Losers: £12,000

Losers: £24,000

Loser: £48,000
Winner: £80,000

High break: £8,000 – S. Davis 127

WORLD CHAMPIONSHIP ROLL OF HONOUR 1927–87

YEAR	WINNER	RUNNER-UP	SCORE	VENUE
1927	J. Davis (Eng)	T. Dennis (Eng)	20–11	Camkin's Hall, Birmingham
1928	J. Davis (Eng)	F. Lawrence (Eng)	16–13	Camkin's Hall, Birmingham
1929	J. Davis (Eng)	T. Dennis (Eng)	19–14	Lounge Billiard Hall, Nottingham
1930	J. Davis (Eng)	T. Dennis (Eng)	25–12	Thurston's Hall, London
1931	J. Davis (Eng)	T. Dennis (Eng)	25–21	Lounge Billiard Hall, Nottingham
1932	J. Davis (Eng)	C. McConachy (NZ)	30–19	Thurston's Hall, London
1933	J. Davis (Eng)	W. Smith (Eng)	25–18	Joe Davis Billiards Centre, Chesterfield
1934	J. Davis (Eng)	T. Newman (Eng)	25–23	Lounge Billiard Hall, Nottingham
1935	J. Davis (Eng)	W. Smith (Eng)	25–20	Thurston's Hall, London
1936	J. Davis (Eng)	H. Lindrum (Aust)	34–27	Thurston's Hall, London
1937	J. Davis (Eng)	H. Lindrum (Aust)	32–29	Thurston's Hall, London
1938	J. Davis (Eng)	S. Smith (Eng)	37–24	Thurston's Hall, London
1939	J. Davis (Eng)	S. Smith (Eng)	43–30	Thurston's Hall, London
1940	J. Davis (Eng)	F. Davis (Eng)	37–36	Thurston's Hall, London
1941–45	No tournament held			
1946	J. Davis (Eng)	H. Lindrum (Aust)	78–67	Horticultural Hall, London
1947	W. Donaldson (Scot)	F. Davis (Eng)	82–63	Leicester Square Hall, London
1948	F. Davis (Eng)	W. Donaldson (Scot)	84–61	Leicester Square Hall, London
1949	F. Davis (Eng)	W. Donaldson (Scot)	80–65	Leicester Square Hall, London
1950	W. Donaldson (Scot)	F. Davis (Eng)	51–46	Tower Circus, Blackpool
1951	F. Davis (Eng)	W. Donaldson (Scot)	58–39	Tower Circus, Blackpool

World beaters: the legendary Joe Davis (left) and Fred Davis.

In 1952, a dispute between the Billiards Association and Control Council and the professional players led to a split and two tournaments were held.

The BA&CC tournament attracted just two players in Horace Lindrum and Clark McConachy, while the professionals organized the World Matchplay Championship in which Fred Davis met Walter Donaldson in the final.

BA&CC Tournament

YEAR	WINNER	RUNNER-UP	SCORE	VENUE
1952	H. Lindrum (Aust)	C. McConachy (NZ)	94–49	Houldsworth Hall, Manchester

World Matchplay Championship

YEAR	WINNER	RUNNER-UP	SCORE
1952	F. Davis (Eng)	W. Donaldson (Scot)	38–35
1953	F. Davis (Eng)	W. Donaldson (Scot)	37–34
1954	F. Davis (Eng)	W. Donaldson (Scot)	39–21
1955	F. Davis (Eng)	J. Pulman (Eng)	37–34
1956	F. Davis (Eng)	J. Pulman (Eng)	38–35
1957	J. Pulman (Eng)	J. Rea (NI)	39–34

Between 1958 and 1963 no matches took place. From 1964 the title was decided on a challenge basis which meant that there was often more than one event per year.

YEAR	WINNER	RUNNER-UP	SCORE	VENUE
1964	J. Pulman (Eng)	F. Davis (Eng)	19–16	Burroughes Hall, London
	J. Pulman (Eng)	R. Williams (Eng)	40–33	Burroughes Hall, London
1965	J. Pulman (Eng)	F. Davis (Eng)	37–36	Burroughes Hall, London
	J. Pulman (Eng)	R. Williams (Eng)	25–22	Match series in South Africa
	J. Pulman (Eng)	F. van Rensburg (SA)	39–12	South Africa
1966	J. Pulman (Eng)	F. Davis (Eng)	5–2	Match series at St George's Hall, Liverpool
1967	No tournament held			
1968	J. Pulman (Eng)	E. Charlton (Aust)	39–34	Co-operative Hall, Bolton
1969	Championship again organized on a knockout basis			
	(Players No. 6) J. Spencer (Eng)	G. Owen (Wales)	37–24	Victoria Hall, London
1970	(Players No. 6) R. Reardon (Wales)	J. Pulman (Eng)	37–33	Victoria Hall, London
1971	(actually held Nov 1970 as a round robin) J. Spencer (Eng)	W. Simpson (Aust)	37–29	Sydney, Australia
1972	(reverted to knockout basis) A. Higgins (NI)	J. Spencer (Eng)	37–32	Selly Park British Legion, Birmingham
1973	(Park Drive) R. Reardon (Wales)	E. Charlton (Aust)	38–32	City Exhibition Hall, Manchester
1974	(Park Drive) R. Reardon (Wales)	G. Miles (Eng)	22–12	Belle Vue, Manchester
1975	R. Reardon (Wales)	E. Charlton (Aust)	31–30	Melbourne, Australia
1976	(Embassy until present day) R. Reardon (Wales)	A. Higgins (NI)	27–16	Town Hall, Middlesbrough, and Wythenshawe Forum, Manchester

Year	Winner	Runner-up	Score	Venue
1977	J. Spencer (Eng)	C. Thorburn (Can)	25–12	Crucible Theatre, Sheffield
1978	R. Reardon (Wales)	P. Mans (SA)	25–18	Crucible Theatre, Sheffield
1979	T. Griffiths (Wales)	Dennis Taylor (NI)	24–16	Crucible Theatre, Sheffield
1980	C. Thorburn (Can)	A. Higgins (NI)	18–16	Crucible Theatre, Sheffield
1981	S. Davis (Eng)	D. Mountjoy (Wales)	18–12	Crucible Theatre, Sheffield
1982	A. Higgins (NI)	R. Reardon (Wales)	18–15	Crucible Theatre, Sheffield
1983	S. Davis (Eng)	C. Thorburn (Can)	18–6	Crucible Theatre, Sheffield
1984	S. Davis (Eng)	J. White (Eng)	18–16	Crucible Theatre, Sheffield
1985	Dennis Taylor (NI)	S. Davis (Eng)	18–17	Crucible Theatre, Sheffield
1986	J. Johnson (Eng)	S. Davis (Eng)	18–12	Crucible Theatre, Sheffield
1987	S. Davis (Eng)	J. Johnson (Eng)	18–14	Crucible Theatre, Sheffield

Song bird: Joe Johnson, the 1987 World runner-up, relaxes with his recording group Made in Japan.

OTHER TOURNAMENT RESULTS 1986/87

Australian Championship

FIRST ROUND: G. Jenkins 6, G. Ganim 2; L. Condo 6, E. Charlton (junior) 0;
J. Charlton 6, G. Robinson 4

SECOND ROUND: Condo 6, J. Giannaros 4; I. Anderson 6, J. Charlton 2; G. Wilkinson 6,
L. Heywood 0; R. Foldvari 6, Jenkins 3
Losers: £423

QUARTER-FINALS: J. Campbell 6, Wilkinson 1; Foldvari 6, P. Morgan 2; W. King 6,
Condo 3; E. Charlton 6, Anderson 2
Losers: £847

SEMI-FINALS: Campbell 8, Foldvari 3; King 8, Charlton 6
Losers: £1,271

FINAL: King 10, Campbell 3
Loser: £1,906
Winner: £3,117

South African Championship

FIRST ROUND: P. Francisco 6, V. Blignaut 3; D. Mienie 6, M. Hines 5; F. Ellis 6,
R. Amdor 2

QUARTER-FINALS: S. Francisco 7, G. Johnston 0; P. Francisco 7, R. Grace 1; J. van
Rensburg 7, Mienie 1; Ellis 7, P. Mans 6
Losers: £846

SEMI-FINALS: S. Francisco 8, P. Francisco 3; Ellis 8, van Rensburg 2
Losers: £1,567

FINAL: S. Francisco 9, Ellis 1
Loser: £3,134
Winner: £5,329

Canadian Championship

FIRST ROUND: G. Watson 6, J. Caggianello 3; F. Jonik 6, G. Rigitano 1;
R. Chaperon 6, J. Bear 3; B. Mikkelsen 6, W. Saunderson 1;
P. Thornley 6, M. Morra 4
Losers: £540

QUARTER-FINALS: C. Thorburn 6, Watson 1; Jonik 6, Chaperon 3; J. Wych 6,
Mikkelsen 3; K. Stevens 6, Thornley 2
Losers: £835

SEMI-FINALS: Thorburn 6, Jonik 3; Wych 6, Stevens 2
Losers: £1,157

FINAL: Thorburn 6, Wych 2
Loser: £1,672
Winner: £2,829

HIGH BREAK: £145 – J. Wych 129

Carlsberg Challenge

SEMI-FINALS: J. White (Eng) 5, A. Higgins (NI) 1; Dennis Taylor (NI) 5,
J. Johnson (Eng) 3
Losers: £5,500

FINAL: Dennis Taylor 8, White 3
Loser: £8,000
Winner: £12,000

HIGH BREAK: £2,000 – Dennis Taylor 138

People's Scottish Championship

FIRST ROUND: S. Hendry 6, B. Demarco 2; John Rea 6, I. Black 1; E. Sinclair 6,
M. Gibson 2; J. Donnelly 6, M. Macleod 2
Losers: £500

SEMI-FINALS: Hendry 6, John Rea 0; Donnelly 6, Sinclair 4
Losers: £1,000

FINAL: Hendry 10, Donnelly 7
Loser: £2,000
Winner: £4,000

HIGH BREAK: £500 – S. Hendry 119

Tolly Ales English Championship

FOURTH ROUND: A. Meo 6, D. Fowler 0; J.Parrott 6, J. Virgo 2; W. Thorne 6,
D. Martin 3; D. Reynolds 6, J. White 5; L. Dodd 6, B. West 3;
M. Hallett 6, K. Owers 2; R. Williams 6, David Taylor 2; J. Johnson 6,
S. James 3
Losers: £1,625

QUARTER-FINALS: : Meo 6, Parrott 3; Thorne 6, Reynolds 4; Dodd 6, Hallett 5; Johnson 6,
Williams 5
Losers: £3,250

SEMI-FINALS:	Meo 9, Thorne 3; Dodd 9, Johnson 5
	Losers: £6,500
FINAL:	Meo 9, Dodd 5
	Loser: £12,500
	Winner: £20,000
HIGH BREAK:	£2,000 – J. White 125

Matchroom Welsh Championship

FIRST ROUND:	W. Jones 6, M. Bennett 3; C. Roscoe 6, C. Everton 2
QUARTER-FINALS:	T. Griffiths 6, W. Jones 2; S. Newbury 6, C. Wilson 2; D. Mountjoy 6, Roscoe 2; A. Chappel 6, R. Reardon 4
	Losers: £500
SEMI-FINALS:	Newbury 9, Griffiths 6; Mountjoy 9, Chappel 2
	Losers: £2,000
FINAL:	Mountjoy 9, Newbury 7
	Loser: £5,000
	Winner: £8,000
HIGH BREAK:	£1,000 – D. Mountjoy 108

Matchroom Irish Championship

FIRST ROUND:	D. Sheehan 5, J. McLaughlin 4; P. Browne 5, Jack Rea 3; P. Burke 5, P. Fagan 3; E. Hughes 5, P. Watchorn 3; A. Kearney 5, T. Murphy 1; J. O'Boye 5, B. Kelly 0
	Losers: £150
QUARTER-FINALS:	Dennis Taylor 6, Sheehan 4; Browne 6, Burke 2; Hughes 6, Kearney 1; O'Boye W. O. A. Higgins
	Losers: £1,000
SEMI-FINALS:	Dennis Taylor 6, Browne 1; O'Boye 6, Hughes 3
	Losers: £2,500
FINAL:	Dennis Taylor 9, O'Boye 2
	Loser: £5,000
	Winner: £8,500
HIGH BREAK:	£600 – Dennis Taylor 129 (Championship record)

TOURNAMENT RESULTS OF PREVIOUS SEASONS

YEAR	WINNER	RUNNER-UP	SCORE

Winfield Masters

1983	C. Thorburn (Can)	W. Werbeniuk (Can)	7–3
1984	A. Knowles (Eng)	J. Virgo (Eng)	7–3
1985	A. Meo (Eng)	J. Campbell (Aust)	7–2
1986	S. Davis (Eng)	Dennis Taylor (NI)	3–2
1987	S. Hendry (Scot)	M. Hallett (Eng)	371–226 (5-frame agg.)

Carlsberg Challenge

1984	J. White (Eng)	A. Knowles (Eng)	9–7
1985	J. White (Eng)	A. Higgins (NI)	8–3
1986	Dennis Taylor (NI)	J. White (Eng)	8–3

Langs Supreme Scottish Masters

1981	J. White (Eng)	C. Thorburn (Can)	9–4
1982	S. Davis (Eng)	A. Higgins (NI)	9–4
1983	S. Davis (Eng)	A. Knowles (Eng)	9–6
1984	S. Davis (Eng)	J. White (Eng)	9–4
1985	C. Thorburn (Can)	W. Thorne (Eng)	9–7
1986	C. Thorburn (Can)	A. Higgins (NI)	9–8

BCE International

1981	(was Jameson) S. Davis (Eng)	Dennis Taylor (NI)	9–0
1982	(Jameson) A. Knowles (Eng)	David Taylor (Eng)	9–6
1983	(Jameson) S. Davis (Eng)	C. Thorburn (Can)	9–4
1984	(Jameson) S. Davis (Eng)	A. Knowles (Eng)	9–2
1985	(was Goya) C. Thorburn (Can)	J. White (Eng)	12–10
1986	N. Foulds (Eng)	C. Thorburn (Can)	12–9

Rothmans Grand Prix

1982	(was Professional Players Tournament) R. Reardon (Wales)	J. White (Eng)	10–5
1983	(PPT) A. Knowles (Eng)	J. Johnson (Eng)	9–8
1984	Dennis Taylor (NI)	C. Thorburn (Can)	10–2
1985	S. Davis (Eng)	Dennis Taylor (NI)	10–9
1986	J. White (Eng)	R. Williams (Eng)	10–6

YEAR	WINNER	RUNNER-UP	SCORE

BCE Canadian Masters

YEAR	WINNER	RUNNER-UP	SCORE
1985	Dennis Taylor (NI)	S. Davis (Eng)	9–5
1986	S. Davis (Eng)	W. Thorne (Eng)	9–3

Tennents UK Open

YEAR	WINNER	RUNNER-UP	SCORE
1977	(was Super Crystalate) P. Fagan (Rep Ire)	D. Mountjoy (Wales)	12–9
1978	(was Coral) D. Mountjoy (Wales)	David Taylor (Eng)	15–9
1979	(Coral) J. Virgo (Eng)	T. Griffiths (Wales)	14–13
1980	(Coral) S. Davis (Eng)	A. Higgins (NI)	16–6
1981	(Coral) S. Davis (Eng)	T. Griffiths (Wales)	16–3
1982	(Coral) T. Griffiths (Wales)	A. Higgins (NI)	16–15
1983	(Coral) A. Higgins (NI)	S. Davis (Eng)	16–15
1984	(Coral) S. Davis (Eng)	A. Higgins (NI)	16–8
1985	(Coral) S. Davis (Eng)	W. Thorne (Eng)	16–14
1986	S. Davis (Eng)	N. Foulds (Eng)	16–7

Hofmeister World Doubles

YEAR	WINNER	RUNNER-UP	SCORE
1982	S. Davis (Eng) & A. Meo (Eng)	T. Griffiths (Wales) & D. Mountjoy (Wales)	13–2
1983	S. Davis (Eng) & A. Meo (Eng)	A. Knowles (Eng) & J. White (Eng)	10–2
1984	A. Higgins (NI) & J. White (Eng)	C. Thorburn (Can) & W. Thorne (Eng)	10–2
1985	S. Davis (Eng) & A. Meo (Eng)	A. Jones (Eng) & R. Reardon (Wales)	12–5
1986	S. Davis (Eng) & A. Meo (Eng)	S. Hendry (Scot) & M. Hallett (Eng)	12–3

Kit-Kat Break for World Champions

YEAR	WINNER	RUNNER-UP	SCORE
1985	Dennis Taylor (NI)	S. Davis (Eng)	9–5

YEAR	WINNER	RUNNER-UP	SCORE

Mercantile Credit Classic

Year	Winner	Runner-up	Score
1980	(was Wilsons Classic)		
	J. Spencer (Eng)	A. Higgins (NI)	4–3
1981	(Wilsons Classic)		
	S. Davis (Eng)	Dennis Taylor (NI)	4–1
1982	(Lada)		
	T. Griffiths (Wales)	S. Davis (Eng)	9–8
1983	(Lada) S. Davis (Eng)	W. Werbeniuk (Can)	9–5
1984	(Lada) S. Davis (Eng)	A. Meo (Eng)	9–8
1985	W. Thorne (Eng)	C. Thorburn (Can)	13–8
1986	J. White (Eng)	C. Thorburn (Can)	13–12
1987	S. Davis (Eng)	J. White (Eng)	13–12

BCE Belgian Classic

Year	Winner	Runner-up	Score
1986	T. Griffiths (Wales)	K. Stevens (Can)	9–7

Benson and Hedges Masters

Year	Winner	Runner-up	Score
1975	J. Spencer (Eng)	R. Reardon (Wales)	9–8
1976	R. Reardon (Wales)	G. Miles (Eng)	7–3
1977	D. Mountjoy (Wales)	R. Reardon (Wales)	7–6
1978	A. Higgins (NI)	C. Thorburn (Can)	7–5
1979	P. Mans (SA)	A. Higgins (NI)	8–4
1980	T. Griffiths (Wales)	A. Higgins (NI)	9–5
1981	A. Higgins (NI)	T. Griffiths (Wales)	9–6
1982	S. Davis (Eng)	T. Griffiths (Wales)	9–5
1983	C. Thorburn (Can)	R. Reardon (Wales)	9–7
1984	J. White (Eng)	T. Griffiths (Wales)	9–5
1985	C. Thorburn (Can)	D. Mountjoy (Wales)	9–6
1986	C. Thorburn (Can)	J. White (Eng)	9–5
1987	Dennis Taylor (NI)	A. Higgins (NI)	9–8

Dulux British Open

Year	Winner	Runner-up	Score
1980	(was British Gold Cup)		
	A. Higgins (NI)	R. Reardon (Wales)	5–1
1981	(Yamaha)		
	S. Davis (Eng)	David Taylor (Eng)	9–6
1982	(Yamaha)		
	S. Davis (Eng)	T. Griffiths (Wales)	9–7
1983	(Yamaha)		
	R. Reardon (Wales)	J. White (Eng)	9–6

YEAR	WINNER	RUNNER-UP	SCORE
1984	(Yamaha) Three-man play-off		
	D. Martin (Eng)	J. Dunning (Eng)	3–2
	S. Davis (Eng)	J. Dunning	4–1
	S. Davis	D. Martin	3–0
	Winner – Davis		
1985	S. Francisco (SA)	K. Stevens (Can)	12–9
1986	S. Davis (Eng)	W. Thorne (Eng)	12–7
1987	J. White (Eng)	N. Foulds (Eng)	13–9

Tuborg World Cup

1979	(was State Express)		
	Wales	England	14–3
1980	(State Express)		
	Wales	Canada	8–5
1981	(State Express)		
	England	Wales	4–3
1982	(State Express)		
	Canada	England	4–2
1983	(State Express)		
	England	Wales	4–2
1985	(Guinness)		
	Ireland A	England A	9–7
1986	(Car Care)		
	Ireland A	Canada	9–7
1987	Ireland A	Canada	9–2

Benson and Hedges Irish Masters

1978	J. Spencer (Eng)	D. Mountjoy (Wales)	5–3
1979	D. Mountjoy (Wales)	R. Reardon (Wales)	6–5
1980	T. Griffiths (Wales)	D. Mountjoy (Wales)	9–8
1981	T. Griffiths (Wales)	R. Reardon (Wales)	9–7
1982	T. Griffiths (Wales)	S. Davis (Eng)	9–5
1983	S. Davis (Eng)	R. Reardon (Wales)	9–2
1984	S. Davis (Eng)	T. Griffiths (Wales)	9–1
1985	J. White (Eng)	A. Higgins (NI)	9–5
1986	J. White (Eng)	W. Thorne (Eng)	9–5
1987	S. Davis (Eng)	W. Thorne (Eng)	9–1

Stephen Hendry, the Scottish kid with the glittering future, stands proudly with the Winfield Masters trophy – surely the first of many tournament wins for this eighteen-year-old from Edinburgh.

Hendry travelled to Sydney, Australia, to become the youngest professional winner after his 371–226 5-frame aggregate success in the final against his doubles partner Mike Hallett.

There had been controversy before the start when Barry Hearn withdrew his seven Matchroom players after a row over air fares with promoter Eddie Charlton. But there was still a quality line-up including Cliff Thorburn, Joe Johnson, Tony Knowles and Alex Higgins.

Hendry's quarter-final victory over Thorburn, the world number 4, was his biggest scalp to date, and he went on to defeat Higgins in the semi-final.

Now snooker will have to wait and see what impact this talented Scottish teenager has on the 1987/88 season. Hendry has no doubts, as he says: 'I want a place in the world's top eight.'

THE OPPOSING CAMPS

THE RISE AND RISE OF THE ROMFORD EMPIRE
by Alexander Clyde

1 June 1982 and 4 May 1987 were two red-letter days in the history of professional snooker. On those dates Matchroom, a word that spells success with a capital S, booked its place at the top of the tree.

On 1 June 1982 Barry Hearn, the fast-talking, fast-moving and fast-thinking accountant, put pen to paper and sold his chain of Lucania Snooker Centres to Riley's for a cool £3.1 million. At the same time he created Matchroom Limited with three of the game's top players in his Romford 'stable' and set up a dream – to conquer the world and make a fortune for everyone involved.

Less than five years later, with four more thoroughbreds added to the stable and a vast collection of lucrative endorsement, sponsorship and spin-off contracts in the bank, the dream was realized. On the evening of 4 May, Steve Davis potted the last ball of the 1987 Embassy World Championship against Joe Johnson at the Crucible Theatre, Sheffield. But he did much more than regain the World title he had been striving to win back since it was agonizingly snatched from his grasp by Dennis Taylor in the amazing black-ball finish two years earlier. He completed the Grand Slam, a Matchroom clean sweep of all the major trophies in the 1986/87 season, a season in which the seven members of manager Hearn's elite squad had topped £1 million in prize money. Yet it was the tip of the money iceberg compared to their vast incomes from off-the-table activities.

Davis, indisputably the number 1 player again with the precious World Championship back on his heaving sideboard, had also pocketed the Tennents UK Open and Mercantile Credit titles plus, for good measure, the BCE Canadian Masters and

All decked out: Barry Hearn's seven Matchroom players take it easy beside the sea at Westcliff.

Benson and Hedges Irish Masters and a half-share in the Hofmeister World Doubles with his partner Tony Meo.

Jimmy White, the seventh and last piece in the Matchroom jigsaw, had completed a splendid first season in the fold with two major trophies – the Rothmans Grand Prix and Dulux British Open. He also established himself as the game's number 2 player.

WHO SAID THAT?

'The way my boys are performing, we could dominate snooker for the next ten years.'

▲

Barry Hearn, manager of the Matchroom squad

Then there was the remarkable Neal Foulds, the young 6-footer from Perivale, West London, who had joined the team in March 1986 and was supposed to be 'one for the future'. Foulds, in his first season among the elite top sixteen in the rankings at number 13, made nonsense of his role as the apprentice by powering to victory in the season's first ranking tournament, the BCE International at Stoke, and reaching two other major finals, the Tennents and the Dulux. The cool determined youngster with the single-minded ambition of a young Davis soared to number 3 in the rankings. Not even a fierce controversy surrounding his use of a type of beta-blocker drug – to combat a heart complaint – could ruffle the temperament of the level-headed Foulds at Sheffield and he reached the semi-finals before finally running out of steam against an inspired Johnson.

Despite the spectacular exploits of the big three – Davis, White and Foulds – the Matchroom operation is all about team-work. The seven players work closely together away from tournaments and, despite the little clashes of temperament and ego that are inevitable with any group of highly competitive sportsmen, the other players did their bit.

Dennis Taylor, who became a Matchroom man soon after depriving Davis of his World title in May 1985, regained some of that form in the second half of the season, winning the prestigious Benson and Hedges Masters title and picking up over £140,000 in prize money. He also collected the Matchroom Irish Professional Championship.

Willie Thorne, the fifth man to sign for Matchroom in February 1986, also topped the six-figure mark. The talented Leicester star was frustratingly inconsistent but still picked up titles in Hong Kong and Peking, proving that he is the emperor of pot in the East as well as the East Midlands. Thorne also upset the form book by beating the favourite Davis in the final of the new Matchroom Championship at Southend in September.

Terry Griffiths failed to win anything and even managed to lose his Welsh Professional title, despite the presence of Matchroom as the new sponsors of the event. But the likeable Welshman was so consistent that he was the only professional to reach the last sixteen of every ranking tournament. His reward was a steady haul of ranking points which lifted him from 10th to 6th in the rankings list.

The one real disappointment was Tony Meo who paid a heavy price for his dismal showing in the ranking events by slipping down from 11th place to 20th. However, Meo was still a winner twice over, retaining his English Professional title and helping Davis to win the doubles for the fourth time in five years. Meo's prize money for the season still topped £100,000.

No wonder Hearn just could not stop grinning. The rise and rise of his Romford empire had the man with a profile as high as the ceiling of the Albert Hall laughing all the way to the bank. Hearn pulled all the commercial and financial strings while his septet of players pulled in all the trophies in one of the great success stories in modern sporting history.

What a haul! The Matchroom players (minus Jimmy White) show off their clean sweep of the game's major trophies.

The ebullient Hearn, who had pioneered the overseas market by sending his band of millionaire snooker missionaries to all corners of the globe to spread the gospel, dropped a typically audacious time-bomb before his fellow directors of the World Professional Billiards and Snooker Association the day after the Sheffield final. He announced that he intended to bid to take over as sponsor of the World Championship when Embassy's contract runs out in 1990. He revealed that Matchroom would be offering a ten-year deal worth nearly £13 million, as long as he was allowed to take over the promotion and TV negotiations. The offer was on the table and, as Hearn put it, 'Unless they can come up with a better offer, they cannot turn me down.' With the arrival of cable and satellite TV, Hearn is well aware of the enormous world-wide potential of such a deal. It is something he has been working on in his various projects, including the planned expansion of his highly successful new

> ### WHO SAID THAT?
> 'We have a fleet of helicopters on emergency stand-by, ready to fly anywhere, any time. I don't care how much it costs – £10,000, £15,000 – I don't care.'
>
> ▲
>
> *– Barry Hearn on the first match of the Rothmans Matchroom League when snow threatened to stop the players getting to Torbay for the first match*

Matchroom League, with sponsorship from a wealthy multi-national like Rothmans.

The League made a highly promising debut in 1986/87 and proved that 'grass-roots snooker' can exist without TV, as attendances were excellent for the matches up and down Britain. Plans are already under way to expand the League across Europe, with matches in places like Marbella, Monte Carlo and Brussels next season.

Any success story produces resentment from those who are excluded from the big-money share-out and Hearn's brash, go-getting approach has attracted plenty of criticism. The Belgian Classic was a casualty when Hearn withdrew his Matchroom men from the event. As a result, Belgian TV wanted to scale down their coverage of what had become a second-rate event and the tournament was eventually scrapped. Hearn was cast as the villain of the piece, accused of selfishly putting his Matchroom League dates before the good of the game in the WPBSA's vain attempt to expand the tournament circuit. But he insisted that his League dates were made long before he was informed of the new date for the Belgian Classic. The fact is that Hearn holds the aces but did not want to be seen playing them to wreck an overseas event. The lines of communication between the WPBSA's Bristol headquarters and Romford had become badly tangled.

WHO SAID THAT?

'I can't work with Mickey Mouse decision making. It's not the start of a breakaway – just a realignment of the game.'

▲

– Barry Hearn after pulling his seven Matchroom players out of the Belgian Classic in Ostend

---

A similar problem arose when Hearn withdrew his players from the Winfield Masters event in Australia in the summer following a dispute with promoter Eddie Charlton. Again there were rumblings that Hearn's allegedly selfish attitude was jeopardizing the chances of other players earning money in lucrative tournaments abroad.

But the name of the game is success and every player wants to jump on the Matchroom bandwagon. Men like Alex Higgins, who had sought and was refused admission to the Matchroom club – 'totally the wrong sort of image' was among Hearn's more printable explanations – and Tony Knowles

have publicly voiced their grievances. But Knowles was, and no doubt would still be, delighted to guest on any Matchroom tours.

Canadian giant Cliff Thorburn had also been critical of the Matchroom set-up in the past, but was more than happy to join last year's pre-season Far East tour and then play as the eighth man in the Matchroom League. Business is business as far as Cliff is concerned, as it should be for any good professional.

Hearn sees his role as that of a 'benevolent dictator'. Discipline goes hand in hand with professionalism. Matchroom men do not turn up late or badly dressed for exhibitions. Image and public relations are as important as the relentless pursuit of trophies and titles. 'Sure, we have made mistakes,' admitted Hearn, usually using the royal 'we' when he means 'I'. 'Nye Bevan once said that if he didn't make seven mistakes by lunch-time, he should have stayed in bed.'

Considering that he is the archetypal capitalist, it is surprising to hear Hearn also quoting the late Socialist when he likens Matchroom to Bevan's creation, the Welfare State. 'Matchroom is a sporting extension of the Welfare State. Our players are looked after from the cradle to the grave. On balance I've got to be happy with the job we've done – things have gone in our favour. The players have shown unbelievable staying power, but I am worried about the workloads they will have to take on as we move into new areas with new and heavier demands,' he says. 'I can't put much more on my existing players, the game is getting harder and more competitive all the time and players are getting scar tissue earlier in this game. All this is apart from all the extra commitments which we are taking on off the table.'

Matchroom have been involved in the men's toiletry business, with their own brand of after-shaves and so on, in association with Goya. But there was a rare and embarrassing whiff of failure when Goya

We're number 1! Steve Davis and Barry Hearn relax in Switzerland.

sponsored a major ranking tournament in 1985. The event was not a success and, what made it worse, none of the Match-room men survived even to reach the semi-finals.

Then there was their excursion into the world of pop music. In harmony (?) with pop stars Chas and Dave they recorded 'Snooker Loopy' which soared to number 5 in the charts in 1986. However, the follow-up, 'The Romford Rap', went down like a lead balloon and never left the mid-90s. Willie Thorne had particularly painful memories of that flop, as he fell off the stage of the Hippodrome while making the video. More than the Thorne pride was bruised.

Now, apart from their massive com-mitment to tournaments, leagues and exhibitions in those vast, snooker-starved acres of space west and east of this tiny island, Matchroom are moving into the time-share business in Spain. And – in keeping with Hearn's magnificent obsession with keep-fit and marathon running – there will be a Matchroom range of vitamins and health foods. Jimmy White and Terry Griffiths, the two Matchroom men who have resisted the pressure to give up smoking, will have to escape behind the bicycle shed if they want to keep puffing while promoting the new range!

Luck plays an important part in any success story and Hearn freely admits it was only his disillusionment with the world of fashion which prompted him to buy the Lucania chain of snooker clubs back in the mid-1970s. He had never even been inside a snooker hall before, but it all clicked into place when he walked into what has become his second home, the Romford club which became his headquarters and is now the nerve-centre of a multi-million-pound operation housing fourteen companies and controlling so much more than seven snooker careers. The interests include such diverse activities as racehorse owning, various property investments and even a forest in Scotland.

The luckiest break of all, however, was that one of the crowd of young hopefuls wielding his cue on the tables upstairs was a skinny lad from Plumstead with straggly red hair called Steve Davis. The two men are now more like brothers than business colleagues and their close friendship was the starting point of it all. The fact that this young man had a unique gift for playing snooker – with a single-minded determi-nation to match – has made it all that much easier. Davis earned over £1 million last season and his exhibition fees are now around £5,000 per night – a far cry from the early days when Barry Hearn was happy to pick up £25 for a night's work for his young protégé.

On a purely personal note, the best part is that Messrs Hearn and Davis are still basically the same two people that I met back in 1978. Despite all their fame and fortune, they are as approachable and helpful as they were a decade ago. Their feet have stayed firmly on the ground, despite the soaring success of Matchroom.

BEACH TO BAIZE: HOWARD'S WAY

A sunny beach in Marbella was the unlikely launching pad for snooker's Framework organization which features, among others, Alex Higgins, Tony Knowles and Joe Johnson. In what is regarded predominantly as a lilywhite world, Knowles displays a permanent suntan befitting his playboy image. Nowadays, he has a villa in Tenerife, where he keeps his colour topped up as often as possible. But when he first met the man who was to set himself up in competition to Barry Hearn's multi-talented Matchroom squad, Knowles was relaxing at the luxurious Spanish resort.

A chance encounter with casual friend Paul Lynott, the ill-fated rock star from the group Thin Lizzie, in the summer of 1985 set the wheels in motion. With Lynott in Marbella was Howard Kruger, the young showbusiness impresario who had music connections throughout the world. Kruger was astonished that Knowles, tall, dark, handsome and, most important of all, footloose and fancy-free, wasn't utilizing his talent and good looks. Weeks later they met again in more businesslike surroundings and a deal was struck. Kruger would manage the Bolton star and take the pressure off him in business while Knowles would teach him the ins and outs of the game.

'Snooker was a natural progression from what I was doing,' said Kruger. 'I was managing two big celebrities and had the full weight of my organization behind me.'

It was the beginning of a firm friendship as well as a sound partnership, but within weeks Kruger found himself dealing with newspaper controversy concerning his charge. A former girlfriend sold a story about her lover, causing Knowles acute embarrassment. However, the matter was handled well by Kruger, fascinated by the intrigue and politics behind the scenes. Soon he was looking to expand and an obvious – though somewhat precarious – choice was Alex Higgins, the colourful, controversial, self-styled People's Champion who had lurched from one crisis to another throughout his career.

Apart from a brief spell with a northern

Mine's a pint: Tony Knowles and Alex Higgins try out the Guinness during a Sports Writers Association lunch in London.

company Higgins had jogged along for years under the protective wing of WPBSA official Del Simmons, the only man, it appeared, capable of handling the Hurricane. But as snooker grew, so too did Simmon's responsibilities as contracts negotiator, and an offer from Kruger to look after Higgins arrived with perfect timing. It was acceptable to all parties and the Irishman himself envisaged a bright new dawn.

Next on Kruger's list was Joe Johnson, newly crowned 1986 World Champion, whose own management team agreed to sign an agency-only deal. It was quite a feather in Kruger's cap because Johnson rejected a lucrative overseas summer tour with Hearn in favour of Framework and their own expedition to the Far East. Hearn retaliated by signing Jimmy White from under Kruger's nose, having taken the London Whirlwind with him on tour instead of Johnson. Framework had acted as White's agents for several months and had been confident of adding him to their squad on a more permanent basis.

Kruger, through his rock music connections, had even launched a record featuring Knowles, Higgins, White and Kirk Stevens to compete with the Matchroom Mob's slick 'Snooker Loopy'. It was no contest. Hearn won hands down, reaching number 5 in the Hit Parade as 'The Wanderer' flopped. It was all in good fun, though, and the rivalry was welcomed by Hearn who had been having things all his own way.

Kruger remained undaunted at losing White and continued building with the addition of John Parrott, the chirpy Liverpool youngster with the Steve Davis approach on the table and a bubbly sense of humour which appealed to fans. It was interesting to note at this stage that Hearn, once content to manage Steve Davis, Tony Meo and Terry Griffiths, was also expanding, White bringing his tally up to seven players. Could Kruger's wheeling and dealing be having an effect on him? The

two men were cornering the market in world-class players, and Irishman Eugene Hughes, based in London and emerging as a serious threat, was also persuaded to join Knowles and co.

All Kruger needed now was a winner but, sadly, his Famous Five failed to deliver. To add to his woes, Higgins found himself in the deepest water of his career. Three separate charges of bringing the game into disrepute, plus a court appearance, did nothing to enhance his reputation. Higgins offered mitigating circumstances in his defence and endeared himself still further to his adoring public on Terry Wogan's TV show only minutes after hearing he'd been given a record five-tournament ban and a record £12,000 fine. With Kruger at his side he told the nation: 'I've never run away from anything in my life and I'm not about to start now. I'll take my punishment like a man and come back fighting.' Not an appropriate choice of words, perhaps, but that's Higgins, who to his credit acknowledges the debt he owes Kruger. From potential commercial 'suicide' Higgins emerged with few scars and, for his own sake, a permanent driver and minder.

Weeks before the ban Higgins, committed totally to Framework, all but delivered their first title of any consequence against Dennis Taylor in the 1987 Benson and Hedges Masters at Wembley. For the first time since the inception of Framework sixteen months earlier, Kruger found himself in direct competition with Hearn for a

major prize. Sadly, one misjudged shot by Higgins cost him dearly as Taylor mounted a rescue operation that was to see him snatch a dramatic victory from the jaws of defeat.

Fortunes improved at Bournemouth in March when Higgins and Hughes joined forces on behalf of Ireland to win the Tuborg World Team Cup for the third consecutive year. Unfortunately for Framework, that man Taylor was captaining the side, but at least Kruger had got his hands on two thirds of a trophy.

Come the World Championship, there was plenty to look forward to. Could Higgins sign off with his third title before the ban was implemented? Could Hughes beat defending champion Johnson in the first round? Could Johnson retain his title? Could Knowles go one better than his three previous semi-final appearances? Alas, the answer was no in each case; although, to be fair, Johnson amazed everyone, himself included, when he fought his way through a minefield to reach the final for a second year, the only player other than Davis to do so at the Crucible.

There were other highlights for Framework. Parrott beat Tony Meo to take his place in the top sixteen rankings and also pushed White all the way in the second round only to falter when it counted most.

Yet Kruger's enthusiasm remained undimmed and he signed three more players to bring the Framework quota up to eight. These were Grimsby's impressive Dean Reynolds, young Welsh prospect Mark Bennett and professional newcomer Martin Clark.

For Kruger the next twelve months should be even more exciting. He was voted on to the WPBSA board of directors in June and is determined to help spread the game. 'I know there is a huge untapped market in Europe and I believe we have to make inroads in the next two years if snooker is to be accepted as an international game and not just a fringe sport,' he says.

Signing on: Framework boss Howard Kruger (third from left) with Joe Johnson, Eugene Hughes and Tony Knowles after signing a deal with Telecue.

'When I first came into it I could see the prospects of it growing bigger and bigger, not just in this country but overseas as well. Barry Hearn has pioneered the game in the Far East, and with two of us both feeling the same way about snooker's expansion, perhaps we can present a strong case for the board in the future.'

Kruger, always willing to accept advice, adds: 'I still have a lot to learn about the game but I'm learning fast. Once I'd signed three or four established stars I decided I would go for the stars of tomorrow, players who weren't set in their ways. I wanted new blood, enthusiastic players that I could model myself. In Eugene I found just the player. We get on extremely well and he's very willing. Mark and Dean are both clean-cut youngsters and also present the right image for my team.'

The walls of Kruger's London office are adorned with gold discs from various rock groups he represents. What would complete the decor is some silverware. Hearn has had more than a decade to polish his act and he also had a nugget called Davis from which to shape his golden collection of stars. Kruger, ever mindful that his original Framework team were dubbed the 'Bad Guys', albeit in fun, is determined to rival Hearn's 'Good Guys' in more ways than one in the future.

WHO SAID WHAT

'Just one and a half hours before the event began, the BBC objected to the blazers being worn by our officials. The BBC finally went to Marks and Spencers to buy new jackets for us.'

— Rothmans spokesman Brian Roach on the behind-the-scenes rumpus over television restrictions on cigarette smoking

'I'm getting too old for this game – at one stage I was just part of the scenery.'

— Jimmy White after scraping through 5–4 against seventeen-year-old Stephen Hendry in the quarter-final of the Rothmans Grand Prix

'Snooker is a game of expression – these laws are denying me that chance. I've cleaned the ball for sixteen years.'

— Alex Higgins on being told that he couldn't clean the cue ball between frames

'I have been invited by so many people to do so many things. It's flattering, but my problem is that I can't say no – I'm too soft.'

— Joe Johnson, speaking a few months after his 1986 World Championship win

'I'm back on a diet of vitamin pills and minerals. In fact, there is one special tablet but I'm not saying what it is.'

— Alex Higgins after his fourth-round victory in the Rothmans Grand Prix

'If I win, I win – if I lose, I lose. I won't be changing my style.'

— Malta's Tony Drago before playing Steve Davis in the Tennents UK Open

'We landed on the football pitch – just inside the penalty area. There were some Cub Scouts there and they gave us some tea. We then caught a taxi to the match.'

— Steve Davis after the helicopter taking him from the horse racing at Cheltenham to the Tuborg World Cup at Bournemouth had to make an emergency landing because of a snowstorm

'I was terrified and didn't want to get on the helicopter in the first place.'

— *Tony Meo who was with Davis in the helicopter*

'I couldn't believe it when they had two referees for each match.'

— *Len Ganley on seeing two officials taking three pockets each at the Kent Cup China International Masters*

'How come, with all these bicycles, a Chinaman has never won the Tour de France?'

— *Barry Hearn while stuck in a traffic jam in Peking*

'I just couldn't concentrate out there. Every time I looked up, I could see my friends.'

— *Canadian Cliff Thorburn after losing the first round of the BCE Canadian Masters in Toronto, his home town*

'I don't like losing but I'll just go away and work on my game.'

— *Steve Davis on his way to Canada for the BCE Canadian Masters after being beaten in the Rothmans Grand Prix*

'Davis sends them to sleep. Spectators have no point of contact. How can you relate to a robot?'

— *Alex Higgins in his book* Alex Through the Looking Glass

'When they made the Hurricane, they must have broken the mould. I'm a one-off who could drive the world's most eminent psychiatrist to his own consulting couch.'

— *Alex Higgins in the same book*

'The time is coming when I might have to risk being labelled "nasty" and start turning things down.'

— *Joe Johnson when he was losing matches last season*

'I would love to retire at twenty-seven because it would be impossible to maintain my gruelling work load forever.'

— *Stephen Hendry*

'It's a young man's game these days. They can knock you off the table.'

— *Ray Reardon*

MAN IN THE MIDDLE –JOHN STREET

John Street, a West Country lad through and through, is a familiar sight on our television screens. Yet this popular international referee was once within hours of death. 'They were even saying prayers for me in church,' said John. 'I wasn't expected to last the night.'

That was back in 1950 in Exeter when John contracted tuberculosis – a killer disease that was to claim the lives of his parents. 'They said TB wasn't contagious but I caught it after my father, Gordon, went down with the illness,' he added.

John was in hospital for fourteen months. When he was discharged, he had to continue treatment for three years. 'I was a very keen table-tennis player,' he said. 'It was a real blow to be told at eighteen that I probably wouldn't play sport again. I was also a member of the local Boys Brigade, and it was when the padre heard how ill I was that prayers were said for me in church. My mother, Ivy, was told she could stay all night with me in hospital because I wasn't expected to last. But I made it until morning and then started to

get better. I am not a religious man, but my recovery began after those prayers were said. Who knows how these things work?' By then, the disease had claimed his father. 'I went down a lot after that,' admitted John.

Within three years, his mother was to die too, leaving John on his own. He moved in with his grandparents, Charlotte and Jack, to try to rebuild his life.

Table-tennis was now certainly out of the question, as were many other sports: an operation to collapse his lung and stop the disease had left him weak. John, born in 1932, had played in the 1949 English table-tennis championship in London. Ironically, years later he was to meet two players who took part in that event – both now associated with the Benson and Hedges Masters, one of the tournaments that John regularly referees: they were Benson and Hedges tournament chairman Len Owen and liaison officer John Lazarus.

By this time John was married – thankfully his mother was able to be at the wedding before her untimely death. John said, 'I met Jean, my wife-to-be, at the usual Saturday night hop in Exeter. We were married in 1953.' His early working career had been curtailed by his illness: being an apprentice engineer was considered too hard, and instead John took a job behind the counter at Horne Brothers, the high-quality men's tailors.

Snooker was another new part of his life. 'After the illness, it was the only sport they would let me play,' he recalled. In those days it was thought to be a very unhealthy game to play. Most snooker halls were seedy establishments that men visited but didn't talk about at home. John's regular haunt was in Waterbeer Street in Exeter: 'It was a real den of iniquity. I used to spend a lot of time down there. It was a good life.'

Standards were a lot lower in the 1950s than they are today, but John still managed to get into Exeter's top ten. That's how he started on the refereeing trail. He said, 'In League matches, we all had to take it in turns to referee. We just mucked in and helped out. I wasn't a bad player and had a top break of 69. That's poor today, but it was good then.'

John had meanwhile changed jobs again – to go back to engineering. It was 1960 when he took his first refereeing exam and passed. He could now call himself a C grade official recognized by the Billiards and Snooker Control Council. In 1961 he was appointed to the B grade panel, and in 1968 he took the final step, passing the tests for A grade and examiner – the ultimate in refereeing. 'I was probably the only A grade official in Devon,' he said. 'That obviously meant I was in demand in that part of the world.'

There was also the Street family to rear – two daughters, Jacqueline and Caroline. Samantha was to be born later. John had also switched jobs yet again – this time he was working behind the counter at a betting shop. Then in 1968 came the final job change before he turned full-time snooker referee – he was appointed district agent for Pearl Assurance. 'I loved that job,' said John. 'The flexible hours fitted in perfectly with my snooker commitments. It also meant I got round to see people, real people.'

There were offers of promotion, but John was happy just to stay in the Exeter area where, apart from being evacuated north during the war, he had spent almost his entire life.

John's big breakthrough came in 1974 when the World Championship was taking place in Belle Vue, Manchester. He recalled, 'A letter was sent to all the snooker associations asking for referees to help them out. I was lucky enough to be invited and that's where it all started. I think my first match involved Jim Meadowcroft. In fact, at that event, there were some thirty or forty referees – not a bit like today.

'Then I got another break when Benson and Hedges began to sponsor snooker in

1975. I was recommended by John Smyth, went up to London for an interview and have been officiating there ever since. The first major final I did was when Alex Higgins beat Cliff Thorburn in the 1978 Masters.'

Street has always been one of the most popular referees on the circuit. He's always looking relaxed – his ability to nod off between sessions is quite legendary. However, despite that calm exterior, John admits: 'I get nervous every time I go out to referee. The butterflies are there.'

Amazingly, he originally turned down the chance to referee the World Championship final between Cliff Thorburn and Alex Higgins in 1980. 'John Williams, the senior referee, told me I was to do the final,' he said. 'I told him that I couldn't do it. He looked at me and said, "Don't be silly. Of course you can. Get out there!"' And Street did just that. There was a bit of history that day as Cliff became the first overseas winner of the World title. John went on to officiate at the 1986 World Championship final when Joe Johnson beat Steve Davis 18–12.

Now John would love to referee a frame when a 147 is scored. 'I've seen three,' he said, 'but I have never refereed a 147. That would be great.'

The year 1986 was also a major landmark in the Street way of life. He quit his job in insurance and decided to take the plunge to become a full-time official. 'I talked it over with Jean and we decided to give it a go. Jean also does some part-time typing to keep things going,' said John.

John spends most of the year refereeing and loves every minute, but he can't wait to get back home to Devon and pursue his greatest hobby – sea-fishing. He has his own boat moored a few miles away from home at Starcross. He said, 'In the summer, I go to sea four or five times a week. It's perfect relaxation for me.' His best fish is a splendid 28lb cod, but his favourite fish is the gleaming, hard-fighting bass. He said, 'They are the real quarry. The biggest bass I have ever caught weighed only 5½lb, but I know I'll eventually catch a much bigger one.'

John often gets stopped in supermarkets. He might not be a household name like Steve Davis but, he said, 'You suddenly notice people pointing at you and saying things like, "There's that bloke on TV – the snooker ref."'

He still lives in his modest semi-detached house in the centre of Exeter, smokes (though he's trying to stop), and sips the odd glass of wine. He is also a consultant at the up-market Exeter Snooker Lodge. His only real luxury is a Rover 213S car; but, he said, 'I do so much travelling on the motorway that I need a reliable car.'

Snooker has transformed his way of life. 'I travel all over Britain,' he said, 'and I like to think that wherever I go, I've got friends. That's the best thing that snooker has done for me.' He's still involved in the Exeter Snooker League where he has filled the posts of player, press officer, secretary, vice-chairman and chairman. He's now the president.

It seems a long while ago when he was lying at death's door. But John prefers to remember the present – his days at sea-fishing and the snooker people who have made him one of the cheeriest men on the pro circuit.

ARE YOU STREETS AHEAD OF REFEREE JOHN?

John Street is one of the game's most respected referees. Here, John sets you some teasers on the rules of snooker. Some answers are obvious, some are not so easy, while one or two questions will make even the most competent official put on his thinking cap.

Just for fun, John has given points for each question. Take your time, work out the answers and then turn to page 142 to check if you were right. Add up your score and see how you compare on John's points table. Who knows? – you might be another John Street waiting to be discovered.

1 What is the highest possible score you can make in one stroke in a frame of snooker? (*6 points*)

2 With several reds on the table a player is snookered after a foul stroke. He nominates the black as his free ball, misses it and hits a red. Is this a fair or foul stroke? (*4 points*)

3 Green and pink are potted in the same stroke but only the green spot is free. Where would you place the green and pink? (*5 points*)

4 Player A pots the green after potting a red and the referee spots the green on the yellow spot. The player then pots another red without noticing that the referee has made an error. Player B then claims a foul stroke on the grounds that Player A has played with the balls incorrectly spotted. Player A disputes this because it was not his fault as the referee has made a mistake. Who is right? (*5 points*)

5 During a frame of snooker a player goes in-off. His opponent, in placing the cue ball in the 'D', fouls a ball. Is the next player now allowed to move the cue ball to another position?(*6 points*)

6 When is the only time you can snooker your opponent behind the nominated ball? (*4 points*)

7 A player pots a red and, instead of taking a colour, proceeds to pot another red. What is the penalty? (*4 points*)

8 If asked, should the referee inform the player of the difference between the scores? (*2 points*)

9 A frame of snooker is just about to start and the player who is going to break off places the cue ball in the 'D', but in doing so moves another ball. Would this be a foul? (*4 points*)

10 How is it possible to score a break of 17, including potting the blue ball four times? (*10 points*)

How did you score?

0–10:	Oh dear! Put away those white gloves for another year.
11–20:	I bet you get into a few arguments when you are playing.
21–30:	It's easier to play than referee, isn't it?
31–40:	Very good – you can referee for me any time.
41–50:	You are a genius! Are you after my job?

THE COLOURFUL STORY
OF TELEVISION AND SNOOKER

by Ron Gubba

When Dennis Taylor potted the most famous black ball in the history of snooker – to win the 1985 World Championship from Steve Davis – the estimated television audience was 18.5 million. That would have been a remarkable figure had the event occurred in prime viewing time, around eight or nine o'clock in the evening. As it actually occurred at twenty-three minutes past midnight, on the eve of a working day, the figure was incredible.

It set three new records for television: the highest viewing figure for televised sport in Britain, the biggest BBC2 audience and the largest British television audience after midnight. It showed beyond doubt the extent to which the British viewing public has become addicted to snooker.

Seventeen days long, the Embassy World Championship is the longest outside broadcast in the BBC sporting calendar. It does not have the same complexity as an event such as Wimbledon, where action is being recorded on numerous courts simultaneously, but the working day is much longer, with play commencing each morning at 10.30 and often going on until after midnight. The BBC screens an average of eight hours' play per day during the Championship, with technical and production staffs having to work a rota system to cover the long hours involved.

The extent to which this sporting telethon had captured the public imagination was illustrated by a story which was circulating at the time of the 1980 final between Alex Higgins and Cliff Thorburn. While they were fighting out their epic battle at the Crucible, a battle of a more sinister nature was being fought out during the siege at the

Centre of the world: Sheffield's Crucible Theatre, home of the Embassy World Championship.

Iranian Embassy in London. The story goes that a man in a pub asked his mate: 'What's the latest news from the embassy?' To which his mate replied innocently, 'Higgins is leading 9–5.' The authenticity of the story hardly matters, but it does reflect the level to which a preoccupation with snooker had taken over the public imagination.

Astonishing as it may seem, the BBC received complaints at that time from some viewers who were annoyed that coverage of the snooker final was interrupted by news reports of the siege. Later that year, as it happened, both 'events' were nominated in the 'Outside Broadcast of the Year' category at the BAFTA awards ceremony. The BAFTA judges gave their award to the news coverage.

Much has been written about why snooker is so successful on television and undoubtedly one important factor is that, unlike many other sports, the game is at least as popular with women as it is with men. Perhaps the spectacle of two elegantly clad and, generally speaking, impeccably behaved men engrossed in a contest which is not only visually interesting, but also appears to have a subtle cerebral dimension too, creates a seductive atmosphere which a great many women, with their penchant for the romantic, find irresistible. Whatever the reason, there is no doubt that the ladies are hooked on snooker.

One immense advantage which snooker clearly enjoys is its compatibility with *colour* television. The game might almost have been designed with the medium in mind. It also takes place in a confined area which is comparatively easy to televise – so that scarcely a moment of the drama need ever be missed. Even the joky asides, which players like Ray Reardon and Dennis Taylor like to direct at the live audience, are usually audible via the effects microphones, giving the viewer at home a feeling of 'being there' more acutely than in practically any other sport.

Snooker is arguably the most popular sport on television today, but it was not an instant success. In the late 1950s and early 1960s both BBC and ITV dabbled with snooker coverage, without the game making any appreciable impact on viewing figures. Transmissions then, of course, were in black and white, and as many of the events televised were challenge matches, specially staged for television, they lacked a true competitive edge.

It was during one such 'match', at Goster Green, Birmingham, in 1962, that Joe Davis made his one and only century break in front of television cameras. Joe was playing a series of challenge frames against John Pulman for *Grandstand*. In one of these, straight after Pulman's break shot, Davis, 'the father of snooker', stepped up to the table to rattle in exactly 100 in just over six minutes. The action was described for viewers by the man who was to become known as 'the voice of snooker', Ted Lowe.

The BBC subsequently mislaid their recording of the event, and as years passed and memories grew hazy there were those who expressed doubts that it had ever actually happened. Joe, of course, always insisted that it had but, as time went by, the sceptics began to think that he must have imagined it. In 1982, however, when some research was being undertaken at the BBC's film library in Brentford, the recording resurfaced inside a dusty old can marked 'rugby'. Unfortunately, Joe had died some years earlier and never knew of the discovery. This unique recording has been televised several times since.

One important development which Joe did live to see was the introduction, in 1969, of the BBC2 programme *Pot Black*. Joe had retired five years earlier but the significance of the development was that, for the first time, snooker was to have its own regular programme. A not inconsequential additional detail was that the series would be in colour.

Genuine snooker tournaments had always proved somewhat unattractive to television due to their inordinate length, with matches – particularly the finals of major events – lasting anything up to a week. The revolutionary format of *Pot Black* was to stage a tournament based on single-frame matches which would be recorded in the controlled environment of a television studio. It is no great secret that the vast majority of professional players dislike the single-frame sudden-death contest, representing as it does no real test of ability. However, this televised tournament, whatever the format, gave players an important 'shop window' which would enhance their marketability for other income-raising activities away from television. *Pot Black* was born.

The number of television sets which were capable of receiving BBC2 in 1969 precluded any possibility of audience figures of the scale now commonplace for snooker. But, by the standards of the day, it soon became apparent that the new series was both popular and successful. With the benefit of hindsight, what *Pot Black* had demonstrated was that for snooker to be televised successfully it needed to be organized in a way which was compatible with the needs of television. Clearly the single-frame format had no wide application for the game in general, but the message was that successful television coverage would require a more manageable package than the cumbersome format on which snooker tournaments were traditionally based.

Throughout the early seventies, perhaps encouraged by the success of *Pot Black*, the television companies continued to provide occasional coverage of snooker tournaments and the tournament organizers began to stage shorter and more compact events. In general, though, the material was still being used primarily in short segments during *Grandstand* and *World of Sport*. Often, because the final of a tournament

was not scheduled to reach its climax until Saturday evening, that climax never reached the television screen.

In addition to these difficulties, there were also problems of a technical nature which needed to be sorted out before snooker could be satisfactorily televised. The lighting shade which hung over the table, for instance, had to go. It obstructed the overhead cameras and provided inadequate light. Television lighting, on the other hand, presented problems of glare and excessive heat. Boffins at the BBC had to devise a completely new lighting rig which suited both the requirements of the players and the needs of colour television.

The balls too had to be modified so that their colouring reproduced satisfactorily on a colour television screen. Little by little, steps were being taken which would eventually turn the televising of snooker into the perfectly routine happening which it is today.

WHO SAID THAT?

'They beam our coverage up to a satellite and then it is picked up by dishes in the bars.'

▲

– Charles Butler, head of sales (sport) for Thames TV, on a £50,000 deal that took snooker to the pubs and bars of Australia on Sky Channel

---

A significant step forward was taken in 1977 when the BBC decided to screen recorded highlights of the semi-finals and final of the World Championship on three successive evenings. This was the first year in which the tournament had been staged at Sheffield's Crucible Theatre, which proved to be an ideal venue. The results of the experiment were sufficiently encouraging for the BBC to take the momentous decision in 1978 to show recorded highlights on all thirteen days of that year's tournament, with live coverage of part of the final. For the very first time the viewing public was presented with daily coverage of a snooker tournament over an extended period.

The result was beyond the wildest dreams of those involved. Happenings at the Crucible became a daily talking point in offices, shops and pubs all over the country. Audiences grew as the Championship progressed until, on the evening of Saturday, 29 April 1978, over seven million switched on to BBC2 to watch a recording of how Ray Reardon had defeated the popular little South African Perrie Mans 25–18 in the final.

The snooker boom was under way, and in the year which immediately followed there was a massive expansion of television coverage. In addition to the World Championship, the BBC already had the rights to the Coral UK Championship and the Benson and Hedges Masters. Coverage of these events was expanded and in 1979 a new World Team Championship was added.

ITV had not, as yet, geared itself up to providing national coverage on the same scale. The difficulty of reaching agreements between the various regional companies meant that, in general, individual companies were still limited to screening what they could of tournaments in their own area. This led, in 1979, to Thames Television suffering the embarrassment of missing the opportunity of screening what would have been the first televised 147.

The calamity happened during the semi-final of a tournament sponsored by Holsten Lager in Slough. Because they were planning to show only limited coverage in their own region, Thames could not justify the manpower cost of recording all of the play. In the event, John Spencer scored his 147 while the cameras and video tape machines were unmanned. The lesson was well learned by the television industry and I do not believe that a ball has been potted since, where television cameras were present, which has not been recorded.

As it happens, ITV did eventually screen the first televised 147 and ironically John Spencer was again involved; although it was his opponent, Steve Davis, who potted the balls during the 1982 Lada Classic, in Warrington.

There have been two other televised 147s – both on BBC. At the Crucible in 1983, Cliff Thorburn became the first man to score a 147 during a World Championship, and in 1984 Kirk Stevens recorded the third televised maximum during a memorable Benson and Hedges Masters semi-final against Jimmy White.

From the early days of Joe Davis's black and white challenge matches, snooker on television has come a long way. Now BBC and ITV each cover four major tournaments and no effort is spared in bringing the best moments of these to the screen. From being a modest 'filler' item in general sports programmes, snooker now commands hundred of hours of air time each year in its own right. Its appeal still seems to be growing.

British television programmes can be

Listening in: ITV commentator Rex Williams.

Nerve centre: behind the scenes with CBC at the Canadian Masters in Toronto.

picked up in some parts of Europe and viewers there, especially in Belgium and Holland, have been fascinated by snooker. One Dutch schoolteacher and her mother make regular trips to Britain for the sole purpose of attending the major tournaments. The Canadian Broadcasting Corporation has been transmitting coverage of the World Championship since 1985, and in 1987 TV New Zealand, too, began comprehensive daily coverage. Many more countries receive recorded packages of snooker from BBC TV. With the world audience for snooker growing continuously, all the signs are that the boom, which began at Sheffield in 1978, has some way to run yet.

Top man: BBC's Nick Hunter.

RUBBING THE LAMP OF PUBLICITY

by Roy Collins

One front-page headline during the 1987 Embassy World Championship removed any lingering doubt that snooker had ceased to be a mere sporting event and moved into the class of a mega-happening – like a General Election or Wimbledon. The headline referred to alleged problems in the marriage of veteran commentator Ted Lowe, a sad little tale that ought to have remained private but which was presented as the most important news event of the day.

Of course, that reflects far more badly on Fleet Street than on snooker. But to make the front page even in the paper concerned, you normally need to be a soap queen or a real Queen. Poor old Ted found himself in this exalted company because,

Innocent victim: BBC commentator Ted Lowe.

as a TV event watched by millions, the World Championship is in the *EastEnders* bracket. And when you're in that league, any member of the circus is newsworthy by association. Anyone who has ever had a walk-on part in *EastEnders* knows that his or her story is of interest to the national press simply because he or she has rubbed shoulders with Dirty Den, Angie and the other stars. That's why the whispers about

Ted Lowe's marriage made Fleet Street editors prick up their ears: Lowe's in snooker, snooker is big news – QED, we've got a front-page lead.

It's also why another national paper carried a big piece about Robbo, chauffeur to Steve Davis and the other Matchroom boys, detailing such important issues as what shoes he wears – Robbo, not Davis – and how much they cost. And why yet another paper ran a whole series on Stephen Hendry, with lengthy quotes from his mum and details of her break-up with Stephen's dad. All about as riveting as an Eddie Charlton century break.

Marriage break-ups seem to be almost as popular as reports of players taking beta-blockers, Ray Reardon also making headlines when he left his wife. He partly blames his steady drift down the world rankings on the resulting press stories instigated by his abandoned spouse.

Snooker brought a lot of this on itself with so many players willing to take Fleet Street's shilling by telling their frank, exclusive and often fairly squalid little tales of life on and off the baize. Most now regret it.

Kirk Stevens, for instance, did a series in which he admitted cocaine addiction and told of his early days hustling for a living in North American bars. Now he is struggling to hold his form and his life together. He poignantly observed after his first-round defeat at Sheffield, 'No matter how hard I tried to concentrate, when I looked down my cue, all I could see were problems.'

Tony Knowles told all about his sexual conquests, while Alex Higgins is another who has got his hands grubby on newsprint, though many of the stories about him haven't been written with his consent.

In print: the past problems of Kirk Stevens.

Another reason why the World Snooker Championship now appears in the diary of news, features and women's editors, instead of just sports editors, is the stories of sex, booze and drugs connected with the game. When snooker was trying to attract mass media coverage, all three were easily available to reporters – the stories, that is. Once you open the door to such prying, which snooker did, it's almost impossible to close it, as the sport is now finding out.

As a result, desperate attempts are being made to present a clean, respectable image. The money brought in by TV and sponsorship has brought professional agents and marketing men in its wake, a move that has made it harder for papers to get their ration of scandal. Players are now discouraged from telling all to reporters round the back of the Crucible. Instead, they appear at properly organized press conferences where they spout the sort of inanities we've come to expect from footballers – things like: 'Joe played really well and I don't want to take anything away from him, but when he missed that fourteenth red . . .'

The TV conference is most important because that's as close as most people get to snooker players. They are not sportsmen who perform weekly in front of home-town audiences – or any large crowds, come to that. They're men viewed almost exclusively through a TV tube because modern snooker is a sport raised by television for television and there wouldn't be room for fans even if they wanted to watch live. Around 12 million people may watch a day's play of the World Championship on television, while fewer than 1,000 people can get into the Crucible Theatre.

Frankly, I don't understand why anyone would want to watch snooker live, because TV gives a much better view than just about any seat at any venue. I know that's true of most sports, but in cricket, rugby,

football and most other games, atmosphere compensates for having to watch the action from the back of the stand or behind someone wearing a hat like one of Mrs Shilling's. In snooker you have to sit in darkness and total silence. If you as much as cough, you're likely to get a black look from one of the players or a bellowed warning from referee Len Ganley. The reason why people put up with this is the same as why Ted Lowe's marriage was considered newsworthy – the celebrity status conferred automatically on people in the game by television.

Players aren't seen so often in the working men's clubs or snooker halls these days. That used to be their main source of income apart from tournaments, but the working men's clubs, or unemployed men's clubs as some could more appropriately be called, can't afford the £4,000–£5,000 demanded for such appearances. The

Double act: Alex Higgins and Tony Knowles.

players aren't keen anyway. Touring the provinces is hard, tiring work and there are bigger business deals to fry, like Steve Davis's £1 million contract with John Courage.

Thanks to TV, there are also far more sponsors willing to back the game and hence far more tournaments, all offering substantial prize money. Tournament earnings can now be the cake as well as the bread-and-butter earnings for successful players in the top sixteen world rankings. Steve Davis made £367,714 from prize money alone last season, including £88,000 from the World Championship which manager Barry Hearn thinks is small beer. He believes that the World Snooker Champion is worth as much as the Derby winner – £200,000.

All this may add to the mystique of snooker players as remote, untouchable, God-like figures, much like Dirty Den and the other characters in *EastEnders*. It's a good comparison because snooker, like all good sport, is pure drama, with plenty of differing personalities and never-ending twists to the plot. There's emotion, too – none more so than when Higgins is in close-up. Higgins knows that he's good television. He says, 'That's maybe why people love me. They can see the pressure I'm under, they can see the emotion and tension coming from me and they relate to that. Some of the players don't show that, but people can see that I'm human, see that I'm vulnerable. And what you see on the table is me.'

Higgins now wishes, like many of the other players, that he could switch off the media focus when he leaves the snooker table. But they all willingly rubbed the lamp of publicity and now the genie will always be with them.

Ted Lowe unwittingly rubbed it, too, back in 1946 when he beat World Champion Joe Davis in an exhibition game, a feat that also made headlines – in Ted's local South London paper. Ted was astonished to find himself in print then, but not half as astonished as when he discovered that his domestic problems were considered worthy of parading before four million readers.

BREAKING DOWN WALLS – CHINESE-STYLE

The referees bowed politely and took up their positions – two to a table! This was snooker, Chinese-style. It was to be an historic week for the game which was enjoying its first ever tournament in Red China in the capital, Peking.

Barry Hearn's seven Matchroom players plus Rex Williams had flown into Peking, not knowing what was waiting for them. The journey over had been typical Matchroom – first-class all the way courtesy of Cathay Pacific, a Matchroom sponsor. More than a day had been spent on that journey and players had reacted in different ways. Neal Foulds just carried on eating. Quail, pigeon breasts and caviare all came and went the same way. No food was refused. The champagne was also chilled to perfection. Terry Griffiths even sipped a few glasses of wine. And he slept a lot. Dennis Taylor sat next to Tony Meo. They chatted a lot.

Matchroom manager Barry Hearn thought a lot. He thought about 1,100

On parade: Willie Thorne gives a few tips to People's Liberation Army soldier Kou Nan.

million Chinese who could turn out to be the biggest snooker market in the world. He thought about the prestige of playing in front of more than 100 million television viewers. He also thought about the money: Kent Cigarettes were putting up £100,000 for the Kent Cup China International Masters.

Every first-time visitor to China notices the lack of cars and the abundance of bicycles. Hearn was quick to ask, 'How come, with all these cyclists, China has never won the Tour de France?'

Our first fears about the quality of the hotel accommodation were quickly ended when we arrived at the ultra-modern Holiday Inn Lido on the edge of Peking. Dennis Taylor was particularly relieved as he had caught violent food poisoning in Shanghai a year earlier.

Eight selected Chinese amateurs were waiting to take on eight of the world's greatest players. The task was daunting and so was the venue: the 5,800-seater Peking Indoor Sports Centre. The hall was

Dennis and friends: Dennis Taylor finds two new fans outside the Forbidden City.

never full but that was hardly surprising with live coverage on Chinese television.

Wang Lin, a Peking Sports Centre employee, had the hardest task – meeting Steve Davis. But Mr Wang was not worried because, he explained, 'There is no need to be nervous when you have no chance of winning. It will be an honour to play and be beaten by Mr Davis.' Davis made sure he received that honour.

WHO SAID THAT?

'There is no need to be nervous when you have no chance of winning. It will be an honour to play and be beaten by Mr Davis.'

— ▲ —

– *Wang Lin, a Peking sports centre worker, before playing Steve Davis*

Jimmy White was the only player to experience a slight hiccup. He lost a frame to Zhang Yanbin, a chef from Shanghai, but came home 2–1. Mr Zhang, it seems, only took up snooker because he 'preferred the quiet atmosphere compared to noisy sports like soccer and rugby'.

Top international referee Len Ganley was looking after the officials. And, for once, he was lost for words when eight referees went out into the arena to officiate at four tables. There was also another problem, as Ganley explained: 'One referee didn't know how to use a ball marker and

Chairman Rex: Rex Williams, complete with cashmere coat, takes a donkey ride to the Great Wall.

he asked Rex Williams to put his finger on the spot while he cleaned a ball. I had never seen anything like it.'

No trip to China would be complete without a journey to the Great Wall. The final ascent to this magnificent monument of yesteryear left the players gasping: it was by donkey! Williams, now known as Chairman Rex, was resplendent in his most expensive cashmere overcoat plus immaculate suit and best shoes. He was, perhaps, overdressed. Ganley, 19 stone and dieting, nearly flattened his poor animal. Someone suggested that he should carry the donkey to the top!

When we had reached our destination, Hearn surveyed the scene and asked, 'I wonder if they want to sell part of the Wall? – I have always told my players to invest in bricks and mortar.' We didn't notice many estate agents in the area, however. Hearn also found time to indulge in his favourite hobby, running, in a race against time, up one part of the Wall. He won.

The second day's play saw the exit of Williams, Griffiths, Meo and Taylor. It

Up the Wall: Barry Hearn, his Matchroom players and Rex Williams.

also saw the removal of Willie Thorne's drink of local Coca-cola (not to be recommended) after a low-flying bat stopped on the rim of his glass and took a sip.

The snooker tables were fine, courtesy of Riley, another Hearn sponsor. There were even two tables in the hotel, which pleased the players. Even when away in an exciting new country like China, players are seldom far away from the practice table. (The snooker room was, incidentally, right next to the ten-pin bowling alley, where Davis was the early champion.) Tables are manufactured locally in Peking and other cities. One company we heard of, called the Sea Swallow Billiard Factory, has a year-long waiting list. In Canton we were told that enthusiasts are using cement tables outdoors because of a lack of proper snooker tables.

East and west: Jimmy White tries the chopsticks while Willie Thorne uses a more conventional method.

Every day seemed to bring a banquet as the Chinese made sure that the party wanted for nothing. The food was a delight to Foulds who devoured a Mongolian hotpot, while Griffiths picked his way carefully through the assortment of courses. But even Foulds drew a line at sea-slugs which he swore were still alive. A Chinese liqueur was also offered to everybody. 'Jet fuel,' suggested White.

Some of the party were selected to play at a top government club where Williams and Davis also put on a billiards exhibition. It appeared that Deng Xiaoping, the country's paramount leader, used to be a

billiards fan when he visited Europe many years ago. He didn't watch in person but no doubt received first-hand reports.

In their spare time Williams, Thorne and Co. spent almost every waking minute playing liar dice: on the bus, in the hotel lobby, at lunch, waiting to play snooker and in the bar the dice never stopped rolling. Meo and White decided to do some

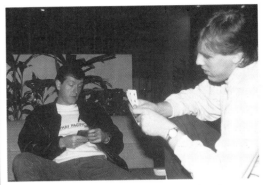

Aces high: Steve Davis and Neal Foulds take it easy between flights.

shopping. Cashmere sweaters were high on the list and both players were on the lookout for Buddha ornaments. White bought just one, while Meo ended up with three of the biggest statues in Peking which somehow he had to get back through Customs in one piece. Apart from a slight hiccup at Hong Kong, and a small chip out of one statue, they all, amazingly, arrived in safety at Heathrow.

Our tournament was organized by Tan Yang Enterprises, a Hong Kong-based company. Tai Wung Wah, Tan Yang's chairman, offered this staggering thought: 'One day snooker will become as popular

Meo's memories: Tony Meo with three 'friends' he found in Peking.

in China as table-tennis.' Now, that would be a breakthrough.

Davis went out of the tournament 4–3 at the hands of Thorne who produced a 75 break to win the final frame. His final opponent was White who was also a last frame winner against Foulds.

The Forbidden City was next on the whistle-stop tour of Beijing, as the Chinese prefer Peking to be known. Then it was back to the final action and more banquets, including the famous Peking duck.

Thorne, who scored a century in every round, did it again in the final as he came home a 5–2 winner. He said, 'The air must be good for me out there. I won in Hong Kong at the start of the season. If they ever switch the World Championship to the Far East, they will make me favourite.' Davis took the high break with a 134 – the biggest score ever seen in China.

Then it was time to go home. We travelled via Hong Kong, where the players did more shopping, played more dice and Hearn discussed more possible business deals. Foulds settled down in the first-class compartment of the Cathay Pacific jumbo to eat more caviare and Hearn reflected on the trip. 'We'll be back,' he said. 'Snooker will be like a locust storm spreading across Asia.'

Going potty: winner Willie Thorne, runner-up Jimmy White and Steve Davis (highest break) show off their prizes.

BREAKING DOWN BARRIERS

TAKING ON THE MALE CHAUVINISTS
AT THEIR OWN GAME
by Gaye Jones

It is a sad fact of life that there are still so many people, both male and female, who feel that snooker is a male domain and that a woman's place is tied to the sink and the children. In this day and age, when women are company directors, pilots and even astronauts, it seems unrealistic to expect them to accept the fact that there are many clubs and leagues in Britain which will not allow them to play in or, in some cases, even enter a snooker room.

Snooker, is, after all, a recreational sport like tennis, golf, cricket, darts and many others in which women participate in their own right and in some cases in mixed company. As many of the more enlightened male snooker players I have met have pointed out, snooker is a game of skill rather than strength and there is no real reason why women should not compete on level terms. There are, however, many men in the snooker world, some of them quite well known, who would disagree, and their opinions will not be dispelled until we women have proved them wrong on the table.

The standard of play on the ladies' circuit, although improving dramatically, is not as high as that of the men. But many people don't realize the reason for this is that men have been playing the game for over a hundred years and it is only in the last decade or so that women have been allowed into clubs and allowed and encouraged to play the game. Combine this fact with the tradition and convention attached to the game and you will understand the reason for the discrepancy in standard which is the mainstay of the critics' arguments.

Although I agree that our standard is not yet as good as the men's, I will qualify that

Watch out world — here comes Allison Fisher!

by saying that the women are now putting in breaks of 70 and 80 in tournaments on a fairly regular basis. In the 1986 Tuborg UK Championship Stacey Hillyard, who was the first woman ever to make a competitive century at the age of fourteen, made a break of 82 for which she received a highest break prize of £25. In the same year Colin Roscoe took the £500 highest break prize in the Zetters Welsh Professional Championship for a break of 81!

Yes, ladies' snooker has been making rapid progress. Changes in the administration structure of the World Ladies Billiards and Snooker Association, the ruling body, together with the continuous improvement in the standard of play on the tournament circuit, have meant that the all-round development has continued to improve.

The increased interest shown by the media has to a great extent been influenced by the remarkable achievements of Allison

Fisher who is, without doubt, the greatest lady player the world has ever seen. Her dedication and practice have started to bear fruit and she is now consistently beating some of the world's top amateur male players in open competition. Last May she achieved her first competitive century break with a 103 clearance in the final of the Billiards and Snooker Control Council Ladies' English Amateur Championship, and it seems fitting that her first century was made against Stacey Hillyard, one of her main rivals at the top of the ladies' game.

I have talked about Allison's achievements but I think it is fair to say that to some extent her progress, which has justifiably received a considerable amount of press coverage, has partially overshadowed the achievements of other players on the circuit. At number 2 in the rankings is Mandy Fisher, founder of the WLB&SA and no relation to Allison. Mandy has consistently proved to be a strong contender for all the major titles and she has met Allison in a number of finals and, indeed, was unlucky to lose on the black in one of them. Like Allison, Mandy has made snooker her career and plays exhibition challenge matches all over the country, losing only three out of the first fifty-seven matches that she played. Sponsored by Sovereign Snooker, Mandy went to Kuala

Women's Ranking List at 1 June 1987		
		POINTS
1	Allison Fisher	340
2	Mandy Fisher	203
3	Kim Shaw	179
4	Ann Marie Farren	175
5	Stacey Hillyard	155
6	Caroline Walch	133
7	Angela Jones	130
8	Georgina Aplin	126
9	Karen Corr	89
10	Maria Tart	84
11	Serena Sinanan	59
12	Gaye Jones	42
13	Sue Lemaich (Can)	40
14	Jayne Heyhurst	39
15	Sue Martin (Aust)	38
16	Allyson Ratcliffe	34

Lumpur on an exhibition tour in the early part of 1987.

Another rising star is sixteen-year-old Ann Marie Farren who reached the quarter-final of the 1985 World Championship, her first ever tournament. She has only been out of the prize money once since then when she played while suffering from glandular fever. Ann Marie has a prodigious talent which, if nurtured, should make her into a fine player in the next few years.

Stacey Hillyard is still only seventeen and has gained herself a place in the record books for her break of 114 (made in less than five minutes!) during a league match when she was only fourteen. The month before she made the break she had won the World title, having beaten her arch rival Allison Fisher in the semi-final before going on to overcome Natalie Stelmach from Canada in the final.

There are quite a number of high-class overseas players from Canada and Australia who are unable to compete in Britain because of the enormous expense involved in travelling. A small number of them, including Sue Lemaich, last season's beaten

On the circuit: world number 2 Mandy Fisher.

World finalist, managed to compete in the World Championship.

Sponsorship of ladies' tournaments is increasing steadily. We now have sponsors for most tournaments, some of whom are sufficiently foresighted to pledge their sponsorship over a number of years. Warners' £10,000 sponsorship of the 1987 World event was a step in the right direction, and we hope that this will lead the way for other major companies to become involved in the ladies' game.

An increase in the value of sponsorship packages is essential to provide sufficient earning power to enable the top players to make snooker their career and to provide stimulus for up-and-coming players. The filming of a documentary about ladies' snooker for network broadcasting in 1988 should prove beneficial in attracting future sponsorship.

The continuous and rapid development in both standard and competitiveness, together with Allison's achievements, indicates that the girls are advancing and have signalled their intention to make it to the top.

ALLISON FISHER: THE GIRL FROM LIMBO LAND
by Jean Rafferty

It was Allison Fisher's first visit to the World Snooker Championship in Sheffield; her first experience of the Crucible atmosphere, as white hot as the steel this town used to make; her first venture into the world that is modern snooker, full of hard-headed businessmen out to make a fortune in the growth industries which have sprung up around the game – marketing, promotions and advertising. To them Allison Fisher was nothing more than a pretty little blonde with baby-doll blue eyes.

But because the doll happens to be the Women's World Champion, she has a certain novelty value to the men of snooker. So, a daily newspaper brought her into the Crucible's empty arena and took pictures of her sitting in the chairs where Steve Davis and Joe Johnson had played their final. As she sat there, Allison felt as if she knew what it would be like to be there for real, with the cameras trained on *her*, every eye in the theatre looking at *her*. She vowed that one day she would make it back there

Looking ahead: Allison Fisher outside the Crucible Theatre.

on her own merit, that one day she would be a professional snooker player competing on equal terms with the best in the world.

If that ever happened, the hard-headed businessmen in snooker would look at Allison with more interested eyes, because for years it has been a snooker truism that the first woman to reach the pro ranks will make a fortune. That won't necessarily be through prize money, but through the endorsements she would attract and the promotional opportunities. Just by being part of the male world of televised snooker, she would become a star of advertising.

So far, nineteen-year-old Allison is the only woman to have even come close to this achievement. She has been Women's World Champion for the last two years and it's longer than that since she was beaten by another woman. 'I'd hate it if I did lose now,' she admits, 'but I suppose in reality you can't win all the time. I'm the sort of person that it would make even stronger if it did happen.'

She's talking in the Winners' Club in London's Southgate, a futuristic snooker club with a gym downstairs and a television relaying not the ordinary news, not even cable, but satellite news beamed from the USA. She likes this place, not just because it has a bar she can relax in and the gym, where she can work off the extra pounds she needs to get rid of if she wants to be an advertiser's pin-up, but because she thinks of herself as a winner.

'There are very few champions who can do it on a consistent level. I think I'm one of those lucky few,' she says. 'There's a gap now, but it's up to me to put the effort in. It's a matter of getting there – that's the hard part for me. But I'm sure I can do it.'

By 'getting there' she means getting her pro ticket, breaking into the magic circle of the 128 players who are officially deemed to make their living out of snooker. Allison has already made it once into the top hundred amateurs but dropped out through not playing enough events.

'A lot of people reckon I should be in the top forty,' she says, the baby-blue eyes innocent of any recognition that the top forty, good though it may be, is still a long way away from the top pros. This is a girl who thinks she can be the best and has the temerity – or perhaps the stupidity – to admit it.

'I could make it right to the top,' she claims. 'Like Steve Davis level. It's not out of reach.'

Allison became hooked on snooker at the age of seven – after sitting on her father's lap one day when he was watching *Pot Black*. She got a small table for Christmas that year and then progressed to a 6-foot one her dad bought off her uncle. Now she has her own full-size table housed in the special extension her parents built on the end of the house for her – taking out a second mortgage to do it.

With two brothers in the house she was always something of a tomboy and happily confesses, 'I was never distracted from wanting to play. I was never told, "You can't do that." The year I got the little table for Christmas I got a little basketball table as well. I had guns and footballs and punch bags. They just accepted it.'

Really Allison's story is not much different from that of thousands of little boys who saw the game on television and dreamed of being the Steve Davis or Alex Higgins – though perhaps not the Cliff Thorburn – of the future. (Cliff, like olives and alcohol, is one of those tastes that adults acquire.) But Allison dreamed only of playing snooker and not of the future.

She recalls, 'I remember when I was eight and a bridesmaid at a wedding. There were five of us altogether – my two brothers, a cousin and a friend of the family – and we went downstairs to this full-sized snooker table. And they said to me, "You score." I didn't want to score, I wanted to play. But they made me. When my mum came down later to collect me, I burst into tears. I wanted to play and they didn't let me.

'Another time I was told I couldn't play on the table in the Peacehaven Social Club, where my mum and dad were members. I was crying in my bed that night when my mum came in and asked, "What's wrong?" I said, "I wanted to play on that table," so they persuaded the owner of the club to let me use it. It was me desperately wanting to do it. It's strange.'

That level of desire for snooker has taken her to the top of the tree in the ladies' game. But, although breaks of 50 and 60 are now not uncommon in women's competition, there are few contenders for Allison's crown, so few that she admits she has gone into some competitions with no real motivation. Stacey Hillyard, who won the title in 1984, is a good player, as is young Ann Marie Farren, the fifteen-year-old who has taken Allison to two black-ball finishes lately. For a long time it has been Allison on whom women's snooker has been judged.

'If I had an off day and was playing bad, everyone would sum up ladies' snooker from that,' she says. 'That's hurtful, because you know you could play better and you just want the floor to open up. I used to go to exhibitions and think, "I wonder how good they expect me to be?" But audiences have always been very warm to me. Usually they reckon I'm better than they thought I'd be.'

How good that really is remains to be seen. Allison has had her successes up against the men, a few frames taken off the pros in one-frame exhibitions, a tournament win on the Isle of Wight where she beat some of the top amateurs, men who had got or were just about to get their pro tickets. But at the moment she really is in what she calls 'that limbo land where no one's ever been before', at the top of the women's game and the bottom of the men's.

'I had a bit of a psychological advantage against the men up until about six months

The champ: ladies' world number 1 Allison Fisher.

ago,' she says ruefully. 'I was a lady player and they were afraid to lose to me, but now they just treat me as any other player.'

Small with baby-blue eyes she may be, but she has a fierce determination to get out of that 'limbo land', to be the first woman to break into the top echelons of the professional game.

'I think if someone else jumped in before me I'd go and shoot them!' she declares. 'Well, I'd be very annoyed, because I was the one that was given that opportunity. I just want to be the first. The first one is like a winner. She'd get remembered. I'm the one that's expected to do it and it would be like a failure for me if someone else did it. I'm the one that's closest to it.'

And if she did do it, she'd be more than remembered. She'd be immortalized in advertising campaigns up and down the country.

THE BILLIARDS REVIVAL

NORMAN'S TRIPLE CONQUEST
by Mark Wildman

The 1986/87 billiards season was significant because, for the first time in the modern professional game, three ranking tournaments were held. The total prize fund of almost £50,000 was the highest ever, which helped attract record tournament entries from committed exponents of the game and billiards and snooker all-rounders. All three titles – the UK, the World and the European – were taken by one man, Leicester's Norman Dagley, who also earned nearly £20,000.

WHO SAID THAT?

'This was our biggest and best season.'

▲

– Mark Wildman talking about the rebirth of billiards

Last season also saw the traditional game of billiards break into the European market with the BCE European Championship taking place in Antwerp, Belgium. It is expected that billiards will eventually prove popular with Europeans who are expert cannon players through their mastery of the Carombole billiards game. This is played on a slightly smaller table but with no pockets. Carombole is arguably the most extensively played green-baize game in the world – it is popular right across Europe and is known in places as far apart as South America and Japan.

On the home circuit, Monarflex again sponsored the World Championship, while PM Sports backed the UK event for the first time. Four more players turned professional: Howard Griffiths of Wales; Mike Russell, an eighteen-year-old from Redcar; and two players from India, Michael Ferreira and Geet Sethi. The Pro-Am Grand Prix League provided a breeding ground for aspiring professionals.

Billiards is still fighting to establish itself in the nationwide popularity stakes and the sport has tended to produce big fish in little ponds. The only chance for hopeful amateurs to meet the top professionals used to come but once a year in the English Amateur Championship. However, this changed with the arrival of the well-organized Pro-Am League. By throwing amateurs and professionals into the pot together over nine one-day events, the League helped overcome what could have proved a fatal wasting disease for the sport. The League venues are spread nationwide and increasingly well supported – a tribute to the concept and the organizers.

The season also saw the first entrepreneurial attempt at marketing billiards

Billiards stalwart: Ray Edmonds, the World Champion in 1985.

players. Peter Mellor, of PM Sports, acquired the services of many of the top players through the UK Billiards Agency.

The WPBSA, through its billiards committee, continues to support the expansion of the game. Billiards will always remain snooker's smaller brother, but there is little doubt that it will grow steadily in the next few years.

Since November 1980, the World Championship has been arranged on a knockout basis following years of an irregular challenge format whereby the champion agreed to play a challenger. This was not an act of self-preservation but rather one of economics. There were so few players that the game was virtually dormant as a commercial sport. Indeed, the only reward in the game was the World title itself. This could assist the all-rounder marketing himself in snooker!

There might not have been a vast following for billiards but the skill was still there – as proved by Fred Davis in May 1980 in the last World challenge match. Davis made a break of 583 and five of more than 200 in his 5,978–4,452 defeat of Rex Williams.

The first knockout tournament later in the same year was met with a veritable 'explosion' in entries – eleven. This was a spin-off from the new liberal response by the WPBSA to player membership which meant that alongside giants of yesterday were newcomers to the professional game.

Despite a break of 519, Williams was beaten in the semi-finals by Mark Wildman who then lost the final to Fred Davis by 3,037 to 2,064. Williams got his revenge against Wildman at the Ashton Leisure Centre the following year, however, and successfully defended the title at Peterborough against Fred Davis in 1983. Anglia Television was there to record the highlights of a one-sided final.

The venue for the 1984 final was the Portsmouth Majestic where Wildman, at his third final attempt, won a close game against the unlucky Eddie Charlton. Charlton, with four minutes to go, was some 50 points behind and in a good position. But the Australian appeared to lose his concentration and, although still in play at the end, was 33 points away from what would have been his first WPBSA title.

In 1985 the Championship, still lacking a degree of stability, changed its format to a matchplay style of 400 up and moved to the Hatton Garden Snooker Centre in London. Ray Edmonds warmed to the new style and beat newcomer Norman Dagley 3–1 in the final.

The following season saw the World event once more on the move – this time to Romiley Forum, Stockport. Dagley was again beaten in the final, this time by Australia's Robbie Foldvari. BBC TV was there to show highlights in *Grandstand* and on BBC2.

Happy Aussie: Robby Foldvari, world number 2.

The 1987 final switched yet again to Bolton Town Hall, where the splendid arena offers superb playing conditions and tiered seating for 550 spectators. The attendances, excluding that at the final, were of modest proportions, but the venue was confirmed for the next three years which will give the event the opportunity to establish itself. Foldvari's defence of his title failed in the wake of some inspired play by Dagley. The Australian made the top breaks (315, 228, 207 and 122), but Dagley collected the game's biggest ever pay cheque of £9,500 by a 3–1 margin.

Dagley had already claimed the PM Sports UK title with a 3–1 win over Edmonds in the final to take the £3,500 top prize plus £400 for the high break of 249. He was to achieve a hat-trick in Antwerp where he again met Foldvari in the final of the BCE European Championship and again came out a winner at 7–5 to take the first prize of £6,000. The format was again changed here to best of 7 frames, 150 up with best of 13, 150 up for the final. The new system produced an average of just over thirty minutes per frame and was greeted favourably by the players. It will surely appeal to the public at large.

Dagley's performance proved that he is the best player in the modern game. As an amateur he took the English Amateur title fifteen times and also won the World Amateur twice. Now he has completed a full set with his remarkable triple triumph in the professional game.

Billiards Ranking List 1987/88

		POINTS
1	N. Dagley (Eng)	18
2	R. Foldvari (Aust)	14
3	R. Edmonds (Eng)	13
4	M. Wildman (Eng)	11
5	I. Williamson (Eng)	5
6	J. Karnehm (Eng)	3
7	E. Charlton (Aust)	3
8	F. Davis (Eng)	3
9	P. Francisco (SA)	3
10	R. Close (Eng)	2
11	M. Ferreira (Ind)	1
12	M. Russell (Eng)	1
13	E. Hughes (Rep Ire)	1

Demon Dagley: Norman Dagley with the BCE European Championship trophy.

PM Sports UK Championship Results

QUARTER-FINALS		SEMI-FINALS		FINAL	
M. Wildman (Eng)	3				
v		Wildman	0		
R. Close (Eng)	1				
		v		Edmonds	1
E. Hughes (Rep Ire)	2				
v		Edmonds	3		
R. Edmonds (Eng)	3				
				v	
N. Dagley (Eng)	3				
v		Dagley	3		
I. Williamson (Eng)	1				
		v		Dagley	3
F. Davis (Eng)	2				
v		Foldvari	2		
R. Foldvari (Aust)	3				

| Losers: £400 | Losers: £1,000 | Loser: £2,000 |
| | | Winner: £3,500 |

High break: £400–N. Dagley 249

Monarflex World Championship Results

QUARTER-FINALS		SEMI-FINALS		FINAL	
R. Foldvari (Aust)	3				
v		Foldvari	3		
F. Davis (Eng)	1				
		v		Foldvari	1
R. Edmonds (Eng)	3				
v		Edmonds	1		
P. Francisco (SA)	0				
				v	
N. Dagley (Eng)	3				
v		Dagley	3		
I. Williamson (Eng)	1				
		v		Dagley	3
M. Wildman (Eng)	3				
v		Wildman	0		
E. Charlton (Aust)	1				

| Losers: £1,125 | Losers: £2,500 | Losers: £5,500 |
| | | Winner: £9,500 |

High break: £500 – R. Foldvari 315

BCE European Championship Results

QUARTER-FINALS		SEMI-FINALS		FINAL	
R. Foldvari (Aust)	4				
v		Foldvari	4		
M. Russell (Eng)	1				
		v		Foldvari	5
J. Karnehm (Eng)	4				
v		Karnehm	2		
M. Ferreira (Ind)	3				
				v	
N. Dagley (Eng)	4				
v		Dagley	4		
I. Williamson (Eng)	2				
		v		Dagley	7
E. Charlton (Aust)	1				
v		Wildman	2		
M. Wildman (Eng)	4				

Losers: £675   Losers: £1,500   Loser: £3,300
                                                 Winner: £6,000

Billiards Prize Money 1986/87 Season (£s)

	PM SPORTS UK	MONARFLEX WORLD	BCE EUROPEAN	TOTAL
1 N. Dagley (Eng)	3,500 400 (HB)	9,500	6,000	19,400
2 R. Foldvari (Aust)	1,000	5,500 500 (HB)	3,300	10,300
3 M. Wildman (Eng)	1,000	2,500	1,500	5,000
4 R. Edmonds (Eng)	2,000	2,500	–	4,500
5 I. Williamson (Eng)	400	1,125	675	2,200
6 E. Charlton (Aust)	–	1,125	675	1,800
7 F. Davis (Eng)	400	1,125	–	1,525
8 J. Karnehm (Eng)	–	–	1,500	1,500
9 P. Francisco (SA)	–	1,125	–	1,125
10=M. Ferreira (Ind)	–	–	675	675
10=M. Russell (Eng)	–	–	675	675
12=R. Close (Eng)	400	–	–	400
12=E. Hughes (Rep Ire)	400	–	–	400

HB = high break

THE OTHER SIDE OF SNOOKER

Snooker is a sport fêted, glamourized and occasionally pilloried by the media — television, radio, newspapers and magazines. But while snooker's top professionals take most of the headlines, those same players are quick to remember their early days as amateurs. The amateur game is very much alive and it is estimated that more than six million people enjoy a frame of snooker. Here we take a look at the structure of the amateur side of the sport.

BCE ENGLISH AMATEUR CHAMPIONSHIP

Mark Rowing came out on top in one of the best BCE English Amateur finals for many years. The twenty-one-year-old from Doncaster finally overcame Coventry youngster Sean Lanigan 13–11 at Bradford's Library Theatre to take the £1,200 prize. But the tussle for this prestigious title hinged on the 23rd frame with the scores level at 11–11.

Rowing opened a 38-point lead after a break of 52, but nineteen-year-old Lanigan fought back only to miss a vital blue. A relieved Rowing returned to the table to take the remaining colours. That was the clincher and Rowing, who now goes into this season's play-offs for a professional place, captured the 24th frame. Rowing, who took up the game seriously after leaving school five years ago, also recorded the highest break of the final — a 56 in frame 22.

The snooker was superb but there were still moments of light-heartedness — like when a pearl earring belonging to referee Vera Selby bounced across the table. Vera is snooker's only Grade A female referee and official examiner.

Winner: Mark Rowing.

AMATEUR RESULTS 1986/87

Snooker

World Championship (New Zealand)
Paul Mifsud (Malta) 11
Kerry Jones (Wales) 9

BCE English Championship
Mark Rowing (Doncaster) 13
Sean Lanigan (Coventry) 11

World Junior Championship (Hastings)
Jonathan Birch (Hyde) 5
Stefan Mazrocis (Leicester) 1

British Isles Under 19
Mark Johnson-Allen (Bristol) 3
Andrew Henry (Glasgow) 2

British Isles Under 16
Jamie Woodman (Bristol) 3
Mark Peevers (York) 0

World beater: Cheshire's Jonathan Birch collects his World Junior Championship trophy from Brian Bennett, chairman of the International Billiards and Snooker Federation.

BCE Grand Masters
Malcolm Cowley
(Ashton-in-Makersfield) 5
Charlie Gay (Redruth) 3

UK Pairs
Stan Brooke (Leeds) & Paul Cavney
(Leeds) 3
Geoff Laney & Graham Lee
(Stonehenge) 2

B&SCC Ladies
Allison Fisher (Peacehaven) 4
Stacey Hillyard (Christchurch) 1

Inter-Counties
Kent 5   Yorkshire 3

Inter-Counties Under 19
Staffs & West Midlands 5   Devon 3

Riley/Tournament Champions/Pontins
Home International
Winners: England

Daily Mirror/Pontins
Home International Junior
Winners: Wales

Hainsworth TopTable (Billiards and
Snooker Foundation)
Robert Mears (Chearsley) 3
Dave Maudsley (Shaw) 2

Billiards
English Championship
David Edwards (Abertillery) 2474
Peter Gilchrist (Middlesbrough) 2244

British Isles Under 19
Mike Russell (Marske) 395
Peter Gilchrist (Middlesbrough) 166

British Isles Under 16
Rod Lawler (Liverpool) 342
Paul Boden (Middlesbrough) 190

Inter-Counties
Cleveland 843   Devon 629

Billiards and Snooker Foundation
Under 16
Darren Kell (Middlesbrough) 225
Jason Doe (Worthing) 120

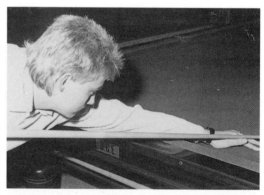

On the move: Mike Russell, British Isles Under 19 Champion, has now turned professional.

THE BILLIARDS AND SNOOKER CONTROL COUNCIL

The Billiards and Snooker Control Council (B&SCC) was established in 1885 and was the world governing body for games played on an English billiards table until 1985. In that year the International Billiards and Snooker Federation took over responsibility as the world body, with nearly thirty countries having an equal say in world affairs.

The B&SCC makes and revises the rules, certificates referees all over the world (there are 5,000 in the UK alone), keeps official break records, is responsible for championship records and organizes the English national competitions for non-professional players. With an estimated six million players in the UK, the Council has the responsibility for administering on an extremely large scale.

Various categories of membership are available to clubs and individuals. Membership not only gives support to the Council but also entitles players to enter the national competitions as well as ensuring that they are kept up to date with all matters relating to the game. A newsletter is published twice yearly which is issued free to all members.

Copies of the rules of both billiards and snooker are available from the B&SCC offices in Leeds at the address below, together with other publications and items which are of interest of followers of the game.

Television and sponsorship have created conditions which delight the players and spectators, and professional players are now firmly established as sporting superstars. It is in the grass roots, however, that the mass of support exists and the B&SCC is dedicated to the interest of this section. Without them there would be no game for anyone to enjoy.

For details of membership and publications write to:

The Billiards & Snooker Control Council,
Coronet House,
Queen Street,
Leeds LS1 2TN.

B&SCC COUNTY SECRETARIES

AVON

Not functioning

CAMBRIDGESHIRE

E. Newton, 39 Coles Road, Milton, Cambridge CB4 4BZ. (0223-861442) (H) (0223-245191 Ext. 227) (B)

CHESHIRE

J. Fidler, The Coppice, Tarvin Road, Frodsham. (0928-33014) (H)

CLEVELAND AND SOUTH DURHAM

W. D. Jones, 2 Frobisher Close, Marske, Redcar, Cleveland TS11 7EG. (0642-478748)

CORNWALL

M. Hugh, 37 Alexandra Close, Illogan, Nr Redruth, Cornwall. (0209-842811)

CUMBRIA

S. Poole, 1 James Watt Terrace, Barrow-in-Furness, Cumbria. (0229-23601)

DERBY

I. Wilson, 36 Morley Street, Derby DE3 3DG. (0332-49894)

DEVON

M. Billinge, 39 Beaufort Road, St Thomas, Exeter, Devon EX2 9AB. (0392-56088) (H) (0626-853108) (B)

ESSEX

M. Smith, 33 Woodhall Road, Chelmsford, Essex. (0245-353312)

GLOUCESTERSHIRE

Not functioning

HAMPSHIRE

A. Hobbs, 155 Wyndham Court, Commercial Road, Southampton, Hants. (0703-36450)

HEREFORD AND WORCESTER

Not functioning

HERTFORDSHIRE

D. Howe, 10 Shelley Close, Hitchin, Herts. (0462-54338) (H)

ISLE OF WIGHT

M. Collingwood, Flat 2, 'Fairholme', New Road, Brading, Isle of Wight. (0983-407777)

KENT

C. Summers, 8 Parkfield, Knights Place, Strood, Kent. (0634-718031) (H) (0634-271681 Ext. 4) (B)

LEICESTERSHIRE

M. E. Jordan, 48 John Bold Avenue, Stoney Stanton, Leics. LE9 6DN. (0455-274071) (H) (0533-50042 Ext. 389) (B)

LINCOLNSHIRE AND HUMBERSIDE

K. Kirk, 35 Broughton Gardens, Brant Road, Lincoln LN5 8SW. (0522-33890) (H) (0522-37361) (B)

LONDON

David Saines, Flat 3, 2 Frithwood Avenue, Northwood, Middx. (09274-28139) (H) (01-422 3434 Ext. 2303) (B)

NORFOLK

A. J. Ampleford, 'Saraja', Chapel Road, Hainford, Norwich NR10 3NA. (0603-898705) (H) (0603-409919) (B)

NORTH EAST

T. Bell, 'Dawnlea', Houghton Road, Newbottle, Houghton-Le-Spring, Tyne & Wear DH4 4EF.

NORTH WEST

R. Tonge, 6 Mendip Close, Bolton BL2 6LG. (0204-387144) (H) (061-273 2524) (B)

NORTHAMPTONSHIRE

J. Yule, 87 Westfield Road, Corby, Northants. (0536-65185)

NOTTINGHAMSHIRE

A. Clowes, 4 Wheatgrass Road, Chilwell, Notts. NG9 4JN. (0602-227966)

OXFORDSHIRE

J. Evans, 4 Glebelands, Headington, Oxford. (0865-68054)

SHROPSHIRE

J. Griffiths, 107 Dalelands Estate, Market Drayton, Shropshire. (0630-4757) (H) (0952-503042) (B)

STAFFORDSHIRE AND WEST MIDLANDS

G. Harding, 140 Hawksford Crescent, Bushbury, Wolverhampton. (0902-725428)

SUFFOLK

P. Fuller, 59 Rendlesham Road, Ipswich, Suffolk IP1 2LX. (0473-210404)

SURREY

R. Mason, 39 Frailey Hill, Maybury, Woking, Surrey GU22 8EA. (04862-66292)

SUSSEX EAST

N. Jay, 14 Croxden Way, Willingdon Trees, Eastbourne, East Sussex. (0323-508619)

SUSSEX WEST

T. Corio, 22 Kingfisher Lane, Turners Hill, W. Sussex RH10 4QP. (0342-715972)

WARWICKSHIRE AND MIDLANDS COUNTIES

S. Martin, 73 Blackmare Close, Winyates East, Redditch, Worcs. (0527 29739)

WESSEX

B. Tucker, 13 Lark Close, Midsomer Norton, Avon. (0761-419283)

WILTSHIRE

D. Lye, 46 Kingsbury Street, Marlborough, Wilts. (0672-53464)

YORKSHIRE

E. Hodgkinson, 3 Eastbury Avenue, Horton Bank Top, Bradford 6.

THE BILLIARDS AND SNOOKER FOUNDATION

The Billiards and Snooker Foundation was formed in 1969 under the joint sponsorship of the Billiards and Snooker Trade Association and the Billiards and Snooker Control Council.

The prime object of the Foundation is to teach young people under eighteen the basic skills of billiards and snooker. To achieve this, it is necessary to train coaches who attend courses at Lilleshall National Sports Centre. Four courses are generally held each year, and coaches who qualify for a certificate may then organize coaching courses for boys and girls.

Jack Karnehm, a former World Amateur Billiards Champion who is now well known as a professional billiards player, television commentator and author of several best-selling books, acts as national coach for the Foundation.

The Foundation co-operates with Pontins Holidays by providing coaches during the summer season and it also organizes the Hainsworth Toptable Snooker Competition and the B&SF Under-16 Billiards Competition annually.

The Foundation is run by a joint committee made up of members of the Billiards and Snooker Trade Association, and officials of the Billiards and Snooker Control Council, together with the development officer and the national coach. Meetings are held four times a year.

The coaching scheme
Each candidate attends a course to be instructed in the basic skills required to coach young persons up to the age of eighteen. After qualifying, a coach is expected to arrange courses in his own area.

Qualifications required
A prospective coach should be a fairly competent player of both billiards and snooker. He should be dedicated to the sport and its advancement, be able to talk freely, clearly and without embarrassment, and be able to communicate easily with others, particularly young people.

Coaching course syllabus
Aims and objects of the Billiards and
   Snooker Foundation
Instructional techniques
Basic rules of billiards and snooker
History, characteristics, care and mainten-
   ance of equipment
Practical demonstration in instruction

Examination
Written examination on the basic rules of
   billiards and snooker
A continuous assessment of candidates
   takes place during the course

How to apply for a place on the course
To apply for a place on the course write to the Development Officer of the Billiards and Snooker Control Council, Coronet House, Queen Street, Leeds LS1 2TN. Every candidate is required to obtain a letter of recommendation from the League or Association with which he is connected in order that it can be established that he conforms to the necessary requirements.

THE BILLIARDS AND SNOOKER FOUNDATION COACHES

Devon and Cornwall

REGIONAL COACH

D. Robb, 14 Hartley Road, Exmouth, Devon.
(Exmouth 6502, after 6pm)

AREA COACHES

W. Ley, 8 Congrams Close, Newport, Barnstaple, North Devon.
P. Davey, 8 Smithy Lane, Carnon Downs, Truro, Cornwall.
W. Hopwood, Abbotts-Kabete, 68 Sidford Road, Sidmouth, Devon.
J. Saxby, 41 Freshwater Drive, Hookhills Farm, Paignton, Devon TQ4 7SB.

Gloucester, Avon, Shropshire and Wiltshire

REGIONAL COACH

C. Handscombe, 8 High Fields Villas, Station Road, Newnham, Glos.
(059-455-429)

AREA COACHES

W. D. Curnow, 16 Alton Road, Horfield, Bristol BS7 9PS.
E. W. Nott, 'Ashcroft', Tilley Lane, Farmborough, Bath, Avon.
P. R. May, 144 Silver Street Lane, Trowbridge, Wilts.
M. P. Stooke, 4 Bedford Road, Salisbury, Wilts.
B. A. Tucker, 12 Edgeworth Road, Kingsway, Bath, Avon.
J. Tomlinson, Yew Tree Lodge, Ogbourne St Andrew, Marlborough, Wilts.
D. A. Gilbert, Flat 23b, Spring Gardens, Ditherington, Shrewsbury, Shropshire.
M. R. Riley, 22 Sweets Road, Kingswood, Bristol.
P. I. Howley, 1 Bracken Grove, Wellington, Telford, Shropshire.
G. Leddington, 28 Golf Links Lane, Wellington, Telford, Shropshire.

R. Nethercott, 3 Yeoman Close, Market Lavington, Devizes, Wilts.
J. Raeburn, 37 Poynder Road, Corsham, Wilts SN13 9NB.
R. S. Dix, 10 The Mead, Statton-on-the-Fosse, Somerset.
N. G. Dowie, 29 Buckland Close, Park North, Swindon, Wilts.
A. Messenger, 78 Windsor Road, Swindon, Wilts.
F. Adamson, 44 Yeo Moor, Clevedon, Avon.

Hampshire, Dorset and Sussex

AREA COACHES

W. Ashdown, 26 Rushlake Road, Coldean, Brighton, Sussex.
E. J. Carroll, 27 Long Water Drive, Gosport, Hants.
P. Jennings, 17 Old Manor Close, Bexhill-on-Sea, East Sussex.
A. J. Davies, 63 Shaftesbury Road, Gosport, Hants.
N. Harwood, 17 Green Walk, Seaford, Sussex.
D. W. Heaton, 6 Sandwich Drive, Filsham Valley, St Leonards-on-Sea, East Sussex.
J. Hughes, 81 Pevensey Bay Road, Langney, Eastbourne, East Sussex.
W. J. James, 12 St Catherines Road, Bitterne Park, Southampton, Hants.
A. Doughty, 70 Amherst Road, Hastings, East Sussex TN34 1TX.
J. H. Quinn, 8 Meadow View Road, Broadway, Weymouth, Dorset.
T. Rundle, 100 Cherrytree Avenue, Cowplain, Portsmouth, Hants.
D. Wells, 'Armwood', 73 Hobb Lane, Hedge End, Southampton, Hants.
P. R. Chalk, 20 Wesley Close, Bewbush, Crawley, West Sussex.
F. Sandell, 65 St Lawrence Avenue, West Tarring, Worthing, West Sussex.
H. Excisa, 18 Chalet Road, Ferring, Worthing, West Sussex BN12 5PB.
R. A. K. Nicholson, Flat 1, Glenview, Station Road, Steyning, West Sussex.
A. D. Phillips, 66 Hangleton Valley Drive, Hove, Sussex.
D. C. Torrington, 18 Owen Street, Southsea, Hants PO4 9PB.

B. Henderson, 'Woodside', Henley Down,
Catsfield, Sussex TN33 9BP.

W. Ogg, 10 George Street, Gosport, Hants.

P. Fox, 4 Hyde Park House, Hyde Park Road,
Portsmouth, Hants.

K. Jones, 3 Welles Road, Chandlers Ford,
Eastleigh, Hants.

Isle of Man, Northern Ireland and Scotland

AREA COACHES

J. J. Herron, 24 Strangeford Park,
Londonderry, N. Ireland.

M. E. McHale, 211 Wellesley Road, Methil,
Fife, Scotland.

B. Duncan, 5 Rosedale Drive, Baillieston,
Glasgow, Scotland.

W. McKerron, 21 Redhill View, Lanark
Road, Edinburgh, Scotland.

S. Pavis, Centre Spot Club Ltd, 1a Lelia Street,
Belfast, N. Ireland.

M. Quine, 52 Barrule Drive, Onchan,
Isle of Man.

P. F. Locke, 3 St Catherines Drive, Douglas,
Isle of Man.

P. A. Reynolds, 54 Tromode Park, Douglas,
Isle of Man.

R. M. McCabe, 30 Glencairn Street,
Camelon, Falkirk, Stirling, Scotland.

E. Gill, 33 Priory Drive, Kylepark, Uddington,
Glasgow, Scotland.

H. Brown, Riverford House, Wylie Place,
Stewarton, Kilmarnock, Scotland.

R. Briggs, 38 Ben Nevis Way, Cumbernauld,
Central Region, Scotland.

J. Halcrow, 5 Oak Drive, Corronvale,
Larbert, Central Region, Scotland.

G. Manson, 1 Hope Road, Kirk Muir Hill,
Lesmahagow, Lanarkshire, Scotland.

J. Caven, 28 Parklands, High Beeches,
Coylton, Ayrshire.

Lancashire, Merseyside, Greater Manchester and Cheshire

REGIONAL COACH

R. J. Hope, 953 Kingsway, Didsbury,
Manchester 20.
(061-445 9991)

AREA COACHES

J. E. Gavin, 75 Withins Drive, Breightmet,
Bolton, Lancs.

K. Rollinson, 6 Witherslack Close, Westcate,
Morecambe.

D. O'Connor, 29 Rydal Street, Newton-le-
Willows, Merseyside.

N. Carter, 23 Selkirk Drive, Walton-le-Dale,
Preston.

R. C. Anderson, 21 Edgewood Drive,
Wistaston, Crewe CW2 6SB.

D. Myler, 273 Bolton Road, Ashton-in-
Makerfield, Nr Wigan.

A. Davies, 52 Sycamore Lane, Great Sankey,
Warrington, Cheshire.

J. Titterington, 20 Grindleton Road, West
Bradford, Nr Clitheroe BB7 4TE.

R. Johnstone, 129 Napier Street, Nelson
BB9 0RB.

J. W. Hurst, 1 Ardmore Road, Bispham,
Blackpool, Lancs.

H. Lancashire, 32 Oregan Avenue, Oldham,
Lancs.

M. D. Jones, 57 Broughton Lane, Wistaston,
Crewe CW2 8JR.

H. McGuire, 96 Irwin Road, St Helens,
Merseyside.

F. J. Sheridan, 23 Harrowby Road, Seaforth,
Liverpool L21 1DP.

D. M. Williams, 47 Serpentine Road,
Wallasey, Merseyside.

D. Rawcliffe, 359 St Annes Road, Blackpool,
Lancs.

F. Barlow, 36 Goldsworthy Road, Flixton,
Manchester M31 2UP.

J. W. Smith, 33 Kirkstone Road South,
Litherland, Liverpool.

D. McDonald, 11 Birkbeck Close, Kendal,
Cumbria LA9 6AY.

W. T. Gent, 2 Bembridge Close, Widnes,
Cheshire.

T. Woodward, 944 Oldham Road,
Thornham, Rochdale, Lancs.

W. Smith, 97 Settle Street, Bolton, Lancs
BL3 3DJ.

J. Stephens, Chapel House Farm, Chapel
Lane, Rainhill, Merseyside.

W. Moore, 224 Water Street, Accrington,
Lancs.

D. French, 284 Crescent Road, Bolton, Lancs.

B. Neild, 2 Lyndale Avenue, Haslingden,
Rossendale, Lancs BB4 4BP.

G. Whittaker, 17 Westside, Halton Gardens, Marton, Blackpool FY4 4XY.

D. Woodburn, 55 Piccadilly Street, Haslingden, Rossendale, Lancs BB4 5LU.

C. Walton, 70 Brecon Drive, Bury, Lancs BL9 9LE.

K. King, 9 Lindwall Close, Northern Moor, Manchester M23 0EF.

R. Davies, 7 Haddon Avenue, New Moston, Manchester M20 PSR.

London and Home Counties – North

AREA COACHES

M. S. Clarke, 82 Greenway Gardens, Greenford, Middx.

J. Brewerton, 40 Green Leas, Sunbury-on-Thames, Middx.

E. A. Driver, 12a Makepeace Mansions, Makepeace Avenue, Highgate, London N6.

H. J. Evans, 4 Glebelands, Headington, Oxford.

H. Wilmot, 340 Cassiobury Drive, Watford, Herts.

T. E. G. Hughes, 2 Burnham Close, Bourne End, Bucks.

R. T. Ford, 24 Cromwell Avenue, Newport Pagnell, Bucks MK16 8DQ.

A. Tanner, 923 Green Lanes, London N21 2PB.

P. G. McDonald, 414 St Johns Road, Kettering, Northants.

B. Dix, 72 Barley Lane, Kingsthorpe, Northampton.

G. V. S. Jones, 33 Fernhurst Road, Ashford, Middx.

J. A. Paton, 45 Bellamy Drive, Stanmore, Middx.

J. Holden, 126 Sandy Lane, Blackbird Leys, Cowley, Oxford OX4 4AS.

G. Armitage, 2 Chessholme Road, Ashford, Middx.

R. Bacon, 96 Kinfauns Road, Goodmayes, Ilford, Essex.

R. Davies, 96 Kinfauns Road, Goodmayes, Ilford, Essex.

London and Home Counties – South

AREA COACHES

I. A. Murray, Flat 7, 13 Sandford Road, Bromley, Kent.

J. F. Carter, 'Jamaica', Fullers Road, Holt Pound, Farnham, Surrey.

C. N. Roberts, 41 Lower Gravel Road, Bromley, Kent BR2 8LR.

F. C. R. Wiggins, 7 Petworth Court, Bath Road, Reading, Berks.

A. G. Glew, 57 Cantley Crescent, Wokingham, Berks.

S. D. Hall, 29 Galleywood Road, Great Baddow, Chelmsford, Essex.

E. L. Bailey, 7 Beulah Road, Tunbridge Wells, Kent TN1 2NP.

R. Barrell, 160 Sunningvale Avenue, Biggin Hill, Kent.

R. Field, 9 Parkwood Close, Tunbridge Wells, Kent.

G. Johnson, 163 Albert Road, Horley, Surrey RH6 7HS.

J. E. Waskett, 9 Rothbury Road, Chelmsford, Essex.

J. H. Luker, 435 Ashingdon Road, Ashingdon, Essex.

R. Mason, 39 Frailey Hill, Maybury, Woking, Surrey.

A. Wix, 99 Merewood Road, Barnehurst, Kent.

D. Harvey, 114 Byron Road, Chelmsford, Essex CM2 6HJ.

R. A. Jones, 130 Canberra Road, Charlton, London SE7.

W. Bridges, 345 Westborough Road, Westcliff-on-Sea, Essex.

North East

REGIONAL COACH

A. Hanson, 121 Charles Street, Boldon Colliery, Tyne & Wear NE35 9BH.

AREA COACHES

W. Ormston, 10 Stanmore Avenue, Beechwood Estate, Middlesbrough.

B. Rawlings, 36 Lingfield Drive, Orchard Estate, Eaglescliffe, Stockton-on-Tees, Cleveland.

T. Scott, 17 Kestrel Court, School Street, Birtley, Co. Durham.

V. Selby, 60 Princes Road, Brunton Park, Newcastle-upon-Tyne NE3 5AN.

H. P. Rooney, 6 Rudston Avenue, Wolviston Court, Billingham, Cleveland TS22.

T. N. Gallagher, 24 Dalton Street, Hartlepool, Cleveland TS26 9EL.

J. Levett, 12 Durham Road, Ferry Hill, Co. Durham.

W. Jones, 2 Frobisher Close, Marske, Redcar, Cleveland.

G. Crook, 28 Pelaw Road, Chester-le-Street, Co. Durham.

Staffordshire, Nottinghamshire, Midland Counties and Leicestershire

REGIONAL COACH

F. Martin, 19 Harvey Road, Handsacre, Near Rugeley, Staffs WS15 4HA.

AREA COACHES

M. H. E. Chapman, 15 Wheelers Lane, Kings Heath, Birmingham B13 0SB.

C. Barnett, 36 Walton Avenue, Windmill Lane, Nottingham NG3 2BS.

P. H. Fisher, 28 Elmsleigh Drive, Midway, Swadlincote, Burton-on-Trent.

D. J. Doherty, 14 Shorncliffe Road, Coudon, Coventry CV6 1GS.

C. J. Mayers, 50 Kings Acre Road, Hereford.

E. G. Palmer, 162 Wolverhampton Road, Cannock, Staffs.

L. P. Meeks, 6 Cedar Avenue, Brickfields, Worcester.

K. Laverty, 4 The Leecrofts, Earl Shilton, Leicester LE9 7BN.

T. D. Spraggett, 4 Blakeley Avenue, Tettenhall, Wolverhampton, West Midlands.

J. Ridley, 9 Thornhill Drive, Boughton, Notts NG22 9JG.

K. Garlick, 16a Wolverhampton Road, Wall Heath, Dudley, West Midlands.

D. Palmer, 46 Walnut Drive, Cannock, Staffs WS11 2NF.

D. G. Burton, 'Kimley', 3 Parkside Road, Chadderston, Derby DE2 6QR.

R. M. Hunt, 11 Bader Road, Bentley, Walsall, West Midlands WS2 0BJ.

E. Gratton, 'Pippenwell', Pippenwell Lane, Chelmorton, Nr Buxton, Derbyshire.

K. Gilbert, 113 Regis Heath Road, Rowley Regis, West Midlands.

G. O'Halloran, 58 Berkswell Road, Erdington, Birmingham B24 9ED.

D. Rees, 37 Back Lane, Chellaston, Derby S45 9PJ.

Suffolk, Norfolk, Cambridge and Lincolnshire

AREA COACHES

E. Brown, 208 Woodbridge Road, Ipswich, Suffolk.

J. MacKenzie, 117 Simons Cross, Wickham Market, Woodbridge, Suffolk.

A. A. A. Howling, 3 Medlock Crescent, Spalding, Lincs PE11 2NG.

C. Steels, Invermark House, 228 Park Road, Peterborough, Cambs PE1 2UR.

H. S. Hall, 14 Middleton Way, Leasingham, Sleaford, Lincs.

C. Smith, 5 Manor Close, Walberswick, Suffolk.

B. Allright, 31 Cliffe Drive, Cromer, Norfolk.

A. J. Ampleford, 'Saraja', Chapel Road, Hainford, Norwich, Norfolk NR10 3NA.

S. Lewis, The Bungalow, Yew Tree Farm, Elsing, Norfolk.

A. D. Schofield, 'Wintons', Clover Road, Attleborough, Norfolk NR17 2JQ.

P. J. Sayer, 68 Cedar Drive, Attleborough, Norfolk NR17 2HN.

D. A. Springthorpe, c/o 70 Oakdale Avenue, Stanground, Peterborough PE2 8TD.

N. W. Watson, Old Post Office, Yarburgh, Nr Louth, Lincs LN11 0PN.

R. Barrett, 80 Hillmead, Catton Estate, Norwich NR3 3PF.

Wales

AREA COACHES

R. O. V. Humphreys, 9 Heaton Place, Colwyn Bay, Llandudno, Gwynedd.

D. I. Lewis, Graig yr Allt Cottage, Cwm yr Allt, Hengoed, Mid Glamorgan CF8 8AW.

F. W. Baker, 31 Adam Street, Clydach Vale, Tonypandy, Mid Glamorgan.

J. Carney, 84 Herbert Street, Pontardawe, Swansea, West Glamorgan.

J. Terry, 13 Cherry Grove, Sketty, Swansea SA2 8AS.

V. C. Jones, 6 Delius Close, Alway Estate, Newport, Gwent NP9 9SL.

J. G. Owen, Browerydd, Caergog Terrace, Aberystwyth, Dyfed.

K. Pask, 87 Brynglas, Hollybush, Cwmbran, Gwent NP44 7LJ.

Yorkshire and Humberside

REGIONAL COACH

J. Ingleby, 33 Bar-Croft, New Road, Kirkheaton, Huddersfield.
(0484 36758)

AREA COACHES

S. Brooke, 80 Winrose Hill, Leeds 10.

J. H. Bayes, Manor Close, 34 Tower Street, Flamborough, North Humberside.

R. B. England, 27 Horsemarket Road, Malton, North Yorks.

R. Ledger, 14 Lime Grove, Harrogate, North Yorks.

M. Lockwood, 10 Mount Avenue, Eccleshill, Bradford.

G. Mellor, 78 Fleminghouse Lane, Waterloo, Huddersfield.

W. E. Reed, Laburnum Cottage, The Park, Woodlands, Doncaster.

D. J. Rourke, 7 Portal Crescent, Mirfield, Yorks.

A. Smith, 55 Chapel Road, Chapeltown, Sheffield S30 4SS.

K. Steel, 146 Haigh Moor Road, Tingley, Nr Wakefield.

R. Stobbs, 115 Ash Road, Headingley, Leeds LS6.

M. Dawson, 41 Milton Avenue, Peasey Hills, Malton, North Yorks.

G. White, 10 Highmill Drive, Scarborough, North Yorks.

H. Hodgson, 3 Stonecliffe Walk, Leeds LS12 5BG.

J. Needham, 'Ashlea', Hope Bank, Honley, Huddersfield.

T. J. Pearson, Bridlington Snooker Centre, Regal Buildings, Promenade, Bridlington.

D. J. Sugden, 11 Kingsway Close, Ossett, West Yorks WF5 8DY.

D. M. Clarke, 20 Weekes Road, Cleethorpes, South Humberside.

B. Mizon, 3 Central Avenue, Beverley, North Humberside HU17 3HL.

D. Townend, Courtfield, 3 St James' Drive, Harrogate, North Yorks HG2 8HT.

S. Bennett, 5 Clarendon Street, Barnsley, South Yorks S70 6AH.

Inner London Education Authority
(Not available for area courses)

E. E. Bacon, 17 Ramsden Close, Orpington, Kent.

P. J. J. Casserley, 66 Langbrook Road, Kidbrooke, London SE3.

J. A. Coleman, 148 Oakridge Road, Downham, Bromley, Kent BR1 5QG.

M. J. Pollard, 130 Southwood Road, New Eltham, London SE9.

SO YOU WANT TO BE A REF?

Millions of armchair snooker fans tune in to watch the major tournaments on television. Many must dream of walking out to applause from a packed arena with the TV cameras following their every move. Though snooker is now Britain's biggest participant sport, there is very little chance of Mr Average Viewer becoming a good enough snooker player to join the professional ranks. Yet there is another way that you can get on TV: as a referee! That, too, is a long tough task, but at least the opportunity is there for all – men and women.

So, how do you become a referee? Your first step is to write to the Billiards and Snooker Control Council at Coronet House, Queen Street, Leeds LS1 2TN (please enclose a stamped addressed envelope). Tell them that you would like to start refereeing and they will inform you of the local examiner available in your area. Alternatively, you can contact your local league secretary or club for details.

John Williams: senior tournament referee.

Your examiner will supply you with a rule book, for a small charge, and will offer coaching and advice before your first examination. The first test will cover the basic rules of the game – for instance, table size, spot positions, and so on. If you are successful, you will be awarded a Grade C certificate. This will enable you to gain experience by officiating at local league matches and competitions.

Now comes the hard slog to the top of the refereeing tree. After a minimum of two years as a Grade C official you may apply once again to be tested with a view to being awarded a Grade B certificate. This test covers all aspects of the rules, including a comprehensive knowledge, understanding and correct interpretation of each one. The test is both oral and practical, and it is then up to the examiner to decide whether you should be awarded a Grade B certificate.

This Grade B award allows you to gain even more experience at a higher level of the game. There is still a long way to go. After you have completed five years officiating as a Grade B referee, your County Association can recommend to the B&SCC that you are upgraded to Grade A.

If successful, you are then eligible to apply for membership of the Professional Referees' Association. You will be offered work at a number of amateur events where you will be under the scrutiny of members of the PRA. Your application will then be formally considered by a panel of three professional referees and three professional players under the chairmanship of Rex Williams, chairman of the World Professional Billiards and Snooker Association.

If accepted, you could one day be refereeing at Sheffield's Crucible Theatre. You could even go on to take charge of the World final – just like Len Ganley last season in the match between Steve Davis and Joe Johnson.

SNOOKER DICTIONARY

ANGLED   If a direct stroke in a straight line to any part of every ball on is obstructed by a corner of the cushion, then the cue ball is said to be angled.

BALL MARKER   A plastic accessory that enables the referee to mark accurately the position of a ball that is to be removed from the table for cleaning or any other purpose.

BALL ON   Any ball which may lawfully be struck with the cue ball.

BAULK   A straight line drawn 29 inches from the face of the bottom cushion and parallel to it is called the baulk line. The area between this line and the bottom cushion is known as baulk. It is used only in billiards but, even when snooker only is to be played on a table, tradition decrees that this line is still put on the table.

BED CLOTH   The green woollen cloth which covers the slate bed of the table and the cushions.

BREAK   A number of pots in succession made in any one turn.

CENTRE SPOT   This is midway between the top and bottom cushions and midway between the centre pockets. It is used for spotting the blue.

CHALK   The material which a player rubs on to his cue tip so that he will get good contact between the tip and the cue ball.

CLEARANCE   A player taking all the balls remaining on the table in one visit.

CROSS REST   An aid to a player who cannot place his bridge hand near enough to the cue ball to be able to cue properly.

CUE BALL   White ball.

CUE EXTENSION   An implement which fits on to the end of a player's own cue, enabling him to reach shots where he would normally be required to use the half-butt cue.

CUSHAID   An innovation designed to assist a player when playing a ball near a cushion. Sometimes the line of the shot is such that the shot is difficult to play when using a normal cross rest. The cushaid is a small grooved plastic block which, when fitted on to the cross piece of the rest, allows the player to cue more easily over a cushion.

CUSHIONS   The rubber which is covered with bed cloth and which surrounds the playing surface of the table.

DOUBLE   When the object ball enters a pocket after first striking a cushion.

EXTENDING CUE   A cue with an adjustable shaft which may be used as an alternative to the half-butt or full-butt cues.

EXTENDING REST   A cross rest with a shaft of adjustable length which enables a player to play a shot more comfortably when the cue ball is in such a position that it cannot be reached in the conventional manner.

EXTENDED SPIDER REST   A version of the spider rest with the grooved portion extended out from the feet to enable a player to bridge over a number of balls.

FOUL   An act which contravenes any of the rules of the game.

FREE BALL   When a player is snookered after a foul, a free ball is awarded and, for the purposes of the next shot, the ball the striker elects to play receives the value of the ball on.

FULL-BUTTS   A cue and rest approximately 9 feet long which have the same function as the half-butts and are used when the player has to stand a long distance from where the cue ball has come to rest.

HALF-BUTTS   A cue and rest approximately 7 feet long, which are used when a player cannot play a shot with his own cue as the cue ball is situated in a position that makes it impossible for him to reach it in the normal way.

JUMP SHOT   This is a foul shot when the cue ball jumps over any ball, either by accident or design, except when it first strikes the object ball before jumping over another ball.

LONG SPIDER REST   A version of the spider rest fitted to a 9-foot shaft.

MAXIMUM BREAK   When a player scores 147 points by potting 15 reds, 15 blacks and all the colours.

MULTI-REST   A version of the cross and spider rests which combines the characteristics of both implements. It has a single forked end which is adjustable to a variety of positions.

NAP   The woollen bed cloth has a pile similar to pile on a carpet. The cloth is fitted so that the nap runs from baulk end to spot end.

NOMINATED BALL   The ball which the striker elects to hit with the first impact of the cue ball.

OBJECT BALL   Any ball which may lawfully be struck with the cue ball.

PLANT   This occurs when an object ball is hit on to another object ball with the second ball going into the pocket. This can be a two-ball plant, three-ball plant, etc.

POT   When an object ball enters a pocket without the striker contravening any of the rules of the game.

PUSH SHOT   This illegal shot is made when the tip of the cue stays in contact with the cue ball after it begins its forward motion or when the tip of the cue remains in contact with the cue ball when the cue ball makes contact with the object ball.

PYRAMID SPOT   Also known as the pink spot, this is situated midway between the centre spot and the face of the top cushion.

SAFETY SHOT   A shot played to give one's opponent the least chance possible to make a scoring stroke.

SCREW   Striking the white ball in such a way that it will travel backwards after impact with the object ball.

SIDE   Striking the cue ball on either the left or right hand side, so that it spins off at an angle after contact with the object ball or cushion.

SNOOKER   When a stroke in a straight line to any part of every ball on is obstructed by a ball or balls not on. Then a player is said to be snookered.

SPIDER REST   An aid to a player who has to play a shot which he cannot reach with the aid of his normal bridge hand or which, because of the position of other balls, he cannot reach with the normal cross rest. The spider rest has a bridge which is shaped in such a way that it is about 3 inches from the bed of the table.

SPOT $12\frac{3}{4}$ inches from the face of the top cushion on a point on the centre longitudinal line of the table. The black ball goes on this spot.

STRIKER   The person in play or about to play.

STROKE   This is made when the person in play strikes the white ball with the tip of the cue.

STUN   Striking the cue ball in such a way that it will stop on impact with the object ball.

SWAN-NECKED SPIDER REST   Sometimes called a goose-necked or billiards spider, which has a single forked end. This implement performs the same function as the ordinary spider rest, but enables the player to play a greater variety of shots from awkward positions.

THE 'D'   This is a semi-circle with a radius of 11½ inches in baulk with its centre at the middle of the baulk line.

TOP CUSHION   The cushion at the spot end of the table. (*See* Spot.)

TOTAL CLEARANCE   A player taking all the balls on the table from the first red to the black with one visit to the table.

ARE YOU STREETS AHEAD OF REFEREE JOHN?
ANSWERS TO THE QUESTIONS ON PAGE 106

1   16 – you are awarded a 'free ball', so nominate a colour as a red and pot this along with all the other 15 reds in one shot. Improbable, but it could happen.

2   It is a foul stroke as the player must hit the ball he nominates.

3   The green would be placed on its own spot by right and the pink would go as near as possible to its own spot between that spot and the top cushion on the centre line.

4   Player B is right. It is a foul stroke because, although the referee made a mistake, it is the players' responsibility to see that the balls are correctly spotted.

5   He must play from where the ball is or he can request his opponent to play from that position.

6   When only the pink and black are on the table.

7   7 points.

8   No. It is up to the player to work out the difference himself.

9   No. It is not a foul as the frame has not started until the cue ball has been struck with the tip of the cue.

10   Player A is taking the colours and pots up to the blue when it is discovered that there is still a red on the table – a foul stroke is declared and he loses 5 points for a foul on the blue. The blue is then replaced on the table and Player B also has a free ball as he is snookered on the red. He takes the blue as his free ball, pots it and scores 1. He then pots the blue (total 6), the red (7) and the blue (12). He then proceeds to take the blue as the next colour (17). That makes four blues. Easy, wasn't it?!

RULES OF
THE GAME OF SNOOKER*

Authorised by
THE BILLIARDS AND SNOOKER
CONTROL COUNCIL

THE BILLIARDS ASSOCIATION
Established 1885

THE BILLIARDS CONTROL CLUB
Established 1908

AMALGAMATED 1919

Chairman: Stan Brooke
Secretary and Chief Executive: David Ford

SECTION 1. EQUIPMENT

1. Table (Imperial)
1M. Table (Metric)
2. Balls
3. Cue
4. Ancillary

SECTION 2. DEFINITIONS

1. Frame
2. Game
3. Match
4. Balls
5. Striker
6. Stroke
7. In-hand
8. In play
9. On
10. Nominated
11. Pot
12. Break
13. Forced off
14. Foul
15. Snookered
16. Angled
17. Occupied
18. Push-stroke
19. Jump Shot
20. Miss

SECTION 3. THE GAME

1. Description
2. Position of Balls
3. Mode of play
4. Play from in-hand
5. Simultaneous hit
6. Spotting colours
7. Touching balls
8. Edge of pocket
9. Free ball
10. Foul
11. Penalties
12. Movement of ball
13. Stalemate
14. Four handed

SECTION 4. THE PLAYERS

1. Time wasting
2. Unfair conduct
3. Penalty
4. Non-striker
5. Absence

SECTION 5. THE OFFICIALS

1. Referee
2. Marker

*Copyright © Billiards and Snooker Control Council

SECTION 1. EQUIPMENT

1. The Standard Table – Imperial

Dimensions

(a) the playing area within the cushion faces shall measure 11ft 8½ins × 5ft 10ins with a tolerance on both dimensions of ± ½in.

Height

(b) the height of the table from the floor to the top of the cushion rail shall be from 2ft 9½ins to 2ft 10½ins.

Pocket Openings

(c)   (i) There shall be pockets at the corners (two at the Spot end known as the top pockets and two at the Baulk end as the bottom pockets) and at the middle of the longer sides.

       (ii) the pocket openings shall conform to the templates authorised by the Billiards and Snooker Control Council.

Baulk-line and Baulk

(d) a straight line drawn 29ins from the face of the bottom cushion and parallel to it is called the Baulk-line and the intervening space termed the Baulk.

The "D"

(e) the "D" is a semi-circle described in Baulk with its centre at the middle of the Baulk-line and with a radius of 11½ins.

Spots

(f) four spots marked on the centre longitudinal line of the table.

       (i) the Spot: 12¾ins from the point perpendicular below the face of the top cushion.

       (ii) the Centre Spot: Midway between the centre pockets and equidistant from the faces of the top and bottom cushions.

       (iii) the Pyramid Spot: Midway between the centre spot and the face of the top cushion.

       (iv) the Middle of the Baulk-line.

1M. The Standard Table – Metric

Dimensions

(a) the playing area within the cushion faces shall measure 3500 mm × 1750 mm with a tolerance on both dimensions of ± 3 mm.

Height

(b) the height of the table from the floor to the top of the cushion rail shall be from 850 mm to 875 mm.

Pocket Openings

(c)   (i) There shall be pockets at the corners (two at the Spot end known as the top pockets and two at the Baulk end as the bottom pockets) and at the middle of the longer sides.

       (ii) the pocket openings shall conform to the templates authorised by the Billiards and Snooker Control Council.

Baulk-line and Baulk

(d) a straight line drawn 700 mm (⅕th the length of the playing area) from the face of the bottom cushion and parallel to it is called the Baulk-line and the intervening space termed the Baulk.

The "D"

(e) the "D" is a semi-circle described in Baulk with its centre at the middle of the Baulk-line and with a radius of 292 mm (⅙th the width of the Playing area).

Spots

(f) four spots marked on the centre longitudinal line of the table.

       (i) the Spot: 320 mm (1/11th the length of the playing area) from the point perpendicular below the face of the top cushion.

       (ii) the Centre Spot: Midway between the centre pockets and equidistant from the faces of the top and bottom cushions.

       (iii) the Pyramid Spot: Midway between the centre spot and the face of the top cushion.

       (iv) the Middle of the Baulk-line.

2. **Balls**
   (a) the balls shall have a diameter of 52.5 mm (2¹⁄₁₆ins) with a tolerance of + 0.05mm–0.08mm.
   (b) they shall be of equal weight within a tolerance of
      (i) 3 gms per Snooker set, and
      (ii) 0.5 gms per Billiard set.

NOTE:
A SET OF BALLS MAY BE CHANGED WITH THE CONSENT OF THE PLAYERS OR ON A DECISION OF THE REFEREE.

3. **Cue**

   the cue shall be not less than 910 mm (3ft) in length and shall show no substantial departure from the traditional and generally accepted shape and form.

4. **Ancillary**

   "Rests" may be used to provide a bridge for the cue.

NOTE:
IT IS THE PLAYERS RESPONSIBILITY TO BOTH PLACE THE REST ON AND REMOVE IT FROM THE TABLE.

NOTE:
A PLAYER SHALL NOT BE PENALISED IF A REST HEAD FALLS OFF AND TOUCHES A BALL. THIS DOES NOT, HOWEVER, ABSOLVE A PLAYER FROM THE RESPONSIBILITY TO ENSURE THAT HE DOES NOT TOUCH A BALL WITH OTHER THAN THE TIP OF THE CUE.

SECTION 2. DEFINITIONS

1. **Frame**
   a frame is completed when
   (a) conceded, or
   (b) the black is finally potted or fouled.

2. **Game**
   a game is an agreed number of frames.

3. **Match**
   a match is an agreed number of games.

4. **Balls**
   (a) the white ball is the cue-ball.
   (b) the 15 reds, and
   (c) the 6 colours, are object balls.

5. **Striker**
   the person about to play or in play is the striker and remains so until completion of the stroke or break (Sec. 2 Rules 6 & 12).

6. **Stroke**
   (a) a stroke is made when the striker strikes the cue-ball with the tip of the cue.
   (b) for the stroke to be a "Fair Stroke" the following conditions must be met:
      (i) At the moment of striking, all balls must be at rest, and where necessary, colours correctly spotted.
      (ii) The cue ball must be struck and not pushed.
      (iii) The cue ball must not be struck more than once in the same stroke.
      (iv) At the moment of striking, at least one of the strikers feet must be touching the floor.
      (v) The striker must not touch any ball other than the cue ball as in section (a) above.
      (vi) A ball or balls must not be "forced off the table".
   (c) a stroke is not completed until all balls have come to rest and the referee has decided the striker has left the table.

7. **In-hand**
   (a) the cue-ball is in-hand when it has entered a pocket or has been forced off the table.
   (b) it remains in-hand until played fairly from in-hand or a foul is committed whilst the ball is on the table.

8. **Ball in Play**
   (a) the cue-ball is in play when not in-hand.
   (b) object balls are in play when spotted and remain so until pocketed or forced off the table.

NOTE:

USING THE CUE TO POSITION THE CUE-BALL
IF THE REFEREE CONSIDERS THE PLAYER IS NOT
ATTEMPTING TO PLAY A STROKE, EVEN THOUGH
THE TIP OF THE CUE TOUCHES THE CUE-BALL,
THE BALL IS NOT IN PLAY.

9.   **Ball on**
      any ball which may be lawfully hit by
      the first impact of the cue-ball is said to
      be *on*.

10.   **Nominated ball**
       a nominated ball is the object ball which
       the striker declares, or indicates to the
       satisfaction of the referee, he undertakes
       to hit with the first impact of the cue-
       ball.

NOTE:
IF REQUESTED BY THE REFEREE THE STRIKER
MUST DECLARE WHICH BALL HE IS ON.

11.   **Pot**
       (a) a pot is when an object ball, after
           contact with another ball, and with-
           out any contravention of these rules,
           enters a pocket.
       (b) if a colour, it shall be spotted before
           the next stroke is made, until finally
           potted under Sec. 3 Rule 3.
       (c) if a stroke is made, with a ball or
           balls incorrectly spotted, and a foul
           is not awarded, the ball or balls
           (i) if on the table will be
               considered to be correctly
               spotted.
           (ii) if not on the table will be
                spotted when the foul is
                awarded.

NOTE:
   (i)   IT IS THE STRIKERS RESPONSIBILITY TO
          ENSURE THAT ALL BALLS ARE COR-
          RECTLY SPOTTED BEFORE STRIKING.
   (ii)   SUBJECT TO SEC. 3 RULES 8 & 12, REDS
          ARE NEVER REPLACED ON THE TABLE
          DESPITE THE FACT THAT A PLAYER MAY
          BENEFIT FROM A FOUL.

12.   **Break**
       (a) if a ball is potted, the same player
           plays the next stroke.

       (b) a break is a number of pots in
           succession made in any one turn.

13.   **Forced off the table**
       (a) a ball is forced off the table if it
           comes to rest other than on the bed
           of the table or in a pocket.
       (b) if a colour it shall be spotted as per
           Sec. 3 Rule 6 before the next stroke
           is made.

14.   **Foul**
       a foul is any act in contravention of
       these rules.

15.   **Snookered**
       (a) the cue-ball is snookered when a
           direct stroke in a straight line to any
           part of every ball *on* is obstructed by
           a ball or balls not *on*.

NOTE:
IF THERE IS ANY ONE BALL THAT IS NOT SO
OBSTRUCTED, THE CUE-BALL IS NOT SNOOKERED.

       (b) if in-hand, the cue-ball is snookered
           only if obstructed from all positions
           on or within the lines of the "D".
       (c) if the cue-ball is obstructed by more
           than one ball, the one nearest to the
           cue-ball is the effective snookering
           ball.

16.   **Angled**
       (a) the cue-ball is angled when a direct
           stroke in a straight line to any part
           of every ball *on* is obstructed by a
           corner of the cushion.

NOTE:
IF THERE IS ANY ONE BALL THAT IS NOT SO
OBSTRUCTED, THE CUE-BALL IS NOT ANGLED.

       if angled after a foul,
       (b) the referee will state angled ball,
           and
       (c) it may be played from in-hand at the
           strikers discretion.

17.   **Occupied**
       a spot is said to be occupied if a ball
       cannot be placed on it without it touching
       another ball.

18. **Push Stroke**
a push stroke is a foul and is made when the tip of the cue remains in contact with the cue-ball,
   (a) when the cue-ball makes contact with the object ball, or
   (b) after the cue-ball has commenced its forward motion.

   PROVIDED that where the cue-ball and an object ball are almost touching, it shall be deemed a fair stroke if the cue-ball hits the finest possible edge of the object ball.

19. **Jump Shot**
a jump shot is when the cue-ball jumps over any ball except when it first strikes the object ball and then jumps over another ball.

NOTE:
IF THE CUE-BALL FINISHES ON THE FAR SIDE OF THE OBJECT BALL, EVEN THOUGH TOUCHING IT IN THE PROCESS, IT IS CONSIDERED TO HAVE JUMPED OVER.

NOTE:
AFTER STRIKING THE BALL ON FAIRLY IF THE CUE-BALL SHOULD THEN JUMP OVER THE OBJECT BALL AFTER HITTING A CUSHION, IT SHALL BE DEEMED TO BE A FAIR STROKE.

20. **Miss**
A miss is when the referee considers the striker has not endeavoured to hit the ball *on*.

SECTION 3. THE GAME

1. **Description**
The game of Snooker is played on an English Billiard Table and may be played by two or more persons, either as sides or independently.

Points are awarded for scoring strokes and forfeits from an opponents fouls.

The winner is the player or side making the highest score or to whom the game is awarded under Sec. 4 Rule 2.

Each player uses the same WHITE cue-ball and there are twenty-one object balls – fifteen reds each valued 1 and six colours: yellow valued 2, green 3, brown 4, blue 5, pink 6 and black 7.

Scoring strokes are made by potting reds and colours alternately until all reds are off the table and then the colours in the ascending order of their value i.e. – yellow through to black.

2. **Position of Balls**
At the commencement of each frame the object balls are positioned as follows: BLACK on the SPOT: PINK on the PYRAMID SPOT; BLUE on the CENTRE SPOT; BROWN on the MIDDLE of the BAULK-line; GREEN on the LEFT-HAND and YELLOW on the RIGHT-HAND corner of the "D".

The reds in the form of a triangle, the ball at the apex standing as near to the pink ball as possible, without touching it, the base being parallel with and nearest to the top cushion.

NOTE:
THE POSITIONS FOR THE OBJECT BALLS ARE COMMONLY REFERRED TO BY THE COLOUR, E.G. BLACK SPOT, PINK SPOT, ETC.

3. **Mode of Play**
   (a) the players shall determine the order of play which (subject to Sec. 3 Rule 10) must remain unaltered throughout the *frame*.

NOTE:
THE PLAYER TO STRIKE FIRST AT EACH FRAME SHALL ALTERNATE DURING A GAME.

   (b) the first player shall play from *in-hand* and the frame starts with the first stroke.
   (c) the cue ball
      (i) must first hit a ball *on*, and
      (ii) must not enter a pocket.
   (d) a ball not *on* must not enter a pocket.
   (e) (i) for the first stroke of each turn, until all are off the table, red is the ball *on*.
      (ii) the value of each red potted in the same stroke is scored.

(f) if a red is potted, the next ball *on* is a colour, which if potted is scored. The colour is then re-spotted.

(g) until all reds are off the table the break is continued by potting reds and colours alternately.

(h) if the striker fails to score the next player plays from where the cue-ball comes to rest.

(j) the colours then become *on* in the ascending order of their value (Sec. 3 Rule 1) and when potted remain off the table (except as provided for in the next paragraph).

(k) when only the Black is left the first score or foul ends the frame, unless the scores are then equal, in which case:
　　(i) the Black is spotted.
　　(ii) the players draw lots for choice of playing.

NOTE: AGGREGATE SCORES
IN GAMES OR MATCHES WHERE AGGREGATE SCORES ARE RELEVANT IT IS ONLY WHEN THE SCORES ARE EQUAL AS A RESULT OF THE LAST FRAME THAT THE ABOVE APPLIES.

(l) The striker shall to the best of his ability endeavour to hit the ball *on*. If the referee considers the rule infringed he shall call foul and miss.

NOTE:
BALL *ON* IMPOSSIBLE TO BE HIT.
IN THIS SITUATION IT HAS TO BE CONSIDERED THAT THE STRIKER IS ATTEMPTING TO HIT THE BALL *ON*.

4. **To play from in-hand**
to play from in-hand the cue-ball must be struck from a position on or within the lines of the "D".

NOTE:
THE REFEREE WILL ANSWER IF ASKED IF THE BALL IS PROPERLY PLACED.

5. **Hitting two balls simultaneously**
two balls, other than two reds or a *free ball* and the ball *on*, must not be hit simultaneously by the cue-ball.

6. **Spotting colours**
(a) if a colour has to be spotted, and its own spot is *occupied*, it shall be placed on the highest value spot available.

(b) if there is more than one colour, and their own spots are *occupied*, the highest value ball takes precedence.

(c) if all spots are *occupied*, the colour shall be placed as near as possible to its own spot between that spot and the nearest part of the top cushion.

(d) if, in the case of the Black and the Pink, the space between its own spot and the nearest part of the top cushion is *occupied*, the colour shall be placed as near as possible to its own spot on the centre line of the table below that spot.

7. **Touching Ball**
(a) if the cue-ball is touching another ball which is, or can be, *on*, the referee shall state TOUCHING BALL.

(b) the striker must play away from it or it is a *push stroke*.

(c) no penalty is incurred for thus playing away if:
　　(i) the ball is not *on*.
　　(ii) the ball is *on* and the striker *nominates* such ball, or
　　(iii) the ball is *on* and the striker *nominates*, and first hits, another ball.

NOTE: MOVEMENT OF TOUCHING BALL
IF THE REFEREE CONSIDERS THAT A TOUCHING BALL HAS MOVED THROUGH AN AGENCY OTHER THAN THE PLAYER, IT IS NOT A FOUL.

8. **Ball on edge of pocket**
(a) if a ball falls into a pocket without being hit by another ball it shall be replaced.

(b) if it would have been hit by any ball involved in a stroke, all balls will be replaced and the stroke replayed.

(c) if the ball balances momentarily on the edge and falls in, it must not be replaced.

9. **Free ball**

    (a) after a foul, if the cue-ball is *snookered*, the referee shall state FREE BALL.

    (b) if the non-offending player takes the next stroke he may nominate any ball as *on*.

    (c) for this stroke, such ball shall (subject to para (e) (i)) be regarded as, and acquire the value of, the ball *on*.

    (d) it is a foul, should the cue-ball
        (i) fail to first hit, or
        (ii) except when only pink and black remain on the table, be *snookered* by, the *free ball*.

    (e) if the *free ball* is potted it
        (i) is spotted, and
        (ii) the value of the ball *on* is scored.

    (f) if the ball *on* is potted it is scored.

    (g) if both the *free ball* and the ball *on* are potted only the value of the ball *on* is scored (subject to Sec. 3 Rule 3(e)(ii)).

10. **Fouls**

    (a) if a foul is committed:
        (i) the referree shall immediately state FOUL and on completion of the stroke announce the penalty.
        (ii) unless awarded by the referee or claimed by the non-striker, before the next stroke is made, it is condoned.
        (iii) any ball improperly spotted shall remain where positioned, except that if off the table it shall be correctly spotted.
        (iv) all points scored before the foul is awarded or claimed are allowed.
        (v) the next stroke is made from where the cue-ball comes to rest.

    (b) should more than one foul be committed in the same stroke the highest value penalty shall be incurred.

    (c) the player who committed the foul:
        (i) incurs the penalty prescribed (which is added to the opponent's score), and
        (ii) has to play again if requested by the next player. Once such a request has been made it cannot be withdrawn.
        (iii) If a breach of Section 3.3(l) occurs, the offending player has to play again from the original position, if requested by the next player.

11. **Penalties**

    the following are fouls and incur a penalty of four points or the higher one prescribed.

    (a) value of the ball *on*:
        by striking
        (i) when the balls are not at rest (Sec. 2 Rule 6).
        (ii) the cue-ball more than once (2–6).
        (iii) with both feet off the floor (2–6).
        (iv) out of turn (3–3).
        (v) improperly from *in-hand* (3–4).
        by causing
        (vi) the cue-ball to miss all object balls (3–3).
        (vii) the cue-ball to enter a pocket (3–3).
        (viii) a *snooker* with *free ball* (3–9).
        (ix) a *jump shot* (2–19).

    (b) value of the ball *on* or ball concerned:
        by causing
        (i) a ball not *on* to enter a pocket (3–3).
        (ii) the cue-ball to first hit a ball not *on* (3–3).
        (iii) a *push stroke* (2–18).
        (iv) by striking with a ball incorrectly spotted (2–11).
        (v) by touching a ball with other than the tip of the cue (2–6).
        (vi) by forcing a ball off the table (2–13).

(c) value of the ball *on* or higher value of the two balls by causing the cue-ball to hit simultaneously two balls other than two reds or a *free ball* and the ball *on* (3–5).

(d) a penalty of seven points is incurred if:
the striker
   (i) after potting a red commits a foul before *nominating* a colour,
   (ii) uses a ball off the table for any purpose,
   (iii) plays at reds in successive strokes, or
   (iv) uses as the cue-ball any ball other than white.

12.   Ball moved by other than striker
if a ball, stationary or moving, is disturbed other than by the striker it shall be re-positioned by the referee.

NOTE:
THIS COVERS THE CASE IN WHICH ANOTHER AGENCY CAUSES THE STRIKER TO TOUCH A BALL. NO PLAYER SHALL BE RESPONSIBLE FOR ANY DISTURBANCE OF THE BALLS BY THE REFEREE.

13.   Stalemate
if the referee considers a position of stalemate is being approached, he should warn the players that if the situation is not altered in a short period of time he will declare the frame null and void. The frame shall be re-started with the same order of play.

14.   Four-handed snooker
(a) in a four-handed game each side shall open alternate frames, the order of play shall be determined at the commencement of each frame, and must be maintained throughout that frame.

(b) players may change order of play at the beginning of each frame.

(c) if a foul is committed and a request made to play again, the player who committed the foul plays again, and ·the original order of play is maintained.

(d) when a frame ends in a tie Snooker Rule 3k applies. The pair who play the first stroke have the choice of which player plays that stroke. The order of play must then be maintained as in the frame.

(e) Partners may confer during a game but not whilst the striker is at the table or after the first stroke of his break.

SECTION 4. THE PLAYERS

1.   Time wasting
if the referee considers that a player is taking an abnormal amount of time over a stroke, he should be warned that he is liable to be disqualified.

2.   Unfair conduct
for refusing to continue a frame or for conduct which, in the opinion of the referee is wilfully or persistently unfair a player shall lose the game. He is liable to be disqualified from competitions held under the control of The Billiards and Snooker Council and its Affiliated Associations.

3.   Penalty
if a game is awarded to a player under this section the offender shall:
   (i) lose the game, and
   (ii) forfeit all points scored, and the non-offender shall receive the value of the balls still on the table (each red counting eight points).

NOTE:
PROVIDED THAT WHERE AGGREGATE POINTS SCORES APPLY, THE OFFENDER SHALL ALSO FORFEIT 147 POINTS FOR EACH UNPLAYED FRAME, TO THE NUMBER REQUIRED TO COMPLETE THE GAME.

4.   Non-striker
the non-striker shall, when the striker is playing, avoid standing or moving in the line of sight; he should sit or stand at a fair distance from the table.

5. **Absence**
    in case of his absence from the room he may appoint a substitute to watch his interests, and claim a foul if necessary.

SECTION 5. THE OFFICIALS

1. **The Referee**
    (a) the referee shall
        (i) be the sole judge of fair and unfair play, and responsible for the proper conduct of the game under these Rules.
        (ii) intervene if he sees any contravention.
        (iii) if a player is colour blind, tell him the colour of a ball if requested.
        (iv) clean a ball on a player's request.
    (b) he shall not
        (i) answer any question not authorised in the Rules.
        (ii) give any indication that a player is about to make a foul stroke.
        (iii) give any advice or opinion on points affecting play.
    (c) if he has failed to notice any incident he may take the evidence of the spectators best placed for observation to assist his decision.

NOTE:

THE REFEREE WILL NOT ANSWER A QUESTION REGARDING THE DIFFERENCE IN SCORES.

2. **The Marker**
    the marker shall keep the score on the marking board and assist the referee in carrying out his duties.

NOTE:

IF REQUESTED BY THE STRIKER, THE REFEREE OR MARKER MAY MOVE AND HOLD IN POSITION ANY LIGHT SHADE WHICH INTERFERES WITH THE ACTION OF THE STRIKER.

Rules of the Game of English Billiards*

Authorised by
THE BILLIARDS AND SNOOKER CONTROL COUNCIL

THE BILLIARDS ASSOCIATION
Established 1885

THE BILLIARDS CONTROL CLUB
Established 1908

AMALGAMATED 1919

Chairman: Stan Brooke
Secretary and Chief Executive: David Ford

SECTION 1. EQUIPMENT

1. **The Standard Table – Imperial**

   Dimensions

   (a) the playing area within the cushion faces shall measure 11ft 8½ins×5ft 10ins with a tolerance on both dimensions of ± ½in.

   Height

   (b) the height of the table from the floor to the top of the cushion rail shall be from 2ft 9½ins to 2ft 10½ins.

   Pocket Openings

   (c) (i) There shall be pockets at the corners (two at the Spot end known as the top pockets and two at the Baulk end as the bottom pockets) and at the middle of the longer sides.

   (ii) the pocket openings shall conform to the templates authorised by the Billiards and Snooker Control Council.

   Baulk-line and Baulk

   (d) a straight line drawn 29ins from the face of the bottom cushion and parallel to it is called the Baulk-line and the intervening space termed the Baulk.

   The "D"

   (e) the "D" is a semi-circle described in Baulk with its centre at the middle of the Baulk-line and with a radius of 11½ins.

   Spots

   (f) four spots marked on the centre longitudinal line of the table.

      (i) the Spot: 12¾ins from the point perpendicular below the face of the top cushion.

      (ii) the Centre Spot: Midway between the centre pockets and equidistant from the faces of the top and bottom cushions.

      (iii) the Pyramid Spot: Midway between the centre spot and the face of the top cushion.

      (iv) the Middle of the Baulk-line.

1M. **The Standard Table – Metric**

   Dimensions

   (a) the playing area within the cushion faces shall measure 3500mm × 1750mm with a tolerance on both dimensions of ± 3mm.

   Height

   (b) the height of the table from the floor to the top of the cushion rail shall be from 850mm to 875mm.

   Pocket Openings

   (c) (i) There shall be pockets at the corners (two at the Spot end known as the top pockets and two at the Baulk end as the bottom pockets) and at the middle of the longer sides.

   (ii) the pocket openings shall conform to the templates authorised by the Billiards and Snooker Control Council.

   Baulk-line and Baulk

   (d) a straight line drawn 700mm (⅕th the length of the playing area) from the face of the bottom cushion and parallel to it is called the Baulk-line and the intervening space termed the Baulk.

   The "D"

   (e) the "D" is a semi-circle described in Baulk with its centre at the middle of the Baulk-line and with a radius of 292mm (⅙th the width of the Playing area).

   Spots

   (f) four spots marked on the centre longitudinal line of the table.

      (i) the Spot: 320mm (1⁄11th the length of the playing area) from the point perpendicular below the face of the top cushion.

      (ii) the Centre Spot: Midway between the centre pockets and equidistant from the faces of the top and bottom cushions.

      (iii) the Pyramid Spot: Midway between the centre spot and the face of the top cushion.

      (iv) the Middle of the Baulk-line.

2. **Balls**
   (a) the balls shall have a diameter of 52.5mm (2¹⁄₁₆ins) with a tolerance of + 0.05mm − 0.08mm.
   (b) they shall be of equal weight within a tolerance of
      (i) 3 gms per Snooker set, and
      (ii) 0.05 gms per Billiard set.

NOTE:
A SET OF BALLS MAY BE CHANGED WITH THE CONSENT OF THE PLAYERS OR ON A DECISION OF THE REFEREE.

3. **Cue**
   the cue shall be not less than 910mm (3ft) in length and shall show no substantial departure from the traditional and generally accepted shape and form.

4. **Ancillary**
   "Rests" may be used to provide a bridge for the cue.

NOTE:
IT IS THE PLAYERS RESPONSIBILITY TO BOTH PLACE THE REST ON AND REMOVE IT FROM THE TABLE.

NOTE:
A PLAYER SHALL NOT BE PENALISED IF A REST HEAD FALLS OFF AND TOUCHES A BALL. THIS DOES NOT, HOWEVER, ABSOLVE A PLAYER FROM THE RESPONSIBILITY TO ENSURE THAT HE DOES NOT TOUCH A BALL WITH OTHER THAN THE TIP OF THE CUE.

SECTION 2. DEFINITIONS

1. **Game**
   a game is completed
   (a) at the expiry of a specified period of play, or
   (b) when the number of points agreed on is first scored.

2. **Match**
   a match is an agreed number of games.

3. **Balls**
   (a) the cue-ball is the ball of the striker.
   (b) the other balls are object balls.

4. **String**
   to string is to play together from the Baulk-line to the top cushion with the object of leaving the player's ball as near as possible to the bottom cushion.

5. **Striker**
   the person about to play or in play is the striker and remains so until completion of the stroke or break.

6. **Stroke**
   (a) a stroke is made when the striker strikes the cue-ball with the tip of the cue.
   (b) for the stroke to be a 'Fair Stroke' the following conditions must be met:
      (i) At the moment of striking, all balls must be at rest, and where necessary, object balls correctly spotted.
      (ii) The cue-ball must be struck and not pushed.
      (iii) The cue-ball must not be struck more than once in the same stroke.
      (iv) At the moment of striking, at least one of the strikers feet must be touching the floor.
      (v) The striker must not touch any ball other than the cue-ball as in section (a) above.
      (vi) A ball or balls must not be 'forced off the table'.
   (c) a stroke is not completed until all balls have come to rest and the referee has decided the striker has left the table.

7. **In-hand**
   (a) A player's ball is in-hand when it is off the table, and
   (b) It remains in-hand until played fairly from in-hand or a foul is committed whilst the ball is on the table.
   (c) When the non-striker's ball is in-hand it remains so until his turn to play or is spotted as in Sec. 3 Rule 7.

8. **Ball in Play**
   (a) A player's ball is in play when not in-hand.

(b) The red is in play when spotted and remains so until potted or forced off the table.

NOTE:

USING THE CUE TO POSITION THE CUE-BALL

IF THE REFEREE CONSIDERS THE PLAYER IS NOT ATTEMPTING TO PLAY A STROKE, EVEN THOUGH THE TIP OF THE CUE TOUCHES THE CUE-BALL, THE BALL IS NOT IN PLAY.

9.   **Hazard**
a hazard is
(a) A pot, or
(b) An in-off.

NOTE:

A POT IS OFTEN REFERRED TO AS A WINNING HAZARD AND AN IN-OFF AS A LOSING HAZARD.

10.   **Pot**
A pot is when an object ball, after contact with another ball, and without any contravention of these rules, enters a pocket.

11.   **In-Off**
an in-off is when the cue-ball, after contact with an object ball, and without any contravention of these rules, enters a pocket.

12.   **Cannon**
a cannon is when the cue-ball hits both the object balls, without any contravention of these rules.

13.   **Miss**
a miss is when the cue-ball fails to hit any other ball.

14.   **Break**
a break is a succession of scoring strokes made in any one turn.

15.   **Forced off the table**
a ball is forced off the table if it comes to rest other than on the bed of the table or in a pocket.

16.   **Foul**
a foul is any act in contravention of these rules.

17.   **Occupied**
a spot is said to be occupied if a ball cannot be placed on it without it touching another ball.

18.   **Push Stroke**
a push stroke is a foul and is made when the tip of the cue remains in contact with the cue-ball,
(a) when the cue-ball makes contact with the object ball, or
(b) after the cue-ball has commenced its forward motion.

PROVIDED that where the cue-ball and an object ball are almost touching, it shall be deemed a fair stroke if the cue-ball hits the finest possible edge of the object ball.

19.   **Jump Shot**
a jump shot is when the cue-ball jumps over any ball except when it first strikes the object ball and then jumps over another ball.

NOTE:

IF THE CUE-BALL FINISHES ON THE FAR SIDE OF THE OBJECT BALL, EVEN THOUGH TOUCHING IT IN THE PROCESS, IT IS CONSIDERED TO HAVE JUMPED OVER.

SECTION 3. THE GAME

1.   **Description**
The game of English Billiards is played by two or more persons, either as sides or independently. Three balls are used, 'plain' white, 'spot' white and red.
It is a game of *pots*, *in-offs*, *cannons* and positional play.
Points are awarded for scoring strokes and forfeits from an opponents fouls.
The winner is the player, or side, who has scored most points at the expiry of an agreed period, first scores an agreed number of points or to whom the game is awarded under Sec. 4 Rule 2.

2.   **Commencement of Game**
(a) The choice of ball and order of play, unless mutually agreed upon, shall be decided by *stringing*, the winner having the option, and shall remain unaltered throughout the game.

(b) At the commencement of the game the red is placed on the spot, the first player plays from *in-hand* and the game starts with the first *stroke*.

3. **Order of Play**

The players play alternately unless a score is made, in which case the *striker* continues the *break* playing from where his ball rests, or, after an *in-off* or as in Sec. 3 Rule 11, from *in-hand*.

4. **Spotting the Red Ball**

(a) If the red is *potted* or *forced off* the table it is placed on the spot. If the spot is *occupied* it is placed on the pyramid spot. If that spot is also *occupied* it is placed on the centre spot.

(b) If the red is potted from the spot or pyramid spot twice in succession in one break, not in conjunction with another score, it is placed on the centre spot. If this spot is *occupied* it is placed on the pyramid spot or if both these spots are *occupied* on the spot.

If again potted it shall be placed on the spot.

NOTE:
IF DURING A STROKE THE RED COMES TO REST ON THE SPOT, IT IS NOT CONSIDERED TO BE SPOTTED.
IT IS THE STRIKER'S RESPONSIBILITY TO ENSURE THAT ALL BALLS ARE CORRECTLY SPOTTED BEFORE STRIKING.

5. **Details of Scoring**

Points are awarded as follows:

(a) for a *cannon*, *pot* white and *in-off* white, two.

(b) for a *pot* red and *in-off* red, three.

(c) if more than one *hazard* or a combination of *hazards* and a *cannon* are made in the same *stroke* all are scored.

(d) when an *in-off* is combined with a *cannon* it shall score two or three according to whether the white or red was first hit.

(e) should both be hit simultaneously the *in-off* shall count two.

6. **To Play from In-hand**

The cue-ball must

(a) be struck from a position on or within the lines of the 'D'.

NOTE:
THE REFEREE WILL ANSWER, IF ASKED IF THE BALL IS PROPERLY PLACED.

(b) be played out of baulk, except that it may be played against a cushion in baulk to hit a ball out of baulk.

(c) hit a ball or cushion out of baulk before hitting a ball in baulk.

NOTE:
A BALL IS IN BAULK WHEN IT RESTS ON THE BAULK-LINE OR BETWEEN THAT LINE AND THE BOTTOM CUSHION.
IF A BALL IS OUT OF BAULK ANY PART OF ITS SURFACE MAY BE PLAYED ON FROM IN-HAND:
IF A BALL IS IN BAULK NO PART OF ITS SURFACE MAY BE PLAYED ON DIRECTLY FROM IN-HAND.
THE REFEREE WILL ANSWER, IF ASKED, IF A BALL IS IN OR OUT OF BAULK.

7. **Limitation of Hazards**

Consecutive *hazards*, not in conjunction with a *cannon*, are limited to fifteen.

If more than one *hazard* is made in the same *stroke* it shall count as one for the purpose of this rule but all points shall be scored.

After ten *hazards* or on request, the referee shall inform the *striker*.

Should the non-strikers ball be off the table as a result of the non-strikers last stroke, it shall be spotted after the fifteenth *hazard* on the middle spot of the 'D', or if *occupied* on the right hand corner of the 'D'.

NOTE:
SHOULD THE REFEREE FAIL TO INFORM THE STRIKER AFTER TEN HAZARDS THE STRIKER IS ENTITLED TO PLAY A FURTHER FIVE HAZARDS AFTER HE IS INFORMED.

8. **Limitation of Cannons**

Consecutive *cannons*, not in conjunction with a *hazard*, are limited to seventy-five.

After seventy *cannons*, or on request, the referee shall inform the *striker*.

NOTE:
SHOULD THE REFEREE FAIL TO INFORM THE STRIKER AFTER SEVENTY CANNONS THE STRIKER IS ENTITLED TO PLAY A FURTHER FIVE CANNONS AFTER HE IS INFORMED.

9.   **Ball on Edge of Pocket**
      (a) if a ball falls into a pocket without being hit by another ball it shall be replaced.
      (b) if it would have been hit by any ball involved in a *stroke*, all balls will be replaced and the *stroke* replayed.
      (c) if the ball balances momentarily on the edge and falls in, it must not be replaced.

10.   **Ball moved by other than striker**
      if a ball, stationary or moving, is disturbed other than by the *striker* it shall be repositioned by the referee.

NOTE:
THIS COVERS THE CASE IN WHICH ANOTHER AGENCY CAUSES THE STRIKER TO TOUCH A BALL. NO PLAYER SHALL BE RESPONSIBLE FOR ANY DISTURBANCE OF THE BALLS BY THE REFEREE.

11.   **Balls Touching**
      When the *striker's* ball remains touching another ball, red shall be placed on the spot, the non-striker's ball, if on the table, shall be placed on the centre spot, and the striker shall play from *in hand*.

12.   **Miss**
      (a) For a miss the striker incurs a penalty of two points.
      (b) a *miss* is a foul except when the striker is *in hand* and there is no ball out of baulk.

13.   **Fouls**
      (a) if a foul is committed
          (i) the referee shall immediately state foul.
          (ii) unless awarded by the referee or claimed by the non-striker, before the next stroke is made, it is condoned.

(iii) any ball improperly spotted shall remain where positioned, except that if off the table it shall be correctly spotted.
(iv) all points scored before the foul is awarded or claimed are allowed.

(b) the player committing the foul incurs a penalty of two points, which are added to his opponents score.

(c) the next player has the option of playing
    (i) from where the balls are at rest (the red if off the table having been spotted), or
    (ii) from *in-hand*, the red and white being spotted on the spot and centre spot respectively.

(d) the following acts are fouls:
    by striking
    (i)   when the balls are not at rest (Sec. 2 Rule 6).
    (ii) the *cue-ball* more than once (2–6).
    (iii) with both feet off the floor (2–6).
    (iv) out of turn (3–3).
    (v)   improperly from *in-hand* (3–6).
    (vi) with a ball incorrectly spotted.
    (vii) a ball other than the *cue-ball* (2–6).
    by making
    (viii) a *jump shot* (2–19).
    (ix)   a *push stroke* (2–18).
    (x)   more than fifteen *hazards* (3–7).
    (xi)   more than seventy-five *cannons* (3–8).
    (xii) by touching a ball with other than the tip of the cue (2–6).
    (xiii) by forcing a ball off the table (2–6).
    (xiv) by using a ball off the table for any purpose.

SECTION 4. THE PLAYERS

1. **Time wasting**
   if the referee considers that a player is taking an abnormal amount of time over a stroke, he should be warned that he is liable to be disqualified.

2. **Unfair conduct**
   for refusing to continue a game or for conduct which, in the opinion of the referee is wilfully or persistently unfair a player shall lose the game. He is liable to be disqualified from competitions held under the control of The Billiards and Snooker Council and its Affiliated Associations.

3. **Penalty**
   If a game is awarded to a player under this section the offender shall:
   (i) lose the game, and
   (ii) if the game was to be decided on a number of agreed points he shall forfeit all points scored and the non-offender shall receive the agreed number of points, or
   (iii) if the game be decided at the expiry of a specified period of play and forms part of a team match the whole match shall be forfeited.

4. **Non-striker**
   the non-striker shall, when the striker is playing, avoid standing or moving in the line of sight; he should sit or stand at a fair distance from the table.

5. **Absence**
   in case of his absence from the room he may appoint a substitute to watch his interests, and claim a foul if necessary.

SECTION 5. THE OFFICIALS

1. **The Referee**
   (a) the referee shall
   (i) be the sole judge of fair and unfair play, and responsible for the proper conduct of the game under these Rules.
   (ii) intervene if he sees any contravention.
   (iii) if a player is colour blind, tell him the colour of a ball if requested.
   (iv) clean a ball on a player's request.

   (b) he shall not
   (i) answer any question not authorised in the Rules.
   (ii) give any indication that a player is about to make a foul stroke.
   (iii) give any advice or opinion on points affecting play.

   (c) if he has failed to notice any incident he may take the evidence of the spectators best placed for observation to assist his decision.

NOTE:
THE REFEREE WILL NOT ANSWER A QUESTION REGARDING THE DIFFERENCE IN SCORES.

2. **The Marker**
   the marker shall keep the score on the marking board and assist the referee in carrying out his duties.

NOTE:
IF REQUESTED BY THE STRIKER, THE REFEREE OR MARKER MAY MOVE AND HOLD IN POSITION ANY LIGHT SHADE WHICH INTERFERES WITH THE ACTION OF THE STRIKER.

THE PUNCH BOOK OF
SEX AND MARRIAGE

Also published by Grafton Books

The Punch Book of Cricket
The Punch Book of Golf
The Punch Book of Health

THE PUNCH BOOK
OF

Sex & Marriage

Compiled by
Susan Jeffreys

Foreword by
Maureen Lipman

A PUNCH BOOK
Published in association with
GRAFTON BOOKS
A Division of the Collins Publishing Group

LONDON GLASGOW
TORONTO SYDNEY AUCKLAND

Grafton Books
A Division of the Collins Publishing Group
8 Grafton Street, London W1X 3LA

Published by Grafton Books 1987

British Library Cataloguing in Publication Data

The Punch book of sex and marriage.
1. Sex——Anecdotes, facetiae,
satire, etc.
I. Jeffreys, Susan
306.7'0207   HQ23

ISBN 0-246-13238-8

Printed in Great Britain by
Butler and Tanner Ltd, Frome, Somerset

The articles by Keith Waterhouse are reproduced
by permission of David Higham Associates Ltd
and the articles by John Wells are reproduced by
permission of Anthony Sheil Associates Ltd.

CONTENTS

FOREWORD

by Maureen Lipman

I do believe I'm perfect casting for writing a foreword to a book about Sex and Marriage. I am, after all, from Hull. I'm forty. I wear glasses and, during several seasons of the year, a vest – and the only sexually-transmitted disease I've had is a headache. In short, what I know about both Sex and Marriage could be written on one side of a curiously strong mint.

Actually, when I accepted this brief (as we say in the world of foreword-writing), I was under the impression that it was for a *Punch* book on *Saxon Marriage*, a subject abnormally dear to my heart. Indeed, I became quite fired by the idea and did some primary research into the ceremony ('Do you, Caedmon, takke thisse woman, Grendel, to bee thy strawful-bedded weaving-machine?') and into the honeymoon – when the bridegroom would swill down a smoked ox with four hornsful of mead, indulge in a spot of bull-baiting and challenge his new mother-in-law to a game of dice to the death played with the ankle-bone of a sheep. How much duller lyfe has become, has it not, since decimal currency came in?

Before leaping on to the wooden nuptial couch, the happy couple would settle down to eight or nine hours of the sagas of their fore-fathers (forefathers being the same as forewords except in direct speech). Then, back to the straw hut for some serious procreation, by which I mean, out of your flea-infested garb and 'Wham, bam, thank you Hengist,' under the watchful eyes of four cows, two dogs and the fierce god Woden (or, three nights a week, Wogan) and his goddess-wife, Frig. Yes, Frig (serious etymologists start here). Those were the days, when men were men and women were . . . had a bit . . . Eate your hearte oute, Mickeye Rourke.

But I digress. Briefly, then, I've read the proofs – and I'm *amazed*. There's not *one word* about the true significance of what's it . . . thingy . . . you know – yes, I'm not afraid to say it – congress, whose aim, as any normal English-man knows, is to bring two people to the emo-tional, spiritual and physical peak suitable for Desmond Wilcox to do a documentary on them. In fact the whole book's a tissue of innuendo, filth and suggestive smut, graffiti masquerading as cartoons and other such naughties.

Nor is there anything *instructive* in the book. No mention of cold showers, bracing walks, nightly dental-flossing or lying back and think-ing of the Humber Bridge. In fact, unless you want to grow hairy palms on your eyelids, you'd be a damn sight better off with a decent hobby such as tatting, synchronised drowning or foreword-writing.

As for the 'Marriage' bits, well again, the trouble with this book is that with all that S.E.X. lolloping about there's little room for marriage, which is a bit like life only the other way round. Very little about the sanctity of wedded bliss, the stroll hand-in-handcuffs through Life's ups and downs. The patter of tiny mortgages, the sharing of burdens and dis-posable razors . . .

Any road up (and aren't they all these days?), I'll be honest with you. Several times whilst reading this book I became distinctly aware of a twitching at the corners of my mouth. On a topless beach with Alan Coren, not literally you understand but, well, – literature-ly – I couldn't help smiling, although it could have been indi-gestion from some braised bean curd I'd had an hour before. And again in bed with some Frenchman and Irma Kurtz – and well, Michael Parkinson had me on the floor – no, you mis-understand! I mean on the floor *laughing* – I mean, oh what the heck!, I can tell you're going to read this book so just don't blame me if it ends in tears. You've been foreworded.

LIST OF CARTOONISTS

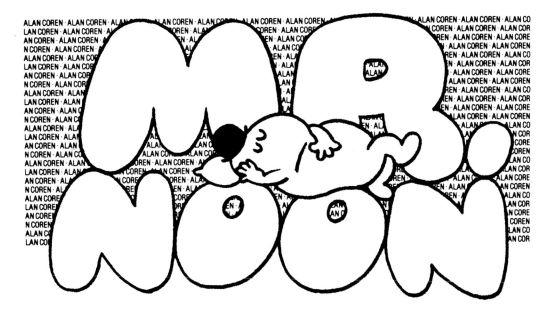

A novel by D. H. Lawrence is to be published by Cambridge University Press next month, 54 years after his death. Researchers found the MS. among papers at the Humanities Research Centre of the University of Texas, Austin.

The new book is called *Mr Noon*. Lawrence wrote it in two parts and hoped they would be published as separate novels, but the publishers found them too short.

Daily Telegraph

Mr Noon lived up to his name.

He did not get up with the cock.

He did not get up with the sun.

He did not get up and collect the nice fat heavy eggs, still warm from squeezing out of the plump chicken loins.

He did not get up and tug the long rubbery-flubbery teats of Daisy the Cow so that the bright hot milk spurted ringingly into the big dark depths of the bucket.

He did not get up and take Roger the Ram down to the bleating sheep to let Roger the Ram go humpity-humpity and make the sheep feel as if great big waves were crashing on the shore time and time and time again.

Mr Noon did not get up in the morning at all. He stayed in his bed until noon.

Mr Noon would stay in his bed in case a visitor turned up.

Many visitors *did* turn up at the little cottage, but Mr Noon would send them away again.

Every day, the Postman would call up to the little open window of Mr Noon's bedroom.

'Good morning, Mr Noon!'

And every day, Mr Noon would call out:

'Eff off, Postman!'

Every day, the Jehovah's Witness would call up to the little open window of Mr Noon's bedroom.

'Good morning, Mr Noon!'

And every day, Mr Noon would call out:

'Eff off, Jehovah's Witness!'

And so on.

Mr Noon liked using naughty words. He did not think they were naughty at all, and he was right. People who object to naughty words are guilty of hypocrisy and cant. Mr Noon hated cant.

'Silly cant!' said Mr Noon, lying in his bed.

He would look at the ceiling all morning, and make pictures in his head. Don't you do that, too?

Mr Noon would see trains rushing into long dark tunnels.

'Whoosh!' went the trains.

'Wheeee!' went their whistles, inside the tunnels.

Mr Noon would see his Dad going to work.

His Dad was a miner. Every day, his Dad went down a long dark hole. When he got to the bottom, he would take out his big shovel.

Dig, dig, dig, went Dad Noon!

Mr Noon would see all this, lying on his bed.

He would also see his Mum. Mum Noon was a schoolteacher. But most of all, she liked riding horses. He would see her, on the ceiling, riding a big black stallion, with her skirt tucked into her knickers, and her nostrils flaring. The stallion's nostrils flared, too. Sometimes they would ride into a tunnel, if there wasn't a train coming.

When they got home, they were all sweaty! So Mum Noon would get out a great big tin bath, and put it in front of the fire, and put the horse in it, and scrub its back.

Mr Noon liked that picture best of all.

By mid-day, when no visitors had called, except the Gasman, and the Man About The Rates, and the Double Glazing Man, and the Reader's Digest Man, and the Tally Man, Mr Noon would at last get out of bed, grind his big yellow teeth, and say:

'Boogger! Boogger! Boogger!'

Then he would clump down the little creaky staircase in his big honest clogs and out into the smelly old farmyard and try to find something nice to worm.

On a good day, it might be Sharon the Sow. But on a bad day, it might only be Corky the Cat.

Then, one fine, ripening, spring morning, with the fat fuzzy pussy-willow catkins jiggling up and down outside his bedroom window and making his throat go all dry and funny, Mr Noon heard an unfamiliar voice call up from below.

'I say!' it trilled. 'Is anyone at home?'

Slowly, the image of tall dark beetling industrial chimneys raping innocent verdant hills faded from Mr Noon's ceiling. The voice was not a Postman's voice or, indeed, anything remotely like it.

'Aye,' grunted Mr Noon cautiously, from the bed (for it was still only ten-fifteen). 'Aye, appen there be.'

'Oh, ripping!' cried the voice. 'Oh, top-hole! Oh, super!'

Slowly Mr Noon broke the habit of a lifetime and, well before mid-day, swung his big hairy feet out of bed and onto the linoleum, and walked, squeak-squeak-squeak, to the little window and looked out.

Mr Noon found himself staring down into the upturned smiling face and almost equally upturned open blouse of a very pretty lady. Mr Noon gripped the little window ledge with his big hairy hands to stop them trembling: it was a Visitor!

'Can ah elp thee, miss?' croaked Mr Noon.

'Oh, would you?' cried the young lady. 'I was just driving past in my motor and I could not help noticing your little chickens. I have a teensy-weensy dinner-party tonight, just a few ripping top-hole chums from the upper classes, and a couple of plump pullets would be absolutely tickety-boo!'

Mr Noon closed his eyes. Then he opened them again, struggled to ungrip his hands from the little window ledge, and retreated, lurching, into the room.

Mr Noon pulled on his thick corduroy trousers.

Mr Noon pulled on his coarse linen shirt.

Mr Noon spat on his big hairy hands and smoothed down his big hairy head.

Then he went downstairs. Clump, clump, clump, went his clogs.

Mr Noon stepped into the unfamiliar morning.

'Pullet?' he said, hoarsely.

'Definitely!' trilled the young lady.

The breeze blew her thin cotton skirt against her legs. Her huge eyes were the deep blue of a faceworker's scars. The sun caught her soft forearm down, reminding Mr Noon of the lioness's belly at Nottingham Zoo.

Mr Noon licked his lips.

'Appen ah'll ketch thee a couple,' he murmured, fighting a sudden dizzy spell. 'Tha'll want plump 'uns, ah tek it?'

The young lady nodded, and winked, and clapped her hands, and giggled.

Mr Noon lunged suddenly, his huge corded muscles bulging, and hurled himself at the squawking chickens.

Scuttle! went the chickens.

Grab! went Mr Noon.

Kof-kof-kof! went the chickens.

Oh! went the young lady.

Mr Noon brought them to her, one in each hand. They were still warm. They were still wriggling, slightly. She touched the plump little bodies with her long slim white fingers.

'So many feathers!' she murmured. 'And I'm late already.' She turned her big blue eyes up to Mr Noon's strong dark face. 'I suppose a pluck would be out of the question?' she said.

Mr Noon fainted.

When he came round, he found the Postman, the Double Glazing Man, the Tally Man, the Reader's Digest Man, and the Man About The

Rates standing over him. They had been watching, the way folk do in those parts.

Only the Jehovah's Witness had made an excuse and left.

'Where be er?' enquired Mr Noon.

'Er be gone,' replied the Postman.

'Funny to see you up and about so early,' said the Tally Man. 'Reckon as how we won't be able to call you Mr Noon no more.'

The Double Glazing Man nudged him in the ribs, and winked.

'Mister Bloody Good Opportunity, more like!' he said.

How everybody laughed!

All except Mr Noon, of course.

Alan Coren 28.8.1984

IN SEARCH OF AN ORGY

I, Charles Septimus Parkin of 23A Jubilee Mansions, Norwood, make this statement voluntarily in the presence of Detective-Sergeant William Cooney and PC Throstle of 'E' Division. I am forty-three years old and a clerk in the employ of British Fat Products Ltd. I am married in name only. I do not wish to add to that.

I first became aware of the permissive society on or about September 5 1969. I remember the date because it is the birthday of my niece Avril, and I had bought her a Kooky-doll as a present. I do not know why the Kooky-doll is still in my possession or why she was in the cistern cupboard. I cannot explain why she is wearing fishnet tights, see-through bra and a PVC mackintosh instead of the après-ski outfit depicted on her box. The Action Man produced by Det.-Sgt. Cooney from the cistern cupboard in my presence does not belong to me. I do not know why Action Man is wearing only his boots. The Polaroid camera is for the purpose of taking holiday snaps. The photograph which I ate before being cautioned by Det.-Sgt. Cooney was a holiday snap.

On or about September 5 1969 I read in a

Sunday newspaper about a wife-swapping ring in Mauncey Road, Birmingham, together with an exposé of certain magazines 'for swingers only', also photographs allegedly taken at a drag party in Leeds before the reporter made an excuse and left. It is not true that from that day on I became obsessed by the permissive society, although what I read was certainly an eye-opener. I did not suggest to my wife Noreen that we should engage in similar activities. The phrase, 'Let's get some fun out of life while we're still young, or are you too frigid?' is not one that I would normally use. I did not place an advertisement in the *Swapper's Digest*. I have never heard of the *Swapper's Digest*.

I now recall that I did place an advertisement in the *Swapper's Digest*. The fifteen back numbers of this publication under the towels in the airing cupboard are for my own use. The advertisement was a joke. It has been put to me that 'Virile husband-and-wife duo wish to meet AC-DC couples, no prudes' does not sound like a joke, but I do not agree. It was an exercise in parody. I know nothing about an accommodation address in Soho. I received no replies to my advertisement.

I have never been in Mauncey Road, Birmingham.

I now recollect that I went to Mauncey Road, Birmingham, on September 9 and spoke to a woman now known to me as WPC Hawkins. My purpose in journeying to Birmingham was to visit an old army friend, 586 Cadger McNally, whose address I cannot at present remember. I asked WPC Hawkins to direct me to New Street Station. I did not employ any words such as 'Are you a swinger?' I recall employing the phrase, 'Where is the action?' This is an idiomatic expression indicating that I was looking for New Street Station.

I did not deposit a suitcase in the left-luggage office at New Street Station. I identify a suitcase produced by Det.-Sgt. Cooney as my property. I confirm that it did not fly to Birmingham of its own volition. The mask, riding-crop and length of rope are all my property. I purchased the mask at a novelty shop in Paddington in case my friend 586 Cadger McNally was giving his annual fancy-dress party. The riding-crop was a present for my married niece June, who is a keen horsewoman. I have no recollection whatsoever

of proposing to my married niece June that I should be her gee-gee and that she should ride me around her living room. The length of rope was in case of fire. I have always carried a length of rope in case of fire ever since reading that Hans Christian Andersen did likewise. It has been put to me that Hans Christian Andersen is the same 'Fancy-pants' Andersen who is now doing bird at the Scrubs for thieving lingerie off of clothes lines. To the best of my knowledge Hans Christian Andersen was a writer of fairy tales. I have been informed what the expression 'fairy' means in common parlance. I have never been that way inclined. I have never been to Hampstead Heath.

It is not true that I was wandering about Leeds in a polka-dot dress and steel-blue nylon stockings on the night of September 9–10. The polka-dot dress produced by Det.-Sgt. Cooney was purchased at Selfridge's for my friend 586 Cadger McNally's fancy-dress party. I regard flushing clothes down the lavatory as a normal method of disposing of unwanted property.

Having been shown certain photographs, I now wish to correct any suggestion I may have made that I was not wandering about Leeds on the night of September 9–10, but I deny that I was looking for a so-called drag party. I was in Leeds for the simple reason that I got on the wrong train at Birmingham New Street Station. I was suffering from flu and had taken some tablets shortly before drinking a glass of beer. This must have made me light-headed. I was definitely not wearing the polka-dot dress, except for a short period.

I admit to having knocked at a door in Victoria Hospital Avenue, Leeds, between 12.30 and 12.45 am. I deny asking the lady now known to me as Mrs Jeanette Henderson if there was room for one more. I deny suggesting to Mrs Henderson that nobody would take her for a sailor. My purpose in knocking at the door was to ask for a glass of water. I was not wearing the polka-dot dress. I had recently drunk a carton of milk which must have splashed over my overcoat, giving it a polka-dot effect. I did not raise my overcoat to thigh level while in conversation with Mrs Henderson.

Having been given an opportunity to reconsider that portion of my statement relating to the *Swapper's Digest*, I now believe that there may have been one or two replies to my advertisement. There may have been 1,753 replies. Certain parcels which Det.-Sgt. Cooney removed from under the floorboards in my presence may contain replies to my advertisement. I have not read any of them. I do not recognise a typewritten manuscript entitled *Kitty's Awakening*. I do not know of any invitation to attend a party in Tulse Hill for sex fun.

I am familiar with Tulse Hill. I may have been there on the evening of December 18. An important invoice had blown out of my office window on that day and I thought it might have landed in Tulse Hill. I may have been wearing a shortie nightdress under my raincoat. I often wear a shortie nightdress in the privacy of my own home as I understand there is no law against it. I wear it because it is convenient. At approximately 10 pm, on the evening of December 18, I remembered that I had not taken the dog for his usual walk. I put on a raincoat over my shortie nightdress and took him as far as the pillar box. The dog having slipped his lead and been run over by a coal-lorry I thought that rather than waste my outing I would proceed to Tulse Hill and look for the invoice.

I may have approached several householders in the Tulse Hill district with the words, 'Have you a French kitten for sale?' I was not aware that this was a password. Owing to the accident to my dog I was anxious to obtain a new pet as quickly as possible. I do not know why I asked for a French kitten. I now think that I may have asked for a *fresh* kitten, meaning one that was only a few days old.

After a conversation with my wife Noreen I now recall that I have never owned a dog. I have been taking pills for a severe migraine and these, swallowed in conjunction with beer or wine, sometimes induce a sensation of owning a dog.

I deny hailing a taxi at Tulse Hill Station at 1.43 on the morning of December 19.

Having been assured that nobody is going to get their collar felt for taking a cab, I now remember hailing a taxi at Tulse Hill Station, but deny asking the driver if he knew anything about blue movies.

The taxi took me to my home. I deny saying, 'Well, here we are at Iceberg Manor.' I deny offering the driver double fare to take me to Hampstead Heath.

Certain evidence having been shown to me, I admit to being on Hampstead Heath at 3.16 on the morning of December 19 and approaching the gentleman I now recognise as Detective-Sergeant Cooney. I regret having prevaricated about this matter, but I was of the impression that wearing false moustaches went out with Sexton Blake. I concur that if I had stuck to false moustaches instead of polka-dot dresses I would not be in the situation in which I now find myself.

I confirm that I mistook Det.-Sgt. Cooney for a sex maniac, and that I asked him for information about any lewd, filthy, degrading and obscene parties that might be going on in the vicinity. I agree that I falsely represented my wife Noreen as being available for sex fun in the event of Det.-Sgt. Cooney being able to assist me in my depraved endeavours. I now understand that my use of the words 'sizzling', 'versatile' and 'hot pants' in respect of my wife Noreen was an offence under the Trades Descriptions Act, and I wish to express my regret for any embarrassment, distress and disappointment caused both to my wife and to Det.-Sgt. Cooney.

Keith Waterhouse 7.1.1970

'Can we go to an orgy at the Bennets after choir practice?'

'Now did you remember to put on a clean vest?'

'Can I take your things?'

'Coffee and biscuits, everybody!'

'So the group profits were £75,000 – interim 5 % already paid, of course.'

'Shy? . . . Me?'

'I could walk from here if you like, Mr Sturgeon.'

'Oh boy! . . . Match of the Day in colour!'

'. . . And thank you for having me!'

ORGY ETIQUETTE

Orgies, as J. B. Priestley once complained, always happen the night before you arrive. Until the other day, when I attended one, I would have sworn Priestley's axiom was inflexible and universally true.

It was my wife who arranged this rather bizarre experience for me, and indeed she was the one who was supposed to attend. It all happened when, in the course of her journalistic duties, she encountered a man called Mick, a local government officer, who devoted his spare time gathering together groups of some dozen or twenty Londoners for guiltless, fleeting, sexual encounters, designed to gratify the gourmet appetites of consummation addicts, rather after the fashion of a Wine and Food tasting.

A fortnight later, my wife being abroad, I was sitting at home watching television with our gay au pair boy, when my mind began to stray to the Party that night. Well, why not? I mean, strictly in search of copy, of course. I rang Mick and was given an address on the western fringes of Hammersmith.

There were around fourteen guests, more women than men, mainly in their twenties and early thirties, but two or three middle-aged males. Not all of the men were good looking, but nobody actually appalling. (I had been having fantasies of the occasional grossly fat monster or a cross-eyed dwarf.) Most of the women were attractive in a nullish sort of way, rather what you expect of the wives of distant relatives, but one or two were really gorgeous.

I was in some vamping-till-ready conversation, barely listening to myself, with a pink, doll-like creature, about gardening I think, when I realised a man behind her was sliding his hand down into her blouse. I stopped in the middle of the word 'delphinium', whatever that is, not wishing to deprive her of full concentration on the sensual experience. But she completed the word, and started on vegetables. Another man, crouched lower down, was now removing her skirt. Soon she was there, being massaged and palped in a tiny pair of panties by two of them, and still her lips moved. Gradually, and with the utmost courtesy, they edged her away, up an open staircase, to a mattress-strewn balcony. When she got to the top, she finished her sentence, gave a tiny wave, and vanished beneath them.

I was accosted by one of the middle-aged men. 'Listen to that,' he crowed. 'She's away.' There was a noise like a lowing cow from the balcony. 'That's my wife,' he said. 'Why don't you try her? She likes eleven chaps in a row. We got her a football team once.'

And then he quailed. I realised that there must have been something in my eye, a look of contempt perhaps, or even worse pity. Anyway, it shrivelled his excitement. Why do I feel this, I wondered. If it is what they both want, and does no harm to anyone else, why shouldn't they? But I realised I felt no arousal at all.

But I was determined, having longed to be at an Orgy since the age of twelve, that I should play some part. Would anything else not be an act of rudeness to my fellow guests? I started to remove my trousers, being then almost the only non-naked person in the room. But suddenly there was a pause, a kind of halftime interval, in the match. The couple under the stairs disengaged. And one by one the bodies trooped down

the stairs and began to re-assemble, in cocktail hour twos and threes, while the host served pieces of Colonel Sanders' Finger Licking Chicken.

I think it was that which put me off. There was somehow an awful congruity between the pink, slightly glistening flesh of the people and the pink, slightly greasy flesh of the birds. If it had been caviar and champagne, I might not have felt an awful snobbish sense of not belonging. There was more Spanish red. I asked for a Scotch (I could see the bottle at the back of the cupboard) but my host, with a puritanical grimace, whispered – 'We don't encourage the hard stuff. Awfully bad for performance, we find.'

The combinations began to rearrange themselves. The husband I'd quelled slapped his wife's bottom – 'Come on, any more offers?' he said. 'Four more to make up her set.' The room began to empty and the balcony to fill. I rezipped my flies, put on my coat, and didn't even make an excuse, but left.

Alan Brien 8.2.1978

'It's nothing personal—it's just the old problem of supply and demand.'

banx:
HAREM
GLOBE-TROTTERS

'Don't look now but I think Ahmed's having a relapse.'

'First cuckoo of spring? I was practising my baritone.'

'The interview was a breeze – it's the
medical afterwards I hated.'

'That's the trouble nowadays – good eunuchs are so hard to come by.'

'Personally I can't think what we ever saw in those wife-swapping parties.'

FULL OF EASTERN PROMISE

On the evening of my first day in Tokyo, during which I had done some shopping and been chased up the Ginza by a small dog, I decided to avail myself of a bath and massage. A number of men, decorously draped in skimpy white towels, were sweating in the establishment's steam room after an immersion in scalding water which had tasted faintly of sprouts. We grunted and hissed and struck manly attitudes, like a Praetorian Guard off duty.

I was lying recumbent upon a bench, contemplating a seaweed and duck dinner, when the masseuse, a small, nut-coloured woman wearing a surgeon's smock and an expression of limitless rage, sprang onto my back and started running on the spot. The resulting sensation was not unlike having one of those ten-ton iron balls they demolish buildings with bounced briskly about my person and, while I realised it was probably doing my clef-shaped spine a bit of good, I also guessed that my kidneys were being speedily reduced to the consistency of trodden grapes or raw hamburger.

When I could summon the breath I yelled

'Get off!' and she dismounted with a small curtsy and the hint of a blush. Across the room, through the whirling wraiths of steam, one of the men looked up then came clacking over on his elevated wooden sandals. 'You are visiting Japan on business?' he said, in the careful tones of those tiresome Berlitz alumni who seize every opportunity to practise their English on the unwary.

'In a manner of speaking,' I said.

'And what business, prease, are you in?' He was skinny and eager-looking, with unusually opaque spectacles; his eyes seemed to be taking my measure from a spot about half a mile behind him.

'I'm a writer,' I said.

He displayed some astonishment. 'Hah!' he said, then he seized my limp, boiled hand and shook it. 'Fujita. I am pubrisher. Meeting between writer and pubrisher always very auspicious.'

'Quite so,' I said and, politely, I asked him what sort of stuff he published.

'Pirrow books,' he said.

I pondered a moment. 'Oh, pillow books,' I said, recalling that I had been leafing through one of those tastefully-bound and erotic little volumes in a drug-store that very day. I had been unable to make much of the story since it was told in Japanese characters, like the footprints of sparrows with fallen arches and hammer toes, but the spidery pen-and-ink illustrations had held my attention for a disproportionate length of time; I had gathered that the plot concerned a student with a wispy beard who had presumably taken a day off rioting to create mayhem among what appeared to be a group of startled lady gymnasts. 'Very interesting,' I said. 'They sell well, do they? These pillow books?'

By way of a reply he simply allowed himself a broad smile, displaying a pair of jaws that had been painstakingly embellished in recycled sovereigns. Then, abruptly, he sat down beside me. 'Rike hot cake,' he said. 'But I most anxious to break into British and American market. Introduce Engrish-ranguage pirrow books to overseas readers but produce them in Japanese fashion. Market here is frooded. Must export to prosper.'

'Shrewd thinking,' I said.

'So,' he said, 'I am seeking writer for experimental book. You interested?'

'You want *me* to write a pillow book?' I said.

'For overseas market. On trial basis.'

'How much?'

'Five thousand.'

'Pounds or dollars?'

'Yen,' he said.

'Oh.' Well, that was still quite a respectable sum. 'Done,' I said. We shook hands.

'Book must be very sexy,' he said. 'But not crude. No unbridled rust. Good strong prot with ten, maybe twelve character, mostry women, and set in Japan. Character must be interesting and story must stimurate and tease. Think of a situation.'

'Now?' I said. A few yards away the masseuse was busily slapping a paunchy, hirsute man into a kind of gratified coma.

'Sure,' he said. 'We run idea up fragpole and sarute it. Okay?'

'Okay.' I sat peering through the steam, brooding. Well, it wasn't going to be the elegant Proustian tome my mother assumed I would one day write, but there would be plenty of time for that. The experience would be useful, and so would the money. The yen, despite recent fluctuations, is still a very strong currency; you can sandpaper furniture with the notes and even mend bicycle punctures with them.

'Right,' I said. 'Let's make the hero an English

shipping magnate visiting Japan to buy a supertanker. His name is Frisby. One evening he wanders into a Yokohama waterfront bar where supertanker persons and others of that ilk and persuasion tend to forgather for a glass or two of saki before bed. The atmosphere is quiet, almost somnolent. Frisby is playing mah jongg with a bosun when, suddenly, he hears the sound of singing out in the street. He finds a woman's choir standing there, accompanied by a puffing lady flautist. "Take off your trousers, Frisby san," they sing, "and prove you are a true Englishman." The bosun tells him that this is the choir of the Yokohama Women's Institute. Well, Frisby is understandably a little bemused. He tells them to return to their homes and families, but they just grin at him. Then they sing, "Heights of happiness you shall reach with the ninety-nine positions we can teach" and Frisby realises that these choristers are not mothers at all, but yumyum girls hired by a rival supertanker shipyard who want his custom. He . . .'

Fujita held up a hand. 'Very good,' he said. 'Now you go home and write, prease.'

'I'll post it to you in the summer,' I said, 'Hopefully.'

He adopted a prim expression. 'Summer?' he said, his eyes receding a further furlong or two. 'You in Japan now. Manuscript must be ready tomorrow night. Ten thousand word. You bring it back here to bath. I will be waiting.'

I returned to my hotel, rang room service for a bottle of scotch and a pile of warm towels, dusted the keys of my malarial-yellow Olivetti and went to work. I got to bed late and started again at the first hint of daylight – which appeared several minutes behind schedule as the sun usually needs a little time to make its presence known in this smoky, smog-bound city. I worked on through the day, interrupted briefly in mid-afternoon by a small earth tremor which threw me off my tilted chair and set the windbells chiming sharply, like a giant cash register, all over Tokyo.

By evening it was done and, although I say it myself, it wasn't half bad. Frisby and the ladies repair to a nearby tea house where they embark on a complicated programme of charades. During the course of the evening's activities he fractures a rib while playing the role of a kamikaze pilot diving his flying bomb, a part-

'The nice thing about it is
they're all volunteers.'

time model called Suki, onto an important target in Eyelure lashes and Strawberry Parfait lipstick. He discovers, too late, that the target is holding a tea tray above her and, in the ensuing argument, she points out that she is the American aircraft carrier *Chesapeake Bay* and makes the barking noise of pompom guns to prove it.

Over the rest of the proceedings, including the final climactic scene in which Frisby and the girls recreate certain surprising aspects of the Japanese Surrender, we shall draw a discreet curtain. Sufficient to say that our hero, despite a perceptible twitch in the right eye, emerges from his experience a more profound and thoughtful man, and next day he buys the rival supertanker as was hoped, together with a couple of dredgers thrown in for good measure.

I gathered up the pages, hailed a cab and arrived at the baths ten minutes later. Fujita was not there. I asked the masseuse if she had seen him but she evidently misunderstood me for she jumped at my knee and, with a worried expression and a ferocious display of energy, tried to detach it from its socket. I shook her free and noted that Fujita had just walked in.

'Good evening,' I said, handing him the manuscript.

'Pages numbered? Double spacing?' he said. 'Yes, indeed.'

He nodded. 'I take it home and read it,' he said. 'Will call you at hotel with decision tomorrow.' He departed with a small bow, vanishing into the steam like a genie homing in on its lamp, while I sloped off to an early dinner and bed. The moment of truth came the next day, at dusk. 'Very sorry,' said Fujita. 'Story not subtle enough, situations exaggerated, too many jokes and all rather raboured. Perhaps you try again another time. Sayonara.'

The phone went dead. After staring at it for a while I went out for a drink. As the evening progressed I told a barmaid the theme of my opus, jokes and all and, shortly before I was ushered to the door by a bouncer with a face like an opencast coal mine, she said it sounded marvellous, just the sort of pillow book that Japan would be proud to export. And she was an intelligent girl. I could see it in her eyes. That's what troubles me, actually; I've got a sneaking feeling she may have been Chinese.

Alexander Frater 23.1.1974

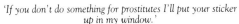
'If you don't do something for prostitutes I'll put your sticker up in my window.'

'Every week I tell him we don't sell the
Church Times or the Methodist Recorder . . .'

MY SOHO

When I first went to Soho it was magic. That was in 1947. I was fifteen years old and I had an elder brother who was a student at St Martin's School of Art in the Charing Cross Road. One day he asked me to join him for a cup of coffee in the cafe in Manette Street that the St Martin's students used and I suppose it was from that day that I got addicted. I've been hooked on Soho now for thirty years and the place gets worse and worse. In the beginning, it was all lovely girl art students, layabouts with something to say – however ridiculous – people who talked absolute rubbish and who claimed to be philosophers, disbarred solicitors, drunken poets, of course, and writers who never wrote plus painters who never painted.

It remained, for me, a sort of social Aladdin's Cave, for the many years until Sir John Wolfenden made his wretched report and cleared the streets. We never went with whores in Soho in the old days because none of us had the funds, but at least we walked down Old Compton Street and looked at real live girls that

people now pay vast sums of money to look at photographs of in pretty tatty magazines. If Wolfenden had let it all ride, Soho would still contain the best cafés and best restaurants in London, like it used to, instead of the most boring and sordid strip clubs, dirty bookshops and so-called 'amusement' arcades.

Actually, I should mention that one of us did go with the whores. He was a small sixteen-year-old student at the Italia Conti acting school in Archer Street who got smaller and smaller every day. We discovered why eventually. It turned out that his mother used to give him 1/- a day lunch money, but he never used to eat any lunch. He saved his shilling a day and at the end of the month, he used to go and have a short time with one of the high-heeled, ankle strapped beauties that paraded up and down Old Compton Street like tigers.

Although Soho was always more 'permissive' than almost any other area of London before that word became fashionable, sex was still pretty difficult to come by if you were a young layabout. And young layabouts made up most of the population. Those of us who were permanently broke and who used to spend all day sitting around in a wonderful collection of cafes

– now sadly gone – occasionally and with luck might manage to pick up the odd art student or two but most of the affairs were conducted with that good old institution, the 'Soho Scrubber'.

These moderately available and sometimes even attractive girls had usually run away from fairly good homes, had a sort of spurious interest in the arts but weren't the sort of girls who'd dream of going on the 'game'.

They attached themselves to us layabouts and would-be artists of one kind or another, but they crawled from bed to bed. Rock bottom were the girls and boys who hung around a coffee stall in Greek St on a bombed site opposite the old Gargoyle Club. I used to go to the Gargoyle Club with the likes of John Minton, George Barker and the Roberts Colquhoun and Mac-Bryde and apart from the painters and poets like them – and myself of course – the place was pretty posh. I actually managed to pull a Duchess in there one night. What made it odder was the fact that it was during one of my rare periods of work on a local building site. I was even wearing gumboots covered in cement when I lurched over to the mink encased Duchess who was sitting by herself drinking champagne. We went off to a hotel and it was fun and slightly wicked and that's just what sex in Soho isn't now. It's tatty in a very nasty commercial way and when I say tatty, I mean ten times more so than the free and incredibly uncomfortable bouts of sex we used to have in odd places like car parks or bombed sites.

Apart from the horrendous ponces and club owners who run things today there is a nasty new sort of whore on the scene. They are called clippers and they get the money from the customer who gets nothing in return since she operates on premises with a back exit she goes through before the naive punter realises what's happened. None of us is perfect, I know, and a gang of us aged about sixteen once emptied a French Letter machine in Archer Street and sold the contents to desperate prostitutes at inflated prices, but some of these girls and boys knocking around now are the end.

Sex available to present day male layabouts on a slightly higher level than that of the stripper, hostess and hooker is made up mostly of the nice girls who work for television commercial production companies and who have three-hour lunches in Italian restaurants and the girls who are fringe literary and who work for publishers and literary agents. In the old days cockneys used to say that the girl at a dance hall wearing a crucifix around her neck was a 'certainty'; now, in Soho, it's the girl carrying the film can.

The death of the afternoon drinking in Soho is also some reason to mourn. In the 1950s, the Mandrake Club and the Club des Caves de France were both happy hunting grounds for people of both sexes with a fear of waking up alone in the morning. I tell you, the village has gone down the drain. If I was Member of Parliament for the place, I'd close down the bookshops and clip joints and invite the French girls back to the pavements. Having done that, I'd offer subsidies to those wanting to open good cafes and restaurants. Then, happily, it would be back to the grindstone.

Jeffrey Bernard 4.5.1977

'. . . five, six, seven . . .'

RATES FOR THE JOB

Councillors vote for legalized brothels

The Times

Hot head throbbing inside his new hat, Mr Arthur Dork groped his uncertain way across the vast foyer of the Town Hall, lurching from pillar to marble pillar.

The dark glasses were as new as the hat. He had crept, hugging the High Street wall, from Dunn's to Boots only an hour before, his head clamped in the encircling vice. It was his first hat, and rather than risk the fearful consequences of long discussions with a salesman who might thus remember his face, he had simply snatched it from the display, banged down the crumpled notes (an identifying cheque being unthinkable), rammed on the hat, and run. It turned out to be perhaps three sizes too small;

but a deerstalker was a deerstalker, and as he laced it tightly beneath his chin, Arthur Dork felt the relief flush through him at the conviction that his ears were now secure from recognition.

The hat had, of course, made for uneasiness in Boots. Indeed, being in Boots at all, in the middle of a weekday afternoon, had induced in Dork so intense a furtiveness as to have almost scuppered the entire exercise there and then: for, in giving the contraceptive display as conspicuously wide a berth as possible while at the same time screwing his head as far away from it as the bonds of his hat would allow, he had walked, unseeing, straight into a Revolv-o-rack of yuletide bath novelties. Tiny lemon-scented ducks rolled around the floor, as Dork gazed, stricken.

A salesgirl mooched up.

'Sorry!' squeaked Dork, in a cracked falsetto.

'Never mind bleeding sorry,' snapped the salesgirl graciously, snatching up the scattered junk. 'Forty-two pound after stoppages and bleeding duck soap under your fingernails smelling all over the Tube.'

Dork, in a moment of what he considered to be inspiration, pointed in mute explanation at his thigh, and then began a grisly limp towards the counter, dragging his leg. If the staff recalled anything, thought Dork smugly, it would be an earless monopode with a eunuch glottis; scant evidence for Mrs Dork to go on.

At the counter, he had selected the darkest glasses available, on the assumption (of, to be fair, a febrile brain) that the less you could see of anything, the less anything could therefore see of you; and limping and squeaking behind his black lenses, had been helped from the chemist's by a small kindly lady who, at the door, had slipped a florin into his palm and wished him a happy Christmas.

And now, here he was in the echoing vault of the Town Hall, poised upon a threshold uncrossed in fifty-three years (with, of course, the honourable exception of a free go on Mrs Dork on the second Thursday of the month); even had opportunities presented themselves, they would have been instantly rejected, so strongly imprinted upon his memory was the brief film he had been shown shortly after his induction into the pay corps, thirty-five years earlier.

But now it was all right. The Council seal of approval lay upon the enterprise. The elected representatives who saw to it that the street lights came on in the evenings and the park croci popped up unblemished every spring were men he could trust.

He felt his way towards the dim outline of the enquiry desk. He stared at the shadowy occupant for some time.

'Yes?' said the ex-Marine sergeant.

'It's – er – it's about my friend,' squeaked Dork.

'Is it really?' said the sergeant heavily. 'About your friend, is it?'

Dork took the clipping from the local paper out of his pocket and offered it to the sergeant. It read: For A Good Time, Ring The Town Hall.

'NORMAN!' thundered the sergeant, 'Gentleman here wants a Woman Licence!'

The cry echoed around the foyer. Behind his shades, Arthur Dork died slightly. An ex-Marine corporal marched up.

'I didn't realise I needed, I mean, I didn't realise,' faltered Dork, 'my friend needed a –'

'Course he didn't!' barked the sergeant. 'Your friend looks to me like something of a prat, doesn't he, Norman?'

'His friend has very likely not bothered to read the small print,' said the corporal, 'in his, what shall I say, repugnant haste for a bit of the other. Your friend is not aware of correct channels.'

'His friend,' said the sergeant, 'doubtless thought he could just slide in here, cut himself a slice of Council property, as it were, and slide out again. His friend would appear to have no bloody idea of Council procedure, would he, Norman?'

'His friend doubtless thinks we keep 'em on the premises,' said the corporal. 'His friend probably imagines we have a slag wing.'

'Would your friend,' said the sergeant, 'care to follow the corporal to Room 418?'

Miserably, Arthur Dork stumbled through the darkness, homing in on the corporal's clicking heels. A door opened, and he went through, into fluorescent light in which he could just make out the serried ranks of grey steel filing cabinets, and two men behind a counter.

'Application for a Woman Licence,' barked the corporal, and left.

'Ratepayer, are you?' said the first clerk.

'Oh, yes,' replied Dork.

'We just slung out a bloke from Camden,' snapped the second clerk.

'Coming down here,' muttered the first clerk, 'trying to sleep with our women. Not in arrears, are you?'

'Oh, no,' said Dork.

'We'll have to check,' said the second clerk. 'Put Mr –'

'Dork,' whispered Dork, after a brief struggle between the twin terrors of discovery and authority.

'– Dork through the computer, Dennis.'

The first clerk punched a number of buttons. The machine beneath the desk whirred and clacked.

'Apparently,' said the first clerk, 'we owe him £7,000,000,000,003.09.'

'That's all right, then,' said his colleague.

'I didn't realise I needed a licence,' murmured the perspiring Dork, 'I thought it was the, er, ladies who –'

'Them too,' said the first clerk. 'We license everybody, don't we, Dudley?'

'If it moves,' said Dudley firmly, 'license it. Next year, it'll cost you a fiver to keep a guppy. What sort of woman did you have in mind?'

'I – I –' Dork's throat dried. 'Could I leave that to you?'

Dudley and Dennis looked at one another.

'Typical,' said Dennis.

'I blame the welfare state,' said Dudley.

'Blonde!' cried Dork desperately.

'Oh, *blonde?*' enquired Dennis. 'What a surprise!'

'A *young* blonde, was it?' said Dudley. 'As it were, Miss Australia?'

Dennis leaned suddenly across the counter, and jabbed a forefinger into Dork's trembling chest.

'It may have escaped the notice of your lust-crazed priorities, son,' he said savagely, 'but we are currently into an ongoing Town Hall cuts situation. You march in here with a requisition order for Dolly bloody Parton, and me and Dudley are sharing a bloody 1974 Allegro!'

'No radio,' muttered Dudley, 'manual transmission.'

'I'm sorry,' mumbled Dork, 'I truly am.'

Dudley touched his partner's elbow.

'It's not his fault, Dennis,' he said. 'The

tribulations of us public servants do not always filter down to the grass wossnames. Look,' he said to Dork, not unkindly, 'how about a nice baldy?'

'What?'

'You can apply for a rate rebate on baldies,' said Dennis.

'No,' said Dork, 'thank you.'

'We had people like him in last winter,' said Dudley bitterly, 'complaining about empty gravel bins.'

'There's always one,' muttered Dennis, lifting the phone. He dialled. 'Madame Foskett? Dennis. You got any of them old brunettes left from the last invoice? Hang on – 674/8392/B. What? No, no, no, I don't see that as a problem, provided she keeps her teeth in. Good. What? I'll find out and ring you back.'

He put the phone down, and thrust a sheaf of variously coloured forms at Dork.

'Right,' he said, 'go over there, fill these in, ink, block caps.'

After half an hour during which Dennis and Dudley occupied their time in evicting a number of small boys in false beards, answering a series of obscene phone calls in like vein (by reference to the department's *Obscene Reply Procedures* hanging from its statutory hook), and dealing with a wild-eyed derelict in a raincoat claiming that his supplementary benefit was inadequate to deal with Madame Foskett's assisted shower tariff, Arthur Dork returned wearily to the counter.

'I've filled in everything except the square footage of our coalshed,' he said, 'which I'm afraid escapes me.'

'You'll have to notify us in writing within thirty days,' said Dennis.

'Including a rough sketch and position of window, if any,' said Dudley. He stared at Dork's strained deerstalker, as if for the first time. 'Here,' he said, 'it's just occurred to me: you're not applying for a Special Services Requirement as laid down in subsection 4, paragraph 9, by any chance?'

'I'm sorry?'

'You're not intending to go in there as Sherlock, er, Thing, are you?'

'Stone me, Dudley, you're right!' cried Dennis, looking over his glasses. 'He is undoubtedly expecting his paramour to slip into Moriarty's overcoat and jump off the wardrobe with her

hands round his throat! We are looking at up to six new buff forms here.'

'Or worse,' said Dudley. 'He could well be expecting her to put on a walrus moustache and do it with a stethoscope in her ears. He'd have to get planning permission for that.'

'You'd have to see the Borough Fantasy Officer,' snapped Dennis. 'It could take weeks! Remember that greengrocer who thought he was Roman Polanski? We had to get the fire brigade to hose him off the roof of the Brownie hut, never mind two vanloads of paperwork!'

Slowly, Arthur Dork took off his dark glasses and unlaced his deerstalker hat.

'It isn't like that,' he said slowly. 'It isn't like that at all.'

They stared at him.

'What is it like, then?' enquired Dudley.

Dork shrugged.

'It's just that after thirty years with Mrs Dork, I thought, that is to say, I rather fancied – oh, I don't know –'

Dennis took off his glasses. He clasped his hands together. His face broke into an enormous and benevolent smile. He lifted the counter flap.

'Arthur!' he cried. 'You should have *said*! If it's a bit of I don't know you're after, we can cut out all this silly paperwork, can't we, Dudley?'

Dudley glared at his colleague.

'You fickle bitch,' he said.

Alan Coren 21.11.1979

THE GAYMARKET, 1880!

Had I the power with prejudice to cope,
The breadth of Byron, or the pen of Pope,
I'd break a lance with Magisterial 'rings'
That strain our laws, and muddle licensings.
Men prate of virtue from their judgment seats,
And turn Sin's gutter flush into our streets;
They close Casinos with a blush – 'tis true!
But make us curse a Place called – Waterloo!

If Vice must dance or dine, and Scandal sup,
Which is the best? Proclaim? or hush it up?
Can stern Morality her models meet
In Piccadilly or in Windmill Street?
Away with cant! Is Gaymarket less vile
With new Criterion, or old Argyle?
Are cesspools worse for health, do you suppose,
Than garbage rotting underneath your nose?
Wherever flesh is weak and spirit willing,
Which is the best? – sin *gratis*, or one shilling?
What have you done, you Magisterial Bench,
Raising in perfect innocence a stench,
To cause on England's forehead to be writ,
In broad phylacteries, – Thou Hypocrite!

This you have done – you've closed in
     summer time
The Garden's purity, the Music's rhyme;
You've crushed, from carelessness, its wit and
     grace,
And given gutter-worship in its place.
You've raised Law's cannons to bombard the
     ball,
And left defiled the modern music hall.
On wives' and daughters' cheeks you've raised
     a blush,
As through the heated streets they drive and
     crush,
To 'scape contamination as they pass
That Gay old Market where young flesh is
     grass!

Be wise, you Senators, be wise in time,
Hide from our eyes Society's worse crime;
Pour disinfecting fluid down the sink
At which the public laughs, policemen wink.
Let us be human only, and despise
That Market festering beneath our eyes –
The painted cheeks, hoarse voices, faces fagged,
Of those who, saved from dragging, should be
     dragged
To silent places where neglect atones
For London's insult on her paving stones!

Anon 9.10.188c

THE GREAT SOCIAL EVIL.

Time: – Midnight. A Sketch not a Hundred Miles from the
Haymarket.

Bella. 'Ah! Fanny! How long have you been *Gay*?'

THE TOP OF THE GAY-MARKET *

About half a mile westward of Mud-Salad Market, as the crow flies, is an unlicensed, ill-regulated, open-air, kerb-stone, midnight kind of cattle-market, called the Gay-Market. We say 'as the crow flies' advisedly, for no crow of respectable habits would probably fly in that direction. The Gay-Market, as it now exists, is mainly the creation of Lord MIDNIGHT BRUCE, the Police, and the Middlesex Magistrates. The Police may possibly derive some profit from this market, and Lord MIDNIGHT BRUCE and the Middlesex Magistrates may be under the fond impression that by turning a certain order of Vice into the open highway under the glare of the gas-lamps, they are forwarding the cause of Virtue.

Does it occur to these theoretical moralists that instead of regulating the few who are

* *The word 'gay' was slang for 'prostitute', c. 1840–1880.*

hopelessly bad, they may probably be corrupting the multitude whose tendency is good?

No city in Europe presents such a disgraceful picture as the top of the Gay-Market between midnight and one or two in the morning. Here is a Metropolis which has worked for years and spent countless millions of money to carry off its sewage unobserved, apparently revelling in a public exhibition of its worst moral impurities. Here the sort of foreign produce which the powerful pencil of JOHN LEECH, years ago, showed that JOHN BULL would willingly dispense with – enters into unholy competition with *Moll Flanders*, who sometimes finds a coronet in the mud, but more often goes to the workhouse. Bullies, betting-men, shop-boys, swells – riff-raff of all kinds – mix with the overdressed females, and block up the pathway with a crowd whose object is unmistakable. The roadway is half filled with lingering broughams and cabs driven by knowing cabmen, while the police look on, like spectators at a show, in speechless admiration, or hopeless bewilderment.

Which is the best system? – a licensing body of some six hundred more or less ignorant and prejudiced gentlemen – chiefly amateurs – who leave London, with its four millions of people, without a Casino or a Music-garden, and thrust our necessary evils under our noses in the most public of our public highways, or a public licenser who knows his business, and provides a few places, under responsible management, where even the most degraded have no excuse for flaunting rowdyism?

John Hollingshead 4.9.1880

STRANGER THAN FRICTION

In Tonga they call it toogi-toogi; in Hawaii it's lomi-lomi and in Charlotte Street it's plain old Finnish. 'Finnish as far as I'm concerned', says Kate Downstairs, an expert at the job, 'is exactly that. You get the "extras"; you come; I go. Finish. No one ever asks for a full massage as

well. No one', she adds confidently, 'ever complains.'

Kate Downstairs (she acquired the name after operating as 'Lovely Young Model Specialises in Plastics' from a basement in Paddington for a number of years) is a qualified masseuse. She pronounces 'masseuse' to rhyme with 'loose' as all the self-respecting operators do. Two years ago, when she saw the way the business was going, she pulled out of plastics and invested £100 in a twenty-week course of massage – an hour a week. She discovered the body is made up of 250 bones – and how to bruise most of them; she received a diploma complete with Latin phrasing and red seal and, on graduation, she took it upon herself to put M.Sc. after her own name. 'It stands for Muscles. That's what you need in this business – stamina and a strong right wrist.'

Kate Downstairs works in one of London's 200 or so (no one is certain of the exact figure) massage parlours offering 'extras'. Her specialities are hand relief (£10), bust relief (£20 a trip) and 'French's' or blow jobs. They come more expensive, she says, because they require concentration – £20. The charges vary from girl to girl but as undercutting is frowned upon, the bargain hunter might find himself frustrated in more senses than one. Kate is also good at pummelling, pinching, effleurage and petrisage, the more orthodox forms of massage. But she doesn't, she says, get much call for those. It's enough to make Mr A. E. G. Kleen of Sweden, author of the authoritative handbook on massage, published in 1895, turn in his grave. No hope now of keeping it Kleen. The massage industry in London seems bent beyond correction.

In the early Sixties, massage had a minority appeal in this country. It was restricted to those who didn't mind being attended to in surroundings resembling a medical appliances factory and by ladies looking not unlike Dr Caligari. Today, while the straight parlours *do* still survive, their illegal offspring, the 'bent' establishment, is doing so much better. Massage has become *the* medium for selling sex in London.

The reasons why are fairly straightforward. To begin with – it makes money. Most parlours offering sexual 'extras' are open seven days a week, twelve hours a day. The masseuses get paid a nominal £10 to £20 a week (they are expected to make the rest in 'tips') and the other overheads are relatively low. An owner needs about £3,000 to set himself up with a few beds, a small sauna ('for show', as one put it), a year's supply of Coca-Cola (the nearest thing to a 'free drink' most punters get) – and a gold fish tank. The gold fish tank seems obligatory. It adds class to the 'relaxing lounge'. It also gives the would-be clients something to watch and *can* work out cheaper than a colour telly. It is in this lounge area that the girls . . . Conchita from the Antipodes, Phoenix Rising from Tooting, Isolda from Clapham and so on . . . wait for 'the call'. They dress very much like holidaymakers at Luton Airport departing for the Costa Brava and – apart from the clients – are the only source of real worry to an enterprising parlour owner.

In addition to the girls and the decor, the good operator also has to fork out about £200 in weekly rent and rates for a good spot in Soho – and he must invest in advertising. The advertising is necessary so that the connoisseur can read between the lines. 'Put it this way', explained Kate Downstairs' boss, 'we need a neon-lit lady with flashing boobs even if it does cost a packet. Because how else is the punter going to know, we're not here to make him better. We're here to make him worse. If you know what I mean.'

All in all, the parlour owner with the right approach ('. . . we give you an experience you won't forget . . .') can expect to make about £100,000 a year in profits with each of his ladies making as much as £200, off their own bat, a week. 'This must be the only business in the world', says Kate Downstairs' boss, 'where a squeeze puts profits up.'

But all is not always hunky-dory. A massage parlour owner does have to take a few precautions to protect himself from the law. In theory, any sexual act which carries a price tag – and it doesn't have to be intercourse – is classed as prostitution. Any massage owner who knows 'that sort of thing' is taking place, can be done for living on immoral earnings. So he never allows 'extras' to be discussed over the telephone – or by his receptionist. 'You want something extra?' says the blonde at the desk. 'We do a nice line in baby oil.'

He also insists that all deals which are done take place in the privacy of the cubicle. The girl

decides her price and keeps the cash. The owner relies for *his* income on the 'legitimate' charge he makes to the customer. That may begin at £7 for a massage, rising to £35 for a massage plus herbal, assisted shower with two topless ladies and a bottle of champagne. (A word of caution; 'assistance' may consist of turning the taps; the 'herbal' element is often the pine in the bar of soap – and the ladies tend to drink most of the champagne themselves. But it may nevertheless still be a relief.)

To boost his sense of security further, the massage operator also knows it is extremely difficult for the police to gather evidence. The police are reluctant to use agents provocateurs – and a raid is likely to produce nothing more than a few gentlemen standing erect by their beds. So even if an enterprising official *does* gather proof that masturbation rather than manipulation is alive and well and being practised in number three cubicle, the owner can profess innocence. No involvement, no conviction. 'Of course', says Kate Downstairs' boss, 'it would make it easier if we could do it the Siamese way. Ask them at the start: with nonsense, or without? But then', he adds with a touch of philanthropy, 'the police need a living too.'

Massage owners have one other slight irritation; the local authority. All thirty-two of the London boroughs operate a licensing system. It is based on an act passed in 1920 when 'Turkish Delight' had more to do with what went on in the local baths than it had to do with the mysterious East. The act, controlling behaviour, insisting on qualified staff and ensuring only the most suitable can receive licences, was impossible to implement in the Twenties and it hasn't improved much since. (Kensington, for example, does not allow qualified masseuses to massage a male below the neck and above the knee – the tropical belt as the girls call it.) Each year, an operator has to renew his licence and in the course of the next twelve months he can expect a 'surprise' visit from the Environmental Health Officer. Kindly, the officer usually gives a fortnight's warning. Long enough for even the most involved to get disentangled.

The pseudo-health connections of the bent parlours is part of their attraction. Men attend them who might not otherwise have bothered.

('After all, it might even do me some good. . . .') And only the nice ladies work in them. Some of the ladies see themselves as therapists, out to cure the world of its ills. It's a hand and mouth existence. Very few regard themselves as prostitutes.

And in the last year or so, an added refinement has appeared on the scene; the visiting masseuse. She needn't be qualified. She can be independent or work through an agency. She can be fat, forty, Scandinavian or skinny. A market exists for every type. All she needs is some subtle advertising – and an A to Z.

Yvonne Roberts 4.5.1977

LONDON SEX GLOSSARY

Adult	Childish
'. . . And they dance!'	And they shuffle round out of time to music
Bawdy	Nudgy
Books and Mags	Unreadable objects covered in unremovable cellophane
Company flat	Flat kept by firm where you can entertain company
Couple	Girls who should know better with man who could do better
Cover charge	Large sum of money levied before you have to start paying for anything
Escort agency	A massage parlour, where, for extra payment, you avoid the indignity of being buffeted by unskilled hands
Exotic	Ordinary
Good time	Short time
'Have you told her yet?'	Most common remark made by girl at next table to her companion. The correct reply is 'No, she hasn't been feeling too well lately'
Head waiter	One who greets you and your wife with the words, 'Nice to see you again after so long, sir,' even though you were dining there the night before. With another lady, admittedly.
Main line station	Large rail link built specially to serve colony of sauna clubs, massage parlours, cinema clubs, etc.
Night Club	Club not open during the day and not much open at night
Non-stop striptease	Striptease performed by girl about to rush non-stop to ten other clubs
Nude	Topless all over
Sauna	(also Showers, Massage, etc.) An establishment devoted to the proposition that sex may not make you happier but by heaven it makes you cleaner
Sensual	(also Sultry, Passionate, etc.) A word applied to films from which someone has cut out all the sensual, sultry, passionate, etc., bits
Sex	Mysterious substance sold in sex shops, apparently made of light rubber
'Show's just starting'	If we get enough people in, and the girls turn up, and the gramophone works, the show will start
Strip club	A doorway in Soho with, outside, an exhibition of photos of girls with 1950s hairstyles and, inside, a man who will take you to a strip club elsewhere
Swinging	Indiscriminate
Unusual	All too frequent
Young	Near retiring age, as in 'Young French model'

'Spaceships landing . . .
hundreds of 'em!
Come quickly!'

'The Fleet's in, girls . . .'

'Is that all you men ever think about?'

ADAM AND EVE
AND PINCH ME

'Sexual segregation has been introduced on the Metro in Mexico City. If successful it will be enforced on all Mexican railways.'

Daily Mail

It's like the toilet arrangements in this Indian restaurant I go to in Notting Hill. You go down the steps to the basement and find two W.C. cubicles standing companionably side by side. Each has a lavatory pan and a lavatory seat, each a cistern, each a toilet roll in a toilet roll holder, each a door that indicates open for vacant and shut for engaged. They are in all respects iden-

tical little cabinets, except that over one door is a skirted pin-person and over the other a trousered pin-person. It always amuses me that the Gents should be quite so manifestly the same as the Ladies, but it's only late on a Saturday night, after the pubs have shut, that you get the full ludicrosity of it all. The queue of men reaches all the way back up the steps, and you see them all standing there, in agony, gazing through the open door of the vacant Ladies, preferring to burst rather than use it.

Mexicans are now prepared to suffocate each other in half a train rather than share air-space with women on a whole one, proving once again that there is no limit to the inconvenience, pain and indignity a semi-conscious misogynist will suffer in defence of his macho integrity. Well, you can't expect much of a Mexican. You wouldn't, for instance, expect him to possess the candour of G. K. Chesterton, who could always get himself a spot of solitude on a train by pressing his nose up against the window and making lewd beckoning gestures to anyone in danger of sharing his compartment, or the simplicity of my friend Barry who achieves much the same thing by raising his hanky to his lips and making small heaving motions with his shoulders.

No, the trouble with your macho Mex is he's too busy being manly to square himself with a perfectly ordinary, wholesome, human longing for the odd switched-off, calmly a-sexual moment. He tries to be repulsive *all the time*. He even succeeds in being repulsive most of the time. What eludes him though, is the absolute and unassailable confidence it takes to be certain that he really *is* repulsive. No matter how hard he tries he somehow can't get enough affirmation of his idea of his own deeply dangerous masculine psychopathy. So, when all else fails, and ladies forget to run screaming and retching from his presence, he simply turns himself in and asks to be locked up.

It's all such a wicked waste. Mexico City is jam-packed with great muscly men all flinching from the dread of what they imagine women to be, all pinching and prodding away at whatever they take to be female flesh, like they're keeping the devil at bay. They've erected this hideous great Thing in the middle of town, the *Monument a los Madres*, they call it; a huge female lump with arms like York hams crouched like a gigantic toad with hundreds of skimpy stone kids festering all over it. You can't live under its shadow and not be profoundly spooked by maternity. You can't even take a five minute taxi ride without your driver turning his head a full 180 degrees as he jumps into the fast lane and offering to father a fine Mexican baby for you. He can't help himself. But you don't have to be spectacularly shrewd to realize that why he can't help himself is he's scared limp of having a woman in his cab. He thinks maybe you're going to do something castrating to him, like lean across his madonna-armoured partition and breathe your awful female breath down the back of his neck, bid him a friendly good-day, act like there's nothing to be afraid of. So he defends his manhood by getting in first with a brutish tongue-lashing designed to keep you in your place, cowering in a corner fearing rape. If you happen to be a fairly heterosexual lady this can be deeply wounding, knowing that he knows, and he knows you know, and you know he knows you know, that he's really saying he doesn't want to have any kind of intercourse with you at all. What he really wants is to have you safely locked up in a compartment marked 'Ladies' so that he can be left alone with his wilfully obscene fantasies of what you might be doing in there.

The idea that the reality of women serves only to disturb the feminine mystique that men are obsessively anxious to preserve is not, least we fool ourselves, an exclusively Latin-American aberration. Our British parallel is that women exist only to stir, tempt and lure men into all manner of ungentlemanly conduct and the only way out of our predicament is to keep out of each others' way. We try, God knows, to be enigmatic about it.

I didn't think too much of it when I went into the public bar of our local the other night, to have my two pint jug filled with bitter ale. I mean, I know as well as the next person that 'public' really means 'men' in this context, but I reckoned I might just get away with it. I made a special effort not to jog anybody's elbow going round the pool table, or walk in front of the darts. I kept my eyes downcast and my voice respectful and I had the right change in my hand so as not to enrage anyone. But they weren't having it. It wasn't so much the rough jostling and mocking I minded, as the way they all went daft in front of each other. 'Here, Ted, I've heard of a jug being called a bottle but this is ridiculous'. 'Here, Tom, I've heard of a jug being called a bottle but this is ridiculous'. 'Here, Bill, I've heard of a jug being called a bottle but this is ridiculous'. And so on. I have absolutely no reason to believe that before I went in they were all being hysterically stupid and repetitive among themselves. It was a special show. In order to dissuade me from intruding upon their orderliness again they were all prepared to make fools of themselves. I was not allowed to unambivalently buy a jug of ale. Not inside the door marked 'public' and meaning 'men'.

The guardians of the British Post Office are particularly well schooled in this enigma. They advise female telephone subscribers to use only the initials of their Christian names in the directory on the grounds that a lady's forename is an incitement to masturbatory calls. Or, as they put it, 'it only causes trouble', and 'you'll have only yourself to blame'. In other words to be blatant about both your femaleness and your contactability is to peg for abuse. It could never occur to the corporate mind that women might sooner take their chances with occasional heavy breathers than be obliged to settle for their own culpability in the matter. Rather we live in thrall to the fiction that women are sexually (a) provocative and (b) vulnerable.

I could have given the lie to that one by the time I was nine years old, had anyone cared to ask me. Growing up in the gutters of London, we little girls were neither promiscuous nor timid. We regarded the abundant displays of male genitalia in the parks and streets with the same phlegmatic indifference with which we viewed everything else. If we wanted to know the right time or the quickest way to Fulham Broadway, we'd not hesitate to ask a flasher if he happened to be nearest. We knew then, as surely as we knew that de Marco's sold lousy ice cream, that it wasn't our fault if a chap wanted to wave his thing about. We wouldn't have wanted him locked up until we were much, much older and had lost our wisdom and our innocence under the pressure of being told we were (a) provocative and (b) vulnerable.

What defeats me is how we came to believe it

so easily. All we're really saying as we slope obediently into whatever ghetto is marked 'ladies' is Men are Silly and it's all Our Fault. And that's no way to run a railway.

Sally Vincent 27.9.1978

MISTRESS MINE

Well, Dr Krankheit, I expect these days you are getting fairly used to chaps lying down in here and telling you the magic has gone out of their . . . Marriages? No, not quite marriages, Dr Krankheit, it was mistresses I had in mind. You must get a lot of chaps lying down in here telling you that the magic has gone out of their mistresses.

I never know why I started going in for mistresses in the first place, Dr Krankheit. You know how it is, one day a fellow is a young, happily married man, playing those endearing little games that newly-weds get up to and everything is going swimmingly. Then one night you jump out of the wardrobe dressed as Bismarck and she says, '*Bismarck never wore ten denier tights.*'

And so pretty soon, with one thing and another, doctor, she doesn't even want to play Marvin The Plumber Comes To Fix The Tumble Dryer or Hi I'm Hy Hyman of Hi Grade Installations May I Interest You In Central Heating? Know what I mean, Dr Krankheit? The bride is no longer the bride, she has become the little woman, the good lady wife, the missus and she starts letting herself go. Suddenly all her tights are fifteen denier and full of snags. I mean, one doesn't even look like Bismarck to one's self, leaping out of the wardrobe in fifteen denier tights with runs in them, does one, Dr Krankheit?

That's right, doctor, that's where the mistress came in. You know the sort of thing, Dr Krankheit, something a little frilly up in St John's Wood. Mistresses were different in those days, doctor. And so understanding. A chap jumps out of the wardrobe dressed as Bismarck

and a chap is a bit worried about the ladders in his stockings and, well, she just says, '*Never mind about that, darling, if Bismarck actually wore black lace stockings they'd be laddered too.*'

Yes, doctor, I've been reading about mistresses. In *The Guardian* and *Daily Mail* and watching TV documentaries about them on BBC2, same as everybody else. But I'm afraid Polly Toynbee and Shirley Eskapa and BBC2 have got it all wrong, Dr Krankheit. They are all behind the times, Dr Krankheit. In fact that whole business about Cecil Parkinson and Miss Keays was like something out of Zola. The little mistress waiting in her lonely flat for the telephone to ring! I mean, what the hell, Dr Krankheit, how *passé*, eh, Dr Krankheit, what? I'm afraid, Dr Krankheit, that Fleet Street and the telly have missed the boat again. Take it from me, Dr Krankheit, I was there when something awful happened to mistresses.

What's that? Do I mean they suddenly got more demanding and rapacious? God, I wish it had been that. But no, not a bit of it, Dr Krankheit. What it was that suddenly happened was that suddenly they started suddenly giving you money and things – that's what suddenly happened suddenly, Dr Krankheit. That's what was sudden. About 1973, I think. Before that, from about, say 1965, say, things were pretty jake, Dr Krankheit. I mean, I'd drop round to St John's Wood, take it out for a show and a little supper and then back to the flock wallpaper.

It didn't cost much, Dr Krankheit, not all that much, but of course you had to give them something a little extra special at Christmas on account of one was back with Bessie Bunter in the bosom of family trying hard *not* to notice how all the issue were getting to look the absolute spitten of the brother-in-law. A gruesome thought that, Dr Krankheit.

That was when a mistress was a mistress, Dr Krankheit, and all they wanted to do was lounge round all day, eating chocolate bon bons and reading the *New Yorker*. I suppose, doctor, that Miss Keays was a sort of old-fashioned mistress. She was *only* a secretary who wanted to be an MP. Nowadays all the mistresses *are* MPs when they're not brain surgeons, test pilots or something big in the City.

What's that? What did you say, Dr Krankheit? Don't I ever feel guilty about leaving these mistresses waiting by the telephone? Gee, Dr Krankheit, *ha ha*, Dr Krankheit. That was dry and bitterly ironic laughter, Dr Krankheit. That's where *The Guardian*, *Mail* and the TV documentary got it all wrong, Dr Krankheit. The trouble with mistresses today, Dr Krankheit, is not that you leave them waiting by the phone but that they leave you waiting by the phone, that's the trouble with mistresses today, Dr Krankheit.

That's right, doctor, you've got it, Dr Krankheit, you've hit the nail right on the head all right, we've all become that new thing, toy boys, doctor. There are 48-year-old men out there, doctor, walking round being toy boys. All the time you thought they were sitting around eating chocolate bon bons and watching the flock wallpaper they were actually taking up brain surgery on the sly.

The trouble is, doctor, it all starts off so innocently. First thing you do is borrow the odd fiver – I mean, what's a fiver to a bull in the City? – for the taxi fare home and the next thing you're doing is asking them if they might not just be able to see you through the quarter's gas bill for your humble flat in Islington which you had to move into ever since Bunjaws ran off with a 13¾-year-old, job-creation, trainee Tesco's bagger. And lonely, Dr Krankheit, I could tell you about being lonely. Sitting round in a pub waiting for her to arrive or at least send a messenger around with the cash to square the tab, only she's all tied up on account of some Arab wanted a rush brain transplant.

I could tell stories, Dr Krankheit, if I wanted to, I could tell stories.

Not that a boy like I would ever complain, not unless I know she has been seeing her husband again and I can maybe throw a bit of a fit and maybe get the cooker fixed or a few nice shirts from Jermyn Street out of it. I'll give you a tip, Dr Krankheit, if you ever take up toy boying, make sure you always buy your own socks. Insist upon it, doctor, insist. Those pastel shades, with clocks! I didn't think anybody ever wore them except in old movies on the telly. And ties! You think those red things they buy their husbands at Christmas are bad, you should see what mistresses buy us. You are, in fact, looking at one. I mean, knicker pink, a knicker pink necktie! I got to wear it just in case she might bounce in

unexpectedly after a hard day concerning wheat in the City. Did you notice the socks, doctor? Peach blossom, with chocolate anchor clocks!

Here I am, 48 years old, with my teeth hanging on to my gums like John Wayne and the US Marines hanging onto the beach at Guadalcanal, and I'm wearing a knicker pink tie and peach blossom socks with clocks, doctor. The trouble is I don't suppose kids today would even know what you were talking about if you said *you* used to pay the rent for the flock wallpaper. You know, Dr Krankheit, it used to make you feel sort of, I don't know, masculine, I suppose, paying the rent and leaping out of the wardrobe up at the popsie's place dressed as Bismarck.

What's that? Do I have a mistress now? Well, there's a woman keeps coming round, her face is familiar but I can't quite place the name. Can you imagine, a 53-year-old woman leaping out of a wardrobe dressed as Kaiser Wilhelm the Second, in fifteen denier tights, with ladders? Well, it pays the rent, Dr Krankheit, it just about pays the rent.

Stanley Reynolds 9.11.1983

'I've found a wonderful little dressmaker round the corner.'

'Notice how they all want to play it safe since the Keeler affair?'

'I don't pay you to think, Miss Bodwell.'

SEXUAL (AND OTHER) INACTION IN THE HUMAN MALE

My own monumental life-work – the Hale
Report on the Human Male
Is the ripe fruit of ruddy
Great weary years of study.
We researchers have found
Fresh ground
In devoting our attention
To what in the matter of sex and other things men do *not* do, or men seldom do, or men do hardly
    worth a mention,
Using the combined analytical methods of Dr Kinsey and Bishop Colenso.
Sunday papers, please copy *in extenso*.

%   %   %

In the matter of sex, now, men
(Up to seventy-three per cent over the age of ten)
Appear to find an absorbing attraction
In simple Inaction.

%   %   %

And whether you put it down to untutored mental haziness
Or just to laziness,
The fact remains that thirty-two-and-a-half per cent have never kissed a lady's patella,
And sixty-six per cent still go to bed swathed in hygienic Soporella,
And quite a number are so sexually childish
That they never go wild, or even wildish,
Over such well-known fetishes as porpoises,
Old boots, bicycle bells, or coroner's corpuses.
(The figure here varies from point-nought-eight per cent in stockbrokers
To ninety-nine-point-nine recurring in Portsmouth stokers:
That's where they largely lack it –
In the lower income bracket.)
And twenty-eight per cent of males after marriage
Have never winked at a lady when alone with her in a railway carriage;
But *per contra* fifty per cent of these twenty-eight per cent have roared
With panic, and pulled the communication cord.

%   %   %

It must also be confessed
That the results of our 'Free Association' test
Came to us as a shock.
Thus, confronted with a stick of seaside rock,
Eighty-nine per cent of males over twenty-one shed only a dim light on
This interesting and evocative subject by promptly replying 'Brighton.'
In Wales, the point was even more sadly missed with
The ninety per cent who answered 'Darro me! Aberystwyth!'

%   %   %

As for Ireland, we nearly abandoned that,
After sixteen hours with a Dubliner (cunningly code-named Pat)
Who sat all day in a snug
With a glass in his hand and his head on his lug,
And when we pointed out the sheer inactivity of being nothing, not even plain hetero,
Said 'For the sake of a quiet life, me boyo, what could be better-o?'

%   %   %

We investigators find little or no satisfaction
In such evidences of sexual inaction.
Moreover, apart from sex, our statistical facts
Reveal that the male commits innumerable Un-Acts.
Thus, forty-two per cent of the less sensitive (or bolder)
Husbands of Pimlico do not even under pressure go to *Tristan und Isolde,*
And the lack of interest aroused by folk-dancing in the Conservative Club of Dolgelly
Is proportionately deathly.
And forty-one per cent in Torbay would not recognize the 'Mona Lisa' or 'The Gleaners,'
And seventy-six per cent of South Shields miners never take their trousers to the cleaners,
And in short the percentage
Of all men (over the Dissent-Age)
Who are not in a state of inaction –
In such matters as mending bath-taps, or paying the radio licence, or taking out decent insurances
for the sake of Wife and Babes, and brushing up their French, and keeping abreast of Mr Graham
Greene's new hem-line for the Roman Catholic Church, and visiting the Natural History
Museum, and remembering birthdays, and putting cigarette-ends in the right-place-not-the-
bath, and loving Mr R. A. Butler for himself, and meeting distant relatives at Liverpool Street,

'He can still turn on the old charm when he wants to.'

and standing up to head-waiters, and in general avoiding a personal premature appearance of
petrifaction –
Our researches prove that in life as in love
The percentage of even moderately active males to be infinitesimal,
Or at any rate down to our last dear, darling, dirty decimal.

%　　　%　　　%

These statistical facts of Inaction in Man
Were always the same since the creature began,
And apply to the high and the low and the middle:
With a toora-too-lay and a fol-de-rol riddle.

Lionel Hale 9.9.1953

'OK, I'm sorry I've been neglecting you – we'll go out to a meal
tonight. That should cheer you up.'

Last-Tango-in-Paris Do-it-Yourself Kit!

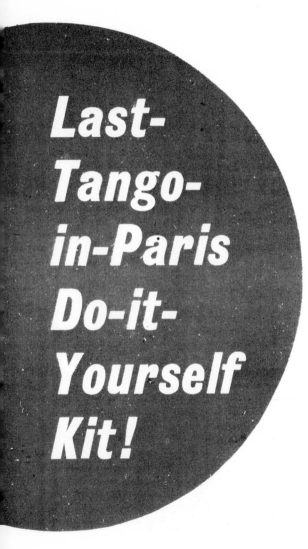

HOW TO TANGO, BRANDO STYLE

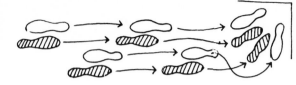

Take your partner roughly round the waist. Follow her as her limbs retreat, until you come to the corner.

Who wants to see the boring, over-publicised *Last Tango In Paris* when you could have so much more fun making your own version? All you'll need is:—

> 1 lb butter
> 1 empty room
> 1 camera
> 1 old friend, 1 young friend (for doing the acting)
> soap and hot water
> anything else that comes to hand

Explain to your friends that they will be representing two people caught in a sudden frenzy to communicate via their bodies in a moving but doomed relationship, and let them get on with it. (Make sure they realise that the reviews will dwell on the essential innocence and agonised purity of the film: that way you can get away with anything.) Oh, and keep the windows closed. What with gas pressure dropping and everything, the last thing you want is a lead actor with a bad cold and goose pimples.

YOU WILL ALSO NEED 10 HANDY EXCUSES FOR NOT GOING TO SEE "LAST TANGO IN PARIS"

1 "I really can't imagine that any film left uncensored by the French will be worth seeing, do you? After all, we cut three minutes from *Trash*, which was bad enough. The French cut twenty-five minutes. They're probably running it as a short."

2 "There's nobody I know in it."

3 "Strictly between you and me, I hear the music's dreadful."

4 "I saw Marlon Brando's chest in *One-Eyed Jacks*. It wasn't that great."

5 "I haven't read the book but I feel I've seen the movie."

6 "It's only *Lolita* without the dialogue, and that was the only good thing about *Lolita*."

7 "I'm going to wait till Ernie Wise rewrites it as a television play."

8 "A friend of my brother's worked on the film in Paris, and he said that it's not Brando at all on screen, it's an authentic life-size replica of him that they moved slightly between each shot, and I'm not going to pay good money to see the first-ever film with dubbed mumbling."

9 "You don't seriously expect me to go and see yet another film about an American tourist in Paris?"

10 "The children wanted to see it, but I couldn't face it myself."

Miles Kington 21.2.1973

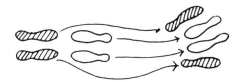

Facing your partner, place your left foot outside her right foot and your right foot outside her left foot. Bend towards her, taking care not to let go. *Keep the knees relaxed.*

Shuffle round the room a bit now, till you are comfortable, placing left foot in front of you, then right foot, then left and so on. Failure to do this may cause falling over. *Do not get out of camera shot.* Now rip her clothes off.

Lots can be done with close-ups of bodies where you're not sure which bit is which. The thing on the right is actually an elbow, or perhaps it's a cucumber.

This is the famous incident where Brando picks up an apple in the thick of the action and surprises everyone by just eating it. What can *you* think of to do with an apple?

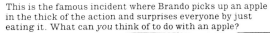

You'll need some sequences like this tender episode where Brando laments his childhood by brutally assaulting the girl.

FRENCH CONNECTIONS

French couples make love once every three days on average . . . during the act one woman in four is thinking not of her partner but of another man . . . according to *Le Matin* . . . ordinary positions for intercourse are considered boring, there is a hint in the poll that nearly everyone is having to try harder and harder to reach an impossibly exotic ideal.

– The Observer

The way a nation makes love is no less idiosyncratic than the way it makes bread, or war, or money. N'est-ce pas, chéri? For example, I've been told by a man who is very high up in low places that Russians couple at amazing speed and whenever they get the chance; this is an attempt to squirrel away a hoard before it disappears from the shelves. They do the same thing with sardines. It stands to reason that in a society where nobody can be altogether sure just how many eavesdroppers are tuned into the pillow-talk, sex takes place in absolute silence. As for fantasies, such terrible things have happened to those Soviet lovers who dared to imagine it might be more fun in Wigan, say, or Tierra del Fuego, that most young people train themselves to think about useful projects during the act such as how to make borscht when the beet crop fails.

'By next summer,' the state guides tell visitors who have noted the lack of ardour in the unions of Soviet Socialists, 'it is planned that we shall be making it better here than any place on earth!'

Americans, on the other hand, refrain from love-making for years at a time so when they are finally laid back enough to get laid they can be sure it will be, like, deeply meaningful. Preferring to leave nothing to chance, the American lover often hires a Sexual Behaviour Modification Expert to sit in on his tryst. This highly-trained voyeur (sometimes a militant Women's Libber) installs her or himself at the head of the water-bed, whence he or she can put the lovers

straight when they are getting hung up, stop them if they are not actualising their potential, alert the male person as soon as sexist tendencies are in evidence, and deposit quarters in the wave-making machine.

Due to all the effort and expense involved in getting their inner space clear for the experience, many Americans make love only once or twice in a lifetime and others, notably North Dakotans, never make it at all. (Well may you wonder why there are so few North Dakotans around and so many Chinese. It is because North Dakotans failed totally to get themselves together. Sad to say, the only North Dakotans left are three maiden ladies in their mid-eighties who eke out a living exporting powdered elk's horn to the fleshpots of Peking.)

When all is said and done, it is as sure as Shakespeare was a German that the French are the world's greatest lovers. And this assessment of French prowess is according to nothing less than their own opinion which, as we all know, has never once in the entire history of mankind been even the least bit wrong. There was a time when Gallic sexual genius was called de Gaulle's *force de frappe*. In those days sex was centralised in Paris, but Mitterrand has expressed his intention to spread it around and you can bet that soon the entire nation will be awash in sexual athletes sweeping as a raging tide towards the Channel and innocent Albion. Mark my words, the fatal day must come when some selfish fool, too besotted to care, succeeds in smuggling just one cuddly little French snookums past the quarantine and onto this uncontaminated island.

Why, you ask, are the French such dazzling lovers? And indeed, so you should ask, my little English cabbages. First of all, because they do it a lot. 'Once every three days' may not sound exactly Rabelaisian but please remember the statistic is *on average*. Consider that French boys and girls until the age of five may do it but ten or twelve times, and French couples over the age of seventy-five may do it only during the month of August, and you begin to see how assiduously every French citizen between five and seventy-five must apply himself to another French citizen in order to raise the national average. Then, too, we learn that one out of every four French-women imagines she is with someone other than the compatriot in her arms, and who can blame her?

However, I must point out that as long as a Frenchwoman keeps her imagination within national boundaries she enjoys a great advantage over the rest of us because the whole of French manhood shares but ten given-names: Jean-Pierre, Jean-Louis, Jean-Claude, Jean-Paul, François, Jacques, Charles, André, Gaston and Philippe; thus, any tiny indiscretion in a moment of passion has a ten per cent chance of going unnoticed.

Not that the man of France seems predisposed to pay much attention to the boring old commodity at hand. Gifted with the famous French *fantasie*, a talent made infinitely potent by the absolute absence of any sense of humour, Frenchmen in bed are busily picturing themselves making love to four *aubergines* during rush-hour on a trampoline at the very pinnacle of Cleopatra's Needle. A little dangerous? Ah yes, my beau brave, and a little – how do you say it? – mad, ees eet not? But 'ow wanderfool! 'Ow absolutely soupair! It may interest you to know that I have it on the French grapevine (and a very good year it was too) that the Pompidou Centre, which has got to be the most wanderfool and soupair example of disposable architecture in Europe, arose from a particularly successful encounter between the then First Man of France and maybe not quite his first lady during which he fantasised a rendezvous with The Alien on the Yellowbrick Road. All of which must go to show that after the French comes the flood. To put it another way: long before you, Gaston, came we.

Irma Kurtz 26.8.1981

NAKED TRUTHS

Ste Maxime, Sunday
There is a gnomic Japanese tale about a prince who dreamt he was a butterfly, and when he woke up he could not be certain that he was not a butterfly dreaming he was a prince. It is, I have no doubt, even more gnomic in Japanese, where it can probably be told in a couple of grunts.

'Funny language,' I said to the Pernod.
'M'*sieu?*'
I looked up from the milky greenness of the glass, into the passing waitress's tawny toplessness.
'*Une langue comique*,' I said, hoarsely, '*le japonais.*'
She smiled. I know, because I was watching her teeth by this time. You cannot actually talk to a bust; not publicly.
'*Moi, je n'en sais rien*,' she said, and glided on through the dotted beach-bar tables, out of my parasol shade, into the searing sun, under the parasol of the next table, changing colour like a travelogue tiger. She put down their bottle of Krug, and that tiny shock as she shed her champagne load rippled her embonpoint just enough to make my hot head sing.

A poised girl. You have to be, nude, and faced with a half-cut Englishman winging in at bust height to raise imponderable points of oriental philology. But then again, I told the Pernod, though not aloud this time, you must expect odd remarks if you're waiting undraped. At least, you must from me; I am still enough unused to toplessness, even after two weeks here on this bizarrely hummocked Riviera beach – the boobs stretch supine to the glittering sea, browning variously, trembling the air above them with ensimmered oil; they are not unlike those puzzle photographs of familiar objects shot from unfamiliar angles, they could be anything, cakes, footpumps, skullcaps, stranded jellyfish – still enough unused, I say, to be confused when unexpectedly confronted with fleshy incongruities.

I tend to say the second thing that comes into my head.

I went to buy a beachball yesterday for my small son; not, of course, without a long shrieking argument about the wisdom of playing football upon this nubile pitch – my French is adequate, but my savoir faire is patchy, and faced with a line of enraged and horizontal Gallic torsoes across which one's *ballon de plage* has just bounced grittily, pinging from nipple to nipple as on some Caligulan pin-table, I doubt that the emollient words would spring lightly to the glottis.

Still, I went at last to buy this beachball; padded up the hot sand, crossed the beachside road, slipped into a shop festooned with dayglo dinghies, balls, inflated Muppets, flippers, all that. And in the shop was a middle-aged French couple with their two pre-teen children, turning postcard racks; but none of them with a stitch on above the waist, save for the man, who sported a white panama. Now, the French, as you know, are both polite and formal, which meant that all five of us said 'Bonjour' to one another, a ritual itself faintly unsettling in the circumstances; but nothing to the one into which we were plunged a terrible moment later.

I reached up to select one of the hanging footballs, and in doing so, the shop being tiny and overstocked, inadvertently brushed, with my elbow, le balcon of the lady customer, who was large and overstocked. I recoiled, with a small shriek; the woman apologised; and her husband raised his hat.

It was a ceremony the frozen memory of which I shall doubtless carry to the grave. It also explains why I am drinking rather more on this holiday than heretofore; it has, too, you will be relieved to hear, not a little to do with the Japanese butterfly-prince.

The plain fact is that I had never until this month encountered mass commonplace nudity, commonplace, that is, to those who constituted the mass; and what has disconcerted me utterly is the shocked discovery that it is not the nudity that makes for awkwardness on my part, but the fact that it is commonplace. I had, that is to say, always assumed that were I suddenly to find myself dropped into an acre of naked girls, the plot would thereafter take a somewhat sexual turn, not necessarily active, you understand, but one in which the lively banter and winking and so forth would somehow take subtle account of the rib-disparity between us. I had imagined that in such a situation I should remain cool, poised, suave, nonchalant, occasionally stifling a yawn when a particularly well-assorted number shimmied past and generally seeing to it that my eyes did not roll around in my head like marbles in a soup-plate.

But it isn't like that at all. The problems, for such they are, are not sexual at all, but entirely social; and I find myself wandering without maps or guides, my social rudder shot away and my behavioural sails in tatters at the broken mast, totally unable to deal with the extraordinary ordinariness around me. For example, if I peer, now, past the rim of this Pernod, I can see a girl some twenty metres away having great difficulty in putting up her deckchair. Were she bikinied, I should shoot gallantly to her side, even her front, and offer my aid. I know how painful it can be, catching things in folding deckchairs. But as I look at the range of things she is likely to catch in this one, I am paralysed, a stoat-pinned rabbit gazing horror-stricken and helpless.

If she traps her bust in the foot-rest, I shall have to phone the fire brigade.

'Quoi?'

'Fire brigade,' I muttered. 'Sapeurs-pompiers.'

I knocked over the Pernod, the waitress laughed, leaned across, began to wipe the table vigorously. I turned my eyes away. God knows how she scrubs floors.

Yesterday, I was sitting on the beach staring at something that was not the stitchless girl five metres to my left blowing up a Li-Lo by mouth, when I was hailed from my right. I turned. It was a French family who had sat beside mine the day before, and with whom we had exchanged brief holiday courtesies, before the four stripped off and dried my throat. Now they were back; they had popped a cork, and invited me to join them.

I moved across, and sat down beside them, because I had no choice. The man is perhaps a little older than I; his wife is large and jolly, the largeness and jollity being unsettlingly inter-related, since every time she laughs, the highlights wink off her oiled and shaking bust like trafficators; his daughter is about seventeen, and has the sort of body over which abbots hang themselves from monastery gutters.

The man is asking me about the Common Market. I AM SITTING WITH HIS NAKED WIFE AND DAUGHTER AND WE ARE TALKING ABOUT THE COMMON MARKET! I AM ASKING HIS NUDE WIFE WHY FRENCH PEOPLE DO NOT BUY BRITISH LEYLAND CARS! I AM EXPLAINING TO HIS RAVISHINGLY AND TOTALLY TANNED DAUGHTER THAT THE BRITISH TELEPHONE SYSTEM IS JUST AS BAD AS THE FRENCH TELEPHONE SYSTEM!

I was not too bad, all in all. I could hear my own voice from several feet away getting genders reasonably right, popping in one or two reason-

ably current idioms. I managed not to look when
Madame began kneading Ambre Solaire into
her superstructure while going on about the
price of vegetables, and I even managed to look
as if I was not managing not to look, if you follow
me. It was not, in fact, until their small boy
arrived and began drawing on his sister with a
felt-tipped pen that I broke away with a light
laugh and hurled myself trembling into the sea.

They are thoughtful at Ste Maxime plage; the
Mediterranean is full not only of salt but of
myriad marine nasties, and freshwater douches
are solicitously provided. I came out of the sea,
and slipped into the nearest cubicle, where a
small nude lady and I shared a cake of soap and
one or two interesting remarks about the
weather. She removed a piece of tar from a
buttock (I forget which), we agreed about
environmental hazards, and we went our separate ways.

That was yesterday. Most of the days have
been like that. I am looking at my new Pernod
now, and realising, with a tiny shock, that I did
not notice the waitress bring it. Interesting.
Perhaps two weeks is enough for one normality
to be replaced by its reverse, perhaps I am almost
ready to help that girl with her deckchair, to
walk through the restaurant kitchen behind this
bar without a second thought (I walked through
it on our first day, and a naked chef was slicing
courgettes, and by the time I got to the third
thought I had to put my head under the tap),
perhaps this will become my own normality,
perhaps it is *the* normality and the case to be
made out for a striped tie and natty grey worsteds

and sensible brogues rests on dubious premises
. . .

I shall be in London in two days. Whether I
shall find myself a butterfly or a prince remains to
be dreamt.

Alan Coren 15.8.1979

'It's all very well, but it makes me feel like a transvestite.'

'You're in luck. The rest of the week I'm liberated
but on Saturdays I revert to being a sex object.'

THOSE HOLIDAY ROMANCES!

A Peek Into Nurse Garsmold's Advice Postbag

Dear Nurse Garsmold:

As a kitchen extractor hood consultant, I meet all sorts, plus a different stratum altogether at my bonsai tree circle (Tuesdays). Furthermore, collecting peculiar headlines, e.g. MAN HAD TURTLE UNDER CARDIGAN, has taught me, over the past twenty years, that life does not hold many surprises for the person who keeps his wits about him.

However, I have been followed to our holiday chalet at Jaywick Sands by a darkie with a medallion and a strange walk who we parked next to in a lay-by on the A 603 to gather from this that I am a family man, and nothing like this darkie has ever happened to me before, except a man with a labrador when I was a scout, and I called the conductor and that was the end of it.

The thing is, though, that he has an interest in midget trees, unlike my wife Yvonne, who cannot stand anything Jap. I know this, because he followed me when I went down The Three Jolly Gulls on our first night and started a conversation, and I did not want to appear prejudiced, after all he might want a kitchen extractor hood one day, you never know in my line. But after I got launched into my favourite topic, the Nikimoto pine, only four inches tall but delivers a full crop of titchy little cones every October, he suddenly put his hand over mine and said I had lovely eyes, they sort of lit up when I got enthusiastic.

I do not know which way to turn. Obviously, I would rather he was a woman, I would leave Yvonne like a shot, but you cannot wait all your life for a girl with an interest in little oriental flora to come along, I am 42 next birthday. What should I do?

Arthur Tenby

Dear Nurse Garsmold,

They have this game in Horremolinos-del-Mar, where a holidaymaker is buried by his wife and the wine-waiter from their hotel,and then the wife and the wine-waiter go off and leave him, and the winning holidaymaker is the one who stays in his hole longest, and he gets a fabulous bottle of Widdlo de Caballo sparkling wine.

I have won this contest five years running. The photo shows me winning this year's one, where I stayed in the hole nine days, with no ill effects except the sun dried up the two ballpoints in my top pocket. The wine waiter's friend come out regular and fed me paella, so a good time was had by all! What I want to know is, is this a record?

R. F. Wiggins

Dear Nurse Garsmold,

I enclose a picture of me, taken in Bognor in 1923. As you will see, the lady on my right bears a striking resemblance to the lady on my left, except for being a head taller. The one on my left is my wife, who I married on the Tuesday of that week, since you did not hang about when you were a member of the Lost Generation etc., you must have read about it, there's been books, films, all sorts of stuff.

It was not till I got home to Waynefleet that I realised I had married the wrong one. My wife wore high heels at the Registry Office, and I never twigged she was short until we got home. I thought I had married the tall one, Wanda I think her name was. My question is: could I change wives at this late date? I think I saw Wanda getting on a bus at New Cross last Friday, she was still tall, if 81, and I wouldn't mind making a fresh start. I know there have been changes in the divorce laws recently, and I thought you would be in a position to advise me.

Edmund Karb

Nurse Garsmold:

Being a typist with some light clerical ... but definitely no tea-making etcetera, ... is what juniors are for, I told them, I ... myself on holiday here in fabulous ...green, and I have a problem, well query, ...ly.

I am not forward, due to a strict Morden ...bringing, Sunday School, father clipping ear, ...d so forth, but I am on the pill, also all ...itted up, and being 32 reckon we only pass this ...way but once and who am I saving it for, as it were.

Anyway, I have met a nice man on this beach we have, well, I say beach, it is more of a sort of large board really, with that plastic grass they have at greengrocers, when they have plums on it and so forth; he is called Pedro and he puts the parasol out of a morning, in its concrete thing due to where the wind comes from Gibralter, I think he said, it is not easy to tell with (a) the wind, (b) him speaking Spanish, mainly, and (c) a growth on his lip, a bit like a cobnut, only with hairs on it.

Anyway, he says I can have the good deckchair he normally saves for special guests, if I go to his hut for a siesta. It is not much of a hut, it has a tin chimney and a dog tied to the doorknob, but Pedro says he has got beer in it and a Li-Lo. What I want to know is, is this "the real thing", or should I wait for Mr Right, as I still have nine days left and have not peeled yet?

Selena Perrins

Dear Nurse Garsmold:

Here I am, just arrived on a Greek island, not sure which, I think it ends in -os, it has Red Barrel and Big Macs and a Berni Inn, so you can probably identify it off a map.

The thing is, I paid £267 in Macclesfield for a singles holiday to meet the man of my dreams as per brochure, but when I got here to see who they had teamed me up with, he was not finished. On the brochure where they had this picture of the men of your dreams, they was all bronzed and muscular with little bums and dark curly hair. Mine is called Cyril and he is still white all over except for his little thin face which is bright red and skinned, he looks like a boiled prawn, and he is virtually bald with no muscles at all, all his bulk is in this sort of oval backside he's got, which he keeps in a pair of baggy black woollen trunks with the label showing. He has also got a Arthur Scargill hat with CHARTERED SURVEYORS DO IT ON THE LEVEL round the peak.

Have I got a claim against Funsingles (Macclesfield) Ltd? I have complained to the courier on Thingos, and he has promised that Cyril will be finished very soon, he will go brown and get his muscles up etc. as per brochure, but personally I have my doubts, I have seen stick insects with better biceps. If I kick up enough stink, would they move me to a more developed specimen? Please advise soonest, I am sick of sleeping in the bath.

Miriam Spofe

THE GOOD SHIP VENUS

Merrily Harpur

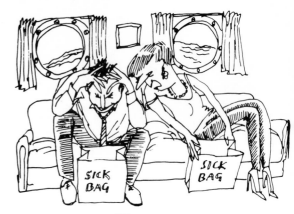

'Who were you eating pineapple with?'

'Fancy you not having been to Hendon.'

'Your husband ahoy!'

'That's the trouble with ships' saunas – you get stowaways.'

'Isn't it neat the way they stow everything away in its place.'

'No, I only do divorces, these days.'

'You're the first iceberg I've ever hit.'

'No, that was the sea that moved.'

'We're hoping to meet again if the wind veers round suddenly.'

'What's happening to our ménage à trois, Jennifer
– are there another deux?'

'He's the best lover I've ever had –
he does body-searches at
Heathrow.'

SEX ANYONE?
A Preliminary but by No Means Tentative Survey

In one form or another, what for the purpose of this work we shall from here on refer to as sex has been with us for a good many years now; and as far as I have been able to make out in the course of my investigations* there seems no reason to hope that we shall ever see the end of it. Certainly not in *your* lifetime. I admit there is the spread of colour television to be considered, not to mention some rather fancy goings-on in test-tubes and the rumoured approach of another Ice Age; but on the whole it seems likely that ladies and gentlemen will continue to look to one another for this particular means of distraction, misery, unsophisticated pleasure or complicated escape for a good many centuries yet. Old habits die hard, and I am confident that once the initial novelty of listening to long-playing records of the works of T. S. Eliot in stereo until all hours of the night has worn off, sex will again take what many people consider to be its rightful place in this sorry scheme of things entire. I'm not saying I approve, and I'm not saying I disapprove. I know perfectly well where *I* stand in the matter, and I'll thank you to mind your own business. Besides, I don't fancy the fate of any man who disparages in print the works of T. S. Eliot in stereo. All I'm saying is, the thing is pretty firmly established, and we might as well make the best of it.

What, we might well ask at the very outset, *is* sex? And it's a damned good question. From the etymological point of view we are in difficulties right away, because for one thing sex strikes a lot of people as being plural, and they may be right. At any rate, misguided or not, there are men and women alive at this very moment across whose minds the question sometimes flickers, 'Where are the sex of yesteryear?' They probably have much the same trouble with scissors, and mathematics, and mumps, and (if you'll pardon the expression: this is, after all, a fearlessly clinical work) trousers. The whole thing is obviously bound up in some way, like everything else, with Zen. What, for instance, is the sound of a single calisthenic?

I cannot help these people, because I haven't the least idea where sex, regarded as a three-letter word, came from, and I certainly don't intend to start prying into musty semantic problems of that nature at my time of life. Such research as I have engaged in has been scholarly enough, I grant you, but there are limits. Besides, people in public libraries tend to inform the custodian if they notice that you have kept a great fat volume of an encyclopaedia open at *Sex* for more than three-quarters of an hour, making notes on the back of an old envelope. It's the same with *Arsenic*. *Forgery* is even worse: I have known the police to be called. *Aphrodisiacs* is all right: people just nudge one another and smile in a lofty way, as though they had caught you trying to forecast the end of the world with a pound and a half of mixed entrails.

So much, then, for sex as a word. More than enough, in fact, except that with regard to synonyms and related words and phrases, I don't mind telling you I've knocked around the world a fair amount in my time, mixing unavoidably with both the high and the low and sometimes noticing the difference at once, and I have heard related words and phrases you'd hardly credit. Most of these are commonly excused on the grounds that they were once used by Anglo-Saxons, a mysterious group who communicated in gruff monosyllables, mainly about the physical aspects of procreation and the elimination of waste matter, and didn't give a hoot who overheard them. (What kind of an excuse this is supposed to be I would not presume to judge.) In the course of time, what with the spread of a new trend called sophistication from the Mediterranean area and the growing number of complaints from waitresses, these Anglo-Saxons were forced to moderate their language, and so they invented the asterisk. In the course of yet

*Thank you, Miss Andrea————, without whose patience, understanding and unquenchably adventurous spirit this book might never have been finished. Thank you, too, Miss Phoebe————, who did the typing so impeccably and then went straight into a nunnery.

more time, the combined efforts of H*nry M*ll*r and the Ev*rgr**n R*v**w put a stop to this effete subterfuge, and today our cocktail parties and methylated spirits soirées alike resound once more with the good old uninhibited lingo.

As to antonyms, there are none. The opposite of sex is something the philosophers have been striving to define for as long as anyone can remember, because this is the kind of thing people expect of philosophers. So far they haven't come up with anything very promising, and if they ever do, I can tell you here and now it's not going to be popular.

Passing to the effects of sex – or, as they are sometimes called, the *side* effects – it may be pertinent to point out that these have included Brahms, Mary Baker Eddy, the present writer, Beowulf, Rin-Tin-Tin, your uncle Stan, Henry Wadsworth Longfellow, and untold millions of others far too tedious to enumerate in a specialised work of this size.

I will go further, and say that sex has been directly or indirectly responsible for decrees both absolute and nisi, separate rest rooms for men and women, the development of the G-string and the drive-in cinema, hereditary frustration among Boston booksellers, eighty thousand letters to editors signed 'Anxious', an alleged war between Greece and Troy, some pretty searching questions about Shakespeare's sonnets, the closing of parks at sunset, the emergence of Red China, the steady popularity of the ruins of Pompeii, the ridiculous price of scent, a number of untimely deaths, eight limericks of a moderately droll nature, the origin of such familiar expressions as 'There is somebody hiding in that wardrobe,' 'I can explain everything,' and 'I don't believe you've met my cousin, have you, dear?', widespread misapprehensions about life in the capital of France, a certain amount of good clean fun, an uncomfortable episode in the history of the Lot family, the Reformation, the side saddle, the permanent wave, the failure of Togetherness, more than one ingeniously phrased item in an expense account return, a misunderstanding between Oedipus and his mother, the eclipse of Charles Stewart Parnell,* the sudden and solemn resurgence of a laughable romance by D. H. Lawrence, the reluctant introduction of

the state of matrimony, bust-worship, bottom-pinching, baby-sitting, bank robberies, beach huts, beauty parlours, Burlesque, and a large and ever-growing number of suspiciously well-heeled psychiatrists.

It is also important, of course, to bear in mind right from the beginning the things that sex is *not*, such as negotiable, inexpensive, tangible, termite-proof, or available on the National Health. It is only intermittently fashionable, and nobody seems to have any clear idea about whether it is habit-forming or not. Some authorities hold it to be expendable, or at best a sheer waste of valuable time; they are apt to know a lot about the private lives of salmon. It is neither chic nor sordid. Nor was it thought up in desperation one rainy afternoon by an advertising man who had been beating his brains out for three weeks trying to find a way of popularising a lawnmower, a soft drink and a cure for halitosis. (This canard has been widely spread, but in fairness to the advertising industry† I feel it should be recorded here that all the fellow actually did was to *equate* sex simultaneously with some ironmongery, a fizzy concoction and bad breath. It was certainly an original notion, and far ahead of its time; but to assert that it involved the downright, deliberate *invention* of sex is to fly in the face of reason. As we have seen, sex had been lying around for centuries doing nothing more useful than to assist haphazardly in the propagation of a species dedicated to the task of perfecting a means of wiping itself out by surreptitiously feeding Strontium 90 to its cows, and it simply fell to this man to be the first to coax it into a more practical channel. Such was the success of his pioneering efforts that today nobody will dream of choosing a motorcar unless some copywriter has subtly convinced him it is good enough to go to bed with. A woman doesn't *buy* a non-stick frying pan, a bra or an automatically defrosting refrigerator: she has an affair with it. A man feverishly taking delivery of the pair of smooth, glossy, perfectly balanced garden shears he fell for in the ad is thinking neither of his *cupressus*

---

*In Ireland this is sometimes classed as a moot point, and so is Sir Roger Casement.

†Craft? Profession? Conspiracy?

macrocarpa nor his privet: all he wants is to get the thing inside and tear its clothes off. Leaving aside religion and the desire for self-government, advertising and sex are the two most lively spiritual forces in the world today, and once the two had been combined there was an almost audible sigh of achievement that stretched from Tokyo to Harrisburg, Pa.* Recently, though, there have been murmurs of frustration; some people are beginning to get the idea that advertising is more exciting than sex itself, and they don't know what the devil to make of it all. I have studied this question too – few indeed are the stones that have been left unturned here, I can tell you – and I unhesitatingly place these people in what we thinkers call the Maladjusted category, if not the Hopelessly Muddleheaded. They are exactly the kind of disturbed people who will complain to the *maître d'hôtel* if the stripper turns out to have no appendix, a fact of which the offending evidence has been cunningly erased on the life-size photograph in the foyer. The next stage is where they turn into people who not only don't want to have their cake and eat it too, but actually prefer to bury it in the garden with cries of disgust, and eat the wrapper instead, together with the carton, the string and the list of certified ingredients. In any case, all this confusion must not be blamed exclusively on advertisements. They form, after all, only one among the many branches of erotica.)

Another thing that sex is not is love, and so is being in the back of a car with the boss's wife, admiring the texture of her handbag while under the impression that it is her knee, and finishing up with a sudden mouthful of ear-ring. The former is a pathological condition, sometimes referred to as possession by demons and frequently brought on by a trick of the light which leads you to believe that you've finally met someone almost as mysterious and fascinating as you are yourself; it can recur, like malaria. The latter is either an unconscious manifes-

tation of the death wish, or just plain ignorance about the peculiar properties of the dry martini with a twist of lemon; one way or the other, you'd better watch it.

You will see from all this that sex could easily prove to be a very deep subject, and well worth a few minutes of anyone's time. Certainly in this day and age it is hardly the kind of thing that should be allowed to pass unnoticed; as a man was good enough to point out to me only the other day on a bus (and I may say he had a brief-case and seemed to be connected with something), there is more than a vague chance that before we know where we are it might be all we have left, apart from a heap of rubble and a wisp or two of smoke. I therefore propose in the course of this work – nay, I regard it as my painful duty – to consider – and sometimes even explore – every aspect, from humdrum problems like The Place of the Orgy in a Normal Healthy Relationship, to such complicated matters as The Use of After-Shave Lotion Considered as a Fine Art. I regret that I shall be unable to enter into any correspondence, cast any horoscopes, or sit listening to case-histories on the telephone all afternoon – except perhaps very short ones, with no strings. I wish to be regarded as neither a Father Figure nor a Mother Superior. If you want to know the truth, I see myself more as a kind of oracle, and you'll just have to be content with that.

Alex Atkinson 31.1.1962

'Well, I don't find it all that titillating being a transvestite.'

---

*The long way round, of course – via Hamburg and Felixstowe but omitting the mainland of China and the USSR, where advertising is still hampered by the influence of dialectical materialism and nobody ever thought much of sex as a lark anyway.

'Captain Martinet, you have made it very plain that I am not welcome aboard the Sea Wolfe!'

'Women are a bad influence on a ship of the line, ma'am!'

'Do you not find me the least bit attractive, sir?'

'Have a care ma'am! After months at sea, it would not take much to set the crew ablaze with flaming passion!'

'See what I mean!'

'I think she's penetrated his façade.'

'He now tells me we're incompatible.'

'Wonderful news, Bernadette – we're forgiven.'

PRACTICAL LOVE-MAKER

THE MAGAZINE THAT SHOWS <u>YOU</u> HOW IT'S DONE

● Find out exactly how to go about it—our simple-to-follow charts guide you through it step-by-step, explaining every detail as you go along

● Discover the fascinating mysteries of it—just how other people go about it, how often they go about it, how perhaps they go about it differently

● Easy-to-grasp instructions in unretouched language teach you all there is to know about it—in no time at all you'll be able to go about it with total confidence

● Our fail-safe methods mean you cannot go wrong—at every stage on the learning curve our fault-finding and diagnostic diagrams are ready to come to your aid

ALL OF IT AND MORE IS INSIDE *PRACTICAL LOVE-MAKER*, AN EDUCATIONAL REFERENCE THAT BUILDS UP INTO A TREASURE-HOUSE OF CLOSER UNDERSTANDING

FIRST STEPS TOWARDS MASTERING IT

In recent years, there has been a revolution in the techniques and capability of modern love-making. It is a revolution which has led many to fear they may be falling behind, losing touch with the rapid advances in this most fascinating of fields.

Yet an awful lot of confusing mumbo-jumbo is put about concerning it. At its simplest, the principle which determines all love-making is not at all dif-ficult to picture—it is about men and it is about women: the so-called *binary* rela-tionship or *operating system*. All the wonderful and amazing things which love can do, all the astonishing sophistication and complexity—it all boils down to this fundamental prin-ciple.

For the moment, it is best to forget all about the confusing jargon—the *floppy nannies*, user-friendly input/output ports, peek-and-poke and so forth—and to concentrate on the basic question of *what you want your love to do for you.*

If, for instance, all that you require is simple shirt and sock processing, a feeding program, or just someone to share your TV monitor, then a relatively cheap and easy-to-manage love-making system is probably all that you need.

As you get more interested in and more confident at love-making, then later you may wish to consider a much more sophisticated set-up, perhaps involving several "peripheral" arrangements.

There is really no limit to what can be done with modern love-making. The first consideration should nevertheless be a cool and honest appraisal of your immediate requirements. Do not be starstruck by the fancy and expensive affairs you often see spread across the media. It is all too easy to be bowled over by the blandishments of attractively packaged love-making partners. *Practical Love-Maker* assumes no previous knowledge—let's set about it together from the beginning.

THE BEGINNING: UNDERSTANDING BASIC

Most love-making buffs begin their fascination with the hobby through basic words and expressions. The words are essentially *prompts* which explain what it is that you are working towards and include ETCHINGS, DRINK, BITE, SLAP and TICKLE. More versatile are the basic operating *commands* which explain what it is that you are trying to get and include OFF, AWAY, MEANINGFUL, OF COURSE and YOU KNOW I DO.

Many beginners take a little time to get accustomed to the *syntax* of basic love-making commands. An expression such as NEVER FELT ABOUT THIS BEFORE WITH ANYONE may not be perfectly understood and could cause a breakdown. An easier method is to understand *Procedures* in which certain moves within moves build up into an easily intelligible way of going about it.

SLOWLY DOES IT

When first they take up love-making, many people find they cannot get enough of it. But it is important to remember that, unless you are used to it, love-making can put unfamiliar strains on your body which will result in back-ache, cramp, crushing, or a squint.

One useful tip is to take a break every hour or so, stretch your legs, perhaps make a pot of tea. It helps to relax muscles and can prevent an unsightly stoop. It minimises the risk of "dropping off" in the middle of an important routine. The technique is called a *Pause.* The *Pause-Off* command is sometimes called a *Hard Break.*

IN FUTURE ISSUES OF PRACTICAL LOVE-MAKER . . .

Establishing a Working Relationship.
Why do some men find it easier to get along with certain types of big, beautifully-finished but not very demanding packages? How can the latest *softwear* help you get more out of your love-making sessions? What does it mean when a man gazes into a woman's eyes then momentarily looks down at her keyboard? Why are some people not satisfied with a single, stand-alone set-up and are always wanting to have a go on the very latest models?

YOU WRITE

Dear PLM,

I've been dating a gorgeous 6ft 2in suntanned millionaire who says he is serious about me and wants us to go on line. My trouble is, I do like him a lot, but I'm not that interested in playing games. How can I tell him that I want to be with him forever, but would far rather we shared an interest in spreadsheets?

—Confused, Staines

Even in these so-called liberated and permissive times, it's up to every young love-maker to make up her own mind how far she wants to go. Many couples feel today that it is OK to go along with a little intimate de-bugging, but sensible girls call a halt when a man says he wants to touch their Winchesters. Why not suggest that you and he have a go with one of the popular simulator programs? The more expensive ones are just like the real thing, but there's no harm done.

VALENTINE CARDS

Valentine's day represents a complete turnaround in the way men honour one simple principle. On Valentine's Day they express themselves in print. They spend the other 364 days of the year strenuously avoiding putting anything in writing to which they might be held, and this holds truer of affairs of the heart than business. Men have been known to launch into print to other men to keep them from committing themselves in ink to women. 'Do anything you both like and anything else you can get away with – but for God's sake don't write to her about it!' would still be advice from any affectionate father to his son. Most men think far more about breach of promise and conduct unbecoming than they do about romance. And it is probably because this has always been the way that we have wound up with one day upon which men are permitted, encouraged and, in some cases, required to express their feelings about their women.

There are, of course, degrees of Valentinism. Setting aside poetry proper, which was a clever evasion because you could be addressing anybody, at the outset it was required that those who were really attracted to one another, in the turbulent way we call 'being in love', used the day to let each other know about it. How the festival of the mating of the birds and the deaths of two early Roman martyrs (who may have been only one, we're not sure) came to result in February 14 as the feast of the protestation of love, is not clear. But, notwithstanding the blood and the birdlime, it becomes the one day when, even if you were of the other sex and a maiden pure, you could express your passion – provided your anonymity was preserved and the object of your affections could be trusted.

Under Victoria, the art of valentine cards flowered and although some were made up professionally, it was more generally expected that if you cared, you'd show it by making your own. In those days, men used the occasion to sound out how the beloved felt, before tackling her father. It was well known that a father usually gave a suitor a rough ride with details about income and expectation, and nobody wanted to have to go through all that if Miss Polly didn't favour his suit from the outset.

Setting aside what you might call the serious valentine, the next stage was rather more exploratory. It was a way of getting a girl to focus on you, rather than all the other men of her circle. It promised nothing except attentions – and who knew where they might lead? It was permission for something a bit more interesting than being a member of the herd; it opened the way for friendship, flirtation, even intimacy. It implied a compliment and few women can ever have enough of those. At this level, too, there was every chance that men received valentines for very similar reasons and they're just as susceptible to flattery.

The third level of Valentinism was rather more general. A valentine might be sent by an old man to his plain nurse or by a little girl to her grandfather. It might be from a sly schoolboy to his sister's best friend, or from a man to his old love, as a sort of remembrance. And it might, too, be sent in mischief to every single woman a man knew to see what would come of it. Nothing appeases vanity more than to have your entire female acquaintance sure that each one is special and striving to put flesh on the bones of that insubstantial fancy. At least that way you find out a bit more about who favours you before you expose yourself further.

But as Victoria receded and modernity advanced, the sending of valentines changed gradually so that more and more women sent them, probably because it was a discreet form of declaration and it still didn't do for a nice girl to be seen making the going. Occasionally a man might send a valentine but it was usually part of the heavier artillery he brought up to secure the end that he had in mind – whether it was breakfast in bed or the wedding banns.

In the meantime, the making of valentine cards became an industry. Today's card is sentimental in the most unaesthetic way, with lots of red heart-shapes or a satin cushion which plays 'I Remember You' when you press it to open on a cloying verse. And in any case, terms no longer mean what they once meant. Declaration has gone out of the valentine card business. 'Be mine!' meant one thing to a suitor of bygone days and quite another to most modern men, of whatever age or background. Nowadays nothing is forever and the speed at which we move and change is reflected in another kind of card quite foreign to its antecedents.

Many more contemporary cards are funny, funny in a deprecating, defensive sort of way, which makes mock of the ideas they were printed to celebrate. Far from the preferable visions of youth and beauty – he tanned and strong, she wistful in white with flowers in her hands – today's cards rib about age, rag about diet, money, fidelity. The big emotional stuff is too heavy for most of us, especially in a form of print more public than a book. Send it up, take the sting out of it – and then we'll see whether the first few nights together lead anywhere. Because most of today's cards reflect not longing for love but intercourse, the pounce, the grab, the getting to grips with the interconnecting body bits. And most of them are completely unmemorable because the main buyers are very young women and for them no valentine is valid for very long.

Barring the office Romeo who'll send out a handful rather in the manner of a hopeful trawler, men buy the romantic cards – and they buy them to say what for the most part they find very difficult to say, out of bed and stone cold sober. Or they buy them to accommodate, because they're involved with the sort of women (of whom there are far too many) who expect to be acknowledged for their attraction, their sexual merit, rather along the lines of a weekly gold star. One week it's a bottle, the next it's a box, but come February 14, it had better be red roses, champagne and a card, because that's what you *should* give the light of your life on Valentine's Day. And no, just taking her out to dinner won't do it, nor will the fact that you've just paid out for something else. On occasions like this there are rules and the card is the most important bit of the ritual, proof positive she isn't losing her lure.

So the unknowingness is rare nowadays. You usually know who has sent you or is sending you a valentine card and, in some cases, you'd be thoroughly put out if it didn't appear along with suitable symbols which signify that you are taken seriously and not for granted.

Well, of course, he's sent you a valentine, hasn't he – I mean, your name's on the front of the car with his, isn't it – Chas and Cheryl? You don't ask much of him, do you – always put up with the sport on telly and keep yourself nice – least he can do is to send you a valentine . . . And of course he writes less in it than he ever has because the verse or the gag is there and all he has to do is to sign his name, with love, and another duty will have been fulfilled, another memorial honoured.

And do you send him a valentine? Well yes, sometimes, if you can find a funny one, one about what he's like when he's had a few or how his eye wanders to anything in a skirt. Does he send you a funny one? No – no, he did once but I told him, that's not a proper valentine card, now is it? He usually gets something more romantic, you know, with flowers and hearts and things. Do you think he likes getting a funny valentine from you? Don't know, never thought about it really. It doesn't mean to men what it means to us really, does it? I mean, it's the thought that counts.

Anna Raeburn 12.2.1986

'We're not goin' steady, we're stuck together!'

Michael Heath
MY PUNKY VALENTINE

'Did you drop this, darlin'?'

LAID BACK

One of the more endearing eccentricities of America's folkloric tradition is that of townships bestowing upon themselves the most curious honorary titles. It's not unusual to drive through the heartland of the Mid-West to find yourself entering the precincts of, say, 'Zilchville, Ohio. Pop 2345. Elastic Bandage Capital of America.'

Or 'Little Vacuum, Missouri. Pop 3456. Home of the Turkey Boot.'

Be it bandage or boot the good citizens are rightly proud of their community's contribution to the Great American Way. If you've got it flaunt it, say I.

Were I a member of San Francisco's ruling Board of Supervisors I would issue an edict declaring that all such signs of welcome to the City by the Bay should bear the legend, 'If you can't get laid here you can't get laid *anywhere*.'

Forget the Golden Gate Bridge, which is painted a severe rust-red in any case. Banish from your mind the cable cars, just as they themselves have been banished from the streets for two years while the entire network is dug up and re-sown.

San Francisco's gift to the nation is sex.

Whatever shape or form your particular sin of the flesh runs to, it's up for grabs, or gropes. Be you hetero-, homo-, or just a plain old-fashioned bi-sexual made for two you'll find yourself accommodated. Not just the sleazoid celluloid offerings in the Tenderloin where you can thrill (or not) to *Wanda Whips Wall Street*, which may be responsible for the sudden mania that has gripped the Stock Market recently. Nor the specialised 'phone services', whereby the obscene phone call has turned out to be profitable for those young women who sit at one end of the line whispering sweet everythings to clients at the other.

No, this is the real thing. Tactile.

In the Fifties it was the Beats who made their cultural mark on the city. In the Sixties it was the hippy influx. The Seventies and early Eighties have seen the homosexual community as the latest nomadic tribe to establish their presence.

Just as the Hispanics occupy the Mission district, the blacks the Fillmore and surrounding streets, so there are clearly-defined homosexual areas in town, most notably Castro, Polk Street and the more affluent parts of Haight Street, the former hippy stronghold.

The mass gay migration to San Francisco has had significant repercussions. Homosexuals make up an estimated 25% of the city's population, so they are not without influence. Woe betide the up-for-election candidate who fails to court the gay vote.

There was a major disturbance in the city in 1979 when a gay Supervisor received a very lenient sentence after shooting and killing the mayor, George Moscone. The residents of Castro swarmed into the city centre, attacking the City Hall and burning ten police cars.

Needless to say the predictable police reaction that night has led to strained relations between the two groups ever since. An interesting side-note to the affair is that the accused Supervisor's defence pleaded that their client was suffering severe mental stress at the time, precipitated by eating too many Twinkies, a favourite American confectionery. A legal first and, I hope, last.

Without doubt San Francisco is 'Singles City USA', a fact confirmed by the just-released census that shows that over 53% of the population (678,974 at the time of counting) live in what are classified as 'non-family' households.

The rest of the country (Johnny Carson) laughs at San Francisco and the gay factor, nightly perpetuating the 'fruit and nuts' myth of the city, with such biting lampoons as 'How many SF straights does it take to change a lightbulb? Both of them – ho, ho.'

A London colleague of the 'persuasion' is convinced I've leapt from my closet as I'm now enjoying my seventh visit in four years. Well, as long as the popular image is maintained, I for one am not complaining. It doesn't need the brain of Mycroft Holmes to fathom that if there's a preponderance of gays in the town it cuts down the heterosexual competition to the point where even an old sexual cynic like myself can have a fairly successful run of luck without having to put himself out too much.

The best advice any financial guru could have offered five years ago would have been, 'Take up thy ferns, take up thy Tiffany lamps and walk

. . . to San Francisco and there open a singles bar.'

Night after night the single persons and per-sonettes gather in the electric glow of Henry's Africa, with more vegetation than the average rain forest, Paoli's, the Holding Company (most apt) in the financial district, and, probably the definitive joint in town, the Pierce Street Annexe (no relation, sexual or otherwise).

If, like me, you have every faith in the maxim that sex is the cruellest form of slapstick comedy, there is a wealth of material to be had treating oneself to a 'night on the pull'.

It is not without its hazards, or its difficulties. The first thing you must do is rid yourself of any misgivings that what you're doing is sexist. It swings both ways, and there's every possibility you'll find *yourself* on the defensive, under siege from some ardent young thing. The role reversal can set you back in surprise, and it's a good lesson for any young buck who thinks he's God's gift to the XX chromosome.

The next hurdle to overcome is that *you* know you're hetero, despite the attempts of gay friends to convince you that inside each man is another man trying to come out, but does she?

Assuming there are two of you out on the spree there's no reason for the brace of lovelies to your left to assume you're not gay, especially if you tend to adopt an English mode of dress. Being a martyr to last year's fashion, I'm pro-hibited from cladding myself in the plaids and sports coats, the 'sensible' shoes, that are the hallmark of middle-American man. Neither is my hair subjected to the statutory blow-dried waves. The Pierce pudding bowl has been handed down through generations and I've no intention of ridding myself of the moptop merely for the sake of sexual gratification. Not just once have I and my companion been asked by some svelte thing, 'You guys faggots?'

'English,' always comes the reply, which can often do more harm than good, many American girls being unable to decide which is the least suspect.

Assuming that you've hooked the victim's interest, now comes the strenuous task of retain-ing it. Her motives for being there are doubtless the same as yours. You may think you're the best thing in black suede shoes to walk into her life but you're just another Joe. Or Mike. Or Duane.

Or Scott. Now must come the crunch tactic. The Big Lie. It's an expected and integral part of the courtship ritual.

OK, so you're a visiting journalist, covering the rock scene, trying to put down roots in the city. Yawn. She's heard it a thousand times. You've told it as many, if not more. Comedian Steve Martin reckons the line best suited to any situation when chatting up an American girl is to amble over to her and without introduction say, 'I make a lot of money.' He's not far wrong. Comics are the best gaugers of the contemporary scene. They make sociologists redundant.

My particular favourite is that I'm checking out the town for the forthcoming tour by the Stones/Paul McCartney/Roxy Music/Anyone Big Who She's Probably Heard Of.

My imagination can really let fly. Rock music is still deified on the West Coast, so any connec-tion, however tenuous, however fabricated, will invariably fall on listening ears.

The routine has become so polished that I am confident that I could offer my services to any band who might wish to employ a reconnais-sance man in the area.

The tale of mystery and imagination is occasionally gilded by the presence of Dave, my flatmate, who bears a vague resemblance to Pete Townshend of The Who (vague is about as far as you'd want), and I have passed him off as the celebrity on a couple of occasions. Strangely enough we ended the evening empty-handed both times.

A lesson I learned early on is not to ply your sparring partner with what you think passes for scintillating English *salon* wit. She'll greet each *bon mot* with 'Sorry I don't understand,' wondering just how she'll rid herself of the inane fool giggling to himself. Worse still, her pupils will distend and with almost Zionist zeal she will exclaim, 'Oh, I just *love* Marnty Pyth'n!'

Sophistication is not the order of the day on the singles scene. Keep the lie big but keep it simple, is the golden rule.

Not even the contagion-level of the dread Herpes (god of sexually transmitted diseases) can quell the enthusiasm of singles devotees.

Real men not only refrain from quiche but they don't let irritating factors like Herpes overly concern them. It's become such a norm that one New York publisher has produced a monthly magazine for sufferers.

And it's in the Big Apple that the singles culture has reached a new state of the art in 'scrufting', whereby you run through the entire proceedings from A to Zee without learning your partner's name. Bonus points if you·get breakfast and your cab fare home the next morning.

If the singles game, and it's little more than that, seems calculated, a sexual exchange for lonely, sometimes insecure people, that's what it is, with the hope lingering that Mr or Ms Right might be the one leaning over the bar clutching his/her Rusty Nail or Whisky Over.

Strings remain firmly unattached 99% of the time, however.

While hardly the most cerebral of exercises it is not without its romance, its intellectual appeal. Once, wishing to impress with my knowledge of the cinematic canon of Woody Allen, I leant across her semi-slumbering body and whispered the closing line from *Sleeper*: 'The only difference between sex and death is that you don't feel nauseous after death.'

The bruises on my ribs should clear up within a few days.

Guy Pierce 3.11.1982

SHEER HYPE

Call me a schlemiel. Or perhaps a Holy Fool. An innocent, anyway. A sexual greenhorn who thought the Shere Hite Report was some obscure work by a dyslexic. Of course, an impressionable teenager, I had read Krafft-Ebing and wept, with the rest of my generation, sympathetic adolescent tears over the man from Linz who fell in love with the liver dumpling. (All the dirty parts in those sexually repressive days, as you probably remember, were written in Latin or worse and so I might have this terribly sad case history a bit wrong.) It was a pretty disastrous love affair anyway because the liver dumpling had absolutely no working orifices to speak of; at least, none to speak of in mixed company although with broads like Shere Hite around a lot of fellows these days are learning to make an excuse and leave the questionnaire.

There are no cowardly flights into the decency of an obscure language with the '7,239 men, ages 13 to 97', who, the blurb on the cover of *The Hite Report on Male Sexuality* tells us, 'speak openly and with feeling about their fears and secrets, their sexual preferences and practices, their profoundest joys and disappointments . . . a new cultural interpretation of male sexuality by the author of *The Hite Report on Female Sexuality*.' The only thing that seems to be missing is the bold-faced type telling us that this is 'NOW A MAJOR MOTION PICTURE' although judging from what I read I rather think

'Just one more question – how often do you sleep with your wife?'

the *Hite Report* will have to ply the home video cassette trade winds.

Taken all around, 1,129 pages of questionnaire answers from men, 13 to 97, coast to coast in the USA, even at a steal price of £9.95 for the limp and £12 for the hard, is a bit heavy-going. But it's not all bad. The fellow who was asked about masturbation and said, 'I enjoy those intimate moments alone with my body,' is perhaps worth £9.95, and likewise the man who said he liked making love because 'it makes me sweat and makes my beard grow faster'.

And yet, as I sat up into the wee small hours – hours usually devoted to making my beard grow fast – and read about the sex lives of those kids from 13 to 97, I kept gently dozing off and a vision of an alternative report,

The Sheer Stan
Male Sexuality Report

kept stealing into my dreams.

How do you rate your sex life with wife/girlfriend/ boyfriend/livestock?

Nine out of ten men said they get headaches just before some female sociologist comes staggering in dead drunk, reeking of drink and demanding questionnaire filling.

Eight out of ten married men said the only sex life they had was answering questionnaires. Some were ashamed of answering question- naires. 'All the guys do it,' one man wrote, 'but as a topic of conversation when the talk turns to sex, questionnaire filling is definitely a no no.' This man, a liberated male, shocked his work- mates on the building site when he admitted, during a luncheon bull session, that he and his wife actually filled out questionnaires together!

How do you feel about the Hite Report?

'I was told you could go blind reading the *Hite Report* and so I guess I'll just read it until I only need glasses.'

'*Is there something wrong with the English language or have I merely been reading too many American sex surveys?*'

'Hello,' I said, 'do you want orgasm?'
'I got orgasm.'
'Gimme orgasm.'
'My girl wants orgasm. Where do I buy orgasm? Or can I just borrow orgasm like a book from the library?'
'Dear Miss Hite, Who is this guy Orgasm that my girl is always saying she wants? Whoever he is he is spoiling my life. What kind of a name is that anyway? Don't sound American to me. Sounds like some kind of goddamn Greek.'

The Sex Problems of the Macho Male

'I am a nice-looking guy, I am two hundred pounds and real macho. I am young. I've still got my figure. I want to put my leathers on and go out and flirt but all she wants to do is sit round filling out questionnaires.'

The Acceptable Face of Pornography

Young persons starting out in life have often asked me, 'How do I become a pornographer?' Anyone can become a pornographer. But to be a pornographer and stay out of the magistrates court is the big one. Do you want to write a best- seller with lots of words like 'erection' and 'titties' and 'bummy' and not have to sink to the level of thinking up some sort of lousy goddamn plot like it was *Forever Amber* or *Lady Chat- terley's Lover* or something infra dig like that goddamn Harold Robbins, with lots of boring dialogue and really passé stuff like character- building and the lousy goddamn weather and all that sort of degrading work a novelist has to go in for? Of course you don't. Who would? What you want instead is a sex survey. Yes, the sex survey is the acceptable face of pornography. It has got all the rude words and lots of dandy descriptions like, 'She was quivering all over and moaning like a bitch,' or, 'Cor, blimey, Guvnor, I never seen such a big one,' just like one of those tacky big best-selling novels and yet it still somehow has got class. For why? Well might you ask. Because of science. And not just science but social science. This is sociology and that, sister, is the gimmick which will keep you out of the police court, while being more filthy than Henry Miller ever dreamed of.

Hurry now. There still is time to get in on the sex survey before they all twig and we have to go back to thinking up 'her nipple grew taut with passion' and all that sort of stuff for ourselves instead of getting the punters to do it for us with the old questionnaire.

How do you feel about publishing sex surveys?

Nine out of ten publishers said although they were quite shy about it at first and didn't like talking about it, not even to their wives, after they saw the sales they realised that publishing sex surveys was a healthy, constructive, positive thing to do.

'I mean,' said Publisher X, 'how many times can you publish Jane Austen? I published Jane Austen about three or four times and, well, it got rather samey, and – and although I really feel embarrassed saying this and would not dare say it if this were not an anonymous questionnaire – I used to fantasize, while publishing, say, *Pride and Prejudice* or *Sense and Sensibility*, that I was actually publishing *The Tropic of Cancer* or even

Last Exit To Brooklyn. Boy, I was so inhibited then that I never even dared dream that some day I would be publishing a sex survey. Wow! Ha ha. It sure seems funny to look back on it now.'

Do you ever feel kind of tacky publishing all this S. Hite?

'I'm awfully glad you asked that, Stan, and I am proud to answer it in the spirit it was meant. There is nothing tacky about a sex survey. There is, in fact, something uplifting, almost spiritual, about the sex survey. People may jeer on street corners in their smutty way but ever since we published our first best-selling sex survey I find that there is something sacred about it. And, after all, remember the sex survey is something people do, not sneakily in the sordid little privacy of their own homes, but right out there in public print.'

What about all that money changing hands, doesn't that make you feel like a goddamn pimp?

'I don't think the act of publishing is debased by the mere fact that money changes hands. There is something sacred and beautiful about publishing, about all publishing. I am even into publishing for children and, yes, for the elderly too. Publishing is beautiful. All publishing is beautiful. Before you start condemning publishing just because money changes hands, visit our insane asylums and prisons, look at the graffiti on our walls.'

What about the appalling, pushy ratbags who write these sex surveys, don't you ever feel ashamed dealing with them?

'All authors cannot be drunken geniuses like F. Scott Fitzgerald or weirdos like Franz Kafka. There is no reason why an author cannot be a pushy dame. Sure, she may be the type of broad who if she was caught in adultery would catch the first stone and throw it back, but the sex survey is the front line and before you condemn these pushy dames, visit our prisons, visit our insane asylums. And what's the use of publishing Fitzgerald and Kafka? They only let you down, they keep on drinking or coughing themselves to death on you. You won't catch a pushy

dame coughing herself to death, not on 15% plus residuals.'

Is there a future for the sex survey in Britain today?

'I'm glad you asked me that, Stan. Frankly, since I've been in Britain I've been looking for surveys to publish but all I see are these things commissioned by the National Health and Ken Livingstone all about old people freezing to death and starving to death and, frankly, I don't think that is much of a turn-on. I mean, if that stuff about old people being cold and hungry turns you on, I mean, well, I feel sorry for the UK because that is, I'm sorry to say this, Stan, a bit sick. Now if the National Health and Ken Livingstone could only commission some surveys about old people having a real and positive and very on-going and beautiful sex life, I mean – and especially with pictures – you have a market area there which could very well be explored. But an old couple simply freezing to death is definitely what I like to call, Stan, pretty iffy.'

Stanley Reynolds 7.10.1981

'I've noticed that these days the only time you ever talk to me is when you're filling in a personality quiz.'

'I thought you knew I'm on a research fellowship.'

THE FACTS
OF LIFE

A Short Story

'It is time,' said my grandmother, 'that the boy knew.'

I looked up from my jigsaw. I was ready for distractions. *The Boyhood of Raleigh* in one thousand two hundred and fifty pieces, and after three afternoons I had just this minute discovered that the sailor's finger had been missing from the start.

My grandmother was sitting rocking in the rocking chair with her back to us. It was an hour this side of Horlicks, and September, and outside the French window the sun was shining on the begonias. My grandmother should have been reading aloud the births and deaths and marriages and for sale. She liked to sit with the newspaper smooth across her lap, an apron of gossip, feeding us with titbits. Occasionally my mother would cluck her tongue when my grandmother's tone changed for a name or a price, but I don't think she was ever really listening.

'Ten,' said my grandmother. 'It is old enough.'

Perhaps they were not begonias, those flowers. I liked the word, though, and still do, though now I think it is a funny word, and then I

didn't. To my young ear, it sounded like a beginning, or something a pale but animated girl might play upon the piano, having to cross her hands for the difficult bits. My grandmother had strict opinions about flowers. When, a little later, I wrote a sonnet about the Greek boy who fell in love with his own reflection, she insisted upon referring to it as my poem about the narcissi. She called the flowers begonias that grew outside the window, and so begonias they were. My grandmother, a widow, was a woman of character.

'When *my* Robert was ten he had sailed to Valparaiso.'

And had been up the topmast three times, I thought.

'And been up the topmast three times,' said my grandmother, rocking. 'In a storm,' she added, and I had not thought of that.

My mother knitted and said nothing. Her eyes were fixed upon the open-heart operation on the television. The Woodbine trembled on her lower lip. No doubt she thought that my grandmother was still reading aloud from the *Southend Standard*. I felt down the back of the sofa for the missing finger. The rocking chair stopped rocking.

'So tell me,' said my grandmother, 'what steps you intend to take.'

Interference zigzagged across our TV screen, spoiling my mother's pleasure in the first incision, making her drop a stitch. 'That Freeman's got his Black and Decker out again,' she said. 'It ought to be suppressed.' She was a quiet woman, my mother, but she took a close interest in televised surgery. She retrieved her stitch. 'Steps?' she said.

'His father,' said my grandmother. 'It would come better from him, wouldn't it? A thing like that.'

My mother averted her gaze from what Mr Freeman's Black and Decker drill was doing to the flesh upon the operating table. She looked at my grandmother. I had seen these looks before. 'Daddy,' she said, nodding so that the cigarette snowed ash down upon her knitting. 'The best course by far.'

And so it was that the following Friday, after supper, my father put on his hat and took me out for a walk. This, I may say, struck me as unusual even at that time. In the first place, my father was not often to be seen with a hat on his head, on account of his dandruff treatment. In the second place, I could not recall that he had ever taken me for a walk before, not even when he came home from the war and my grandmother told me that we had won. I remember, to be fair, that he did give me a whole bar of milk chocolate, but he did not take me for a walk on that occasion.

It was a very long walk indeed. We went down Valkyrie Drive and along Westcliff Avenue and Prittlewell Avenue and Thorpe Bay Avenue and then up Chalkwell Park Road and right round the park including the cricket pitch and the putting green and the Garden of Remembrance. I cannot remember thinking anything in particular, except how proud I ought to be to be out walking with my father, and how glad I was that it was not raining and that none of my friends had seen us. Here we are, I thought to myself, a son and his father out walking on a fine Friday evening in September, man to man, stride for stride, just like *Life with the Lyons* or Abraham and Isaac or any normal family. When we had circumvented the cricket pitch and came to the Garden of Remembrance I added to this thought the observation that the sun was shining on the begonias. They were probably real begonias in the Garden of Remembrance, because I had heard my grandmother complimenting Old Smiley the park-keeper on the display and he had not denied it.

My father said nothing at all on the outward journey, but on the way back he took a deep breath in Chalkwell Park Road and cleared his throat in Thorpe Bay Avenue and Prittlewell Avenue and then again in Westcliff Avenue. All up Valkyrie Drive he was clearing his throat and taking deep breaths as if for a conversation, but it was not for a conversation, it was for athletics because abruptly as we drew level with the monkey puzzle tree in the garden of 46 he quickened his stride. I quickened my stride too. My father looked at me balefully out of the corner of his eye. He managed to add another inch to his stride as we got to the garages. He goose-stepped, in fact, all fleeing and flinging arms and legs, down Cranleigh Road, in the direction of our house. I broke into a trot, then sprinted, trying to keep up with him. It was no use. He burst away from me. His hat fell off and rolled in the gutter but he did not stop. He was a lamppost ahead when he reached our garden gate and headed up the path for the pink front door.

Before my father could get the key from his trouser pocket, the door opened. It was my grandmother. She had a carpet beater in her hand. She took one look at the two of us. We stopped in our tracks – or, to be precise, I stopped in my father's tracks, holding out his hat as though that would explain everything, while he stood gangling, shifting from foot to foot, gazing up critically at the roof as though he expected a tile to fall.

My grandmother called softly to my mother over her shoulder:

'He hasn't told him.'

'Listen,' said my father. 'Wait.'

My grandmother took one step forward and my father took two steps back.

'You tell him,' she said, 'Don't you dare bring that boy back till you've told him.' She slapped her side with the carpet beater. 'It's time he knew,' she said. 'When your father was his age he'd been round Cape Horn.' She turned and went into the house and slammed the door shut. Three times, I thought. 'Twice,' she screeched through the letterbox.

With a weary but manful sigh, my father turned and took his hat from my hand. He dusted it and put it on his head. Then he went to look at his reflection in the front room window to make sure that the hat was on straight. But my mother and grandmother were standing there behind the lace curtains waiting and watching, so my father spun round and grabbed me by the ear and then off we went away down Valkyrie Drive again.

I had less pleasure in the walking now. The sun had gone behind a cloud. In Prittlewell Avenue a fat man with no shirt on was snipping at his hedge with a pair of shears and the smell of the privet got up my nose and made me sneeze on and off all the way to the park. My father grunted and walked daintily. I think he was pretending that this sniffing, sneezing, long-legged brat in wide white shorts had nothing to do with him. For my part, I felt guilty. Whatever it was that my father was supposed to tell me no longer seemed important. What was important was that it was now getting too late for his game of brag at my uncle Oswald's. My father had not missed his Friday brag at uncle Oswald's since the night when the chimney caught fire, and here he was having to miss it because he was out walking me round the streets of Southend-on-Sea because my grandmother would not let us in until he had told me.

If I had been a cleverer boy I would have suggested that we called it a day, and that we both retired to uncle Oswald's for a game of brag. As it was, I shuffled and snuffled unhappily around the putting green in my father's wake, wishing that I had a handkerchief.

'Blow your nose,' he said, and then he started mumbling.

'Beg pardon?' I said.

'Blow your nose,' he said.

'No, not that,' I said, 'the other.'

We had reached the Garden of Remembrance, with its stone that said that They would not grow old as we that were left grew old, and that at the going down of the sun and in the morning we would remember Them. I knew who They were. My grandfather who had maybe been to Valparaiso and Cape Horn, before he was my age, had without doubt been to Ypres and not come back, before my father was born. He was gassed and he was dead in No Man's Land, my grandfather, before he even knew that his wife was going to have a baby.

I wiped my nose on the back of my hand. 'I haven't got a hankie,' I explained.

My father looked at me. Then he fumbled in his pocket and produced his own handkerchief. He unfolded it with care. Tears started to my eyes. My father blew his nose and stuffed the handkerchief back where it had come from.

'You'll go mad,' he said. 'You'll go mad and all your teeth will rot and your hair will fall out so that everyone will *know* and you'll end up dribbling in a wheel chair.'

'Beg pardon?' I said.

My father fixed his gaze on the going down of the sun. 'I speak of excess,' he said. '*Excess.*' He paused. His face shone. Under the brim of the squashed hat his eyes were blazing hot. A butterfly settled on his lapel. 'The damned thing,' he said, 'is unavoidable.' The butterfly warmed its wings on his brown serge. My father's hand came up tremblingly as if to touch it. I held my breath. I had never seen anyone stroke a butterfly, and

my father was not a great stroker of any kind. If he strokes this creature, I thought to myself, I will *really* believe about God and the Virgin Mary, and Spike Langdon's dad and the au pair girl.

My father flexed his right forefinger against his thumb and flicked the butterfly into the begonias. '*Don't touch it!*' he hissed. 'That's all I have to say after a lifetime of experience.' He shut his burning eyes, and swayed on the balls of his feet. 'I found tennis some help,' he confided, 'when I was your age.' He opened one eye. 'Always remember,' he said, 'it takes as much out of a man as three hard sets played in the midday sun.'

I was impressed. All the way back along Westcliff Avenue and Valkyrie Drive I thought about what my father had said. When we passed the monkey puzzle tree, I said, 'Dad.'

'Enough,' said my father.

'Yes,' I said. 'But –'

My father jammed his hat down over his ears and fell upon the garden gate like a Roman soldier falling upon his sword.

'But no buts,' he cried.

He swept past my mother and my grandmother in the hallway.

'Now he knows,' he said.

My grandmother looked at me. My mother looked at my grandmother. My grandmother looked away. 'No, he doesn't,' she said.

'Look, he wouldn't listen,' said my father, leaning on the banisters. 'I tried to tell him, but he wouldn't listen.'

My shoe lace was undone. I wanted to say that I was sorry, but the word wouldn't come out, so I did up my shoe lace instead.

'He just kept sniffing,' explained my father.

My grandmother shook her head. She looked at my mother. My mother looked at me.

'We know you don't know,' my mother said grandly, taking the Woodbine from her mouth. 'You don't know and you don't want to know. Well, now you'll never know. You'll go through life and you'll never know. And that's an end of it.'

It wasn't.

Robert Nye 11.10.1978

No point teaching children something unless there's an exam at the end of it, is there?

GENERAL CERTIFICATE OF EDUCATION

June 1971

Ordinary Level

SEX

Three hours   (Questions 1 and 2 are compulsory. Answer TWO others. Be gentle.)

1. *Read the following passage carefully, and answer the questions below:*

When the ****** descends on the *********** the pressure within the ******* is rapidly reduced; also, as the ***** ****** past the sideways position, the leverage is reduced so that, beyond a certain point, little useful *** is being done. Advantage is taken to increase ********* by arranging for the ****** to open before the **** reaches bottom dead centre, so that the remaining pressure assists in expelling the ****** from the ******. The latter process is known as **********. Finally, in order to encourage the rapid influx of fresh *******, the ******* is opened before the end of the ******** stroke, so that the outgoing **** of ******* creates a follow through effect. To complete the *******, the ****** is not closed until a little after top dead centre. It will be noted that for a short period both **** and ****** are open simultaneously, and this is known as **** overlap. The ***** and ***** are shaped to reduce the tendency for the incoming **** to escape via the ******.

   (i) How does the author keep up your interest?
   (ii) What influences, literary or otherwise, can you trace in the style?
   (iii) Can you fill in the asterisks?
   (iv) Does the passage now seem an accurate account?
   (v) Could you describe it in your own words?
   (vi) Would you be surprised to learn that it was taken from *The Penguin Car Handbook*, p. 34?
   (vii) Why?

2. Write an essay of not more than five hundred words on ONE of the following:
   (i) What I did in the holidays *OR* What I'm going to have to do about it.
   (ii) A bird in the hand is worth two in the bush.
   (iii) "Choose thou whatever suits the line: call me Sappho!" (S. T. Coleridge)
   (iv) "Pat-a-cake, pat-a-cake, baker's man,
   Bake me a cake as fast as you can;
   Pat it, and prick it, and mark it with B,
   Put it in the oven for baby and me!"
   (v) My favourite form mistress *OR* My favourite mistress's form.

3. "Oscar Wilde was a great writer but a bad queen." Discuss.

4. According to Macaulay, Catherine the Great of Russia frequently entertained young subalterns on the sideboard. Will you draw the sideboard, and answer any THREE of the following by marking the details on your sketch?
   (i) When the Seven Years' War broke out on August 29, 1756, what was Catherine the Great's position?
   (ii) Do you consider her to have been too close to the bookcase?
   (iii) Was the candlestick a "heroic gesture that all but succeeded" (Brückner) or a "tactical error of the first magnitude" (Waliszewski)?
   (iv) When Vasili Mirovitch attempted to restore the imprisoned emperor Ivan VI in 1764, how did Catherine come between them?
   (v) How often?
   (vi) Where was the fifth riding-boot, and whose was it?

5. Answer any TWO of the following:
   (i) Tom is taller than Maureen, but shorter than Mary. Mary is shorter than Arthur, but thinner than Jim. Freda is fatter than Jim, but taller than Tom or Arthur or Eric. Eric is twice as fat as Mary, but shorter than Freda or Horace. Horace prefers Jim to Maureen, but Maureen prefers Arthur and Eric to Tom. Tom prefers May to Freda, but Eric to Maureen. Jim is left-handed. Draw a diagram in which everyone in bed is happy.
   (ii) Two vans are approaching one another. Van A is travelling at 30 mph, van B is travelling at 45 mph, and the vans are nine miles apart. In the back of van A are Maurice and Beryl, who normally reach a satisfactory conclusion after 8 minutes 7 seconds. In the back of van B are Herbert and Winifred, who normally take 6 minutes 8 seconds. What will be the distance between the two vans when
   (a) Maurice and Beryl finish?
   (b) Herbert and Winifred finish?
   (iii) Edward is fifteen years younger than his father, but two years older than his sister and one year younger than his twin brothers. The sum of the ages of their mothers is the same as the age of their paternal grandfather, which is two-and-a-half times that of their father. How old is their father?

6. Find the odd man out in the following groups, illustrating, where necessary, the reasons for your choice:
   (i) Troilus and Cressida; Dido and Aeneas, Abelard and Eloise: Mr. and Mrs. Jilly Cooper.
   (ii) T. E. Lawrence; T. E. Shaw; J. H. Ross; Peter O'Toole.
   (iii) Parkinson's Disease; Reiter's Syndrome; Bell's Palsy; Portnoy's Complaint; Todd's Paralysis.

'Not tonight! I've got a headache!'

'No! No! She fended him off again . . . Now he's gone to sleep.'

'God! How I hate Sunday afternoons!'

WHEREFORE ART THOU RONEO?

Discord in the office and declining productivity figures could be the result of office romances, according to researchers from Strathclyde Business School.

Daily Telegraph

Dear Sirs,

We thank you for your DHL/BS of the 16th inst re your valued order No. H/40639/14 for Qty 2,000 Type B-000001 Item 664/239/C118 in dull metal, and regret non-delivery of same due to our computer being down and our inability to concentrate on our work, relax, sleep or keep anything down.

We note your esteemed proposal to gas your good self in the event of the lady to whom your DHL/BS was dictated not undertaking to desist seeing that Customer Accounts executive identified by your Firm's reference RNA/BS on the evenings you are unable to borrow your Staff Welfare office reference GHN/TD's little pad in Ebury Street, and would now cordially extend our gratitude for the favour of past custom.

Whilst appreciating the urgency of your requirements and assuring you that we are fully cognisant that the Qty 2,000 Type standard fitting Item 664/239/B262s already despatched in a happier accounting period than the current one are useless without the Qty 2,000 Item 664/239/C118 as indented for, we regret that we are not in a position to give the matter our immediate attention as requested, as we are sick with worry.

As previously advised in our GN/DP of the 29th ult, we are Qty 100 times more than we have ever been before Type head over heels Item in love, the object of these affections being the latter portion of the above-quoted reference. We would advise you that this is not simply infatuation as was the case in respect of our reference on correspondence previous to that date, namely GN/TC, but the real thing.

We regret to inform you, however, that the personage herein identified has, subsequent to our taking your esteemed Company into our confidence on this matter, become enamoured of one of our junior management personnel in Invoice Processing. Our LNT/DP of the 7th inst in response to your esteemed colleague's RNA/BS of the 5th inst, wherein attention is drawn by the signatory to the pouting lips and upwardly tilting breasts of the combination of initials under discussion, refers. Nevertheless, we wish to stress that notwithstanding the distaff side of our reference driving us mad by flaunting her LNT/DP liaison all over the above premises, that is not in itself the reason why we have not drawn a sober breath since the 6th inst.

With reference to your DHL/LB accompanying your original order, we regret our failure to acknowledge same owing to the indisposition at that time of the second half of our then reference GN/TC, who had gone home in tears. Continued non-acknowledgement of your communication was the consequence of acute apprehension on the part of the undersigned while awaiting further developments subsequent to a statement by the TC portion of the aforementioned reference to the GN portion of same, to the effect that something which should have happened had not happened.

It should be realised that by the date under discussion, following upon a programme of office reorganisation whereby a system of pooled secretaries came into being, our previously sole reference GN/TC was now regularly alternating with GN/DP as above, and the writer of this letter had fallen hook, line and sinker for the reference differential just quoted. Learning of the affair via a photocopy of our GN/DP to Messrs Farley, Speight and Drummond dated the 28th ult which was circulating throughout this department, the TC half of our previous reference, out of sheer spite, point-blank refused to attend a clinic for tests until such time as we should have washed our hands of the DP segment of our subsequent reference. This, it must be stated, is despite the undersigned having gone down on bended knees to implore her to stop playing silly buggers and expedite matters before it is too late.

Meanwhile, having learned of her colleague's possible condition via the file copy of a routine inter-office memo to Personnel seeking morning sickness leave which an anonymous mischief-maker (we suspect our typing pool's part-reference /MD, who is going through a mid-life crisis after the breakdown of her long-standing affair with RTN/ of Bills Inward) had pinned to the notice-board, the only reference we have ever loved went berserk, severing our GN/DP relationship for all but office correspondence purposes, and at once throwing herself headlong into the LNT/DP connection mentioned in a previous paragraph.

The recipient of this communication might imagine that this development would have had a stabilising effect on our reference GN/TC, in that now that the GN/DP combination was effectively severed as demanded by her before consenting to attend the clinic, the lady in question would have been willing to resolve the anxieties which have led to the non-fulfilment of your esteemed order No. H/40639/14. Not a bit of it. Herself having had a mad, passionate

'Why can't I get married in the firm's time? I got pregnant in the firm's time!'

LNT/TC understanding prior to her disastrous involvement with the undersigned the stupid hysterical bitch quoted in our erstwhile reference GN/TC is now threatening to throw herself in the river, having first typed a memo to the coroner accusing the present half of the said reference of having put her in the Club.

Therefore, whilst sympathising with the problems created by the shortfall in our delivery of goods ordered, as well as with the unfortunate personal situation summarised in your DHL/BS above, we would impress upon you the realisation that if you think you have got troubles you do not know you are born.

Referring to the penultimate paragraph of your DHL/LB under discussion, we note that you seek our opinion, without prejudice, as to whether you should leave Mrs DHL and set up an establishent under the reference DHL/BS, if she will have you. Unfortunately, as manufacturers of components for the trade and not agony aunties, we do not feel we have the specialist knowledge to deal with this query. However, informally as between business acquaintances of long standing, we would remind you of our Buying Dept's NPR/JDV of January 21 last, which you may recollect was in pornographic verse, with particular reference to NPR/JDV thrashing about on a bed. A copy of this letter having been posted anonymously to Mrs NPR – again, the aforementioned twisted soul/MD is suspected – that lady came down to the present premises unexpectedly, where she discovered NPR/JDV *in flagrante delicto* in the first aid room – a location, be it said, for the proximity of which the personnel involved were to be duly grateful by the time Mrs NPR had finished separating their initials.

In response to your enquiry, therefore, we would draw your attention to the couplet reference Congreve/Mourning Bride III viii:
Heav'n has no rage, like love to hatred turn'd,
Nor Hell a fury, like a woman scorn'd, and would advise continuing the relationship DHL/BS as constituted, omitting any cross-reference to Mrs DHL.

Finally, noting that the reference DHL/LB has been appearing ever more frequently on correspondence emanating from your department subsequent to the deterioration of your esteemed relationship DHL/BS as first outlined in the PS to your self-billing VAT invoice 23906/85 of December 19 last, we trust that you are not proposing to make the same mistake as the undersigned and get emotionally involved with one reference before you have satisfactorily disentangled your good self from the other, otherwise you truly will have something to put your head in the gas oven for.

Assuring you of our best attention at all times, we remain, yours &c &c &c.

Keith Waterhouse 8.1.1986

'To be honest, Mr Grand, this isn't at all what I expected.'

'God, I hate being treated as a sex object.'

'Greedy!'

'Him and Miss Edthorpe, they don't
care **who** sees them!'

'I can't decide what to wear for the office party.'

TAKING OFF

Ever since the Casino de Paris in Denman Street closed the art of striptease has been in a parlous state.

Salomes with their eyes on classier things than a five-minute flash at a Hen and Stag Gala or a beat-the-clock race between El Sexy Show and the Paradise Club are left with a choice of the Nell Gwynne in Dean Street or Raymond's Revuebar. Even Paul Raymond, however, is feeling the draught.

'It's more and more difficult to find good acts,' he declared recently. 'Italian girls, Chinese girls, French girls, yes. But where are the English girls? They don't seem to know what their bodies are for.' It was to meet this national crisis that a small film company called Amarant Productions Ltd decided to mount and shoot *The Great British Striptease Festival* in Blackpool ten days ago.

The venue was an intimate aircraft hangar in the Norbreck Castle Hotel. Here, three hundred members of the public were served with a Burlesque Burger and a Bombe Titti Bombe ice cream, and invited to select the winner, who received a cash prize of £500.

On the afternoon before the contest the sixteen entrants sat slouched on stools knocking back vodka to give them Dutch courage while Amarant productions – a troupe of swarthy young men from minor public schools wearing trick T-shirts – cannoned into each other with requests to 'take it from the top'. Five of the girls had never stripped before and talked darkly of making a break for it while there was still time.

'Have another drink,' one of the producers urged.

'I don't call this showbiz,' said a stoat-faced Liverpudlian blonde. 'I bet they don't realise I was one of Ken Dodd's Diddy Men in 1971.'

The original concept for the film was a wholly amateur contest but as successive Blackpool housewives flunked out, Amarant talent scouts combed the country for the crème de la crème of striptease talent. These included two Page Three girls from the *Sun*, a topless waitress from Blackpool's Gladray Club, a fire-eater from Soho, an apprentice motorbike mechanic and a Miss Brighton who on closer investigation was suspected to be Miss Hove. In addition to this first division there was a clutch of bleached blondes with knee-length breasts and miscellaneous glamour models (*Penthouse, Knave, Hustler, Fiesta*) two of whom had such graveyard coughs the compere offered to throw them a raw fish. Rumour had it that the one with the bubble cut and the vaccination mark was really a feller. 'Why else should she do the splits *over* that feather boa?' conjectured the topless waitress. The most attractive of the bunch was the motorbike mechanic, an eighteen-year-old with waist-length blonde hair, breasts like cupcakes and a bolshy behind she rotated at the camera. The previous day she had been fined for indecent exposure at a rock concert. 'I'm doing this strictly for political reasons,' she told a cameraman with a castrating smile, 'So up yours, mister.'

The press were discouraged from attending rehearsals. 'It's a low budget movie that'll be bags of fun without exploiting the girls,' another of the producers explained as the camera zoomed in for a crotch shot of a knicker-whirling French maid. On the day of the contest, however, *The Sun*, the *Daily Mirror* and *People* were allowed in. After a brief conclave round a couple of stroppy blondes, they sped off in a shower of dandruff to report the Girls Did Not Know They Had to Strip Scandal.

'Ladies and Gentlemen,' the compere intoned to the empty hall, 'welcome to the Great British Strip Festival. We've got a very mixed bag here tonight. And here she is, Miss Peaches on Regalia.'

'Couldn't she do anything with her hair?' the director appealed, 'She looks as if she's run under a low bridge.'

'It's a small budget movie that aims to be lighthearted but wholesome entertainment,' a third producer told me as he disappeared with a frisky forty-five-year-old in a school uniform.

In the dressing room the talk was all of the rigours of the Go-go life. The topless waitress had just returned from a dancing stint in Iran where her passport was confiscated, she was locked in her room every night to prevent her from escaping, and her salary consisted of a whip-round with a bottle. 'Nothing wrong with that,' commented a Germanic blonde 'You just say, "Give us a fiver or I'll smash your face in." They soon cough up.'

'Not in Iran,' said the Go-go dancer. 'We only kept 75 pee out of £10 anyway and then we had to do a private show afterwards for the manager of the club.' The Gladray to which she had thankfully returned was Blackpool's first topless bar. 'But I wasn't the first topless waitress,' she assured me. 'That was Gloria. She's doing a live sex show now in Amsterdam.' An envious silence fell.

By the evening of the contest it had taken a fresh crate of Scotch to prevent mutiny in the ranks. There was an unexpectedly large audience turn-out, most of whom had not realised that their view of the stage would be obstructed by a crane-sized camera, a stills photographer and myself. I was on the verge of a punch-up when I discovered that the splayed nose suggesting I move myself elsewhere was none other than retired boxer Brian London.

'Now now, don't let's make an 'amburger out of it,' soothed his friend, a scrap metal dealer wearing a knuckle-duster of signet rings, but by this time the whole audience was restive and out of hand.

The show was a success. 'There's not an artiste among them,' the scrap metal dealer slurred as his eyes riveted on the two Page Three girls churning arhythmically round the podium ecstatically as a ferocious brunette, just back from a gruelling Go-go gig in Jakarta, wielded her G-string with a baleful stare.

A black model from the Seychelles collected the most cat-calls. Her slinky cool and appendix scar were well set off by the Go-go dancer who swung her bathrobe about and did a strenuous Can-Can. The black girl won. 'We don't see many darkies in the buff up here,' the scrap dealer explained with a deprecating smile.

Afterwards, the French maid and the schoolgirl entered into a business transaction with a stag party of visiting Arabs, the two blondes had a date with cocktail waiters in their room and the motorbike mechanic squeezed her high breasts into a tight T-shirt and said, 'It was about bloody time they had a union.'

It was one a.m. when the last of the producers took the lift up to the hotel suite where the wine flowed fast into the small hours. 'It will be,' he told me, 'a low-budget upbeat movie which proves the art of stripping isn't dead.'

Tina Brown 4.10.1978

'I didn't pay good money to come here and look for contact lenses!'

'Gone are the days when a double first led straight
to a plum job in Whitehall.'

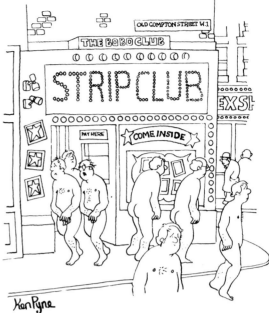

'To be honest, I was expecting something slightly different.'

'OH, FREDERICK, ISN'T THERE SOME PLACE
WHERE THERE ARE FEWER FISH?'

IT'S LOVE THAT MAKES THE RAIN COME DOWN

What men or gods are these?' cried Keats to his Grecian urn: 'What maidens loth? What mad pursuit? What struggle to escape?'

What struggle to escape, indeed. The maidens are obviously far from loth, and aren't escaping at all, merely beating a temporary tactical retreat.

After all, if they're not there for a spot of jolly rustic rape, what *are* they there for – skipping winsomely about like that in the undergrowth, draped in bits of ill-fitting scarf, bared bosoms bouncing about like beanbags? Clearly such saucy misses were always hanging about in Arcady waiting for some godling to ride by, or even a herd of corpulent satyrs to come thundering out through the olive grove with twigs in their hair and bunches of grapes dangling about their privates.

No, the maidens' anxious glances obviously are not directed at their pursuing lovers, but at the terrain: any minute now, if they don't pick up speed, they'll be flung down in some nettle-patch or bit of dank bog and used as a sex-object-cum-lilo – and too bad they didn't quite make it to that cosy patch of ant-free moss ahead where they'd planned to sink prettily to earth in strategic surrender.

It's about time really that the liberated nymphs of the seventies turned rapist in order to avenge woman's centuries of ordeal by alfresco sex. Womanhood must now wheel around and leap off in hot pursuit of yelping lovers as they scamper desperately over cow-pat and thistle, felling them with neat karate chops and seeing how much *they* fancy being ravished in a gorse bush for a change.

Of course, you could reach some kind of compromise by suggesting the use of a ground-sheet – although such a measure tends to be viewed with lofty contempt as being yet another, typically feminine attempt to destroy the essential spontaneity of outdoor eroticism. Moreover, it's a direct attack on his virility: how dare you *even* suggest that being impaled on a bramble bush could materially diminish your ecstasy once he's treated you to the full splendours of his sexual technique?

Back home in Barons Court, your feller may well have been mugging up on the secrets of the 143 positions received under plain brown cover, but let him come within sniffing distance of meadow or copse and you can forget all about that: as far as Man is concerned, Woman's sexual position in the great bug-filled, horsefly-haunted outdoors is always, quite literally, inferior. A chap feels so much safer that way . . .

I once had a boyfriend whose principal erotic ambition was to make love naked in the snow. I was to peel down like a grape glacée, but he'd be all togged up as usual, snug as a bug in his Lillywhites' oiled socks, ski-boots, string vest, fair-isle woollies, long coms, y-fronts, stretch pants, furry mitts, anorak, pompon hat and goggles.

Okay, I said sourly I'd do it, but only if he took off his clothes as well. He found the suggestion profoundly lewd: 'Me? Take off my *clothes*! Who

do you think I *am*? And besides', he added in pained reproof: 'You *know* I get chilblains.'

I retorted rudely that *my* joints would play up something horrid once he'd deepfrozen me into the Eigergletscher, and how about *that* lover-boy? and he retorted sulkily that I wasn't very romantic was I, no imagination, in fact down-right *frigid* he'd say. And I yapped back that I certainly *would* be frigid if I went in for many such Sex-on-Ice Spectaculars, and he said very funny, ha, ha, and eventually went off, mascu-line modesty still intact, and found himself a massive Finn who simply adored roguishly romp-ing about in snowdrifts while being beaten on her big pink botty with a birch-twig . . .

If snow is nasty, beaches are nastier. There's nothing less passion-provoking than lying prone in the freezing spume, with seaweed making rubbery squawks and pops beneath you and little sudsy waves playfully filling your eardrums with gritty foam and rendering you deaf as a post for hours. You emerge rubbed raw, beaten flat and encrusted with sand like some jumbo-sized wienerschnitzel ready bread-crumbed for the pan.

In fact sand is highly inimical to enjoyable sex. One girlfriend of mine, having reached the age of twenty-five, got bored hanging around Saving Herself for Mr Right, and decided to go on holiday to pick herself the sexiest Mr Wrong she could find.

She lit upon a Spanish squid fisherman called Miguel – who surged about in the gigolo's regula-tion crotch-strangling jeans, raking every female under ninety with his fierce, steaming glances – and decided she'd have to surrender her All to him on the beach, since that's where he seemed to spend his life when he wasn't actually out at sea, or under it, or surging profitably in and out of wealthy widows' bedrooms.

The experience was horrendous and she swears she's been right off sand, and virtually off sex, ever since.

Boats aren't much better than beaches. Small boats have skittish ways and tend to tip you both into the harbour oil-slicks, more often than not in full view of shrieking boat-loads of unspeak-able schoolboys with braces on their teeth. Large boats are generally better – although it does rather depend how many devotees of love-making under the stars are crammed on to any one boat at any one time.

I was once on a working cruise round the Adriatic islands with a bunch of randy travel-agents of both sexes who, swiftly awash with slivovic and freed from the pruderies of home life in Crouch End and Potter's Bar, paired off – and then spent the whole of the first night reluctantly playing Sardines en masse on deck.

All night long, the yacht rang with muted thumps and twangs and clonks as frustrated lovers softly ricocheted off steel ropes and anchor chains and fire-buckets, desperately hunting for a patch of unoccupied deck, occasionally uttering stifled grunts and hisses like 'Ouch!' and 'Oops!' and 'Muriel!' and 'Sorry old chap!' and 'What the hell . . .?' and '****!'

From below one could dimly hear them blundering about like a herd of blinded elk, and none of us on board got a wink of sleep that night, and judging by the uniformly filthy tempers of the star-crossed adulterers next morning, they'd not been able to get a wink of anything else either . . .

Incidentally, have you noticed how people still wax absurdly lyrical on the subject of outdoor sex in our rural past? One can still stumble across sentimental parlour-Rousseaus who'll bore you rigid with explanations about how all those lads and lasses having it off in haystacks were, in some primeval way, acting out folk memories of fertility rites among the ancient corn gods.

Actually I think they were always having it off in haystacks because it was more convenient than having it off at home – what with the place being full of cattle and pigs and hens having fits and the wimminfolk a-guttin' rabbits and the menfolk a-packin' dung and Grandma stickin' pins in wax dolls and some spavined cousin a-layin' of the hired girl behind the butter churn as usual.

Spirituality scarcely reared its pretentious head one suspects, in truly bucolic sex: you got yourself a good woman if she had all her own teeth, proved to be good breeding stock by dropping a lusty son every nine months – and then stoutly shaking her skirts and going straight back to work again, bashing beets and strangling chickens.

Idealisations of rustic lust were still being produced until relatively recently, largely by middle-aged litterateurs whose slim volumes on rural Venuses tended to be financed by Papa's liver-pill fortune or great-aunt's Brazilian holdings, and whose knowledge of nature was pretty well limited to what they saw out of train windows on day trips to Box Hill.

Oddly enough one *can* be made to feel dimly guilty about not liking sex out there under the skies, in the great embracing bosom of nature.

For after all, is one not Woman – whose great groundswell of spirit apparently answers to the ebb and flow of the seasons, whose blood is said to rise with the sap, wild calling to wild in the core of her being, whose soul they say lies deep-rooted among the burgeoning mysteries of bog-myrtle and bladderwort? Whose breasts are like the hills, whose eyes like stars, whose hair like tangled moonbeams; who's as capricious as the summer's day, and yet full of deep intuitive wisdom; the fleshly expression of the universal life-force from whose fecund loins springs the eternal Man-child . . . and all the rest of that Earth Mother codswallop.

And do you mean to tell me that this mighty mysterious spirit isn't keen on a bit of slap and tickle among the bog iris *merely* on account of it's cold and it's wet and the sea fog's rising?

Yes, I do.

Ann Leslie 16.6.1971

'The price they are these days, you wonder how she can go on affording footballers.'

'But I've **said** thank you.'

'You don't often see a real silk
lining, these days . . .'

WHERE IN THE WORLD CAN YOU LOVE A LOVER?

The best place for a broad is abroad, as any
professional bachelor will tell you, bringing out
his little black book, full of first names and
telephone numbers, supplied by his friendly
neighbourhood branch of Interpoke. But where
do you go, *together*?

What you need is somewhere which will
mirror your fantasies about each other. After all,
you have the characters for your charade. The
dialogue can be ad-libbed as you go along. The
plot is simple – boy gets girl – one act, in several
scenes, with lots of intervals. All you are looking
for is the correct back-drop.

It's not that the scenery at home is less
beautiful. But when all around you is strange,
new and unpeopled with memories, you stand
out more clearly as a couple. The lovers' illusion

that only you two are really real is easier to sustain there. You want a place where the camera eye can identify you as the stars as it pans across the crowd. The rest are just walk-ons, bit players, spear-carriers and rhubarb-rhubarb mutterers. With an occasional eccentric comedy-cameo role as taxi-driver, head waiter, carpet seller, rickshawman or police officer written into the script for a character actor to show off his heart of gold as he beams at the handsome couple you make.

So first of all, it is often advisable for you to find a spot where you only speak enough of the language to find your way (and get your way) and where you never overhear conversations more interesting than your own and your dialogues are never overheard even in a crowd. Bad linguists carry our own privacy with us everywhere.

For noises off, and light under the door, I like water. Mountains and forests and grassy slopes are all very well on picture postcards – indeed they soon become picture postcards, only the colours are less bright, the sunsets less original and the clouds not so operatic. Water provides the essential movement out of the corner of your eye, like a fire in a room. It is restless yet soothing. It gives you that cosy feeling that something is at work while you are doing nothing. And if it does spur you both to action, then it is likely to be the action you are after, the wish devoutly to be consummated.

The four settings for two that I recall most fondly are in France, Italy, the Lebanon and the Bahamas. The first, in Duclair, anyone can find in the *Michelin*. It has one rosette for food – but it should have three stars for its autumnal dinners on the wrought-iron terrace hanging out over a dark, lost garden, just four tables in the misted glow from the steamy kitchen window.

Serious lovers are always serious eaters – at least, mine are. And few things are more sexy than a pre-bed silence broken only by the heavy breathing and faint sighs of the diners, the clink of the bottles, the slurp of the glass, as the *pâté de canard* is slid aside after a third helping, and the fortifications of *moule* shells and *crevette* heads grow around each place setting.

And I would award a pink double-bed in any guide for those upstairs rooms where you sit next morning, propped against a pregnant pillow, warming your already warmed lap with a bowl of coffee-tinged milk and rustling-fresh *croissants*, while on the wall ahead, as on a giant home-movie screen, the window is filled with the image of the swiftly-sliding Seine and its noise-less traffic of cargo ships.

The second, in Venice, may seem more predictable but it comes far down in the Italian *Michelin* listing, among modest but acceptable *pensions* on the unfrequented side of the Grand Canal.

Ruskin lived here once and the food is appalling. But just round the corner is a *trattoria*, entered through a grotty bar, which opens out into one of those rare Venetian gardens, almost an orchard, where you sit under an awning of flowering trees, like Milton's Adam and Eve, while petals fall into your hair and *pasta* as a gentle, slow-motion snowstorm.

The bedroom has three windows, on two sides. At the foot, the vast, busy Giudecca, with its booming cruise liners. To the side, a narrow frothing waterway where beeping taxi-boats polish each other's paintwork as they just avoid collision at 25 m.p.h. It seems about as private and restful as a mattress perched below Eros in Piccadilly Circus. Until you close the shutters, laddered with sun-baked cracks, and the Venetian light, buffeted and bent by the sequin-scaled sea, projects on your ceiling a flickering, *camera-obscura*, panorama of the passing show.

The third place, Tyre in southern Lebanon, is on no one's list (except perhaps pinned to the wall of an Israeli operations room) – a crumbling, cavernous hotel, its taps pouring rust into cracked wash basins, its lavatories overflowing, its bathrooms simply cells with perforated pipes, holes in the floor, like decontamination chambers. And its public rooms empty *salons* with cracked glass roofs bending over a few scattered rugs and collapsing divans. It most nearly resembled an abandoned Crusader fort, lately camped in by a raiding party of the Golden Horde. We were the only guests and met no other visitors to the warren except a naked wandering Nubian.

But it backed onto a more populous open-air restaurant, by the side of Tyre's shallow harbour where waves occasionally lapped across the floor almost, if never quite, dowsing the diners' toes. Great spreads of saffron-yellow rice-and-shell-fish served by the light of candles guttering in the warm, spicy, night breeze. Strange fishes, with the lacy flapping wings of submarine butter-flies, lined up to watch us. The wine was laboratory alcohol, faintly flavoured with sweet red grape juice.

But all night long, under our windows, which lipped the Mediterranean like the breakwater of a lighthouse, the sea pounded and chewed a few feet from our unsleeping heads.

Tyre may have changed since then. Four years ago, we had returned from a newly-shelled Arab village on the border, where coffins still lay in the streets, pools of dried blood were relief maps in the market, sobbing women in black threw dust on their heads. The road back was criss-crossed with barricades, manned by guerillas with tommy guns and necklets of grenades. We passed lorry upon lorry of refugees, buried alive under furniture and chickens.

Death quickens sensuality. Loving couples seize upon places from which tourists have fled and inn-keepers open up for you alone, so long as you pay in advance, make your own bed, and demand no service. Something of the same feeling invests even seaside resorts out of season which also have that air of being deserted in advance of occupying troops, so conducive to instant intimacy and mutual dependence.

My fourth, the Bahamas, can provide that world-well-lost atmosphere at any time. Outside Nassau, where British exiles sit in their huge American cars, unable to drive more than 10 miles and 25 m.p.h. without falling off the edge, there are a thousand improbable islets. Each seems to be for sale in some part and you can be flown or sailed there, free, for a day of Crusoe seclusion with your hamper and bottles amid pantomime palms and sands.

But it is almost impossible to produce an exhaustive summary of bolt-holes for holidaying lovers. Often it is easier to be together in a modern hotel, even on the coach-tour circuit, especially if there is a Party conference or business convention, than in that forgotten back-water at the end of an unmade road where the locals eat strangers alive for a taste of company.

Remember the honeymoon couple who, when their friends cooed 'Ooh, it's lovely in Paris,' answered innocently – 'Ooh, it's lovely anywhere.' Even, I remember once, in the Strand Palace.

Alan Brien 30.1.1974

'Be a sport, Mr Gray – say you saw me ploddin' 'omeward.'

RITES OF SPRING

Spring is OK for snowdrops. After the long fight through the iron-hard ground, all they have to do is bloom and look beautiful. It's harder for the rest of us. There seems to be a venerable consensus of opinion about spring being the time when a young man's fancy, etc. etc. I wonder, in view of the recent Arctic temperatures, whether an enthusiastic tumble is not less to do with passion than with warmth, and furthermore, if man could emulate the animals he resembles and sleep away the long dark days of winter instead of being their painstaking witness and guardian, whether his sap wouldn't rise a little less desperately and a bit nearer home. The trouble, perhaps, is that the horrendous heating bills become confused with the image of his wife, a fairly effective antidote to connubial amity, and as a result, he'd rather expend his sap anywhere other than where it best belongs.

As a season, spring is about renewal and revitalisation. Too often, when used as a metaphor for human doings, it means starting again – and few things hit men worse than starting again, unless they're only ever starters, in which case they're stuck in a permanent state of never getting anywhere quite. No man really wants to have to start all over again. He doesn't mind a quick adventure down a by-way or an interlude in a cul-de-sac but once he's taken in everything of interest on the detour, he wants to come back to where he left off, on the main road. Starting all over again implies things lost more than gained, and I've never met a man who wanted to lose anything which might be for his comfort, regardless of season.

Spring wouldn't be such a risky business if it didn't follow winter. But the days have been long and cold and dark for so long that, come the first blast of warmth, we all shed garments like mad and become overwhelmingly aware of each other. It should be acknowledged at this point that there are two kinds of people in the world as far as spring is concerned – those who love it and those who hate it. Those who love it cling to it as the light at the end of winter's tunnel, aligning it in their minds with the return of life proper, green buds, fluffy animals and effulgent catkins. Those who hate it know it's even more of an endgame than winter was: cruel spring of high hopes and harsh light; sneaky spring, when men have flings and women walk out.

Part of the trouble has been the abandonment of our sensible pagan ways when the warm days of spring were the time for coupling in the furrows to encourage the crops. But, of course, you would be hard pushed to find a furrow in urban Britain and an office desk is not nearly so *simpatico*. And as the ice-cap extends, if you found a furrow, it would be freezing. Part of the trouble, too, is that few people of any sexual proclivity couple with simple warmth and transitory affection any more. Nowadays the act is fraught with the threat of unfriendly germs and analysis. Numbers have made everything more complicated than it used to be. But nobody has told large sections of the population or their media and so, even if your sap is not rising, you feel it should be or that there's something wrong with you. And, of course, there *is* something wrong with you. You either have winter depression or spring fever. You're as peevish as a convalescent child. You're tired of everything, but beneath the tiredness is a febrile energy. Women turn upon their surroundings, you turn upon – well, that depends upon how far you want to take it.

It begins with the purchase of unusual gar-ments, more brightly coloured than is your wont – or else completely irrelevant, like waders or a topee. It spreads to expensive hobbies. Many a woman has come home from shopping one March morning to find the makings of a swim-ming-pool or £500 worth of camera equipment being delivered. No matter that he can't swim or doesn't know one end of a camera from the other. It's the February fidgets, he's as mad as a March hare.

If this particular form of scratching doesn't calm the itch, you begin to look at women with new eyes. Actually, it's not so much that your eyes are new as that you can see the female sex for the first time in several months as they shed scarves and boots and Grandmother's beaver lamb. Sometimes looking is enough. But look-ing was never enough for everyone.

The problem is that your approaches to your wife or female partner fall on deaf ears. She is exhausted by thinking up new ideas for any one of the many businesses which ritualistically require them as spring hails over the yard-arm. Or she has been shopping for hours to find something you can afford which she likes, which *Vogue* featured and in which she doesn't turn blue. Or she's been spring-cleaning. She has no sympathy with your inflammation. 'The bath-room needs painting,' she mutters as she falls into a sleep from which an earthquake wouldn't waken her. The risky thing is that this missed close encounter only applies within the marital (or otherwise regularly maintained) unit. Other men's wives and girlfriends seem to be a good deal more enthusiastic towards you, which per-plexingly means that your partner may be feeling just as frisky about somebody else. The motto at this stage should be 'Do nothing in the spring that you can't live with in the summer'. Every-thing passes, even spring, though there's little doubt that few women recognise the essentially temporary nature of spring fever.

But like most fevers, it gets worse before it gets better. In the next stage you lash out on new aftershave, contact your gym or start up some sport again, worry about your weight and your wardrobe. You part your hair closer to your ear to drape it across your head, wear a brooch on your lapel, drink margueritas (although they give you savage indigestion) and generally pursue fleeting youth until spring isn't so new any more and your temperature comes down. If you're really lucky this will coincide with the cessation of housework hostilities at home, thus giving you an excellent opportunity to sample the wisdom of Paul Newman's remark about not bothering to eat hamburger out if you've got steak at home.

If you've really got style, you'll cement the new treaty with a weekend somewhere roman-tic, just the two of you, so that you can sit and watch the world go by, making just as big a fool of itself as you were three weeks ago.

Anna Raeburn 12.3.1986

'*Beats me how the crocuses ever get through.*'

HELLO, YOUNG LOVERS

Double standards from British Telecom, all right. What's going on there? On the one hand the bob-a-throb sex phone-ins. On the other, I see, they are ripping the doors off Cornish call-boxes to stop 'courting couples' getting in there out of the cold. Or at least staying in long enough to warm up. Actual getting in there is easier, with no walking round the thing looking for the door, then a grope to find the handle when your tiny hand is frozen.

BT shareholders who managed to grab a bit of scrip and a few quid knocked off the next quarter's bill, are saying that nothing of this kind happened when John Stonehouse was Postmaster-General, and asking who looks after things under the new management. There's never been an answer to the heavy breathing syndrome, in or out of the kiosk, but now it's a PLC there's clearly a policy split in its Moral Measures Advisory Sub-Committee, some members favouring a dirty talk service, others loud on stamping out any unbridled slap and tickle. Tickle, anyway. Try a slap in there and you could break an elbow on the coin-box.

Whether the last is just a seasonal move I don't know. The spring is nearer than we think, especially if we're in the West Country at the moment, with snow and drifting, where we think it's not going to come this year. It will though. Cheer up, Cornwall. Hello, young lovers. Get out into the primroses, and stuff the snogging in a crowded booth with the sleet blowing in. If it's seasonal, and the doors go back, they might consider sticking up a This Way In notice outside. Speaking personally, a This Way Out notice inside wouldn't come amiss either. I'm not much in call-boxes, it's true, even for telephoning. When I am, it takes me a day or two to lose the shoulder bruise from barging at the three non-exits. And I'm not even blind with love.

The quotes embracing the courting couples, para 1, above, are because I filch the phrase from the *Daily Mail* report on this act of administrative vandalism. It's pleasing to find a smart,

modern, on-the-ball paper talking in this demure way. None of your nudge-nudge as in the Diary page, where Dempster people may be described outright as 'being seen about together', but no raunchy suggestions of a call-box tryst. The word has a tinge of Jane Austen. No hint of the blood running hot in the veins. Or perhaps of Wimpole Street, where Bob Browning courted Liz Barrett and not even Charles Laughton caught them up to anything.

But if there isn't a lot of courting practised these days – waiting down in the hall with a bunch of gladioli while the girl upstairs gets herself ready to swoon just at the sight of your trousers – it doesn't mean today's average couple are any better off for places to go when they want to do it, whatever they call it now.

It's a long time since those top communications men, perhaps a top token woman, were members of an average couple, who shall be deemed, for the purpose of these remarks, to be starry-eyed, aged $14\frac{1}{2}$, tormented by facial blemishes, and still not too sure of getting their noses the right way round when kissing. No statistical breakdown is available, but I'd say that's about it, and in this, despite recent developments in the way of space-labs, spare-part surgery, the car-phone, the compact disc and Habitat, not much has changed since Adam and Eve were teenagers.

And at least they had somewhere to be private. A rude hut. The long grass under an apple tree. Until, on pretty thin grounds, it always seems to me, they got flung out into an unsympathetic world with frightful problems on what to do about Cain and Abel, problem kids the both of them.

That policy-making Telecom gang has forgotten such earlier frustrations of life, now as remote to them as the separate-earpiece telephone. Wasn't there a time, if they look back for a moment, when they themselves, incredible as it seems, had nowhere to speak their confused hearts but shop doorways, or pressing their suits against cold railings? Perhaps they were the lucky ones, though you wouldn't think so to look at them now, and had access to the back seat of the family Mini – which even Sir Alec Issigonis, that early designer-knight, hadn't got quite right for courtship purposes.

This is clear from their double-standard sex

thinking. They are at the age when the fire has died. All passion spent. So it's gone these two ways. No necking in the kiosks, so rip off the doors. But for those who need their passions pumped up a bit, dial the dirt. As to the doors, at any rate, they can fool their consciences with feats of hypocrisy. No, no. They aren't against the courting couples. It's the booth-using public they have in mind, with every right to get in there and call the number zoned as erogenous. (See your phone book. I can't see it in mine, unless it's under Bedtime Stories. In case of difficulty, dial the operator, but you won't get anything too salacious from her.)

Meanwhile, a word to you shareholders in all this. Your next AGM is scheduled for September. What I want to urge on you is not to miss it, even if it means crowding into the Albert Hall if Westland aren't using it. These are your phone-boxes, remember. Any threat of the torn-out doors spreading from Cornwall, until no misted glass nook in the kingdom will be available for courting, and you must make a firm stand.

It will mean thinking young. Even too young to need the sex-line. Raise the banner of youth. Alas, I can't be with you, as a non-investor. I regret that.

It would be nice to find the years rolled back, as I hope yours may be, to bleak embraces on the windswept dunes of Skegness, the uncomfortable but undistracting penetration of woodland pine-needles in Epping Forest, never mind an acrobatic refuge in the back of a pre-Issigonis Morris Minor. And that was in the springtime. The only pretty ring time. Not that any pretty ring changed hands as a result of such encounters. That's no reason why you shouldn't give me one, pledging your support. My number's in the book.

Basil Boothroyd 5.3.1986

'And to my wife, Joan, I leave my mistress, Valerie.'

'We'd better report back to Colonel Ivanov for Instructions!'

'OF COURSE WE MUST FACE FACTS. IT'S
GOING TO MEAN WAITING.'

Pont, Punch, May 12, 1937

'You don't even take me to the youth club with you any more!'

MALE and female prisoners should be imprisoned together with shared facilities and supervised by staff of both sexes, according to an independent inquiry into women prisoners to be published this week.

The Observer

Dear Claire Rayner,

Oh dear me, I am in a pickle! Since 1981, I have been walking out, not literally, ha-ha, with a wonderful guy from E wing, he is strong but never smelly, and very considerate, for example he has promised that as soon as he gets out he will have *Terence* tattooed on his left bicep with a little ring of teeth round it in memory of our first date

But suddenly, horrors, this has all changed! Last week, they introduced women into our nick, since when he has been all over a fat redheaded bitch doing three for dishonest handling, and seeing her standing next to him in the slops queue this morning, I am here to tell you the jury were not wrong!

I am at my wits' end to know what to do. He seems to have lost all interest in me. Worse, my attempts to win back his undying affection seem doomed. Last night, I stuffed a couple of oranges up my singlet in the hope of beating her at her own game, but he just pulled them out, gave one to her, and they ate them in front of me

I don't mind humiliation, as a matter of fact I have made a bob or two out of it in my time, but what I can't bear is not understanding. Up until last week, he was a normal, healthy prisoner. What has made him go peculiar, all of a sudden?

Weepy, Strangeways

Dear Claire Rayner,

I am at my wits' end. I was recently moved here to Broadmoor from Holloway because I kept shaving my hair off, and they put me in with a very attractive arsonist, slim, little moustache, nice personality, likes Chinese restaurants – apparently they're very slack on fire regulations, you learn something every day, don't you? – and we have been getting on like a house, anyway, to cut a long story short, he wanted to know why I had no hair, and I didn't like to tell him it was only because I had nits and didn't want to let on at Holloway because they make you wash in Lysol etc, so I told him it was because I was Joan of Arc, she is always bald in pictures e.g. Ingrid Bergman, Jean Seberg, I thought that might impress him, due to where most of the women in here are Florence Nightingale and Queen Victoria and Edwina Currie and boring old rubbish like that.

I think it was a mistake. It has made him fall in love with me. Every time we are alone, he starts breaking up the chairs and putting them into a pile and throwing me on top. It is not really risky, because they do not allow him matches, so he has to get down and start rubbing two chairlegs together, which gives me plenty of time to run, but that is not my problem.

My problem is: if I tell him I am not Joan of Arc, will he stop respecting me? I suppose I could tell him my voices had suddenly come to me and informed me that I was non-inflammable, but would he believe me? Worse, if he did believe me, would he stop loving someone he could not get to light?

Desperate,
Broadmoor

Dear Claire Rayner,

Please use your enormous influence to help me!

On our top corridor, the authorities are shoving four women in with every four men. Do people outside have any idea what conditions can be like with eight prisoners crammed into a titchy cell originally intended for four, all pressed up against one another?

Well, down here they have given us sod-all! We are four blokes rattling around like wossnames in a bloody pod.

The undercrowding is a scandal.

Disgusted,
Durham

Dear Claire Rayner,

I am doing a ten stretch for using a hammer on my wife without due care and attention, i.e. failure to throw same off bridge, and I have recently took a fancy to a nice big woman who is in for running a disorderly launderette.

Recently, she took 2oz best snout off of me, so I know I am in there with a chance, there is a romantic language of snout, and I have asked her to come away for the weekend to a nice little place I know behind the boilers. But I have been in here since 1981, and I know fashions change, and I do not wish to look a prat, so can you tell me whether I should knock her about on our first date, or would it be more sensible to wait until we know one another better?

Confused,
Brixton

PS I mean failure to throw the hammer off a bridge, not failure to throw the wife off.

PPS Oh, I don't know, though.

THE SILENCES OF PASSION

In certain areas of life, I am told, love moves like a great and gifted fish from the current of one desire to the next. I have a strong feeling that I have been hanging about on the banks of the wrong streams, staring at the wrong seas. In the social contexts where my identity was fashioned, love, where it should have left a memorable radiance, created as often as not a mildewed quietness.

In any fairly ravaged industrial area, the face of love can be clobbered beyond recognition. Passionate liking is such an absurd and tenuous relationship it needs strong hints of grace and sophistication to provide it with a reasonable frame-work.

The early films provided us with many a shock as we saw the sheer floor space in which the better-provided were allowed to develop their pre- and extra-marital antics. It created a fixed bitterness in young lovers who had a narrow choice to make between a back lane and a parlour in which an immovable uncle was tickling 'Abide With Me' up to a Sunday gloss on the harmonium.

In the South Wales of the '20s politics and religion twisted the arm of the libido with a consistent ferocity. We subsisted on speeches, sermons and hymns which declared that the only authentic love was the urge to unite socially with the rest of the species.

Sexual love came into it only to be denounced as an indecency, an irrelevance, a betraying and bathetic bit of farce, a sheltering in stupid shadow, while the vast body of the army was advancing in light towards the uplands of total liberation. The nearest we got to the foot of Juliet's balcony was a demonstration. And we landed on the balcony itself only when we had some letter of scalding protest acknowledged on heat-proof vellum by the Prime Minister's secretary. Many a smooching amorist was dragged from a protective doorway by a father beating him half to death with a knout of knotted pamphlets.

Love needs an oxygen of confidence and when one has known an ambience of grotesque indignity one approaches personal love as warily as one would a gaol-break. The adulterers I recall from my childhood were few, although I admit that I was not at that time watching out for them. The ones who were brought to my attention by relations anxious to point out to me in a cautionary way the various paths to hell, were jolly, roaring outlaws, not giving the sliver of a damn for their shattered respectability, and defying the pious to apply to them the execution by dog, stone or exile prescribed in the rougher pages of the Old Testament. They were, too, heavily dependent on drink for their excesses and in days of slump tended to crawl back into an autumnal restraint, and the places where extra-mural love throve, like the warmed wall of the old steam-fan and the back of the dance-hall, fell silent.

We followed these sinners about with praise, encouragement and building foods. They and the revivalists were the only people whose signatures we sought, thinking that in handwriting might be some clue to success.

From the numberless chapels which had splintered off from the Established Church flew many fragments of further dissent. These new persuasions settled themselves in small huts, usually on the moorland fringe of the town. The religious idiom in these places was much more passionately assertive and individual than in the conventional temples. I suppose starting up a new sect is classically a crypto-sexual act, for it is simply a desire to introduce some sensational novelty into one's relations with others. One is looking for a new and astonishing posture, a new chime of echoes for a voice maddeningly muffled.

I did a fair amount of research into these break-away conventicles, usually on winter nights when sensual fervour ran thin. The sectaries reached a high degree of excitement. They did not favour long, set statements by a chosen preacher or hymns decorously sung. Their fancy ran to accordions, to dancing of a stamping kind, and self-revelations delivered in gibberish and a half-delirium. If the drug coca had been cultivable in those hills I would say that they had stumbled across a fair plantation of it.

My envy of them had edges of unforgettable anguish. Their ecstasy would move swiftly from the mystical to the sexual. The accordion would keep playing, because musicians of this type get their own kinds of satisfaction which are not explicable in terms of other love-techniques. It must have something to do with those straps and a swiftly manipulable key-board. But many couples would leave the hut, yap up in joy at the frost-bright stars, canter up into the darkness of the hillside, then find bliss disperse abruptly as their bodies touched the freezing surface of the moor.

We wished them well, for they appeared to have reached a superb synthesis of the two passions we most admired, preaching and kissing. And the sight of their slow, sad progression from the heights back down to the blinking censure of the valley bed's streets, led us to the discovery of one of our first principles, that the levels of heat on this earth are disastrously and inextricably uneven.

In the lives of many of the women in that time and place there must have been caves of yearning. Men whose maturing was too often a simple rejection of tenderness, over-large broods of children, tormented by a lack of space and calories into muttering insurrection, hutchhouses where a wish for privacy passed as something sinister, a symptom of contempt or eccentricity, these things did a perfect Jack the Ripper job on more women than even Jack ever dreamed of. Death could often be seen backing in shame from such a lack of fulfilment.

On to the lives of such women the reasoning of demagogues and revivalists fell like an appeasing dew; their candent perorations warmed like brandy. The great revivalists came to revive something more than a limping theology. At their best they relieved more sieges of coldness than the gulf stream. They shattered silences that threatened to become funereal. They set lights swinging in dreams that had slipped betimes into a penultimate shroud.

I am thinking of one such wizard who lived well into my own life-time. During one summer, when he was in his middle twenties and supremely handsome after the fashion of Henry Ainley, he burst forth from some Calvinistic Death Valley in the far Welsh west, his eyes mesmeric with conviction, his tongue a thunder-clap of sonorous hallelujahs. Every crouching heart in the land rose in a full ecstasy

of response. Men paddled into the harbour of salvation after years on a broad lagoon of booze. Four members of the local quoits team, athletes of depravity, confessed their sins publicly and asked for admission into the orbit of grace. The whole audience wept as they saw these scamps sob and forswear quoits, sex, ale and the gleegroup. They lapsed that very night, somewhere between the chapel and their homes, lured into a sawdust bar by some voter who had big gambling money involved in a quoits contest which the four converts stood a chance of winning.

But for the women it was a more serious thing. Their need for beauty, which a man can drown in a pint or stifle with a jest, is in them organic and abidingly disquieting. For them our revivalist was a combination of Valentino and Lloyd George; Latin frankness set squarely in the midst of a hymn-singing and Radical democracy. The less timid went down to his enchantments like skittles. The pulpit on which he stood was less a platform and lectern than a protective screen. He spoke of the sun of warmth and love that was shortly to rise over the stricken tundra of their days. The brilliance of his invocations exploded with blinding force between them and the image of the muffled necks and belted bellies of their shuffling and beer-logged mates.

There was an occasion when he was found in a fern-bed, in flagrant delight with one of his younger worshippers. It was a great mistake. When one is stoking a communal libido it is tactless to particularise. That evening, a whole army of enraged lovers assembled in the chapel and a mood of lynching was in the air. The deacons refused to take any part in the opening hymns. Two sidesmen soaped the rope. Two hundred pairs of female eyes did not leave his blushing face. He dangled from the grudge they bore him. We small ones in the gallery heard dreams topple and hit the ground so hard we wondered if it was just life again or a fresh onset of subsidence.

The revivalist stood up for his sermon. This, we thought, was one torero who would gladly ask the bull to get on with it. He opened his arms and leaned towards us. He said nothing. He was inviting us to brood upon all the places in the lives of men and women where love needed to go and, sometimes, inscrutably went. We brooded. Our spirits went towards him like lemmings, fascinated by the cliffs of his confessed anguish. He began, softly, to conjugate the verb 'to love' in Welsh and English. His voice had a quite unearthly timbre and reach. The precentor, a megalomaniac and a hard man to stop when he felt the mood was with him, began to hum one of our lovelier songs of lamentation. At least three women left the place, weeping, to mark the falling from the sky of yet another love.

At the end of that summer the revivalist, his larynx and most of the rest of him spent, retired into private life. He took with him a curious seraglio, a group of exquisite hand-maidens, his favourite gospel-singers. And he left behind him a land that he had come to salve and left even more scarred and apprehensive than it had been before.

I fancied the revivalist line myself. Indeed I fancied anything that would make me a magisterial and admirable fellow, letting off storms of compassion in the female breast, flanked by women groaning for a fresh sound, sight and touch of me. I practised a few perorations in the kitchen and thought I was doing fairly well until my brothers found a soporific herb and three wrestling grips that kept me out for the count for days on end. Also, my faith withered, and most of my carnal urges with it.

For me, Spurgeon dropped out of sight at about the same time as Casanova. On a blazing day in 1924 I was bitten by a rabid student of Bradlaugh who was crawling about in the Free Thought section of the Library and Institute. I lost my urge to preach and to impress my name and wishes on the melting hearts of women.

Which is a pity, for I, too, can conjugate the verb 'to love' in Welsh and English. And Spanish, too, if the thing ever went on tour.

Gwyn Thomas 2.1.1963

'Isn't it a small world, Lionel! The Gribsons' daughter once worked in the same strip club as Melissa!'

'It's about time we got those warts sorted out, Brother.'

'I'm sorry, my dears, but I'm afraid the Reformation won't go through without job losses.'

THE VICTIM
A Short Story

It was the 7.40 train from Munich to Rome and there were four of them. It was as though their young limbs hadn't yet set – their inability to sit upright, four square in the four trim seats, two facing two, in the second-class compartment. The two girls faced each other next to the window. But they seldom sat erect, leaning, lounging, collapsing, hugging, stroking, each was engulfed in the indolent caresses of the young man beside her. It was done without effort, without strain. Even without sensuality – the easy fondling and nosing of a litter of young puppies. But adult. And discrete enough not to transgress the barriers of pairs.

They were German. It was high August and they were heading south. But they were dressed for drab cities, dark in colour, sombre. The boys' jeans were dark navy, stiff with newness. But tight. The taller of the girls wore dark trousers too, tapering narrowly below the knee, with brass studs down the side seams. Above, she wore a shaggy grey sweater, a winter garment, through at the elbows, puckering unravelled wool from the hole. She didn't notice. Unexpectedly, she had very long finger nails that gave her hands the exaggerated gestures of Siamese dancers. They were painted silver and she cleaned them from time to time with a dirty penknife.

The other girl was small and chubby and as drab, though her garments, because of their softness and fluidity, offered some acknowledgement of summer. But they were black: a wide cotton skirt speckled with tiny mauve flowers reached to her ankles where bare dirty feet swung blue flip-flops from the big toes. Her top was gauzy and thin, a black smock edged with mauve lace. Funereal colours, but pretty.

They had been up since early morning. But had obviously dressed with little attention. They were careless of such things. Whatever impulse had brought them together each to each, it was independent of modish attractions. Their looks were their own. They could, but for differences of bone and contour, have been siblings. It was a group look: dark, shared, menacing even. Though they laughed a good deal. And often. At almost nothing. A donkey seen from the train wearing a straw hat against the sun. Yelps of laughter. A fat porter struggling to urge a bulging case from the platform up the flight of steps to the carriage floor. Eager bubbling giggles. Their joyfulness was alert and watchful, taking pleasure from around them. But there was much they did not see. Did not care to.

Other people they ignored, except as they presented themselves as passing entertainment. Each avoided the eyes of outsiders. A deliberate unspoken conspiracy. It made for curious imbalance. For a while they perceived no one, actually avoided looking; everyone else sensing their unity gazed at them the more. Their very self-containment made them a spectacle. People stared, and then unrebuked, stared harder and continuously, hostile at not being acknowledged, by the young four. Who persisted in not noticing. It had the effect of keeping all other persons out of their compartment. Travellers, passing along the corridor with luggage and children, looked in questioningly at the two empty seats remaining in the compartment. But noisy laughter, the coiling limbs of the young people and most particularly the fact that not one of them registered the strangers' existence, not one turned to confront their gaze from the corridor into the compartment, all prevailed on the uneasy traveller to seek a place elsewhere. Their self-absorption set them apart, made them alien, disliked.

The train pulled in to Florence station. And it was there that she joined the train, she who would venture into their private world, into their private compartment. It was not clear at first that this would happen. Observing the crowded platforms, the upturned faces clamouring loudly, mostly in Italian, but a good deal in American tourist twang too, the group took action to remain isolated. They pulled down the sun blinds on the corridor windows, hooking them under the brass holders at their lowest point. But the four were no match for the flock of nuns at that very moment invading the train two carriages along.

The nuns occupied the train as an evening gathering of starlings occupied a row of telegraph wires. With much twittering, acknowledging the natural hierarchy of their caste. Some of the sisters were immediately found seats. Others swooped, their long brown habits flapping around them, in and out of doors, their light voices girlish, their banter that of schoolchildren. It was an outing of great occasion. People stared at them, too, as they had at the young German travellers, but comfortably, without suspicion. And always met with smiles from the nuns, from their bland, clear faces. The gaggle of noise swept along the corridor and, presented with the drawn blinds, a hand, spotless with much washing away of sin, pulled open the door. Reverend Mother brooked no ignoring.

A belch of laughter exploded in her face. No one looked up: but her authority withstood their indifference. She stood her ground, upright, appraising the slouched figures before her. It might have been a zoo, so detached was her curiosity, so casual their ignoring her. One of the boys was talking in a soft German lisp, one hand round the shoulders of the dumpy girl, reaching inside her lace smock where his fingertips cupped her full breast. Both ignored this easy intimacy. His other hand held a long thin cigarette. That then was it: her opportunity. In an instant she was into the compartment and upon them. It was the very excuse Reverend Mother needed.

Towering over their prone bodies: 'I'm sorry, but I must explain. We don't allow that in Italy. No. You can't smoke. It's not how we do things. You're in our country. You must respect our ways, our laws. Please put it out now.' Suddenly and with one movement they were staring hard, all four of them. It gave their lack of comprehension an aggressive air. Then as the nun continued gesturing fussily towards the cigarette, wagging a stubby finger, they responded. Slowly, contemptuously and with the minimum of movement the smoker pointed his cigarette towards the international symbol below the window that designated this a 'smoking permitted' area. The shock of her mistake stunned her into silence.

Drawing herself up to her full height she put one starched hand across her breast and offered them in gracious and aristocratic phrases the most abject apology. She did it without smiling. She did it without any humility. And her awareness of this prompted into existence a corner of unease. It was an apology she did not feel. The words were dry with dishonesty, dusty with formal courtesy. It wasn't enough to speak so, to apologise without meaning it. She must make her apology meaningful. The mistake called for a correction, an absolution. A sacrifice. Penance must be done. She must make them an offering to salve her foolishness, her haughtiness, her hatred. She left the compartment and went in search.

Sister Theresa was 21 and olive skinned, with the brooding beauty of an Indian film star, and the passivity of a watchful bird. She alone among the nuns had not found herself a seat. Ideal. The blanched hand that had wagged its disapproval in the face of the young Germans

now took the young nun's elbow and with maternal concern and giving no option, steered the compliant girl towards the enemy. Her voluble reassurance – 'four young people, Germans not Italians, an uncouth group, so at the slightest hint of anything disagreeable . . . remember I am three compartments along . . . and you are next to the door . . . quite safe. Ignore them. Sit still and calm . . . they will admire your discipline . . . there you are go along in . . .' All this gave Sister Theresa no chance to speak. Nor, given the opportunity, would she have done so. She was quiet with a quietness that was totally ambiguous. Whether of blind obedience or blank contempt Mother Agnes could never be sure.

This sullenness, the mystery of the young girl gave Reverend Mother a private satisfaction at having placed her among the aliens. 'Let her and they cope with each other for four hours,' she might have thought, if she had allowed herself such malice. As it was she smiled grimly as she slid the glass door with its drawn blind closed behind the demure girl.

The train was rattling now through the hills between Florence and Arezzo. A landscape of forested slopes and every so often the white stone and square shape of a country palazzo, the cool hillside residence of some Florentine banker, some Roman merchant, occupied perhaps by his family throughout the summer heat or hired to parties of holidaymakers who came now in large groups to the larger villas of the area each August. Sister Theresa knew this because this was her own country. Her father had a smallholding on the slopes above . . . Carpannole where her mother and four brothers helped him tend the grapes. A dusty life in the fields and in the open. Beyond the train window. Their skins were brown, their hands were gnarled where hers had stayed white and smooth – and would stay that way all her life. The familiar landscape revived a yearning she had learned to master within the cool stones of the convent. Gazing now beyond the young people at the train window, her spirit opened to the skies beyond. Her senses throbbed. Even the tensions of her taut body relaxed a little.

How natural they were, she thought, her dear family, in their bronzed skins, their weatherworn bodies . . . ageing like trees before the elements, bending over vines, reaching to garner harvests. Her loved ones living on those slopes. How beautiful they were in the natural sensuality of their lives, close to crops and fruit and grasses. While she had been set apart. By her mother. And by God too. To be upright, contained within herself, to move in stone courtyards, kneel in carved cloisters, gentle and generous in her devotions, but controlled always by the discipline of her will. She did not find it natural. Indeed the strength of her faith came from this very difficulty. At night, sometimes, she allowed herself the remembrance of the fall of chestnuts in autumn, the bronze shine on each fruit and how her mother would heap them carelessly in a cracked earthenware dish. The recollection brought her close to God – her God. She gazed still at them in her mind, out there on the hillside – yearned to be absorbed into them, to partake of their very nature. It was a joyful yearning. A yearning she continually strove to tame. Turning now she looked upon the grubby limbs of the four city strangers.

None of them looked up for some time. Quieter in her presence, they huddled round the window, joking and pointing out the passing landscape. Suddenly a jolt of the carriage caught them off balance. The whole train lurched badly, awkwardly, at some unevenness in the line. The boys fell like babies, relaxed, safe from injury, against the soft shoulders of the squealing girls. Sister Theresa, alone, rigid and upright, had no time to think before putting out her neat hand, involuntarily steadying her tense body against the shoulder of a blond boy. He turned warily and looked at her. She, appalled, looked steadily back. She gestured an awkward regret, but no words came. Instead a gentle, eager and beautiful smile. He, tense now, infected with her anxiety, caught its radiance and suddenly smiled back. Then disentangling his arm from round the plump shoulders of his girlfriend, he placed a solicitous hand on the forearm of Sister Theresa. 'Are you all right, then, sister?' She hadn't known what she had expected. Something of Reverend Mother's own neurosis had planted an unease. Was this smile then a deception, a mistake, a false lead, a disguise? Was his question ironic, contemptuous, a prelude to some insult, abuse? There was no trace of such in his clear gaze and where Reverend Mother might choose to impute deviousness, Sister Theresa chose to match his openness with her trust.

Besides, whatever his action meant she was overwhelmingly pleased with it. More pleased than was in any way legitimate. Pleased in a way that surprised her, even shocked her slightly. And then the thrill of rejecting that shock pleased her even more. This young man, his naked forearm, the dirty hand, bitten fingernails. Had he been of this country, the hills beyond the train's windows, he would have been weathered brown in the fields, his hands would be grained with earth. Instead it was city dust that coated his wan skin. But for that he could be a young man from the fields out there, known to her family. Approved by them. She lifted her own neat fingers and placed her other hand momentarily upon his. A gesture of thanks, she explained to herself.

The girl with the long silver fingernails had watched the exchange with detached curiosity, amused, at first, intrigued, then gradually pleased. As the conversation meandered on, she swung a boot across to nudge the flip-flopped toe of her friend, who looked up sleepily from the corner where the boy had dumped her. She too turned towards the smiling nun.

Fumbling in the gathered folds of her skirt she found a crumpled packet of cigarettes and lifting one half out, reached across to Sister Theresa and gestured her offer. There was no malice here either, and the young nun, surprised by their candour, even hesitated for a moment over the proffered cigarette lest her refusal seemed to reject their generosity. Instead she grinned broadly, a peasant's smile, indicated her habit and laughingly declined to smoke. There was laughter in the compartment now and the four of them lit up. Some code had been broken. They had found a strange friend unexpectedly. Even an ally perhaps, among the foreign crowds. And she was young like them. Like them stared at by others, misunderstood perhaps.

Normal? What was normal? Flesh, skin, the flush on her cheek, the wanness of theirs. Her greedy gaze into the lush countryside, their private conspiratorial look. Her neat cleansed fingernails. Their own. Her heavily clad clumsy feet: theirs. Her tense response to the train's lurch; their easy comfort in their own bodies.

Hers relaxing too now. At ease. With them. They making her so. Happy with her tentative friendship. They unhooked from their intense privacy. The growth of something between them. Not a great deal. Not much that was actual. But contact – limbs, smiles, broken phrases across language, laughter. And so it continued as the train hummed south into the heat.

Reverend Mother was not enjoying the journey. It created too many anxieties. Albeit the crowd of young nuns selected to go to Rome had been chosen for their docility and sweetness of nature, yet there was a tremulous excitement associated with the expedition that alarmed her. The break with daily discipline itself made her uneasy. She missed the routine of devotions. Instead she took reassurance from the train's steady rhythm and hourly refuge in her small prayer book and rosary. She had been in the convent so long she could only enjoy the predictable. Now she was determined to control the tempo of the visit to Rome, to let nothing go amiss. The smooth running of the stay would be her reward. The train rocked, and lurched suddenly, hardening Reverend Mother's resolve to maintain her grip, her ascendancy over the volatile minds in her care. Feeling the burden of her responsibilities, she clung close to the familiar cadences of inwardly-spoken prayer, held each bead in the grip of finger and thumb as though drawing strength through its actual surface.

In the compartment with her, other nuns talked a little, among themselves, gazed in a desultory way at the hills and villages, and occasionally, upright in their separate seats, dozed in the heat. For although the afternoon was lengthening the heat remained intense. The broad window opened fully from the top, the thin blind drawn against the sunlight did little to keep them cool. The air itself, blowing on their white skins, was hot. They sat, stoically, like statues, waiting for it to become less so as the evening mellowed. And the time for food came.

Each of two nuns carried the small leather satchel that held neat bread rolls, sections of cheese and trim fruit, enough for herself and another. At the correct hour and at Reverend Mother's bidding they began to share out their regulated portions. A chorus of chatter broke out from compartment to compartment.

It was only then, and with a sudden spasm of alarm that Reverend Mother remembered Sister Theresa. Alone and suffering the humiliation of those brutish foreigners. She thought with a shadow of guilt how she had left Theresa to their mercy. But then hadn't she deserved as much, always keeping to herself, taking and accepting any treatment the world offered with almost insolent docility. Peasant background: that was it. Placid like the oxen, but with the guile of beasts too. How could someone of Reverend Mother's character, from the best family in Piacenza, expect subtlety of mind and sensitivity of feeling from such a girl? And her beauty – that was the last straw, the final insult to the Piacenza family and their plain daughter. Abruptly Reverend Mother rose and strode with jealous steps directly to the closed compartment. Without pausing she wrenched open its door with a single resounding crack.

The sight that spread before her at that moment was to remain in her mind's eye ever after. Its impact was like a blow, a physical shock that rocked her body, and though she stood rooted in stillness to the spot, her mind raced, screaming with panic, at having to make sense of what she saw.

The young people had picnicked earlier and on the empty seat and the narrow window table lay scattered crusts, greasy scraps of curled and pungent salami, the pulp of soft tomatoes. An empty wine bottle rolled from side to side of the floor with a regular purr and thump. There was a smell of ripeness and sweat. Among the debris of food, their bodies lay asleep – some lolled, half upright, one slouched against another, hands, arms, legs, crossed intertwined, caressed. Except that now there were not four of them. But five. For Sister Theresa lay coiled alongside the others, like a small nestling on the narrow seat. Her heavy shoes sprawled discarded beside the wine bottle. Below her brown habit the frail tips of her stockinged feet showed white and pink like molluscs. And then Reverend Mother's stare reached and held the compartment's centre of shock. Sister Theresa had removed her coif from her brown hair and now lay with her head cradled in the spreading lap of the blond boy. He, hunched intimately against his girlfriend, slept too – but with one indolent and free arm circling the shoulders of the sleeping nun.

Appalled, Reverend Mother caught at her own breath, gasping and slammed the door shut again on the lascivious sight. Whose fault, then? Who to blame? Had this not been her sacrificial lamb, the price of her own sincerity? A momentary frown, then hesitant and thoughtful, she returned to her own compartment determined that nothing had happened.

But the slam of the door had stirred the young people. The boy's thigh shifted below Sister Theresa's head and woke her. Slowly she sat up. The door was closed but she knew it had been opened. She looked about her at her new but familiar friends, smiled at their easy sleep, surveyed the scattered remains of their meal together. Finally and unsurprised she noticed the tidy satchel of food left for her on the empty seat opposite. As she reached deliberately for her nun's portion she was not to know that within the year she would leave the convent, returning at her own request to her brother's fields. And that Reverend Mother would be found early one morning hanging from the beam in the convent refectory.

Joan Bakewell 31.10.1979

Lady (to elderly and confidential maid). 'I'VE OFTEN WONDERED WHY YOU'VE NEVER MARRIED, SIMPSON?'
Simpson (disdainfully). 'I DON'T LIKE MEN IN ANY FORM, MY LADY.'

'When we first met he was tremendously rampant.'

A SNIP IN TIME
SAVES NINE

Not that our foreign correspondent is all that reliable on anything unconnected with levity, but it would seem that while Indira Gandhi lay back and thought of India, henchmen scoured the public railways for folks resembling males, flung them into sidings and divested them of future fatherhood without so much as a transistor radio for a keepsake. A trifle coarse-grained, don't you think, even for the technologically backward, but there is a certain quiet dignity in the aftermath. 'Right, Mrs,' they could say, pulling up their dhotis and limping off into the twentieth century, 'there's another dozen votes you're not getting.'

How much less direct the approach of our own dear system, where a vote for anyone is a vote for the FPA, know it or not, like it or not, and where the intricacies of a highly civilized guilt-and-dread society offer mature choices enough to make your tubes boggle. Time was – and, forgetful as I am, I count myself privileged to have come to nubility at such an age – when chaps had haircuts and barbers would say, all discreet and man-to-man, 'Anything more for you, sir?' and everything was cut and dried. The available gent had this thoughtful little oval embossed on his wallet to denote presence of rubber goods. It was all part of the sportif ever-readiness of the fully-kitted stud-male – petrol tank full, spare tenner in back pocket, corrugated soles on shoes for non-skid agility, the whole Erroll Flynn movie, in fact, always at your service.

Of course you couldn't help noticing, even then, that it was all a bit overtly boy-scoutish. I mean, some of those ovals weren't just embossed, they were sort of wearing through. This tended to suggest that there was less action around than a chap would have his chums at the bar believe. It was more of a talisman, really, like string-backed gloves and go-faster tape on the motor, more for you-butch-me-butch security than for real.

Married blokes though, according to my brother, used to keep their condoms in their bedside tables, which I remember we thought of as wonderfully stable of them. And one paragon apparently made quite a fetish of peeling them out of their foil and plopping them into a little screw-top jar full of scented oil. Like little jellyfish floating there. His: for the use of.

Fact is, though, in those dark but ordered days, he was in charge. Fear of pregnancy and awareness of sin being what they used to be, a lady was effectively celibate unless he chose otherwise. If he slipped up, or a pretty girl happened to be serving in Boots that afternoon, he'd be obliged to mutter something hoarse in the dark, 'Are you all right?' which roughly translated meant 'Excuse me, madam, but have you been sufficiently adult and responsible to calculate the days of your fecundity or would you like to dash off to the bathroom for your secret stirrup-pump or whatever horrible contraption you have standing by for emergencies?'

But there, the whole business is, and always was, much more than a matter of birth control. It is, in all its forms, a totem; the symbol of precisely who is in charge of what and of whom. Possession is nine-tenths of contraception. And whatever else it did, the Pill robbed man of his most precious one. For the first time in the history of human intercourse, the female could call the tune, and my God, what kind of symphonies might she get up to while he was away for the weekend cup-tie? Ah, the fears that raged unspake. How swiftly did the Pill become synonymous with Permissiveness. And all the time Permissive meant Without Permission.

Without His Permission. Such were the agonising . . . *pensées métaphysiques* which beset a chap.

How then to wrest back full sexual control and return to the golden double standard without too much hassle? Naturally his first ploy fairly shimmered with brute force and ignorance. Under cover of avuncular solicitousness he put it about that the Pill Kills. And if not that, then it makes you fat, flat breasted, varicosed, spotty and bearded. The threats were legion but aimed in one direction. She who takes the Pill is unattractive to men. So there!

Earlier the earth moved, as Ernie had said, and it was good. Only the earth moved again and so violently he quite lost his foothold. From here on the only way a chap could get back on top, as it were, has been to make sacrifice. To wit: vasectomy. But it's not that simple, except insofar as it is a very easy little snip job (I could do it myself) which has been possible for a good century.

So why now, if not to recover lost power and control of the bedchamber? Not that it doesn't have its romantic side. I think. Here, he says, is a token of my undying love and esteem and my awareness that you could take the Pill and be available to anyone you fancy. No, wait a minute, that can't be right. Here, he says, is a pledge of my honour with which I attempt to vouchsafe a similar pledge of faith from you. I will-if-you-will and I won't-if-you-won't and where else, for God's sake, did eternal love ever rest its case but in the subtle little dramas of terror and counter-terror, threat and counter-threat, bargain, exchange-deal, your fear for mine, mine for yours and we'll con-join happily ever after? Anyway, with this small operation scar I thee worship. With this small disability I set the seal on our children's inheritance.

Of course, it took the middle-class male to pioneer vasectomy, but it wasn't long before your plain working chap joined the queue. The compensations were somehow too *macho* to be missed. Not just having a white-golliwog tie and knowing that Mr Parkinson has one just like it in his wardrobe, but the whole business of feeling himself the quiet hero of his time. He couldn't exactly slap it down on the bar for a round of applause, but he could smile in a small way, and there's no denying those two little white spots are the closest he could get these days to the old duelling scars a gentleman suffered for a lady of yore. And yes, it's courtly, to say the least. But then chaps do have a way of alternating 'Man gotta do what he gotta do,' with 'I did it for you, darling,' meaning the acquisition of golf clubs, Lamborghini and cabin cruiser (none of which she trusts herself to drive) plus the ulcer to which it all drove him.

Who's to envy modern man? Either he takes it upon himself, Fifties-fashion, and risks the raucous derision of the free-wheeling hussy who laughs at his little rubber goods and wonders where he found it – some kind of museum? Or he goes the whole hog and finds that sometimes even a faithful wife prefers not to have her options closed quite so firmly. And certainly, if my consensus is anything to go by, most ladies Don't Like, Can't Say Why and Just Don't Fancy it. Whisper it low, though, we do sound a bit like those early Pill-knockers. And yet – lives there a lady so liberated she can forget that the most touching definition of maleness is He Who Fathers – and not be squeamish about the knife that takes even that away?

Still, one must explore these things. 'What do you think,' I asked the brave soldier who shares my life, 'of a nice vasectomy now that we're so nicely settled and all?'

'Gandhi off,' he replied.

Sally Vincent 30.3.1977

'If this is love at first sight, don't you think it would be a sensible idea to end it now before it all turns sour?'

A LOVE STORY

It was the kind of party at which nobody got introduced. The room was dark, lit only by candles in bottles, and although a certain amount of feeble shuffling was going on in the centre of the floor, most of the guests were grouped around yelling in a more or less cheery fashion to people whom they were lucky enough to know already. There was a lot of noise, both musical and conversational, and the general tone seemed to Humphrey to be rather high, a kind of cross between the intellectual and the artistic. He could hear from time to time words like 'defence mechanism' and 'Harold Pinter' being bandied about above the deafening body of sound. He supposed, upon reflection, that one might have expected this kind of thing from his host, a young man whom he had met in a pub the week before, who had been most pressing in his invitation, but who had hardly seemed to recognise Humphrey at all when he had duly arrived, some time ago. Now, after half an hour of total neglect, he was beginning to feel rather annoyed. He was in many ways a conventional young man, and had not the nerve to go and accost a group of strangers, who anyway seemed to be getting on quite nicely without him, simply in order to add his own unoriginal views on Harold Pinter. On the other hand, he did not really want to go.

The situation was made even more annoying by the fact that everyone looked so interesting. That was why they were all getting on with each other so splendidly, of course. The only people who were not shouting or shuffling were extremely boring-looking people like himself, who were propped up sadly in dark corners. And the girls, one could not deny it, were most impressive. He liked artistic and intellectual-looking girls, himself; he could never see what other people had against all these fiercely painted eyes, these long over-exposed legs, these dramatic dresses. They all looked a little larger and brighter than life, and talked with a more than natural intensity, and laughed with a more than natural mirth. He found them most exhilarating. He gazed with frank admiration at one exotic creature with long pale hair and a long maroon velvet dress: her legs were not over-exposed but on the contrary totally enclosed, though she made up for this modesty elsewhere, displaying to the world a vast extent of pallid back, where angry pointed shoulder-blades rose and fell as she gesticulated and discoursed. All he saw of her was her active back: her face and front were bestowed upon others.

Even she, though, had nothing on a girl he could see at the other side of the room, far away and perched on top of a book-case, whence she was holding court, and whence she smiled serenely above the heads of others and above the sea of smoke. Her slight elevation gave her a look of detached beauty, and her face had a cool superiority, as of one who inhabits a finer air. She too was surrounded, naturally, by hordes of friends and admirers, who were plying her with chat and cigarettes, and constantly refilling her glass. And she too, like the pale girl, had long hair, though hers, as far as he could distinguish, was not pale, but of a dark and fiery red. He decided that he would cross the room and distinguish a little more closely.

This decision was sooner made than executed. It was remarkably hard to cross the room: instead of parting to let him pass, people seemed to cluster closer together at his approach, so that he had to force them asunder with his bare hands. They did not seem to object to this rough usage, but continued to ignore him altogether, and managed to talk uninterruptedly as though he simply were not there, as though he were not standing on the foot of one and sticking his elbow into another's chest at all. He steered his course by taking the face of the red-haired girl as his beacon, shining dimly for him above the raging social waters, and finally, a little battered, he reached her vicinity. When he got there, he found that his luck was in: by squeezing himself into a small gap between the book-case and a table, he could get very close to her indeed, though he was of course directly behind her, with no view of her face at all, and with his head on a level with her waist. Still, he was near, and that was something; so near that he could have stroked with ease her long descending hair. Not that there would have been any future in such a gesture. In an atmosphere like that she would not even have noticed. In fact, now he had got there, it struck him that there was not much future in anything, that this was really as far as he was likely to get. He had given up hope that somebody would come along with those oft-scorned but now desired words, 'Hello, Humphrey old chap, let me introduce you to a few people.' This lot were clearly far too *avant-garde* for a bourgeois convention like introduction. He wondered how they had all got to know each other in the first place. What was one supposed to do? Surely one couldn't go up to someone and say, 'Hello, I'm Humphrey, who are you?' It seemed, apart from anything else, a positive invitation to rudeness.

The red-haired girl seemed to be called Justina. The name suited her, he thought: there was something finely dramatic and vital about it, and yet at the same time something superior. As well as remarkable hair and a remarkable face, she was the lucky (and conscious) possessor of a remarkable voice, which she was not at all afraid of using. From where he was standing, directly behind her, he could hear every word she uttered, so deep and clear and vibrant were her tones. She seemed to be fond of brave abstract assertions like

'Well, in my opinion, the abstract is a total bore, anyway. I like things that *happen*, I don't like *talk*, I think that action is the only true test, myself.'

He was so entranced that he was content to listen to this kind of thing for a few minutes, but then he began to get a little restless, for, like Justina, he preferred action to talk, especially when the talk in question wasn't directed to him. He began to think of imaginary witty replies, things that he might have said had he not been such a non-participant. He even thought at one point that he might say one of them, loudly, just to see if Justina and her admirers would turn round, but by the time he had summoned up the courage the remark was no longer appropriate, and he had to start thinking up a new one. Then he wondered what would happen if he really took action, and pushed her off the book-case. That would make them notice his existence, at least. She might even like it. Or perhaps he might just grab her from behind and shout gaily 'Hello, let me introduce myself, I'm Humphrey.' And then again, he thought, perhaps not.

Sadly, for the twentieth time that evening, he reached for a consolatory cigarette and put it in his mouth, the miserable last of a miserable pack. And he didn't seem likely to get offered any more, either. When I've finished this, he said to himself, I'll go home. Then, reaching for a match, he found he had lost his box: for some reason the eternal introduction of 'Have you got a light' never even crossed his mind, occupied as it was on far more desperate levels, and he reached to the table behind him for one of those candles in bottles that served as illumination and decoration to the whole dreary scene. He lit his cigarette and stood there, candle and bottle in hand, staring gloomily into the small wavering flame. Thoughts of dramatic calls for attention continued to flow before him: what about that chap he had once known who had put a cigarette out on the back of his hand because some girl said he was a physical coward? He had been drunk at the time, of course, and it had left a horrible scar, but the girl had been most impressed: indeed she had screamed loudly and burst into tears. Humphrey reflected glumly that he could have put out all twenty of his cigarettes all over his person and nobody would have batted an eye-lid. One had to be introduced first, before one could embark on that kind of thing. One had to have an audience.

When it happened, it happened so suddenly that he never quite knew whether it was inspiration or accident. As he did it, he did not quite know what he expected to happen: clearly he could not have hoped that she would go up in a sheet of flame, nor even that she should sustain any injury, however mild, for he was a kind and unmalicious person. She did not go up in flame, anyway: hair is not a particularly flammable substance, not even long flowing fiery-red hanks of it, and he did not apply the candle with much violence. But it did singe and scorch, with a most alarming and dangerous smell, strong enough to cause a great commotion.

'Good Lord, Justina,' said one of her admirers, 'you're on fire!' and he only just had time to put the candle down before she twisted round to clutch at the singed ends, shrieking with dismay and delight, and lost her balance and fell into his arms.

'You did it,' she said, challengingly, from a breath-taking proximity. 'You did it, you set me alight.'

And he, reading in her face nothing but pleasure at having created so large a disturbance, held on to her tight and said:

'Let me introduce myself, my name is Humphrey.'

'What did you do it *for?*' she cried, in a positive blaze of admiration, the kind of excitement kindled by duels or the *Rape of the Sabine Women* or indeed any violent and decisive action taken in the cause of passion.

'Oh well,' he said, with nonchalant pride, as though such inspirations came to him every day of the week, 'I just wanted to attract your attention, that's all.'

Margaret Drabble 28.10.1964

SUGAR AND SPICE AND ALL THINGS NOT NICE

The very dim and misty memories I have of my father – he died when I was only seven years old – do not include a picture of a benign, old, bearded man lowering himself down a chimney with his arms full of presents and his face wreathed in smiles. No, he was a little too crusty for that, and the only Christmas memory I have of him is of his bursting all our party balloons with the lighted end of his cigarette.

Pity about that. It was very traumatic for me and drove me first into my mother's arms and then Nanny's. It probably drove me to drink as well, but that is another story: suffice it to say that I have ended up in the arms of women as frequently as is humanly possible.

The incident also convinced me that there was no such person as Father Christmas but, better still, there was a Mother Christmas. Cynical men, nervous of feminists, are now agreed that God is a woman, but I knew years ago that the reindeers were driven by a woman too, and many's the night I lay crouched in the fireplace of my nursery hoping to get a look up her skirt as she came down the chimney.

But, more than anything, it was the presents of books at Christmas which moulded the disgustingly infantile and regressive attitude that I have towards women today. In fairy stories, they were untouchable, mysterious and exciting in a way that I could not then understand. They aroused the unconscious sexuality in me that we are all born with. Of course there were some wets, and I never could understand how that boring little Snow White could bear to clean up after seven disgusting little dwarfs. The Wicked Queen, though, was a tremendous turn-on, as was the Ice Queen or any Queen north of a line drawn from Glasgow to Moscow.

Dangerous women still appeal to me and I never liked the twee element in fairy stories. At first I fancied Goldilocks quite strongly, and I still have a penchant for blondes, but could you live with a compulsive porridge-eater who has a subconscious hankering for bestiality? And how I wished the wolf had got Red Riding Hood, a horribly sycophantic little girl who was probably hoping to borrow half a crown from her grandmother. A woman I did love quite seriously for a while was the Lady of Shalott, about whom I had several fairly obscene fantasies far in advance of my age. I often found my way to her room at the top of that turret; and she had a mirror on the ceiling as well.

But, as I say, it was the *threatening* women in children's stories that fascinated and excited me. I don't remember exactly but I don't think it was actually stated in Hansel and Gretel whether or not the wicked witch really was ugly, but even if she was, we have it only on the say-so of the Brothers Grimm. She could be interesting and other people's children can be a nuisance. Quite how she would have tempted me, me being diabetic, is something I ponder from time to time, but I think she had the right idea. At least she wasn't cosy, and it's cosiness that I can't take in Hans Andersen. I assume that the Ugly Duckling was, in fact, a girl, though Andersen didn't have the guts (or was too repressed) to say so, but it's very tame stuff. Anyone with eyes would have recognised her potential, and those without an insight as to what a few bob and a good couturier could have done with her would have promptly stuffed her with oranges.

Which brings me to the curious psychology of Beatrix Potter. Some of her stories are far from tame and are, without doubt, about men and women. I suppose it is a nasty, sadistic streak in me that wants to get its own back on women – what the hell for, I wonder? – that makes me revere Mr Tod, probably one of the greatest con men of all time to have failed through sheer bad luck. When he entertained and entirely captivated Jemima Puddleduck, it was so right that he should have been an actor. Jemima loved him as women tend to love ne'er-do-wells, and the wretched farm dog should have minded his own business. But that a fox could persuade a duck to go and pick some sage and onion is to me the most touching case of heart over head I have ever read.

Hot on its heels comes the classic story of requited love, when Pigling Bland runs over the hills with his bride-to-be, hand-in-hand, and into the sunset.

But dear God, how I hate princesses who moon about. I would guess that Cinderella never cracked a joke in her life. Her so-called Ugly Sisters were almost definitely a couple of extremely witty gays and Prince Charming was simply a Sloane Ranger of the bread-roll-throwing variety. No, I still like the baddies and the witches the best, although, heaven knows, they've ruined me.

These stories have stuck and I still keep falling for witches. I found a true Ice Queen last year in Marylebone. In fact I didn't need ice. All I had to do was to get her to glance at my vodka. I made her melt, though, one day, and thought that we were going to run away over the hills, hand-in-hand, into the sunset. Unfortunately, she went through my pockets, saw that I had only some small change, and left me for a property dealer. That is a *real* fairy story and that is why I still believe in them.

Jeffrey Bernard 4.12.1985

'. . . And that won't wake me either.'

'Not now, Gawain – the neighbours will hear you undressing.'

'Dammit, Cleopatra, d'you have to let it sleep on the bed?'

'So – Captain Thin Lips plays his ace!'

*'I can't get Joe to make any sort of
commitment. He won't even be tied down to
coming and going as he pleases.'*

BROAD SHEET: LUNCH

Why is lunch allegedly so innocent? Do we seriously think that because there's light in the sky and others around us are foolish enough to be toiling, it follows that we can't or shouldn't or mustn't do any of those things we feel like doing and which are, for the most part, a great deal more life-enhancing than *cuisine minceur* or a double helping of strawberry shortcake? The wonderful thing about a man taking you to lunch is that it can be as ordinary or as special as dinner but without any of the connotations. Because the Almighty has not yet flicked the celestial light switch, people feel innocent even when they are not.

There are all sorts of reasons for a man taking a woman to lunch, ranging from curiosity to necessity to cowardice, but it is one of the social areas where a man still holds his own without much serious competition. A man asking a woman to lunch has quite a different charge from a man and a woman agreeing to have lunch together. The first transaction is about encounter, the second is about food, but even the encounters vary a good deal.

A man will take a woman to lunch to prove how hardworking he is. They will go 'just to that little place round the corner' and it usually is. They will stay for an hour and a half if she's doing well. He will look crumpled and anything more than a fresh coat of lipstick on her part will be regarded as an overstatement.

A man may take a woman to lunch to prove he esteems how hardworking she is. This is usually to a slightly better class of little place. They're still crumpled but in better gear. She'll wear something a bit more affirmative but still working model, and enhance the proceedings with perfume as well as lipstick.

A man may take a woman to lunch to get to know, as it were, the lie of the land. This has many variations:

1) She is the new secretary and he's quite happy whatever he is. The setting is middle-of-the-road Franco-Italian; they just stay for the hour to show her how businesslike he is. He offers no confidences, gets her to talk about her husband/boyfriend. Altogether super-kosher.

2) She's the new secretary, they are both 'happily married'. They might have a special understanding, ostensibly because they're both married, actually because they're both open to suggestion. Same setting, same timing. Just as businesslike but for a different reason.

3) They've been colleagues for some time. He's not impressed but his boss thinks she's wonderful. Smart place, smart suit, timing strictly according to how long he can get away with it and still make his boss feel he gave her a chance before turning her down.

4) They've been colleagues for some time and he kissed her rather hard after a dinner party given by some mutual friends a week ago. This is testing time. Was it just that rotten Rioja or did a bell ring somewhere? Place where he's known; duration as long as it takes to find out whether this is going anywhere.

5) His wife's just left him. Will she hold his hand or bank the home fires? Off-beat place (no witnesses if he makes a mess of it); he does his best to look devastating as well as a bit shell-shocked and he wants her to look feminine above all else. He won't notice the time for at least two hours. Women, be warned: take tissues, he'll probably cry over the brandy.

6) He's going to offer her a job. Depending on the field of employment, the venue will be either 'in' or grand. He'll look good but comfortable, she has to put on the dog – but nothing *outré* unless he's a movie producer. Timing – anything from two to four hours. Women, be warned: unless sired by a boilermaker, stick to mineral water or spritzers.

A man will take a woman to lunch to tell her he loves her. Could she care if it's at a coffee stall or the smoothest place in town? Relax. Few men tell a woman anything personal in public unless they're very comfortable and few men are comfortable where they can be overheard on the subject of anything romantic. He'll probably take her to a steak house. He needs nourishment while making a major commitment. Or he'll take her somewhere he thinks she'll like. If the attraction's mutual, they'll be there for a long, long time and it won't matter what anybody's wearing until at least six months later.

A man will take a woman to lunch to tell her

it's over. He'll choose somewhere pretty with excellent powder-rooms, in case either or both of them have to withdraw.

A man will take a woman to lunch to tell her he's fallen in love with someone else. And few men seem to have got this sorted out. It is extremely unkind to expect a woman to eat while you break her heart (unless she's one who eats when she's miserable) and if she can't eat, you may be tempted to mutter about her extravagance, which would be caddish to put it mildly. Also, conventional cutlery may incite the more fiery to physical violence. Accordingly, the ideal setting for this lunch is a traditional Chinese restaurant where the waiters neither know nor care what you're saying to one another – and it is very nearly impossible to stab anybody with a chopstick.

A man will take a woman to lunch to show her that she has registered as a woman but not for him. He may take her to lunch when his best friend, her husband, is out of town. He may take her to lunch to make her feel better or to discuss her overdraft. He may take her to lunch because he can't think of anything else to do with her. He may take her to lunch because he can't get through the day without a glimpse of her. He may take her to lunch because once it's over, he won't have to do it again for quite a while.

And sometimes, when a man asks a woman to lunch, daylight or no, work or no work, hang the exigencies of time and place, glory hallelujah, what he really wants is her. And if there will be no more pain than awkwardness and no regret at all, and he has the panache and the wherewithal, then the very best of British luck. But don't expect to remember where you met for lunch, or what you wore or ate. There were more important things on the menu and other appetites to be fulfilled. As a woman, the only problem is distinguishing one of these lunches from the other, given that the man himself doesn't always know how he wants things to work out in the end. Perhaps the best rule of thumb is that lunch with a man may not always be something but it is rarely nothing, and calories have little to do with it.

Anna Raeburn 7.5.1986

'I've just come to the conclusion that the only thing we have in common is the same lunch hour!'

BRINGING UP GRANDAD

If you're like me you don't know anything about yourself until you're told.

'But if we go to bed,' this lady said, 'then I don't see you again for three months. It takes that long to get yourself back.' Yes, by God, I thought, that's exactly what I have to do. Get myself back. What are you giving away when you penetrate that rare and unbearably exquisite catacomb? Oh my darling, I love you I love you I love you (don't move!) no, no, n o . . . .SSSSCCCCC ZZZZZZHHHHHPPPAAAAHHH– phew.

'Don't take it out, let it pickle,' this other lady used to say. 'You're a very shallow person, aren't you,' said another, rather older woman, whom I suddenly realised was a total stranger and rather middle-class. We had nothing in common whatever except a bottle of Scotch. But it's not even this. This is a corny and clichéd conception of going to bed with a princess and waking up with your wife's mother. The terrible thing is if you're like me, as I keep saying, you have nothing in common with anybody. Nobody. I have never in my life met anybody that I have even the least thing in common with.

What do you talk about when you've made love to a seventeen-year-old girl? Nothing, that's what you talk about. And it's a bloody sight worse if they're thirty and expecting something meaningful. One older woman, around thirty-five, slapped my face hard. Bam! Right across the chops. 'Whatja do that for?' I always do that if I don't get an orgasm – it's perfectly all right. Oh yeah? Then you're supposed to telephone the next day?

Go into hiding. I've made love about six times. No, seven. One was a Greek when I was sailing back from Gibraltar with Anna Neagle. 'Who's done this to you?' she kept saying, this Greek girl. She kept a baby in a cot under her bunk. Husband waiting at Tilbury. 'This is Jack – Aris, Jack's a writer.' 'Please to meet you very much. You gotta come and have some food in Camden Town.' He must be kidding. I wouldn't go anywhere there was a knife.

Make love not war?

My son Lee was once chased through Covent Garden when it was a garden by a famous editor with a knife. All he had done was he came back from Norway with this chap's wife. Me and Ross, that's Lee's mother, the novelist Catharine Tracy actually, had from our different parts of England buzzed off twenty pounds each to the police station at – what's that Norwegian port on this side never mind – Gothenburg, that's it – and they had deported him from his holiday and this nice lady on the boat said come and see my husband some time – maybe he'll give you a job on the magazine. I'm sure this was said after the phew bit.

Never ever act on anything that happens after sexual intercourse. Unless you are with somebody who is equally bowled over by the transcendencies of the occasion, that is, has also done it about six times before, then forget it. Some people, and it took me forty years to realise this, are not bowled over by it. For a lot of people, love is something nice that has happened again. Oh boy, I could live a quiet normal life if I felt like that about it.

'You think making love is a victory!' Molly Parkin once said to me. This is a fairly public woman and novelist who is not afraid to say quite openly that she had had it more than seven or eight times. 'I get considerably more than a cup of tea!' she screamed, laughingly, when I was explaining my various achievements with women. You see it always becomes domestic with me. Sex is such an enormous thing that once it has happened I get married. Other men perhaps buy a box of Black Magic.

'You realise we haven't made love for two months?' Elaine says, quite without rancour, but speaking as a fairly careful diarist. 'No, I know. I'm getting myself back.' The point is, you see, for a few moments there, sliding heaven as Rupert Brooke called it (though in fact talking about fish), you have given the lady the false impression that you have nothing else to do. It is a fatal thing to let another person think this for even ten minutes. I used to listen to Jay Lewis talking to his wife on the phone – and to his mother the same way.

'Yes. Oh? Good. I will. 'Bye then . . .'

You would get the impression he was in the middle of balancing a kitchen chair on his chin. I learned a lot from film directors like Jay Lewis and Mario Zampi and Basil Dearden and Sol Siegel and Herbert Wilcox (never mention anyone who's died, his daughter said), but I learned it in that way you still don't do it. All I try to do is not see them for a few weeks. Nothing can be repeated – when you're with another person that's not repeating it. When I say I am sixty-two and I have made love seven times I mean with seven ladies – love is only the first time. After the first time you are imagining some ghostly future.

I get up every morning of my life full of hope. But if I meet somebody beautiful, that is with a mole perhaps or a way of not knowing you are waiting to use the only Biro in Wolverton post office, then I chicken out. Maybe if she faints I can do something introductory, say. Last winter I comforted a girl who was lying under her machine in the snow after an accident in which the car had not even stopped.

'Can you move your feet still?' I asked.

She said: 'If you could just stop leaning on my bike, I'll get up.'

With most of the fanciable girls I know around here in Milton Keynes I just say hi there. I can't think of anything else to say without intruding on my privacy. NO TO YARDLEY

CHASE brought a slight flush of conversation for a time but nobody dragged me away. I'm beginning to think I could do without the whole thing. Could always have done without it. I don't know about you but I think myself into exciting situations sometimes where this very nice lady (who has never said more than good morning) and you are shipwrecked on a desert island with no books or paper or with a typewriter but no ribbon and she has twisted her ankle trying to signal a passing ship.

'Hold my shoulder. I'll have to put my hand on your waist. Is that all right? Lean on me.'

'Good morning,' she keeps saying.

I mean if you've never heard her say anything else for Christ's sake. To have that great resonant peak of sexual union with a person she has got to be almost unattainable – which is precisely why it can't happen twice. Marriage of course has to be the end of sex – indeed if it didn't end after the party last March. Making love to your own wife becomes incestuous, embarrassing, somewhat rude if there are children in the house. Glen Cardno cut this point of view out of my Barbara Cartland interview – Glen edited the *Love and Marriage* film. 'He can't do that, can he?' I protested to the producer. They get scissor happy. To make the visuals work then he had to rescue a bit of film off-cut from the Death episode. Anything that fitted.

'People are bewildered and frightened when their loved one has passed on and they want somebody to turn to,' says David Webb, the undertaker.

If it had been the BBC instead of ATV you would have seen Barbara Cartland's horrified expression. 'Incestuous!' she cried. It's amazing what they can do though. One day I am playing the guitar when Bud Freeman the famous tenor horn man drops out of the sky in a hot-air balloon basket and I go to the window and look out. Unfortunately the Musicians Union would not allow us to use the solo from the sky. So instead one day I am playing the guitar when Paul Nasty and Maggie drive past in a motor car and I go to the window and look out. Amazing – the same film, no Bud.

Sexually then, people keep telling you, you're not much good. You've got this great horny reputation on six or seven times. Seven years

I've been living with Elaine and yet somebody's mother (I mean you know the gang but their mothers are really out of touch) stooped to say to her and did you know about Jack's family before you saw the film, dear? Seven years rubbing my palpitations while I read the bedtime bit of Gatsby, entertaining my various families, gossiping periods and Pills with the daughters and daughters-in-law, remembering authors' names for me, arguing for me. Some stone-age guest wants to bring back hanging.

'Elaine!' She comes in with the coffee. 'Hanging,' I say. That's all I have to say. She can talk fast Geordie anti-hanging for thirty-five minutes without repeating herself, including ape faces and der-type dialogue of the people who think that killing should be made legal and carried out in our name. On intensive farming she's got hens, pigs, calves and all wild and domestic animal cruelty sewn up. I'm not much good in verbal non-typed argument and debate – I start saying fuck. I'm so humane I could kill.

'Let me tell him,' she says. She is talking to my eldest grandson, Howard, who thinks the boat people from Vietnam should be sent back. I hear them in the background of a hubbub and young Howard is saying: 'All right so I read the *Daily Mirror*! You people take *The Guardian* and think you're God! Why should you be right right right all the time! This is our country!' I'd never heard him open his mouth before.

'He's been drinking,' Jackie explained.

'He's very good,' Elaine said when she came back to us. Wrong, but good. 'Let's talk about religion,' says son Pete to change the subject to something facetious and soon everybody's laughing again until somebody says to Elaine: 'Are you still out of work?' And she turns pale. Out of what? She rents our flat (I'm her lodger), does the herb garden, most of the fine weeding amid the flowers and vegetables, takes care of the chickens, manages the video recorder, organises my VAT, income tax, expenses, receipts, the washing machine every day, cleaning, cooking and her own yoga and French. Unfortunately, and I blame the North-East, she is five-foot-one and looks sixteen. On the screen she is the park warden in *Fear*, the girl on the beach in *Money*, the girl in bed with me (our bed) in *Love and Marriage* and etc – so you can see for yourself the troubles we've had with a 39-

year age gap since 1972. At the Electra for *The 39-Steps* last week the cashier said:

'One and a half?'

At the Cock or the Bull at Stony Stratford (this is where the Cock and Bull story originated) on the A5 Elaine is in trouble with the landlord. It was probably her large Canadian Club. 'I'll get you a nice lemonade,' said the Italian waiter at The Swan Revived at Newport Pagnell. When our private garden and orchard was invaded by the public at Whitsun (we live on an exhibition farm) Open Day, Elaine got fed up and took a tub of wet knickers and pants out and hung them on the line – the public withdrew, one by one, family by family and never came back.

'Why don't you just put up a Private notice?' I asked her. But that's fascist. We are trying to teach Queenie the dog to bite but she doesn't seem to understand yet.

'Aaaeh! Like that!' says Elaine. 'If she would just eat kids it would be a start.'

'Why don't we get married?' she asked. 'Give me a bit of status.' I've been a widower since Evelyn died last year.

'I may want to marry that girl at the garden centre,' I pointed out. Because, I don't know if you're like me, but you don't know anything about yourself until it happens.

Jack Trevor Story 29.8.1979

'Has this film been heavily cut, or is copulation really that jerky?'

VERSES VEGETARIAN

(By a Disillusioned Bachelor)

When I was young – as everyone agreed –
   And when my gladsome heart no burden carried,
I had a very near escape indeed
     Of getting married.

My income was diminutive, it's true,
   Yet that was but a small consideration.
I met my love and fell a victim to
     Her fascination.

The day arrived when I resolved to try
   If my persuasive eloquence could win her,
For to her father's house, one evening, I
     Was asked to dinner.

Although I took some other female down,
   I did not mind at all, for I was able
To watch my fair adored one smile or frown
     Across the table.

Now half-way through the dinner we had got,
   And pit-a-pat my frenzied heart was beating,
When suddenly I chanced to notice what
     My love was eating.

Asparagus, that coy, elusive thing,
   She swallowed with an energy most frantic
(Although it may be very nourishing,
     It's not romantic).

The nodding heads, when lifted from her plate,
   Towards her ruby lips she started thrusting.
The scene that followed, I don't hesitate
     To call disgusting.

I felt that I must gaze at her, perforce;
   Ah! how the recollection of it lingers!
The melted butter ran its wayward course
     Along her fingers.

She even smacked her lips, devoid of shame;
  But, as the pile of heads before her dwindled,
Within my heart there flickered out the flame
  That love had kindled.

The mad, delicious moments of the past
  For once and all were absolutely ended.
I left the house much sooner, at the last,
  Than I intended.

*   *   *   *   *

Young men, if any maidens you adore,
  Be guided by a sensible suggestion,
And watch them eat asparagus before
  You put the question!

Percy Greenbank 15.7.1903

PRIMUM VIVERE, DEINDE PHILOSOPHARI.

'IS FLORRIE'S ENGAGEMENT REALLY OFF, THEN?'
'OH, YES. JACK WANTED HER TO GIVE UP GAMBLING AND SMOKING, AND GOODNESS KNOWS WHAT ELSE.'   (*Chorus.*) 'HOW
ABSURD!!'

A SHORT HISTORY OF MARRIAGE

PREHISTORY

According to Professor Leakey, the earth is 4,600,000,000 years old. The year 400,000,1981 AD will therefore be a really big anniversary, possibly Plutonium, and it would be unwise to forget it. Civilisation could end up not talking to you for weeks. Start thinking about a suitable anniversary present now, even if you end up rushing out to buy it at the last minute. Something personal, certainly nothing for the kitchen.

2,000,000,000 BC Unicellular life appears. It reproduces by parthenogenesis, involving no one else. It is therefore pretty happy, especially as nobody asks it where it has been all night.

30,000,000 BC Earliest apes appear. This is the Oligocene Period (from Gk. = 'few'), and the handful of apes thus has a very good time, since you can lope for weeks without running into an ape of the opposite sex, which means that when you eventually do, you are extremely grateful. Ugly apes have as much fun as attractive apes, and do not have to stay in all the time washing their hair. As a result, however, apes naturally begin to proliferate, so that within hardly more than about six million years, some apes are starting to get choosy. Thus, the more repulsive apes take to trying to hang on to their mates permanently, in case the chance doesn't come again. It is the dawn of matrimony.

1,700,000 BC Earliest known hominids appear. Hunting and food-gathering begins. Slight shift in bonding-patterns emerges as female hominids able to make lizards taste good gain edge over female hominids with nice legs.

400,000 BC *Homo Erectus* stage. Body hair starts thinning. As big busts therefore become more evident, there is a commensurate swing away from lizard cuisine again.

350,000 BC Date of Heidelberg jaw. From its size and elaborate hingework, palaeontologists have now been able to sex it with confidence, and also attribute to it the beginnings of domestic conversation. Phonetic experts believe it to have been capable of delivering complex structures at rapid speed, viz. 'What time do you call this, I have been slaving over this bloody lizard crumble all day, I was given to understand you were out gathering moss for afters, it does not take eight hours, whatever they are, to pluck a few handfuls of lichen, doubtless you have been lurching around after that top-heavy slag up the cliff, what is that curly red hair on your club, well I have not given you the best years of my life in order to . . .'

350,000 BC (*later the same evening*) Date of Heidelberg headache.

200,000 BC Discovery of fire. It is now possible to get a decent steak. An entirely new area of marital discord is ushered in, since it is even more possible to get a lousy steak.

80,000 BC Neanderthal Period. Tools become much more sophisticated: the needle is refined, making it possible to invent the nightdress. Cohabitation enters its darkest phase to date.

50,000 BC The First Ice Age. Neanderthal man, maintaining that it was Neanderthal woman's job to get the firewood in, bloody hell have I got to do every little job myself, and while we're on the subject it wouldn't kill your mother to get up off her backside now and again, becomes extinct.

30,000 BC Emergence of Cro-Magnon man, and the Aurignacian culture, bringing with it cave-painting and violent arguments about what colour to do the dining-room. Chisels become more sophisticated, and Cro-Magnon woman suggests that a shelf be put up in the kitchen.

25,000 BC Cro-Magnon woman asks how the shelf is coming along.

18,000 BC Last Ice Age. Cro-Magnon man reckons that it is hardly worth putting up the shelf now, and becomes extinct.

12,000 BC Rise of Proto-Neolithic civilisation. The wheel is invented. The woman is not allowed to roll it.

THE MODERN ERA

3,500 BC Sumerian civilisation flourishes. Cuneiform writing is invented, radically changing the whole nature of marriage, since it is now possible to write notes saying: 'I miss you my darling, when is that ratfaced husband of yours going on nights again, S.W.A.L.K.' As it is also possible to find them lying around in pockets, a new vitality enters married life, together with surgery.

3,000 BC Cretan civilisation. First recorded example of bridegroom saying: 'It is a small thing, but Minoan.' The period is also remarkable for the rise of gold, silver and copper ornamentation: the sweet-dish is born, and becomes the first example of an item made not for using but for giving. Such is the glut of production that weddings alone will not mop up the fearful flood, and the engagement party is invented. This is an extremely successful marketing operation, and even allows the silversmiths to diversify into cruets.

2,000 BC Abraham leads the great emigration from Mesopotamia into Canaan, but it does not help, his mother-in-law finds out where he is from the butcher.

1,988 BC God commands Abraham to slay his son Isaac. His mother-in-law commands him to make the boy a solicitor. It is no contest; by 1,982 BC, Isaac has eight junior partners, plus a branch in Hebron specialising in corporate financing.

1,184 BC Menelaus goes to Sparta on business, and while he is away, Paris comes in to service the dishwasher. He then persuades her to elope with him to Troy, whereupon the Greeks lay siege to the city. The siege lasts ten years, which means that, while Helen was undoubtedly the most beautiful woman in the world at the start, by the end she is lying third, behind Miss Guatemala and Julia Morley. Menelaus takes Helen back to Sparta, but sees a lot of Miss Guatemala on the side.

753 BC Rhea Silvia, left short of housekeeping

by her husband Mars, takes a part-time job in a Latium boutique, but has nowhere to leave the twins. She contacts a domestic agency for a child-minder, but because of a misunderstanding they send a wolf. It does not matter, the wolf is very good with kids and knows some terrific games, plus being a stickler for neatness.

Anyone leaving toys lying around is liable to lose a leg. In consequence, Romulus and Remus grow up right, and found Rome. Dr Spock may have known a thing or two, but he wasn't in the wolf's league.

432 BC Outbreak of appalling marital disorder in Greece: not only are the divorce courts run off their feet with cases in which the evidence leaves even hardened barristers vomiting, but the genetic consequences afflict society for years to come, as sisters find themselves to be uncles and men turn out to be their own grandparents. Sociologists blame it on watching too much Sophocles.

46 BC Carpet containing Cleopatra delivered to Caesar. *Cleopatra:* 'Have you told her yet?' *Caesar:* 'She hasn't been feeling very well

lately.' This is the first recorded example of this popular exchange.

0 BC Breakthrough in attitude to one-parent families.

60 AD Revolt of Boadicea, who fits sword-blades to her chariot wheels and leaves a pitiful trail of Roman sopranos in her wake. Later, she edits *Guardian Women*.

618 Foundation of the T'ang Dynasty in China, ushering in the 128-piece dinner service. This is to revolutionise marriage, since the only way anybody can afford one is to have a formal ceremony, a large number of guests, and a list at Harrods.

663 Synod of Whitby installs Roman Christianity in Britain, which causes many problems, not the least of which is that very few people can spell 'rhythm'.

868 Earliest printed book appears in China. However, since several hundred couples suffer serious damage attempting page 32, it is quickly withdrawn.

879 Following the second Danish invasion, King Alfred seeks refuge in a peasant woman's hut. Her husband, who has been asleep in the garden, is awakened by the smell of a neglected oven, but proves an inferior swordsman to the king. This comes as no surprise to his wife.

1000 Leif Ericsson discovers North America. He is met by a tall woman with wonderful teeth who is prepared to enter into a one-to-one meaningful relationship in which both partners respect one another as persons. Leif Ericsson gets back in his boat.

1066 Normans introduce contraceptive to Britain. It is called garlic.

1099–1204 The Crusades, or I Have To Go Abroad On Business. It is hardly surprising that the English contingent fares so badly: of the 18,400 crusaders who set out, 9,200 are secretaries, and only a handful get further than Brighton.

1327 A bad year for marriage. Edward II, King of England, comes out of the closet. Since he is subsequently killed with a red-hot poker, it is also a bad year for coming out of the closet.

1536 Execution of Anne Boleyn radically changes English sexual mores. Husbands are encouraged to believe that it is no longer necessary to bring home bunches of daffs or engage in enervating foreplay: all you do is stick an axe on the bedside table. Women, however, respond by waiting for

1558, when Elizabeth I introduces the fashion for virgin spinsterhood. Nobody gets married, and there is very little sex, which is particularly hard on Sir Walter Raleigh, who has just invented the cigarette for afterwards.

1590+ The rise of English drama. Hardly have people begun marrying again when they have to start going to the theatre all the time. In arguments about who had the tickets, where to park the horse, who fell asleep during the first act, whether to eat before or after, and whose turn it is to take the baby-sitter home, thousands die.

1669 Nell Gw

1981 Hack's wife bursts in, enquiring whether hack realises it is now 3.30 a.m., not of course that it is a question of hack choosing between her and typewriter, hack exclaims bloody hell,

politely, I have only got to 1669 and not yet dealt with rubberwear or mortgages either, hack's wife says what is hack writing about, hack says marriage, hack's wife goes ha bloody ha.

Alan Coren 22.7.1981

WITH THIS PINT,
I THEE WED

The first thing to understand about north country weddings is that they are the same as north country funerals, the only difference being that at a funeral only one person is being buried. That apart, the cars are the same, they use the same church hall for the 'do', they hire the same teapot, and the same women who laid Grandad to rest are the ones who made the wedding cake. Sometimes you heard the same dialogue.

When Grandad died, we all went back to his house where Auntie Ada said to my old man:

'Has tha' found his bank book then?' Father nodded.

'How much did he leave then?' she asked eagerly.

'Threepence ha'penny and six Craven A', said my old man.

'Pity you don't smoke', he added.

It was the same cast of characters in the same room eighteen months later when our Jessie got married. We were having a few after the wedding when Auntie Ada asked Jessie:

'Has tha' seen his bank book then?'

Jessie looked at her for a moment, then said:

'He doesn't believe in banks, he keeps it buried in a steel box in t'allotment'.

I don't know if Auntie Ada believed her or not, although I have a cousin who swears he once saw her heading for the allotment carrying a shovel.

I don't much go for weddings of any kind, but if it were obligatory that everyone went to at least one a year then I would want it to be a north country wedding. North country weddings, at least the sort I went to, do not entail a visit to Moss Bros. nor polite chit-chat over the top of a champagne glass. They are occasions on which one gets roaring daft drunk on whatever you fancy (excepting Champagne).

When I got married we accommodated overnight 50 people in a three-bedroomed council house. This miracle of hospitality was achieved by letting people lay where they fell. The position was eased by the fact that some chose to sleep in the garden! Next morning the lawn looked like a field in Flanders after a dawn attack.

On the question of dress, the convention was that everyone should look as smart as possible, but no-one raises an eyebrow at the odd eccentricity. For instance, one uncle of mine attended my wedding wearing his best suit, white shirt and silk scarf knotted round his neck – the scarf he wore when he went whippet racing. It wasn't that he didn't own a tie, he just wanted me to know that he liked me as much as he liked his whippets. And I still have a photograph of the wedding which shows my Auntie Florrie looking a million dollars in a smart dress, big hat and posh gloves. The effect is somewhat spoiled if you look at her feet, which are encased in a large and battered pair of carpet slippers.

I became an expert on north country weddings soon after I left school and started work as a reporter on a local newspaper. Like most local newspapers, it based its circulation effort on the amount of wedding reports, funeral details and beetle drive winners it could carry in any one issue. It was during this period that I first became aware of the aforementioned similarity between north country funerals and marriages. For one thing, when I called at a house which was going to have either a wedding or a funeral, there was always the same ritual to go through. The wedding dialogue would go:

'Come in, love. Would you like to see the wedding dress?' And you'd be led into the best room where they kept the piano and never lit the fire, to inspect a wedding dress knitted by some mad Aunt in Barnsley.

'Lovely', you'd say, and they'd thank you for your kindness and give you a tot of rum. If, on the other hand, it was a funeral they were expecting, you would again be shown into the best room, where the deceased would be laid out by the local Co-op with a frill round his face. You would be invited to inspect the undertaker's art by peering at the dead face, as smooth and unlined as a balloon.

'He does look peaceful', you'd say, and they'd thank you for your kindness and give you a tot of rum.

Simple though it may seem, there were hazards to this kind of reporting, particularly at Easter and Christmas time. These were the periods when most people got married, and when my working day was one long round of inspecting wedding dresses and collecting reports. In those days, being just a raw sprog reporter and having seen too many American movies, I fancied myself strongly as Humphrey Bogart. The fact that I was 16 years old, didn't smoke or drink and spent my time cycling round my area on a drop-handled Raleigh in no way dissuaded me from my fantasy. I even went to the extent of buying myself a snap brim trilby such as Bogart wore. The difficulties of keeping a trilby on my head while travelling downhill at 30 m.p.h. with a following wind need no explaining, and I overcame them by attaching an elastic chinstrap to my hat, thus inventing a new fashion in headwear.

This particular Easter, celebrated by my new bonnet, I called on twelve people and collected my wedding reports. At each house I accepted a drink because I thought Bogy would not have refused. The consequence was that I became drunk for the first time in my life, went to sleep in a bus shelter near Barnsley, and when I awoke was minus my trilby and my bike. The end of this saga of misfortune came at the end of the week when, scanning the paper for signs of my handiwork, I came across this line in one of my reports:

'As a wedding gift the bride presented the bridegroom with an electric cock.'

Like I said, north country weddings are different.

Michael Parkinson 7.4.1971

'*Aren't we perhaps being a little premature?*'

Merrily Harpur:

SPRING WEDDINGS

'I didn't realise she was a
career woman.'

'Well, he certainly isn't on **my** side
of the family.'

'I can't help it – I always laugh at weddings.'

'It's a shotgun wedding. They have to
marry before his insurance policy
matures.'

'Strike out "in sickness" and "for poorer". It's too depressing.'

I'M GETTING MALLIED IN THE MORNING

The Japanese yesterday turned their attention towards the traditional English wedding. Twenty-three leaders of the multi-million pound Japanese wedding industry descended on Britain, intent on finding out what makes the girls back East so enthusiastic about an English marriage.

Sunday Telegraph

To many of our highly prized and respected readers the Englishman is a funny coot.

All too often the cultivated Japanese traveller, however intelligent, sensitive and adventurous he or she may be, will be tempted to dismiss Joe Bull as a mobile-faced big pink hooligan, the traditional butt of so much wartime humour.

But perhaps it is time, with the greatest possible respect, that our readers took a short passionate look at Mr Bull with a view to exploding, as the Englishman himself would say, a few French ducks.

Consider the very ancient English Wedding Ceremony. In England, when a man and woman, or any similar combination, wish to 'have a fack' it is not the simple business it is in Japan.

Oh no.

Leading Japanese anthropologist Wassamata Wichu has written: 'In more virile and dynamic societies sexual coupling is a hurdle we go flying over with the greatest of ease. In England, thanks to long centuries of decay and energy-draining, a great song and dance is necessary to land Percy in the Pudding.'

The Ceremony we were able to study took place in the charming city of Reeds, in the Northern province of York-shah.

Despite warnings from our delightful English hosts in London that 'you litre baggers' – an affectionate term meaning 'small friend or companion' – would not understand a word they said in Reeds on account of their pronounced Celtic accent, we found the old ritual both illuminating and as easy to comprehend as falling off a house.

Three weeks before we arrived, the 'Buns of Marriage' had been exhibited at the local Materialist shrine.

We were unable to discover the exact nature of this part of the ceremony, but natives we questioned described it as 'a rot of hokey-pokey,' suggesting that some form of dance was involved, perhaps to exorcise the 'Boon in Tooven,' or unborn child conceived as a result of a previous Wedding.

The day of the main ceremony began dark and wet, provoking much gesticulation at the sky on the part of the assembling natives, together with exaggerated facial contortions and exclamations in a tone of lugubrious fatalism to the effect that a sky-spirit referred to as 'It' was urinating on them.

Despite the inclemency of the weather, grotesque costumes were much in evidence: feathered head-dresses, terrifying face-paint, and many large silver and gold bags, used, we discovered later, as offensive weapons.

The centre of the ceremonial is a mock battle between two teams of champions selected by the couple, and known respectively as 'Blide Sparrans' and 'Glume Sparrans', which is believed capable of exciting them sufficiently to 'have Itway'.

In ancient times this battle was fought to the death, but today, in keeping with the sleepy, easy-going mood of these carefree islanders, the 'poonjub' is very perfunctory, resulting usually in little more than a few broken noses and the loss of a few teeth, and both teams demand liberal supplies of the locally brewed 'Newcassa Blun' before they will go into action.

The drink, which is passed from hand to hand in brown bottles, is believed to possess aphrodisiac qualities, and produced very alarming symptoms as the day progressed, including violent eye-movements, apparent demon-possession, frothing at the mouth, rolling on the floor, loss of memory, incontinence and subsequent nausea.

We requested to taste it, and were at first told that this would not be possible in the small quantities we were asking for, 'not for nips'.

Later however we were offered a bottle by an elderly female celebrant, and found it warm, sweet, and tasting a little like oatmeal soup.

The Materialist shrine had been decorated with flowers for the ceremony, martial music was played on a pipe-organ, and a Materialist monk, flanked by flower-maidens and dressed in what appeared to be a Victorian female nurse's costume with a black petticoat and a white plastic punishment collar, greeted the Wedding celebrants with much upward eye-rolling and clasping and unclasping of his hands.

Materialist teaching is almost incomprehensible to the foreigner, involving as it does repetitive invocation of the sky-spirit in a ritual distraction of the worshippers' attention while the so-called 'sacred element' is rathered in collecting-bags. But its contribution to the Wedding ceremonial is direct and to the point.

The couple being excited to sexual congress are invited by the monk to think about the other's 'Woldy goods,' and to prove their credit-worthiness by exchanging golden rings, worth only a few yen but the equivalent in England of half a dozen oxen or twenty sheep.

The couple are dressed for this holy moment in traditional erotic costumes, the female in a 'baby doll' lace veil and nightdress, suggesting innocence combined with great wealth, and the male in the outfit of a nineteenth-century 'toff' or 'Johnny', the feared hero-villain of melodrama and pornographic film since time immemorial.

On a blast from the pipe-organ, the couple then turn to face the rival armies, drawn up on either side of the shrine and facing to the East, home of the sky-spirit. A march is played, and as the couple pass down through the centre of the shrine the eyes of the two opposing factions converge. Their collective 'woldy goods', or so they believe in the trance-like state induced by the 'Newcassa Blun', are being taken away from them by the opposition.

Eyes glassy and teeth bared, the participants move unsteadily off to the formalised mutual abuse, ripping of clothes and colourful York-shah violence from which the couple will, it is hoped, emerge to perform the final act, boots, dead cats and old tin cans tied to their ankles for luck.

John Wells 5.7.1978

THE WEDDING INDUSTRY
by THELWELL

'It's from my ex-husband. An automatic toast-scraper.'

'She'd like to see some rings.'

'That looks great! Now, what do you fancy for your bridesmaids?'

'Here it comes! Bridegroom hasn't turned up, can we make any reductions?'

'Have you any ready sliced?'

'That was lovely! Could you hold him up just once more?'

FOND AND FOOLISH.

Edwin (suddenly, after a long pause). 'Darling!'   *Angelina.* 'Yes, Darling?'
Edwin. 'Nothing, Darling. Only *Darling*, Darling!'   (*Bilious Old Gentleman feels quite sick.*)

THE FIRST TWO WEEKS ARE THE WORST

I'm told that along the rainswept pier-heads of English summer-seasons, the damp souls of comics are still sprouting honeymoon stories, knowing that a joke about newly-weds has the effect of instantly galvanising old ladies in deckchairs – like hitting them on the knee with a hammer. 'No, see, eh?, no, don't laugh, there was this honeymoon couple see . . . ooooh, *naughty*, I can see you darlin', put 'im *down* . . . anyway, this honeymoon couple . . .' Nudge, nudge, ho, ho. Maeve and Else cackle joyously through their toffomints remembering how Fred's mates at the bottle-works put frogs in Alice's wedding bed and gave her such a turn. In those days,

honeymoons were epic events in one's life, something worthy of being laughed at . . .

Mind you, it was always working-class honeymoons which were supposed to be ipso facto screamingly funny: never upper-class ones. Working class honeymoons were spent in boarding houses with noisy bed-springs which rang out like tocsins across the prom. Upper class ones were apparently always Romantic, spent by limp-wristed young things called Charles and Amanda at Cap d'Antibes, surrounded by champagne buckets and portly Hungarians playing passionate fiddles under the trees. Curiously sex didn't seem to come into the latter sort of honeymoon at all, whereas in the first type, it was the only thing that did.

But on the whole it looks as if the honeymoon joke is gradually losing its place in the joke-book pantheon, along with all those other sure-fire rib-ticklers, Scotsmen, sporrans, mother-in-law and public loos. Permissiveness has probably killed it off.

After all, the whole point of the honeymoon joke was that it was the First Time they'd Had It. Now, by all accounts, everyone's Had It almost as soon as they've cut their milk teeth.

I remember being told by one world-weary little thirteen-year-old in California, how much she deplored the declining moral standards of today's eight-year-olds. 'Sex, sex, sex, that's all they ever think of. Why, when I was their age I was still playing with dolls,' she said, as she popped Tuesday's pill out of its easy-dial packet and set off for another hair-bleaching session at the beauty salon.

Now *I* was brought up – ah, what innocent aeons ago – by nuns who told their spotty little charges that a man who Truly Loved you would Respect you until the wedding night, whereupon, apparently, appalling disrespect would take place, which was unfortunately the price you had to pay for the privilege of frying his fish-fingers and soaking his smalls for the rest of your days.

We heard a great deal about woman's Finer Feelings and man's Lower Instincts but never had a chance to put the theories to the test since the only males for miles around our convent were Ron, the scrofulous gardener's boy – and gloomy Father Flaherty, the parish priest, fresh from the bog, with a face like a fist, a hot line in hellfire, and a habit of tying his gloves to his wrists in case he lost them, so that during his passionate sermons on Fleshy Lust, they bobbed and weaved hysterically about his body like giant bees . . .

But nowadays of course it's all different and the whole sexual initiation part of a honeymoon has gone. Now the honeymoon is meant to be nothing less than a divine, star-spun interlude for you both before you get down to the real nitty-gritty of life among the Squezy mops in Spanland.

Of course, you're still supposed to spend most of it joyously tumbling about in bed together, only none of that beginner's stuff: it's got to be a really jazzy production number these days, real high-wire acrobatics. The whole thing imposes an intolerable strain on a couple who've only just managed to pull through the horrors of the wedding reception.

Most of my married friends swear they all came nearest to divorce during their honeymoons.

Like a girl-friend of mine who spent her wedding night tramping about Dawlish and district in the rain with a husband who said he swore he remembered the hotel they'd booked into was called Seaview, and for Christsake, stop moaning, there couldn't be more than twenty Seaviews in Dawlish, *could* there . . . Well, there could, and actually it was called Seacliffe, and by the time they got there Mrs Potter said she was ever so sorry but she'd disposed of the Bridal Suite to a commercial traveller, and some hours later the bride barked coldly at her spouse as she boarded the coach home to mother 'I'm having THIS annulled for a start!'

Surviving the honeymoon is probably the first great hurdle in a marriage. I was once despatched to Canada on a ship which, my editor was erroneously informed, was a Honeymoon Special, groaning at the gunwhales with 1,500 emigrating newly-weds.

In fact there were four. The first couple had inadvertently been booked into separate cabins by the steamship company: she sharing with three Jehovah's Witnesses, and he with four members of a construction gang heading for Saskatchewan.

The other couple, who'd won their 'dream' honeymoon in a cornflake contest, were together, but only just, as she spent most of the time being sick in the cabin while he glumly downed Guinnesses and played shove ha'penny in the bar. Beneath us the wintry Atlantic heaved like a peptic whale. After a honeymoon like that, married life in Moose Jaw or Calgary could only be a blissful improvement . . .

Of course, the over-selling of honeymoons has even begun to worry social workers. One of them, the secretary of the Fulham and Hammersmith Citizens Advice Bureau, no less, recently quoted by the News of the World as blaming 'honeymoon blues' for the break-up of so many young marriages. 'The proceedings' she said 'aren't as romantic as they would like them to be.'

Well of course not. Honeymoons are a time for the destruction of illusions, particularly those appertaining to the naturally dewy-fresh beauty of the bride. Before marriage you could maintain your beauty was a gift from God and didn't come expensively bottled by Max Factor.

Many's the young husband who must have suffered a cold frisson of fright on first glimpsing his wife minus eyebrows and eyelashes and all greased up like a Channel swimmer in Orange Skin Food. Of course, in America they've already thought of that, and the bride can buy sex-prufe lipstick, eyelashes and wigs, and in case you've got the sort of droopy boobs which hit your knees with a thud when you shed your bra, you can buy nightdresses with built-in foundation garments: 'So soft, so subtle, He'll never Guess!'

To keep the illusion going, you can also book into that ultimate sexual depressant, the Honeymoon hotel, complete with heart-shaped bed, heart-shaped bath, heart-shaped swimming pool, heart-shaped skating rink, and heart-shaped jokes pinned over the dining room exits saying 'We know where you're going!' Over the beds, there's a heart-shaped mirror so you can watch yourself in action, if, that is, you've got the heart for it any more . . .

The only honeymoon I've had so far doesn't encourage me to try another. Ever. We were married in Compton and squabbled furiously all the way down to our hotel in Midhurst.

On arrival, my husband, who puts his all into rows and consequently finds them very debilitating, sank exhausted with rage onto the fourposter and fell asleep, while I went downstairs and watched James Mason in 'Five Fingers' on the hotel telly. Actually this was rather appropriate as I'd been in love with Mason for years and had always dreamt, while doodling on my Latin Primer, of spending my wedding night with James anyway. I once wrote him a poem in which I described his voice as 'soft footfalls in the dark' which I thought amazingly good, but which inexplicably failed to bring him panting to my side. My husband had always felt the same way about Anne Bancroft, but well, there you are. James and Anne always seemed to be otherwise occupied, so we'd had to settle for each other instead.

THE HONEYMOON.

Mary. 'Charles, dear; now we are Married, you know, we should have no Secrets. So do, like a Love, hand me the Bottle of Hair Dye; you will find it in my Dressing-Case.'

The next day we flew to Switzerland to ski, where I promptly broke my leg, due to being hit by a tree which sprang out of the ski-slope, narrowly missing my husband but pole-axeing me. It probably knew I was on honeymoon. By then suffering from honeymooners' paranoia, I felt sure I heard it rattling its cones with sadistic glee as I passed out in a red haze at its feet.

I spent the rest of our honeymoon – all ten days of it – in a plaster-cast lying on a playdeck half way up an Alp wedged between motionless rows of old ladies wrapped in blankets mummifying in the sun, with plastic 'beaks' sprouting from their sunglasses to save their noses from peeling. They resembled a lot of up-ended owls and none of them were great conversationalists – except for the lady who told me every day that she could forecast avalanches by the excruciating twinges she got in her lower intestine, and her friend, who apparently owned three-quarters of Peru and had an understandable thing about Communists.

After three days of this, the sight of my husband, bronzed, merry, magnificent, shussing down the mountainside surrounded by gaily carolling girls made me long to shove him down a crevasse, hobble home and collect on the life insurance.

Things are improving now, but the honeymoon scars took some time to heal and I can't say I've ever quite forgiven him yet . . .

Ann Leslie 7.4.1971

HONEYMOON HOTEL
by QUENTIN BLAKE

'You know, it's funny to think you've probably never seen me before I've shaved in the morning.'

'Room 302 as usual, Madam.'

'See anything you fancy?'

Q. E. D.

'WHAT'S UP WI' SAL?'   'AIN'T YER ERD? SHE'S MARRIED AGIN!'

THE DOUBLE LIFE

What is to be the fate of
Matrimony, the State of?
That much-visited but still inscrutable land
Beset on either hand
By the sabres
Of derisive neighbours?

Many say
It's had its day,
No two ways about it.

Others doubt it.

Joined today, tomorrow put asunder . . .
You can't wonder
That parsons at the altar
Tend to falter
Halfway through the so-called solemnization
At the realisation
That they're only legalising a temporary shack-up
Doomed to an early pack-up.
How often do the young and emotionally supple
Couple
Really put their heart
Into the bit about Till Death Us Do Part?

Perhaps the very twosomeness
Connotes gruesomeness:
A State with only one ruler
Might play the thing cooler:
It's working au pair
That heats up the Matrimonial air
Into the haze
That plays
Such tricks with the visibility
That you can't ever quite discern the divisions of responsibility:
And some think, indeed, that the whole situation
Depends on clear demarcation,
Such as who puts the cat out,
Shakes the mat out,
Gets the ice,
Buries dead mice,

Remembers to turn down the central heating
Or send the birthday greeting,
Cooks
The domestic books
(Without being funny
About what actually is and what isn't supposed to come out of the housekeeping money),

Has the casting vote
Over buying a boat,
Or, where the State's living standards are lower,
A new mower,
And, in general, right across the board,
Which of the twin Heads of State is making a genuine contribution to the smooth running of the
    Realm, and which is a layabout and a fraud.
Well, the battle of who-does-what
Is no comedy spot,
But highly crucial
To any married State seeking to attract the adjective trucial:
Nevertheless, I personally take the position,
After long experience as the other half of a coalition,
That only fools
Make hard and fast rules.
It may seem a good idea
To say your territory ends there and mine starts here,
I'll be Chancellor of the Exchequer,
Handle the Black and Decker,
Order the booze,
Clean the shoes,
While your zone
Is answering the phone,
Buying buns,
And opening the front door to nuns,
But there are days when the phone can ring
And the appointed answerer would rather die than go near the bloody thing,
Or when the accepted writer to the administration's Cheltenham aunt
Simply can't;
When the gorge rises
At the prospect of going to see some ass give away the school prizes,
Or spending all morning on the knees
Wrapping up immense and unmanageable brown paper parcels for unspecified refugees:

And this is no juncture
For the other one to go out to the garage and begin tracing a slow puncture,
On the ground that spheres of constitutional activity have been statutorily allotted,

And those who can't cope can get knotted.
It's standing on rights
That starts fights;
So instead,
If the bed-maker can't face making the bed,
Just make it,
Or baking a cake, bake it.

I hold it to be a fact,
Though its validity may well be attacked,
That an accumulation of these internal defiances
Are a worse threat to the stability of the State than the occasional unilateral outside alliances:

To get briefly fond
Of the odd blonde
Or hanker
After a passing banker
Is supposed to be the traditional way
Of throwing the domestic government into total disarray –
Well, it's clear,
I fear,
That seven year itches
May be deemed by the appropriate international court to disqualify for Dunmow Flitches,
But at least, once they've been scratched,

Rifts can be patched,
And it seems only right and proper
To come back to Momma or Poppa,
A thing that doesn't usually occur
When the break-up came because she/he won't lift a finger to do anything that's supposed to be done
    by him/her.

Naturally, I can only touch
On just so much
In the space available:
The State, I agree, is assailable,
But it's still my opinion
That joint dominion,
Provided you work at it
Has the edge over the loners who smirk at it,
Who argue that a House with only you in it
Puts no bars on what you do in it,
That you come home at the end of the day,
Monarch of all you survey.
All right, so it's true
That you have the run of the loo,
And no scattered slippers,
Stuck zippers,
Or disgorged contents of handbags to mar
The stark symmetrical orderliness left behind by the char,
No outpourings about the stink
In the sink,
The kids'
Ids,
No bravely suppressed grimaces
Which prove on enquiry to be caused by pains in strange places,
None, in fact, of the running anxieties
That make the married state the far cry it is
From that blithe autonomy so easy to win
By either living on your tod or in what used so quaintly to be called sin . . .

On the other hand,
Though this mysterious land
Is despised by the sophisticated and snooty,
It offers certain features of rugged natural beauty:
And though the fate
Of the State
Is held to be sealed
By all the most vocal commentators in the field,
Those of us who happen to find it OK
Never seem to bother to say.

Why not put out more flags,
Some of you old married lags,
Proclaiming your choice?

For a start, anyway, here's one small voice.

Basil Boothroyd 7.4.1971

'WHERE ARE YOU OFF TO?'
'TO THE DOCTOR. I DON'T LIKE THE LOOK OF MY WIFE.'
'I'LL COME WITH YOU. I HATE THE SIGHT OF MINE.'

THE OLD FORMULA.

Wife. 'Look, George – my new respirator.'
George (preoccupied). 'Oh! By Jove – yes! Suits you devilish well, my dear.'

REVELATIONS

'Tell me about yourself,' said the subaltern, gazing at her in admiration; 'where you were born and all that. No, really? I knew some people there. Did you always live there?'

'No; when I was seventeen my father's business went bust through the War and I had to earn my own living.'

'You poor old thing. What did you do?'

'I taught at the High School.'

'You didn't! What did you teach?'

'Mathematics.'

'Good Lord, what a clever old thing you must be! What high school was that? No! Why then you must know the Petersons?'

'Why, Kitty and I left school the same term, only I went back to teach.'

'So you know Kitty. I was sort of engaged to her at one time.'

'You're not "*Bob*"? – don't tell me that!'

'By Jove, yes; she often spoke of – Why, it must have been you! What was your father, by the way?'

'Architect.'

'Really? I never knew that. By Jove, old thing, we are finding each other out.'

They had been married two years – War years, though.

Captain W. P. Lipscomb 27.3.1918

TO MY LADY
IN SPRING

(After much reading of Communiqués from the Western Front)

If no artillery of vows
    Nor creeping barrages of prayer
Compassion in your breast may rouse,
    But I am still a stranger there
On bended knees with outstretched hand
    In No Man's Land;

If, when I only wait the sign
    To compass with outflanking curve
The chosen portion of your line,
    You summon up your coy reserve
With rosy S.O.S's flame
        And spoil my game;

If labouring thus I may but win,
    Prepared by batteries of art,
A temporary footing in
    The outpost trenches of your heart,
That is not good enough for me,
        Hermione.

For somehow I must surely seize
    The full objective I desire;
The buds have raided all the trees
    And Spring has burst the Winter's wire;
A strong offensive round us thrills
        Of daffodils.

The lark has stormed the skies with song,
    Delivering each time the goods;
Last Sunday as I strolled along
    I found a primrose in the woods;
It gave no kind of warning shout –
        It just came out.

Then plague on all cajolings sweet
    And drumfire of continued woe,
I'll rush you, lady, off your feet
    And take you prisoner ere you know;
Triumphant, forcible and frank,
        I'll play the Tank.

E. V. Knox 27.3.1918

Fickle Young Thing (revisiting Tattooist.) 'ER – DO YOU THINK
YOU COULD POSSIBLY ALTER THIS BADGE ON MY ARM? YOU SEE,
I'VE – ER – EXCHANGED INTO ANOTHER REGIMENT.'

Extract from list of recent decorations. 'PRIVATE ATKINS, FOR
ACT OF GALLANTRY NOT IN FACE OF THE ENEMY.'

THE HAPPY MARRIAGE

(A Ballad)

[A sensation has been caused in Portland, Oregon, by the arrest of two ladies and their husbands for highway robbery. Evidence was brought to show that the ladies used to stand beside their husbands while the robberies were being committed, and help to rifle the victims.]

WHEN EMERSON K. WASHINGTON met SADIE Q. VAN POTT,
Her numerous attractions bowled him over on the spot:
At first distinctly timid, gaining courage by degrees,
He rushed into her presence, and addressed her, on his knees:–

'Oh, SADIE Q., I worship you, and not as other men;
My love had proved a worthy theme for Poet SHAKSPEARE's pen;
My groans and sighs excite surprise, whene'er I pace the street;
I really cannot sleep at all. And, worse, I cannot eat.

'For ham and eggs (Virginia style) I've ceased to care a jot;
No strawberry shortcake tempts me now, nor Boston beans, served hot.
The oyster-stew I wave aside: I cannot touch a clam:
From these remarks you'll judge in what a wretched state I am.

'So do decide to be my bride; oh, heed a lover's prayers;
Admit some sunshine to a lot, which now is dark with cares.
But lest without reflection you are tempted to decline,
I'll picture what will happen should we form the said combine.

'Most husbands treat their wives as dolls, and, sorrowful to state,
Refuse to let them take a hand in things of any weight:
Myself I mean to act upon a widely different plan;
For Lovely Woman's duty lies, I hold, in helping Man.

'If you elect to marry me, my angel-bird, you'll be
As partner in my business quite invaluable to me.
And what that business is, without preamble I will tell:
You see in me a footpad. And I'm doing very well.

'Way out in pleasant Oregon my humble trade I ply;
Few highwaymen have got a larger *clientèle* than I;
Think not that these are idle words. With truth my claims agree;
You may have heard of "Sand-Bag BILL"? Exactly. I am he.

'So, if my proffered heart and hand you'll but consent to take,
You'll come with me on every expedition that I make;
Together, hand in hand, my love, at night we'll roam about,
Entrap the guileless traveller, and – briefly – clean him out.'

His speech was scarcely finished, when quoth SADIE, 'Wal, I vum!
What, marry you, my EMERSON? I calculate! Why, some!
Stray travellers in Oregon will soon be mighty sick;
Ring up the parson on the 'phone, and get it over slick.'

The parson put the service through without the least delay;
And EMERSON and SADIE Q. were wed that very day;
Their happiness, I'm glad to say, is wholly free from cares;
I never knew so prosperous a married life as theirs.

For every night, when dinner's o'er, and darkling shadows fall,
They take their knuckle-dusters from the hat-stand in the hall,
And EMERSON says, 'SADIE, have you cartridges, my pet?
Your iron, is it clean and bright?' And SADIE says, 'You bet.'

And then through quiet streets they prowl, through dim-lit squares they roam,
They intercept the passer-by, as he is hurrying home;
And EMERSON's destructive club upsets him with a crash,
While SADIE's nimble fingers gather in the needful cash.

So on they go from day to day, as happy as can be,
And in this simple tale, I think, a moral we may see:
The married state can never be completely free from strife,
Unless a man's profession also interests his wife.

P. G. Wodehouse 9.12.1903

'Nothing has come over me, I've
merely made one or two last-minute
adjustments to my behaviour pattern.'

ANNIVERSARY

My hair was flaxen-fair, lad, my silken hose were green,
I'd sex-appeal to spare, lad, when I was seventeen;
I gobbled up the *savoir-tout* of smarties in *The Queen*
And still had lots of time for bottle-parties in between.
Oh, life was long and love was strong and all our hopes were keen,
But you were young as well, lad, and hadn't got a bean.

The years have had their fill, my lad, my looks have gone to pot,
My hair is flaxen still, lad – but Heavens, whose is not?
My scanty reading seldom strays above a Christie plot
And at a party nowadays my shoes are tight and hot;
But through the murk of middle age there shines a silver spot:
You earn ten times as much, lad, which somehow helps a lot.

Pamela Sinclair 31.1.1962

'*Marvin still has plenty of virility, although of course
these days most of it goes into real estate.*'

'We both made it to the breakfast table so I won't ask you how you are if you won't ask me how I am.'

ROGUE MALE

When I look over my shoulder and see that I've had four wives it doesn't frighten me half as much as the recollection of four mothers-in-law. Think about it. Gives you goose-pimples, doesn't it?

Actually, I didn't know the first one since she snuffed it just at the time her daughter seduced me and pushed me down the slippery slope, but the other three were and are quite something. You couldn't play 'find the lady' with that pack. Mind you, they liked me quite a lot. One of them even went so far as to tell her daughter that I was a 'treasure'. That's because I always did the cooking and washing-up whenever she and her husband came over for Sunday lunch. What she never realised was that (a) I cooked and wouldn't let her daughter in the kitchen because she was such a lousy cook and (b) I did the washing-up to get away from their dreadful cackling and gossiping. In other words, I used the kitchen as a hiding-place. What was a little dodgy, though, was the fact that I strongly fancied that particular mother-in-law, Dolly, who had legs that put me in mind of Cyd Charisse.

It's an odd thing, that. I knew an actor once called Ray Smith who was very good at what male chauvinist pigs call 'pulling birds' and he invariably ended up with their mothers who, he said, were always a great improvement on the original target. Dolly was really rather special but she went over the top a bit when she told my daughter's mother that she didn't deserve me. Of course, Dolly never saw me arrive home at midnight after a day at the races, so she could be excused for thinking that I was pure gold. By the same token, it must have been light years since she had heard her daughter waffling over the breakfast table, as I was trying to concentrate on *The Times* and *Sporting Life* in an attempt to win the rent and rates. She still sends me her love does Dolly, while her daughter, I suspect, sticks pins into a doll-like model of me. I bet you know where she sticks them, too.

Mother-in-law number one, though, was a very different person. She hated me. That was in the days when I was either bumming around Soho or doing nasty odd jobs like navvying or dish-washing. She wanted an officer and a gentleman for her daughter and she simply couldn't understand how I'd slipped from a public school into the gutter where I'd met her daughter. I exaggerate fractionally but I'm sure you get my drift. We all four of us once had a holiday together in the South of France and I got drunk one night and the silly woman got it into her head that I was like that every night. But I'm told she's been very odd about me since we got our divorce. Now, the ex-wife tells me that Mum is inordinately impressed to see the occasional by-line and keeps asking her, 'Are you sure it's not too late to get him back?' She can have little idea of what freelancers earn in Grub Street.

My most recent mother-in-law is a lovely old bird from Dulwich called Gladys. When she refereed title fights between me and her daughter, she would always say, 'You must be very unhappy, Jeffrey, that's all I can say.' This remark, probably nicked from some awful Hollywood movie, was meant to hurt deeply. The biggest fight she ever supervised, like all big fights, was over next to nothing. It was Christmas Eve in the country and at breakfast I asked my wife to put the piece of hot bread she had given me under the grill again for another minute. We had instant 'lift-off'. They drove off to London in the car, leaving me stranded with a 20lb turkey, some Tio Pepe and unopened parcels of presents consisting of chocolate liqueurs and Janet Reger knickers. As they sped off into the east and the sunrise, Gladys lowered the car window and said, 'You must be very unhappy.' For once she had hit the nail on the head.

Mistresses' mothers are a rather different kettle of fish. They look at me with something bordering on disgust or loathing and then turn to their daughters and say, 'I suppose you know what you're doing,' or, 'I suppose you know what you're letting yourself in for.' If these people could only be the flies on the walls when their wretched daughters are doing a command performance it would really open their eyes.

Fathers-in-law are much more reasonable. One of them lent me a tenner five minutes before I married his daughter to buy a wedding ring – subsequently thrown at me, it missed and cracked a window – and he bunged me a further tenner after the deed was done to buy a round of drinks. Of course, I'm going back to when a tenner was a tenner. Come to that, I'm going back to when a wife was a wife, rolling-pins and all. But I'll tell you one thing I've noticed and that is that sisters and brothers-in-law are a very snotty lot who tend to gang up on you, or me, anyway. Usually they seem to be employed in something far more gainful than I am. I've had a neurologist, a publican and a barrister, any of which seem to me to be more attractive ways of earning a living than hiding behind the bushes on Newmarket Heath to find out what's buzzing, or staggering into Fleet Street to insult various editors. Don't they know it, too!

But, to go back to mothers-in-law, you can get them eating out of your hand if you don't mind stabbing wives in the back. I used to find that saying things like, 'I wish she was more like *you*,' would have them purring instantly. And flattering them would always lead to them telling their daughters, 'Why don't you listen to Jeff, he's *so* sensible.' Nevertheless, I don't think I could take a fifth mother-in-law, let alone a fifth wife. But, by now, any woman daft enough to have me would be too old to have an existing mother anyway. In a funny sort of way I miss them. Playing on the jealousy between mothers and daughters is a little like pulling the wings off butterflies, but I can't help being fascinated by watching the female half of the human race struggling without success to be loyal to each other. Give me a good father-in-law who will stand a round of drinks anytime.

Jeffrey Bernard 26.2.1986

'Oh, stop being so jealous, darling – he was a lover from a previous marriage.'

'Mother! Stop prying!'

'My wife doesn't understand
me either!'

MRS CAUDLE'S CURTAIN LECTURE

MR CAUDLE HAS NOT ACTED 'LIKE A HUSBAND'
AT THE WEDDING DINNER.

'Ah me! It's no use wishing – none at all: but I do wish that yesterday fourteen years ago could come back again. Little did I think, Mr Caudle, when you brought me home from church, your lawful wedded wife – little, I say, did I think that I should keep my wedding-dinner in the manner I have done to-day. Fourteen years ago! Yes, I see you now in your blue coat with bright buttons, and your white watered-satin waist-coat, and a moss rose-bud in your button-hole, which you said was like me. What? *You never talked such nonsense?* Ha! Mr Caudle, you don't know what you talked that day – but I do. Yes; and you then sat at the table as if your face, as I may say, was buttered with happiness, and – What? No, Mr Caudle, don't say that; *I* have not wiped the butter off – not I. If you above all men are not happy, you ought to be, gracious knows!

'Yes, I *will* talk of fourteen years ago. Ha! you sat beside me then, and picked out all sorts of nice things for me. You'd have given me pearls and diamonds to eat if I could have swallowed 'em. Yes, I say, you sat beside me, and – What do you talk about? *You couldn't sit beside me to-day?* That's nothing at all to do with it. But it's so like you. I can't speak but you fly off to something else. Ha! and when the health of the young couple was drunk, what a speech you made then! It was delicious! How you made everybody cry, as if their hearts were breaking; and I recollect it as if it was yesterday, how the tears ran down dear father's nose, and how dear mother nearly went into a fit! Dear souls! They little thought, with all your fine talk, how you'd use me! *How have you used me?* Oh, Mr Caudle, how can you ask that question? It's well for you I can't see you blush. *How* have you used me!

'Well, that the same tongue could make a speech like that, and then talk as it did to-day!

How did you talk? Why, shamefully. What did you say about your wedded happiness? Why, nothing. What did you say about your wife? Worse than nothing: just as if she was a bargain you were sorry for, but were obliged to make the best of. What do you say? *And bad's the best?* If you say that again, Caudle, I'll rise from my bed. *You didn't say it?* What, then, did you say? Something very like it, I know. Yes, a pretty speech of thanks for a husband! And everybody could see that you didn't care a pin for me; and that's why you had 'em here: that's why you invited 'em, to insult me to their faces. What? *I made you invite 'em?* Oh, Caudle, what an aggravating man you are!

'I suppose you'll say next I made you invite Miss Prettyman. Oh yes; don't tell me that her brother brought her without your knowing it. What? *Didn't I hear him say so?* Of course I did; but do you suppose I'm quite a fool? Do you think I don't know that that was all settled between you? And she must be a nice person to come unasked to a woman's house? But I know why she came. Oh yes; she came to look about her. *What do I mean?* Oh, the meaning's plain enough. She came to see how she should like the rooms – how she should like my seat at the fire-place; how she – and if it isn't enough to break a mother's heart to be treated so! – how she should like my dear children.

'Now, it's no use your bouncing about at – but of course that's it; I can't mention Miss Prettyman, but you fling about as if you were in a fit. Of course that shows there's something in it. Otherwise, why should you disturb yourself? Do you think I didn't see her looking at the cyphers on the spoons as if she already saw mine scratched out and hers there? No, I shan't drive you mad, Mr Caudle; and if I do it's your own fault. No other man would treat the wife of his bosom in – what do you say? *You might as well have married a hedgehog?* Well, now it's come to something! But it's always the case! Whenever you've seen that Miss Prettyman, I'm sure to be abused. A hedgehog! A pretty thing for a woman to be called by her husband! Now you don't think I'll lie quietly in bed, and be called a hedgehog – do you, Mr Caudle?

'Well, I only hope Miss Prettyman had a good dinner, that's all. *I* had none! You know I had none – how was I to get any? You know that the only part of the turkey I care for is the merry-thought. And that, of course, went to Miss Prettyman. Oh, I saw you laugh when you put it on her plate! And you don't suppose, after such an insult as that, I'd taste another thing upon the table? No, I should hope I have more spirit than that. Yes; and you took wine with her four times. What do you say? *Only twice?* Oh, you were so lost – fascinated, Mr Caudle; yes, fascin-ated – that you didn't know what you did. However, I do think while I'm alive I might be treated with respect at my own table. I say, while I'm alive; for I know I shan't last long, and then Miss Prettyman may come and take it all. I'm wasting daily, and no wonder. I never say any-thing about it, but every week my gowns are taken in.

'I've lived to learn something, to be sure! Miss Prettyman turned up her nose at my custards. It isn't sufficient that you're always finding fault yourself, but you must bring women home to sneer at me at my own table. What do you say? *She didn't turn up her nose?* I know she did; not but what it's needless – Providence has turned it up quite enough for her already. And she must give herself airs over my custards! Oh, I saw her mincing with the spoon as if she was chewing sand. What do you say? *She praised my plum-pudding?* Who asked her to praise it? Like her impudence, I think!

'Yes, a pretty day I've passed. I shall not forget this wedding-day, I think! And as I say a pretty speech you made in the way of thanks. No, Caudle, if I was to live a hundred years – you needn't groan, Mr Caudle, I shall not trouble you half that time – if I was to live a hundred years, I should never forget it. Never! You didn't even so much as bring one of your children into your speech. And – dear creatures! – what have *they* done to offend you? No; I shall not drive you mad. It's you, Mr Caudle, who'll drive me mad. Everybody says so.

'And you suppose I didn't see how it was managed, that you and *that* Miss Prettyman were always partners at whist? *How was it managed?* Why, plain enough. Of course, you packed the cards, and could cut what you liked. You'd settled that, between you. Yes; and when she played a trick, instead of leading off a trump – *she* play whist, indeed! – what did you say to her, when she found it was wrong? Oh – It was impossible that *her* heart should mistake! And this, Mr Caudle, before people – with your own wife in the room!

'And Miss Prettyman – I won't hold my tongue. I *will* talk of Miss Prettyman: who's she, indeed, that I shouldn't talk of her? I suppose she thinks she sings? What do you say? *She sings like a mermaid?* Yes, very – very like a mermaid: for she never sings, but she exposes herself. She might, I think, have chosen another song. '*I love somebody*,' indeed; as if I didn't know who was meant by that 'somebody'; and all the room knew it, of course; and that was what it was done for – nothing else.

'However, Mr Caudle, as my mind's made up, I shall say no more about the matter to-night, but try to go to sleep.'

'And to my astonishment and gratitude,' writes Caudle, 'she kept her word.'

Douglas Jerrold 5. 7. 1845

Affectionate Husband. 'COME, POLLY – IF I AM A LITTLE IRRITABLE, IT'S OVER IN A MINUTE!!'

EXPERIENTIA DOCET?

Wife of Two Years' Standing. 'OH YES! I'M SURE HE'S NOT SO FOND OF
ME AS AT FIRST. HE'S AWAY SO MUCH, NEGLECTS ME DREADFULLY, AND HE'S
SO CROSS WHEN HE COMES HOME. WHAT *SHALL* I DO?'
Widow. 'FEED THE BRUTE!'

AFTER A FEW YEARS

Normally, I don't take the route through Beechwood. I have been taking the road that by-passes
it every Wednesday for nearly six years now, but
I don't go through it. This is not simply because

of the by-pass; there are other small towns on my
normal Wednesday route, just as there are
other, different, small towns on my other routes,
on other days, and I frequently come off the
trunk roads for them. I stop for coffees I leave
half-finished in the cup, I stop for cigarettes
when I already have two packs in the glove
compartment, sometimes I pull in for gas when
the tank is three-quarters full. Occasionally, I
just park at a meter, and walk around for a while,

look in windows, check out house prices, ask a cop for directions to streets I already know. Sometimes I try on shoes, or try to find out if they can repair a calculator while I wait, and if they say yes, sure, then I tell them I'm going to collect it from the car, and I make a note not to go in that shop again.

I'm not too sure why I do all of this. It isn't as simple as boredom, if it were just boredom I'd go into bars; it certainly isn't curiosity, I have very little curiosity about anything. Some of it's about lying, I know that: I like to construct an elaborate lie about why the tank will only take three gallons, about why it is dangerous for me to drink an entire cup of coffee. When I do that, my skin moves. It's best when I put on a fake accent, South African, perhaps, or a muffed German consonant: I am a foreigner in a strange town, a little lost, I need shoes, a flashlight battery. People are nice to me.

Once or twice I have asked a cop directions and then deliberately walked in the opposite direction, feeling myself shaking, waiting for him to come after me, redirect me, perhaps more slowly, if it's one of my foreign days. On one occasion, I went into an out-patient department and told the girl behind the admissions desk that I was a registered addict, but I was a long way from home, the other side of the country, and could they please help me, and when she told me to take a seat I waited for her to leave her desk and go through one of the three white doors behind her, and then I left, running after I got out the door, and driving like hell until I got back on the by-pass.

Well, it breaks up the day. It breaks up life, introducing possibilities, danger, alternatives. After a few years, you need that kind of thing; you need to flirt with alternatives, since it is too late to adopt them. I could, after all, have *been* a foreigner, all I had to do was go somewhere else, I could have been a junkie, I could have been the sort of person who gets through calculators at a remarkable rate. Had I chosen, twenty years ago, to slit my mother's throat instead of going into sales management, for example, I could now be getting ready to come out of jail, into an unknown world, a new life, a person feared, probably, a person unfathomable, certainly, a person for whom every relationship would have been totally different from those I currently

enjoy, or do not enjoy, by simple virtue of the fact that, in one brief second, I had snatched up a cut-throat razor and. But I would have been the same person, at root, that I am now. Isn't that odd? After all, the decision to go into sales management took far longer, involved far more, than cutting a throat on impulse.

I have made a lot of deliberated decisions like that, and hated pretty well all of them. Hated the *process* of making them. You could say that that was the reason I avoided Beechwood for so many years, when it would have been so easy to take a conscious decision to turn off the highway, make a left at the Presbyterian church, take the second right off Walnut Street. I have the whole plan of the place laid out in my head, I have studied large-scale maps of the town, it is as familiar to me as my own. But I did not want to plan to go there.

I did not tell the whole truth earlier. I am quite sure why I spend so much time screwing around in all the other little towns. It is to avoid going to Beechwood. They take the heat out of my anguish at refusing to make a conscious decision to go to Beechwood. I get excited, driving the trunk roads, knowing that I am answerable to no one in my present position and can go anywhere I damn well choose during the course of my professional day; can therefore go to Beechwood anytime I decide to, and see her.

I just decided not to decide to, is all.

But I was forty yesterday, and this morning I took the route through Beechwood.

It was not a decided decision: my heart clanged in my throat, and I made the exit.

Why should forty do it? A liver-spot on the hand, an ache in a crown (they have to be replaced regularly, after forty), a vein on my instep that displays a varicose corddedness, low back pain when I swing my legs out of bed gingerly on a birthday morning, when once I might have sprung? The sense that life has two pivots, one at half forty, one at half death?

Anyway.

I had expected my blood to race rather more, I had expected to become dizzy, as I passed the Presbyterian church, but I did not, it felt quite normal, it felt as if, say, I were going to Redwing or Danville to ask an undertaker if they could quote me for burying my child or a chemist if he could suggest a bath-oil for someone with eczema. Beechwood is a little town just like those, grass verges, few cars over three years old, middle-aged men raising their hats to women, white laundry vans, no buildings much over ten storeys, plane trees, blacks hardly in evidence, a small park, a library with glass walls.

I took the second right off Walnut Street, drove past her house quickly, noted the navy blue door, assessed its rough market value. Her husband had not done particularly well. I drove to the end of the street, made the block, came past her house again, more slowly, drove again to the end of the street, stopped. I felt sick, lit a cigarette, coughed, brought up a little pale bile, folded it into a Kleenex.

There was a call-box across the street.

'Sarah?'

'Who is this?'

'Has my voice changed that much?'

'My God.'

'I had to come to Beechwood. There was a, that's to say, my company is thinking of opening up here. Expansion, all that, times are very good if you have nerve, don't let anyone tell you different.'

'My God. Well, *my God!*'

'I only have an hour or so, could we meet, have a drink, coffee, that kind of thing?'

'I – what do you think?'

'What do I *think?* After a few years, I think it would be nice to have a cup of coffee.'

'Do you have my address?'

'It's in the phone book. They usually are.'

'Of course. I didn't, well, *my God!*'

'Five minutes?'

I redrove the road slowly, as if searching for the house, parked outside, walked briskly towards the door, like someone just dropping in for coffee on a chill day. There was a blue Datsun in the drive with a broken tail-light, but I did not take this as evidence that her husband was home, since this was not a street inhabited by men who drive damaged compacts.

'Don't say *my God* again,' I said. I could see past her, indeed was *looking* past her, at the paper in the hall, a faint apple-green stripe, one of ours, middle of the range, but not cheap, if perhaps vulgar in its very unostentatiousness.

'What should I say, then?'

'You should say: *If I should meet thee after long years, how should I greet thee? With silence and tears,* and I should reply: Jesus Christ, *Shelley!* I haven't read Shelley in – what is it? – twenty years, I haven't read Shelley since you and I used to read it together in college, for God's sake! That,' I said, smiling one of the smiles that has made me not only popular but commercially, I think, successful, 'is what you should say and what I should reply, but it's a hell of a lot to get through standing on the mat, on a cold day, so why don't you just say *my God* again?'

'You handle mat talk pretty well,' she said.

'I had a lot of practice.'

We went inside. The hallway smelt of recently aerosoled violets.

'But then you got successful.'

'But then I got successful,' I said. 'Now I control the decor of half a state.'

She led me into a split-level parlour, old Sahara paintwork, Navaho Sunset walls, reproduction Colonial furniture with all the software in colour-co-ordinated browns, the curtains in one of our cheaper golds, but faked with double-linings. They probably ran short of money when they got to the curtains, a lot of people do.

'I didn't even know you knew my married name,' she said, 'let alone where I live.'

'I keep tabs on all, well, kinds of people. Then there's my memory. I even took a course in it.'

'There's an ashtray somewhere,' she said. 'We don't smoke.'

'Don't we?'

'What?'

'I'm sorry. It slipped out. Other relationships, other conspiracies. We say we at home a lot, too, it gets automatic. I'll use this saucer, I can tell it isn't much, it has earth in it, I'll use it till your plant gets back, it won't mind. They can take more punishment than people realise, plants. All that stuff about talking to them, that's just, well, crazy people. Lonely people, I mean.' I put the cigarette out. 'They made us read whole pages of the encyclopaedia.'

'Who did?'

'On this memory course I did. I got to be able to read a whole page and memorise it in under three minutes. I still know more about lepidoptera and charged particles than practically anybody in the world. How about that?'

'You look thin.'

'I rush about a lot.'

'I'm sorry. It was a silly thing to say after twenty years.'

'What isn't?'

'Do you have children?'

'No, I don't. You have three, right? Cora and Joseph and little Alison.'

'Dear God!'

I tapped my forehead.

'All up here with *argynnis paphia*, largest of the fritillaries,' I said, and laughed, and she laughed, too. There was a dull small thud from beyond the room.

'Percolator,' she said. 'It does it.'

'They do.'

'I'd have it fixed,' she said, 'only there's nothing wrong with the coffee it makes, so let it, you know, thunk.'

'Remember that percolator we had at 1197 Chestnut with perfect pitch?' I said. 'Didn't it used to resonate with Kid Ory solos?'

'You must tell me about your work,' she said, after a few seconds.

'Yes,' I said. 'It's wonderful. If you'd stayed with me, you'd have got to see many of America's finest furnishing fabrics months before they even reached the shops. You see how unexpected life can be?'

She smiled. The percolator grunted. In the room, I could smell the long presence of her children. I know what these fabrics smell like when they come fresh off the mills.

'I'll get the coffee.'

When she was no longer there, I called: 'You're still very beautiful.'

She called:

'Cream and sugar?'

'This is a nice design,' I said, a little later. I turned the saucer over.

'We bought them in Germany. We try to get across to Europe every three or four years. I mean, not just to buy things, of course.'

'No, no,' I said, 'I realise that.'

'Do you go at all?'

'We went on our honeymoon. We hired a VW and went all over. I had a bad time in Venice.' I waited, but her eyes were neutral. 'Do you remember how you and I planned to live in Venice? Why did we pick on Venice, for God's sake?'

'I pass. I don't have your memory.' She did that funny old thing with her eyebrow. 'What I

know about butterflies you could put on a pin. But then again – are you all right?'

I put the cup down on a little fake side table, just in time.

'Sorry. An involuntary tremor. Someone walked over my life. These carpets don't stain, they're impregnated. I still love you, Sarah, there hasn't been an hour in twenty years when I didn't know that.'

'Please.'

'It's all right, I have no plans to embarrass either of us,' I said. 'It isn't a statement I want to elaborate on, and there isn't anything else I want to talk about, the only plans I ever made about coming here and saying it were those in which I determined never ever to come here and say it; up until now my best decisions were always my negative ones.' I got up, and my knee hit the fake table, but it did not fall. 'As a matter of fact, my real plan for this afternoon was to be in East Camden speaking to an oculist in broken French, or possibly getting a quote from a caterer for a really big party I shan't be throwing, that just shows you how much of an accident my being here is, doesn't it?'

'Please don't rush off like this.'

'You don't really mean that.'

'I don't really know what I mean.'

'What I'm afraid of is staying long enough to ask whether you ever loved me, back when. After a few years –'

'Twenty.'

I opened the door.

'Sleet,' I said. It was coming out of the slate sky, slanting. 'I ought to be going anyhow. When it's icy, my husband worries.'

Daniel Sirico 3.6.1981

TAKE THE RING IN THE LEFT HAND AND RUN

Marriage, you had better understand from the very beginning, is no joke. Those strip cartoons of domestic life, where the wife is always buying new hats or signalling a right-hand turn in order to dry her nail-varnish, and the husband is forever marooned in one corner of a newly-painted room, have as much to do with the real thing as your cheapskate engagement ring has to do with the Koh-i-noor diamond.

Married bliss is grim and married bliss is earnest, as you will find before you have even had time to tip the confetti out of your shoes. The problems facing two people about to live under the same roof, let alone share the same bed, are so complex and terrifying that even the kind of manual they send out in a plain wrapper prefers to gloss over them and distract the reader with unprintable euphemisms.

We will attempt to deal with some of these problems here, provided it is understood that we are merely skimming the top of the iceberg, and that Mr and Mrs Newlywed, sooner or later, will have to learn the hard way.

Making sucking noises

When the excitement of the honeymoon has worn off and you settle down to a lifetime of quiet evenings in front of the telly, it will slowly dawn on you that your partner is in the habit of making sucking noises, either through the medium of a hollow tooth or by introducing the tongue to the roof of the mouth.

There is nothing obscene or disgusting about this; indeed some Polynesian tribes do it all the time. But what is normal to one person may be distressing or even frightening to another. If these sucking noises are really getting on your nerves, and you are quite sure that they are not a reprisal for your own knuckle-cracking or whistling through the teeth, have a quiet word with your partner. Explain gently that if you had really wanted to spend night after night after night listening to a repertoire of barnyard imitations, you would have married an intelligent cocker spaniel.

Tensions in marriage

'Will I be able to satisfy her?' is supposedly the question that worries young bridegrooms most. What should worry them even more is, 'Will she be able to find the end of the Sellotape after I have finished using it?' Nothing is more infuriating than a husband or wife who, having taken solemn vows before an ordained minister to make life as cushy as possible for the party of the second part, puts the Sellotape back in the right-hand drawer of the desk without folding the end bit back to save wear and tear of the other partner's nails. It is even more infuriating when the Sellotape is put back in the *left*-hand drawer of the desk, where even a child of four ought to know it does not belong.

Preparing for bed

Ringing the changes is what keeps a marriage fresh and interesting, and nowhere is this more important than in the approach to the marriage bed. If, at precisely eleven o'clock each night for fifteen years, you have been in the habit of stretching elaborately and announcing, 'Ah, well, me for Bedfordshire,' try surprising your partner with some new or daring variation. Say, 'Ho, hum, me for beddy-byes.'

Chewing pencils

If you chew pencils, so that whenever your partner wants to scribble a note to the milkman or to a lover, that partner is forced to handle what looks like a thin cylinder of ossified bacon-rind with a convention of death-watch beetles going on inside it, you are asking for trouble. You are asking for even more trouble if you chew ballpoint pens.

Every kind of gratification may be acceptable in marriage, *provided that it is acceptable to both sides*. Chewing pencils is not. Chewing pencils is a filthy perversion. As for chewing ballpoint pens, people like you should be put away for life.

Telephone bills

In even the most deeply-satisfying partnership of minds and bodies, there may come a moment when one or other partner is arrested on suspicion of knocking the district nurse off her bicycle and interfering with her clothing. Or perhaps, God willing, the crisis may be of a more homely description: the eldest boy has been expelled for unspeakable practices behind the gymnasium (there is a separate booklet available about these), or the baby has been bitten by a poisonous spider.

Be sure, anyway, that tragedy will strike at some time or another. And at times like this, it is only natural that the wife will want to spend hours on the telephone while she acquaints her mother or closest friend with the news that this time she is leaving the swine for good. This must inevitably lead to a high telephone bill, and sardonic remarks by the husband in the order of, 'Since when has your mother been living in bloody Australia?'

Many couples solve this problem by keeping a piggy-bank next to the telephone. This item, if thrown forcibly at the wall by the husband when he discovers it to contain nothing but hairgrips, will do much to alleviate hurt pride.

Adjusting to each other

Like the mating dance of the praying mantis, marriage is a quadrille or, if you are unfamiliar with old-time dancing, a Palais Glide, in which each partner responds almost unconsciously to a pattern of preconceived movements. Thus it will quickly become established that every time you are watching television together, one partner will keep leaning forward and turning up the volume control a fraction, whereas the other partner will keep leaning forward and turning it down again.

It is best to allow these automatic and largely nervous gestures to become part of the background routine of marriage, so that eventually they are hardly noticed by either side. Open discussion on the lines of, 'Wassamarrer, you got cloth ears or something?' may encourage rather than diminish the tension.

Leaving combs on the dressing table with tufts of hair sticking out of them

See our confidential leaflet, 'Leaving screwed-up tissues under the pillow in marriage'.

Keith Waterhouse 7.4.1971

'We have a perfect marriage. Why spoil it by whining for a divorce?'

'What do you mean, grounds for divorce?
Those are my idiosyncrasies!'

ROGUE MALE

After quite a few years of being married to someone or other, it is quite a pleasant change to be on the outside and looking in. In my present role as roving dinner guest – friends are either pimping for me or I am making up the right number – I am the fly on the wall of marriage and the spy behind the net curtain.

Of course, I get to eat some very good meals this way but it really is rather depressing to listen to and watch the wheels fall off mine hosts as the evenings wear on. The dangerous game of 'home truths' is usually begun with the cheese or, in the case of more down-market households, with the guttering of the candles and the circulation of After Eights. The antagonists open fire with the coffee and by the time the brandy arrives, when the verbal flak is reaching a crescendo, I find myself wondering just how the hell they've managed to stay married to each other for twenty years, never mind why on earth they got married in the first place.

Last week I went to dinner with a literary couple who had invited half the literati in London to their table. Most of the women there had written books or had novels under wraps and their husbands, even if they weren't quite in the Nobel Prize for Literature bracket, had at least appeared on *Call My Bluff* or *Start the Week*. Inevitably, the conversation got around to sex, although everybody called it 'personal relationships'. That started it, just like a referee calling two fighters into the middle of the ring and telling them that he wanted a good, clean fight without a chance in hell of getting one.

Then, my host suddenly said to his wife, Cynthia, 'Of course, the trouble with women is that they have no imagination, which is why they've achieved so little.'

Stifled screams from the ladies and our hostess counter-punched with, 'Funny you should say that, darling – after all, you've achieved so much, we can't even pay the rates.' Then, turning to me – and it's awful being picked out to be the middleman – she said, 'D'you know, Jeffrey, marriage is so disgusting, I really wish I was dead.'

I protested feebly, mumbling something about what a dreadful loss she would be to all of us, and she said, 'No, I really mean it. I want to die.' She took another gulp of brandy and lit a cigarette.

'Yes, I look forward to it. Just think of all that peace. Anyway, I've done everything. What's left? I've written books, had children, been in love, not for bloody years I might add,' she said, looking daggers at her husband, 'and I don't really see anything else to do. Yes, I'd really like to die.'

There isn't a lot you can say to that, so I poured myself another drink.

'If you really wanted to die,' said her husband, 'then you would.'

'Not just to please you, you bastard, I wouldn't.' Then, turning her venomous eyes away from her husband, she said to me, 'You have to admit, Jeff, that men are pretty bloody disgusting, aren't they?'

'Well, it's about fifty-fifty,' I said nervously.

'Why are we so disgusting to you?' ventured an academic who had once appeared on *Down Your Way*.

'Well, for a start, you're all so bloody selfish; secondly, I loathe the way you can go to bed with someone without being in love with them, although, mind you, I bloody well could *now*,' she said with another poisonous look at the husband, 'and, thirdly, you're all so bloody patronising. You think women can't *do* anything.'

'But of course we think you can, darling. It's just that a farmer doesn't expect much else of a chicken than that she lay eggs.'

'I've laid my last bloody egg for you, you sod, and as soon as the youngest egg, as you like to call her, leaves home, then I intend to die.'

'R.I.P.,' he said, as she threw a piece of Camembert at him.

'Well, *I* think Cynthia's absolutely right,' said a lady cellist from Hampstead. 'I mean, let's face it, you are all complete and utter pigs, aren't you, Jeff?'

'If you say so.'

'Oh, come on. We're kinder, more gentle, more loving and . . .'

'But darling . . .' her husband tried to interrupt.

'Shut your face, you. As I was saying, we're

not called the gentle sex for nothing. Could you bring up a baby, Jeff?'

'Yes,' I said, 'and I have. Well, for three years or so, some time ago.'

'I bet he can iron shirts, too, and cook and sweep a floor,' said Cynthia's husband. I suddenly wished I had a riot shield.

'If you men are so good at cooking then,' said Cynthia, 'why didn't you cook dinner?'

'I thought paying for it was sufficient.'

I made that forty-thirty to him. Match point and a breathless hush in the close tonight, I thought. I couldn't take a lot more and so I telephoned for a taxi. As I was leaving, Cynthia was again expressing a desire to embrace death. Her husband was detailing the defects of women. As I got into my taxi I could hear Cynthia's voice from the basement reiterating woman's war cry: 'You make me sick.'

In the morning I telephoned Cynthia to thank her for the dinner.

'Oh, I'm so glad you liked it,' she said, 'it was a lovely evening.'

'And how's the old man?' I asked.

'Fine, just fine. He's just left for work. He can be so *funny* sometimes, can't he?'

After we rang off, I wondered about that. I suppose that one of the blessings of brandy after dinner is that it does make for amnesia. Had she forgotten already that the old man was disgusting and did she no longer want fervently to die? I suppose so. I can also only suppose that women like Cynthia start every new day with a clean sheet, as it were. They are addicted to these disgusting things called husbands and the doves don't turn into shrikes until the coffee is served.

Shall I get married again? I don't think it a very good idea but, should some miracle occur and I meet Miss Right yet again, then you must all come to dinner and have a cosy chat about 'personal relationships'.

Jeffrey Bernard 27.11.1985

'Wilbur and I always tell one another when someone has attracted us, and that tends to nip things in the bud.'

'Do you mind. You are holding up our divorce arrangements.'

Albert:
DIVORCE –
LIVERPOOL STYLE

'I bet she can't strangle a pigeon like you can, pet!'

'Our Ronnie's getting suspicious –
we went electric last November.'

'The wife thinks I'm at the match!'

'There never was any kung-fu evening class, was there?'

'I should have known when she started using my aftershave.'

'Who got custody of the whippet?'

'That judge was bloody harsh, thirty pints of Guinness a week maintenance!'

LOVE
is a multi-departmental thing

Take your secretary home to meet the wife, says a psychiatrist, and avoid tense situations.

It was a beautiful morning. It was a sizzling, swashbuckling morning. It was the sort of morning that makes people want to take their clothes off and run down Regent Street towards the sea. The policeman in Piccadilly Circus could hardly believe his eyes.

I took the morning mail into my boss.

'I see mid-summer madness is in the air again, sir,' I remarked.

'Yes indeed, Miss Lefebvre,' he sparkled. 'In fact, a time to throw off restraint and listen to the call of the bloodstream. How would you like me to reserve a bench in St James's Park at lunch-time, just for two?'

'Oh yes please, Mr Preston,' I breathed. 'And after that a week-end in Brighton, with the curtains flapping timelessly in the breeze and the never-ending sound of the cicadas outside our window!'

Mr Preston drew on his thick spectacles and stared strictly in my rough direction.

'Miss Lefebvre, you sadden me. I need hardly tell you that for the second Friday running you have failed the Company's weekly personal standards test. From where I sit your moral fibre looks sub-standard. This is not good.'

'No, sir.'

'But I have faith in you. I know that somehow next Friday you will prove yourself to be strong, and good, and resolute.'

'Oh sir!' I cried. 'But I am so frail and weak and the Company is so firm and manly. Shall I ever be worthy?'

'Of course you will, Miss Lefebvre, but it is a long and hard path. The Company is praying for you. It is also paying for you, so we shall do some letters.'

The day grew hotter and hotter. Word came along the grapevine that several Australian citizens had been arrested in Trafalgar Square for surfing in the fountains. A police car arrived in the street below to prise the traffic policeman out of his patch of melted tar. From where I sat I could hear their strong, upright voices floating up to me and suddenly I found myself standing on the poop deck of a two-masted brigantine, watching the lithe sailors flashing silvery through the waves. There was a man at my side and even before I turned to look at him I knew it was Mr Preston.

'In two days we shall be in Martinique, Miss Lefebvre,' he said, 'and when we arrive I shall put my strong brown arm around you and show you the plantation I have bought for us.'

'I am sorry, Mr Preston, that you should have strengthened and browned your arm to no avail. I must ask you to turn the boat around and take me back immediately to Lower Regent Street.'

His handsome face grew dark and he bit his moustache.

'As you wish, Miss Lefebvre. But you are the first woman who has ever said nay to Jack Preston. I would deem it a favour if you could keep this matter a secret.'

I gave him my word and all through lunch in the canteen I breathed no hint of my narrow escape. The workings of a large corporation are not made easier by the temptations which spring from hot weather and when I thought how near I had come to hurting the shareholders' feelings, a blush came to my face.

I took the afternoon mail in.

'This is indeed a time to be thankful for our calm Nordic temperaments, Mr Preston,' I remarked.

'Darling!' he said. 'All through lunch I couldn't stop thinking of you . . . three times I addressed the chairman as sweetie pie. I have booked our room at Brighton. Do you want a pink, blue or plain hot water bottle?'

'Oh Jack! I don't care what colour it is, as long as it's warm, resilient, durable and reminds me of you!'

'Then you'll be on Platform Three at Victoria at 5.37?'

'There's no other platform I could possibly bear to be on.'

'Miss Lefebvre, you are no doubt aware of the Company's monthly ethical spot check-up. I only mention it now, because you have just failed it abysmally. I cannot understand your lapse, especially when only this morning you promised me to be chaste for the Company.'

'Oh sir! Believe me, when you are not here, I am off-hand to you to the point of rudeness. It is only your presence that affects me.'

'You must learn to control it, Miss Lefebvre. An ecstatic firm is not a happy firm, you know.'

'No, sir.'

The afternoon became golden and somnolent. The traffic in Piccadilly Circus had come to a standstill in the absence of the policeman, who was later found in a Trafalgar Square fountain waiting for colonials to go surfing. The owner of the cafe opposite brought chairs and tables out on the pavement, where they immediately disappeared into the pockets of passing French tourists. From multiple transistor wirelesses came the lilting rhythms of a drawn county cricket match. But I hardly paid attention, obsessed as I was with proving that I was second to none in my devotion to duty.

My chance came sooner than I expected. I was taking an afternoon stroll in the convent garden. The birds were singing in every bush and from the nunnery buildings came the soft murmur of a thousand vows of silence. Suddenly, a face appeared from behind a bush. It was a white hawthorn and Squire Jack Preston.

'Sister Lefebvre!' he said urgently. 'I have come to get thee from the nunnery. I have a pony and trap waiting without.'

Furiously, I produced my pad and pencil and wrote NO!

'Then at least come behind my hawthorn bush with me.'

'I am a Sister of God!' I wrote. 'Would you ask God to sell you His sister?'

His face darkened and he toyed with what was left of his moustache.

'You are right, Sister. I have sinned and see the error of my ways. I would deem it a favour if you were not to pass a memo on my lack of success to any third party.'

As the sound of his horse's hooves faded in the distance, I rejoiced that I had proved strong. Then I put away my things, covered up my typewriter for the week-end and hurried into the rush hour crowd.

Half an hour later I made my way on to Platform Three at Victoria, and there stood Mr Preston.

'My own!' he said. 'So you really came!'

'I really did,' I said.

'I have the tickets here in my pocket. I have reserved a compartment facing west to catch the setting sun and anything else of interest in that quarter. I have asked the attendant to put two gins and tonic on ice. Now all I need is your assurance and signature that you really truly wish to come with me.'

'Oh yes, Jack. Yes, yes, yes.'

'Miss Lefebvre, I'm afraid I must tell you that the Company has today decided to institute a new staff relations adequacy test. It is perhaps unfortunate that it should occur on a day in which you have already twice shown yourself unworthy of the firm, but it cannot be helped. I will be frank with you. You are fired.'

'Oh sir!'

'Yes, Miss Lefebvre?'

'I would just like to say that even if I am far from the Company, I will go on being faithful to it.'

'I think I speak for all of us if I say that the Company will go on loving you in its own way, Miss Lefebvre. So no hard feelings?'

'No, sir.'

'Good girl.'

He glanced at his watch.

'But look at the time! We'd better hurry if we're going to catch that train, my darling.'

Miles Kington 27.5.1970

'Be honest with me, John – is there another woman seeing you without your glasses on?'

'I'm going to feel terribly guilty, Mr
Dodsworth, if you tell me this means cutting
the firm's development programme.'

'Can't it wait until tomorrow, Simpson? I've been running
behind schedule all day, and I still have to ravish Miss Cooney.'

'Fortunately, it says less about me than an American
Express card ever can.'

CONQUISTADOR

A short story

And now here. Look. Friday, January 21, 6:15
pm. The dim, pinkly lit Costa del Sol Lounge
just off the main entrance of the Conquistador
Motor Inn in Bethel Park, a suburb 20 miles
north of Woodland. A solitary woman at the
bar, in a high-necked but backless dress. A
blonde woman. Attractive. Smoking a cigarette
thoughtfully. Not frowning, not melancholy or
troubled, but thoughtful. Mysterious. A woman
of substance. Character. Sitting at the nearly
deserted bar, pert and straight-backed and somehow provocative on one of the little leather
stools, her waist and hips clearly defined in the
clinging black silk dress, her naked back
defiantly white: a woman Edwin Locke has
never set eyes on before, smoking a cigarette
languidly and stirring the ice in her drink.

Look. It is happening as he has planned. As
he has rehearsed.

He enters the lounge hesitantly, almost
timidly, though he knows that his appearance,
this evening, is impressive (a new sports jacket,
brown with brass buttons, and new dark
trousers; his most attractive necktie, a beige
knit; his hair freshly cut, shampooed and blown
dry). A few of the patrons glance around, the
bartender gives him an indifferent appraisal, but
the woman does not seem to notice.

Edwin wonders. Is she alone at the Motor
Inn? Or is she simply awaiting a husband or an
escort? Or a lover? Sitting at the bar, waiting for

a man. Her lover, perhaps. A woman like that *would* have a lover. Lovers.

He sees with a small thrill of excitement that her left hand is ringless. (She is wearing an oversized dinner ring on her right hand, possibly a topaz. Is it in bad taste, or is it merely daring, a flamboyant gesture? It seems clear from the way she plays with the swizzle stick in her drink that she is an independent, perhaps even a somewhat spoiled woman.) Unmarried. Solitary. Very attractive – very. And so, timidly, and boldly, Edwin Locke approaches the bar. His silly heart is pounding. Veins at his temples are pounding.

The risk of it. Once again. The blind gasping plunge.

Cheerfully he has said to himself, up in the room, dabbing cologne on his throat, his jaw: What can I lose? What can I lose?

Ah, the woman *is* attractive. Heavily but skilfully made up. Sharply defined lips, very red. Stylish hair, wavy, shaved up the back of her slender neck. Tiny gold earrings for pierced ears. A somewhat snubbed nose. And that bare, palely gleaming back, the tiny knuckle-bones of vertebrae, a sight that Edwin finds mesmerizing, as if he has never seen anything like it before.

'Are you . . . May I join . . .'

He swallows his words miserably. So timid! Such a fool! The woman finally looks around, her lips parting damply, in expectation. Her carefully arched eyebrows register a cool, almost contemptuous curiosity. Edwin repeats his question, smiling like an adolescent boy, and the woman stares at him in silence. Her eyes are thickly outlined with black pencil, brightly keen. She is young. Well, fairly. A mature woman with a glowing, youthful, sensuous face. It is obvious from the way she sits at the bar, her breasts pressing against the leather rim, that she is a sensuous, experienced woman, a woman of mysterious substance and character. It is obvious that . . .

Edwin pulls a bar stool over. Sits. Sweating, smiling. He orders a scotch from the bored bartender, who is dressed in a toreador jacket. He asks the woman if she is alone. Or waiting for someone. Alone? Yes. Alone. Asks her what she is drinking. And would she like another. Yes? The lounge is quite attractive, isn't it. The black leather, the red and pink lampshades. The bullfighting motif in a bronze bas-relief above

the bar. The Conquistador itself is quite attractive, one of the newer motels in this area. The restaurant, they say, is quite adequate. Overpriced (aren't they all) but adequate.

The woman nods but her manner is still somewhat haughty, withdrawn. Edwin tries to think of something to say, to ask. He *could* inquire about her background: is she married, has she ever been married, has she any children, has she been, well, *wounded* by life, as he has? But she is so coolly remote, so tantalizingly distant. Ah, she knows him – she knows how to tease! He hears himself saying something about the weather. Ever since early December it's been so grim and cheerless, hasn't it. And that blizzard on New Year's Day. Funny, as you get older time is supposed to go more rapidly, and in many ways it *does* (now why in Christ's name am I saying this, Edwin wonders in dismay, but cannot stop, and cannot change the subject), but that isn't true of the weather, is it. In fact the winter seems to hang on forever.

'Yes. I suppose so,' the woman says neutrally.

What to say? He tries to remember what he has rehearsed. In his imagination the woman was far more acquiescent, her face was turned fully toward him, her lips and eyes melting . . . He fumbles in his pocket for cigarettes. But with an exquisitely casual gesture the woman pushes *her* pack toward him.

'Hey. Thanks. That's very sweet,' he whispers.

The woman's smile is wry and knowing. She is not young, nor is she pretty any longer, despite her clever make-up; but Edwin feels almost faint with excitement and apprehension. He leans toward her, smiling. He inhales her perfume with gratitude. Something musky, something very provocative. And the look of her naked back, the tiny bones appearing to shiver slightly beneath the fine, pale envelope of skin.

'You're very . . . You're . . .' He swallows suddenly. Has to fight an impulse to cough, 'a very attractive woman. *Very* attractive.'

Her nostrils widen as she draws in her breath, considering his remark. Then she says with admirable evenness: '*You're* a very attractive man.'

Edwin sips his drink. Says quickly: 'As soon as I came in the doorway I noticed you. And wanted you. I mean that – just the way it sounds.

I saw you sitting here and I wanted you, just like that. I'm the kind of man who . . . who . . . I'm the kind of man who knows what he likes, in a woman. Who is able to appreciate . . . who is able to appreciate a womanly woman. A woman who knows . . . who knows about certain things. Who isn't coy. Who isn't self-conscious. As soon as I saw you here I *knew*.'

The woman laughs lightly, but Edwin can see that he has startled her. 'Is that so,' she drawls.

'I imagine you know what you want too. In a man. I imagine you aren't shy about . . . about expressing yourself,' Edwin says softly.

Half-closes his eyes. Waits. What will happen next, what *should* happen next? He is quite excited. The woman is too, or should be. Sexual tension: unmistakable. The way she is sitting . . . the way she avoids his eye. She *should* be excited. Is. Is excited. Must try to imagine the sensations arising in her, in the pit of her belly, between her thighs, would it be an ache, would it be a nervous tingling feeling, a sense of . . . of yearning . . .? Yearning to be filled? Completed? By him? By *him*?

He lights a cigarette. Bloody damn nuisance: has to flick the lighter several times before a flame catches. One two three four *five*.

She lifts her glass. Drains it in one long swallow.

'A woman like you, with a . . . a body like yours . . . a mature, sensuous, *knowing* . . .'

'Mature?'

'Experienced. Widely and, and variedly . . . and knowledgeably experienced.'

The woman considers his words, staring at the glass in her hand. Edwin sees that her fingernails have been painted a dramatic golden-bronze. How odd, how beguiling a colour! He doesn't think he has ever seen it before, close up, on a real woman, a *real* person. 'And you,' she whispers, 'what about you?'

'Me? Oh. Well. *Me*,' Edwin says, going blank for a moment. 'I am . . . I am the kind of man . . . I am the kind of man, honey, who knows what he likes. I mean I can appreciate . . . I can *see* . . . Well, there are things that another man might not notice, but . . . I have had some interesting experiences with women. Some very, very interesting experiences.'

'Have you,' she says, a trifle sharply. And then, in a more subdued throaty voice: 'Oh.

Have you.'

'And the one thing I learned, the one thing I absolutely learned, was . . . the one thing I am in fact *still* learning . . . is that a woman's sensuality is far deeper and more complex and . . . and astonishing . . . and even alarming . . . than a man's. This is something all men should –'

'Alarming, why? Did you say alarming?'

'Astonishing. Amazing. Just fantastic,' Edwin says, shaking his head. 'I mean *fantastic. You* know what I mean.'

The woman giggles suddenly. 'I'm not sure if I do.'

'Yes, you do. *You* know.'

'Do I?'

'With a, a body like yours . . . Those hips and . . . and breasts . . . Your mouth . . . oh you know, you know,' he says, giggling himself, trying hard to resist a sudden spasm of coughing. 'I mean it stands out. It announces itself. Why, as soon as I came in the door, the doorway, as soon as my gaze fastened on . . . Well I mean I knew. I just knew. And,' he says lowering his voice, trembling, 'I wanted you. In that instant.'

'Did you. Did you really,' the woman says.

'Obviously. Can't you tell?'

'Another drink?'

'Yes. Certainly. What time is it?'

'Early.'

'Early . . . Fine. Another drink. Two more, in fact. And then, do you think we might, do you think you'd enjoy . . . well, coming upstairs with me?'

'To your room?'

'To my room. Where we can continue our discussion in privacy.'

'But we hardly know each other. I don't even know your name.'

'Is that important? Are names so important to you?'

She smirks. No, it is a smile, a frightened little smile.

'No. Of course not. You should be able to tell that, just by looking at me,' she says slowly, vaguely.

'The room is a very attractive one. In fact it's a honeymoon suite, I believe . . . At a special discount.'

'What sort of discount?'

'A sunken bathtub, of marble, an enormous

heart-shaped bed, a dozen pillows, a thick plush rug, lamps with shades of pink and scarlet, flowers, fresh flowers, and candles and incense. And on closed-circuit television, if we should want it, certain films, certain frankly *erotic* films . . . as the advertising brochure says. But I don't really think, do you, that we will need such things,' Edwin says breathlessly.

'Is there music? There must be music,' the woman says, blushing faintly.

'I think so. Yes. Piped-in. Throbbing and sensual. Spanish, I think. Spanish flamenco. I think.'

'But we don't know each other. We don't know each other's *name*.'

Edwin laughs, raising his glass in a toast. His laughter becomes wheezing but he manages to get it under control. 'Name? Why? Such an outmoded convention . . . And you don't look at all like a conventional woman.'

'Maybe I'm not. But still.'

'Beneath your clothes, for instance.'

'Beneath what? Why?'

'In your flesh. In your skin. *There* you aren't a conventional woman, are you? But all women. Sharing in their secrets . . .'

She giggles suddenly. Finishes her drink. 'And now,' Edwin says. 'Now. I think it's about time, don't you?'

'Well –'

'I *think* it's about time we adjourned to room 255.'

'Do you have the key?'

'Of course,' Edwin says, patting his pocket. The key is attached to an oversized Spanish coin of plastic; he slipped it into his pocket on the way down. But though his fingers fully expect to touch the key they come away baffled. 'That is I think . . .'

The woman snatches up her purse. Opens it. Takes out a compact. Dabs at her nose with a powder puff, rather impatiently. 'Have you lost the key?' she asks.

'It's here somewhere. It must be,' Edwin mutters. He searches the pockets of his sports coat. Odd. Very odd. He tries his trouser pockets. No? But where? *Is* it lost? Did someone pick his pocket on the way down? Or? 'Oh Christ,' he says, 'I put it in my other coat. I was going to wear my other coat . . . Not that it matters, of course. I can pick another key up at the front desk.'

The woman closes her purse with an angry snap. Edwin sees, surprised, that her expression is stiff with bemused contempt. 'Can you?' she whispers. 'Can you really?'

'What do you mean? I don't . . . I don't understand . . .'

'Tonight of all nights. Deliberately. And you're drunk, aren't you. You were drinking before you met me. And you saw to it that I'm drunk. Didn't you. And that tie – the dry cleaner never got that gravy stain out of it, can't you see? Can't you for God's sake *see*? I thought I'd thrown that thing out years ago but somehow you still *have* it, you must have *hoarded* it . . .' She begins to cry, her shoulders shaking, her face distorted. Tonight of all nights. Oh Edwin, *tonight of all nights.*'

'But . . . but . . . But I can pick up another key at the front desk, can't I?' Edwin asks, astonished.

Joyce Carol Oates 8.11.1978

'Be quiet, James – I am talking to the floozie. Now then, floozie! Is this your idea of sisterly behaviour?'

My husband is the kind of man no one notices when he enters a room.'

Harpur:
A BIT ON THE SIDE

'Good evening, sir, are we seeing tonight, or being seen?'

'I'm glad we don't live in Iran; a cigarette afterwards beats being stoned to death any day.'

'Well, you're a better cook than my wife, but **still** not quite as good as Mum.

'Whoever she is she's devoted; I keep finding lipstick on his shoes.'

'Darling!'

'We've decided to stay together for your sake.'

'That may be so but I bet he's not better at mowing the lawn . . .'

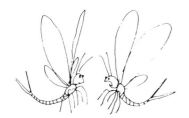

'. . . And to think I've given you the best seconds of my life.'

'Now let's get this straight – you're having an affair **with** the DPP.'

MARRIED MEN – WILL THEY EVER DIE OUT?

The married man is the bane of the single girl. He belongs to a particularly predatory and cunning species that preys upon the unsuspecting, unprotected female. (Very few of us, in fact, get safely through to matrimony unscathed.)

The main trouble is that the married man in full cry is often so much more attractive than the single one. He has to be, of course. After all, he is not in it for amusement, he is in it for real profit. He has no time to waste and everything to lose. And he knows so well the incalculable value of the tender word, the unexpected considerateness.

However boorish the Married Man may be at his own hearthside, he is all thoughtfulness when on safari for big game at, say, a cocktail party. Note the quick 'Here, let me hold that heavy ashtray' of the man who can sit unperturbed while his wife staggers past him with a loaded coal scuttle.

Scrabbling for his next toe-hold after the ashtray ploy, he may use one of the banal but successful follow-ups, such as, 'You are that rare combination, a stimulating conversationalist and a sympathetic listener.' Compared with the arrogant, take-me-or-leave-me-for-the-next-lucky-girl attitude of the bachelor, this is fairly heady stuff.

When it is time to go, the M.M. sends his wife upstairs to fetch her wrap, gives his victim's hand a quick, furtive pressure, and murmurs, 'I must see you again. May I ring you?'

This is the point of no return. Clearly, what the victim should do is smile and say briskly, 'That would be nice. I'd love to see you and your wife again,' but it is surprising how rarely this happens.

Still smarting from the bachelors' disdain and flattered by the urgency in the eyes of this absolutely charming man, she is more apt to murmur her telephone number. Some have even been known to rummage in their handbags for pencil and paper but these are girls who cannot wait for fate to make the decisions, rather older girls, perhaps, who know that their only chance is to catch some man on the second time around.

Once the M.M. has secured the telephone number he has scored a tactical advantage. By surrendering it, in a low voice which her hostess cannot hear, she has revealed her willingness to go on to the next stage. She fully intends that the next stage will be the last. A pleasant dinner somewhere, good food in amusing company, an intelligent choice of wines and words, perhaps a nudge of a knee under the table or a brushing of fingers on the tablecloth. Afterwards, a handclasp, or perhaps a kiss on the cheek, then home alone in a taxi, feeling dreamy and warm and pleasantly desirable.

Naturally it does not turn out like this. There is, if not a sordid fight, an argument, unless her particular M.M. is one of the more patient ones who is prepared to wait until a third meeting before cornering the victim for a kill.

The chosen restaurant is inclined to be somewhere rather dark and unfashionable, where the waiters are known for their indifference. My own sister was once persuaded into going to the theatre and on to dinner with an M.M. Whether or not she was trembling on the brink of an indiscretion I do not know but whatever romantic and foolhardy notions she may have been harbouring died a quiet death when, during every interval of the play and afterwards as they dined and danced, her M.M. insisted on wearing dark glasses.

The M.M. is especially dangerous because he knows what pleases a woman and what does not. He is aware, for instance, that to comment on her dress, even unfavourably, is infinitely better policy than to ignore it. A most successful M.M. who is shared by two very dear friends of mine is fond of saying things like, 'I wonder if that style will ever come back into fashion,' and 'Those Tate and Lyle sugar bags do make up remarkably well, don't they?' and 'I must say this new Holloway uniform is very serviceable.'

The victim is not used to the solicitude of the M.M. For years she has been shivering on wind-raked rugger pitches and crossing roads all by herself and drinking beer out of chipped mugs.

She has become resigned to the expected date who never arrives, the promised phone call that never comes, the three-weeks-late birthday card, the casual escort who meets the boys and forgets that he came in with a girl. So the compliments of the M.M. fall upon fertile ground, and often bear fruit.

But the deadliest of the species is the ex-M.M., or the semi-ex-M.M. This carnivore has the polish, the know-how, the gambling fever and the set-up.

The ex-M.M. is never short of a quick answer. Find a hair-pin on his pillow and he will exclaim, 'Damn that slovenly cleaning woman. She'll have to go!' Discover an ear-ring down his armchair and he will say sadly 'So that's what happened to it. I gave them to my wife just before she left me. She flung them in my face.'

The ex-M.M.'s ex-wife is a shrew. Whereas the M.M. has to restrain himself to 'We don't hate each other, we just go our separate ways' or even the still-popular 'She doesn't understand me,' the ex-M.M., having successfully disposed of his, can paint her any colour he likes.

The ex-wife is invariably a spendthrift, a nagger, an iceberg, a fiend. She has left the ex-M.M. just disillusioned enough to be a challenge, yet not beyond saving by a beautiful emotional experience.

The M.M. has only one advantage over the more resourceful ex-M.M. The M.M.'s wife is excellent protection. 'My wife and I are through but we stay together because of the boy. Whatever happens, he mustn't suffer,' murmured in a grave voice and delivered with a candid look provides him with a handy escape route.

The ex-M.M. may have to fall back on a sudden business trip abroad, or even an unexpected plea from a humble wife who wants to 'try again'. This is much less convenient, for business trips cannot last for ever and make-believe reconciliations are a strain on the imagination.

Although the pace is gruelling and the risk enormous, the M.M. often remains active well into his sixties. He becomes, if anything, more deadly as he matures. It must be the practice.

Sally Hurst 20.9.1961

'*Peggy, it's me. I've left my wife.*'

'*Let me say this, Jennifer, in parting. If you can't appreciate the love of a mature person, you'll just have to run along and play with the other children.*'

*'That's fascinating, George. I had no idea
the ancient Etruscans were polygamous.
Thank you! Now suppose you tell me who
she is.'*

BACHELOR'S SOUP

Make no mistake, as Primavera once again
strokes the crocus bulbs into new life, a bachelor
is a wonderful thing to be. Look at the Pope.

Being a bachelor, I stress, whatever image of
sulky, kohl-rimmed eyes and high-uplift but-
tocks in pink needlecord churning mesmerically
along in the twilight of the Old King's Road the
word may conjure up in the contemporary mind,
is the very essence of masculinity. Light and
sprightly, Samson before Delilah got the shears
out, ready on a roll of drums to explode Houdini-
like out of the chains and padlocks of any
emotional entanglement and land graceful and
poised to a touch on the cymbals, ready for fresh
feats, bright-eyed and unencumbered: he travels
fastest who travels alone.

He may ultimately, to quote whatever fop in a
curly wig and frilly furbelows said it in the first
place, by degrees dwindle into a husband, but as
a practising bachelor he is God before the Creation, Michelangelo up the ladder with a drip-
ping brush and a bare ceiling, Man before the

Fall, enjoying the Golden Age of the Imagination before the miseries of commitment.

Not so Big Doris in the Typing Pool. She has
plumped, as they say in the restaurant reviews,
for the *Papabili Piccolini Cosa Nostra di Arthur
Mullard* at £4.95 without the vegetables.

The bachelor feels pain, somewhere long ago
and far away, like a patient under the anaes-
thetic vaguely aware that an extraction has
occurred. Because the restaurant, the bachelor's
natural habitat, is the place where he has come
to escape that kind of thing. Here he is, leather-
bound menu open in front of him, a familiar
prop in his Sophisticated Perusal act, eyebrows
half lifted, eyes being dragged back like dogs on
the leash from looking at the right-hand column
where the prices are: Lugosi the Head Waiter
hangs hunched like a question-mark, pencil
licked over his order-pad, his mobile face turned
aside to semaphore a welcome of fiendish intensity to the well-dressed couple at the door. The
bachelor could not be in a more characteristic
and contented attitude: the choice unmade,
every possibility left open, lips pursed, about to
ask how the quails are tonight, and Big Doris has
taken the high dive into the *Papabili Piccolini
Cosa Nostra*. So.

The bachelor is not entirely certain that he
likes Big Doris anyway. Were he in the position
of his married friends, sitting down at this
moment to a nourishing supper at one tenth the
cost of Big Doris's main course without the
vegetables, he would probably have settled for
half an hour of *Charlie's Angels* and the News.
Then after lunch Big Doris reached out for the
Tippex, the lift of a breast in a sweater, and here
we are. There is also something wrong about
supper assembled out of familiar cupboards,
however easily, between the evening paper and
bathing the baby or between one nervous breakdown and the next, inevitable and too much
like real life.

For the Prospero and sole inhabitant of his
heterosexual fairy-land, the bachelor's dinner
has to materialise, like the cloud-capp'd towers
and indeed the great Globe itself, by magic. No
squabbles with Big Doris or anybody else about
who Brillo-pads the burnt saucepan, no guilt, no
crinkly fingers, so the restaurant.

This is after all the prelude to the bachelor's
greatest unpainted ceiling of all, the wide-screen

extravaganza in teeth-jarring Sensurround, in which Big Doris falls a victim to the Thousand Loving Thrusts, the Congress of the Mad Gorilla, or whatever else the Manual may recommend for afterwards. Admittedly the first time Doris said she wasn't feeling very well and thought she ought to have an early night, and on the last occasion her mother was staying. No matter. No grim edge of reality must be allowed to protrude in this opening movement of the fantasia, the heady gastronomic helter-skelter ride that will unlock the gentle floodgates of lust, even in Big Doris. The bachelor, like God before the Creation, is an optimist.

Lugosi takes the order, and after various patronising enquiries from the bachelor about Lugosi's wife and children, clicks his heels, inclines his head with a little knowing turn of the chin, and vanishes.

Patronising is the key word. There is only one *patron*, in the bachelor's scheme of things, who *mange ici*. Every night of the year, in some dream-palace or another: paying single-handed for the roof to be rebuilt, for Lugosi to perform as Court Chamberlain, for what his bank-manager would recognise, in terms of personal economics, as a three-dimensional fiction.

Few women, oddly enough, going to a restaurant of their own accord, would dream of treating Lugosi – a man who by daylight no-one would risk having in the house even to read the gas-meter – like a long-lost friend, or going through the grisly old charade with the wine-list: but then few women are to be found dressing up in dirty macs to cluster round the Explicit Films Books and Mags. Men are the masters when it comes to works of the imagination – witness Beethoven, Bach etcetera – and the imagination from time to time needs shoring up. Hence the insane expense of the restaurant, where the bachelor for a brief moment every night can be acknowledged Lord of the Manor.

Admittedly the decor may not be exactly what he would choose for his own dining room, which he could build three times over for the money he spends in a year: admittedly the company he finds there, even overlooking Lugosi and his band of two-faced thieves, is of the kind he would, in his right mind, pay good money to avoid sharing a taxi with, let alone eat with. And Big Doris is about to break the news

about her boy-friend arriving on the eleven ten from Inverness.

Standing on the pavement, with all the glory gone, can it ever occur to him that somewhere in a darkened bedroom, mere mounds under the bedclothes, his married friends, the fortunate fools, are fast asleep? And that it might be time, even for Prospero, to break his magic wand and get down to a bit of serious Dwindling?

John Wells 21.3.1979

'Hello, George – remember you said that although I was going to marry Martin James you'd always be waiting for me if ever I should change my mind?'

'If you're thinking of waking the sleeping princess with a kiss, mate, you're a bit too late.'

THE AGONY AND THE ECSTASY

Love's the name of the game, handsome. And you're looking at the girl who knows all the rules. I guess you're wondering how an individual of my obvious refinement ever got into this line of work. Don't worry, big boy, I know time is money (who knows that better than me?) so I'll make it short and sweet. Let's just say that one night a few years ago I heard myself yet again telling someone I'd just met what to do about her husband's infidelities ('Develop a hobby of your own,' I told her, 'or take up hospital visiting'), when suddenly I was granted a revelation.

'Kurtz,' says I to myself, 'why not start getting paid for what you've always been giving away free?'

Now, my advice column is syndicated in two English-speaking countries, if you count America; and I am often invited to pontificate on television or make impertinent comments about the private lives of celebrities I've never met. It is to me they come: the frigid and the febrile, the homo, hetero, and bi, the burgeoning, the sterile, the flat-chested, the broad-beamed, the hirsute and the bald. Gee, but they weigh me down.

In America I'm called a Miss Lonelyhearts and in Britain I'm an Agony Aunt. This difference makes sense to me. The American women who write to me are almost all looking for a man. The English women are frequently trying to get rid of one. Sometimes I dream I have a magic wand to wave that will send all the unwanted husbands of Britain to all the unmated women of America (and, while it's at it, maybe it could deliver a smattering of Bristol's 38D to 32A of Bournemouth). If I ruled the world, imagine all the good I could do! For a start, I would not allow any but the middle-aged ever to get married, and even then only if they solemnly swore they were *not* in love.

'In love,' I tell my ladies, 'is for making love, but not for getting married!'

Love has ruined more marriages than hell has hot sinners. As a matter of fact, to be in love is the human equivalent of being on heat: it is to be temporarily obsessed, driven, befuddled, astigmatic and trembling much too hard to tie a safe knot.

You'd think people would know that by now, wouldn't you? But the purple torrent keeps pouring across my desk: 'Why doesn't he love me?', 'Why don't I love him?', 'If he really loved me, wouldn't he stop snoring?', 'Why shouldn't he leave his paraplegic wife and their three handicapped kids? After all, we *are* in love.' Love, love, love! Speaking as an Agony Aunt, I can only say, 'Phooey!' Love is a villain. And marriage is only one of the crimes love commits. Divorce is another. Infidelity is a third. But the worst of all is stupidity.

'Dear Worried of Liverpool, you tell me he swears he loves only you and he hasn't slept with his wife in six years. He would leave her tomorrow, you say, but his two-year-old twins need him and another baby is due next month. Never mind, Worried, you're fortunate to have such a good career. Women brain surgeons are few and far between.'

I'm afraid I have to admit to you that my American readers are sillier about love than the others. Maybe it's all the red food colouring. Probably, it's cholesterol. American women in love who write to me throw around words like 'eternity' and 'forever' as if there were no tomorrow. They have this cock-eyed notion that men and women are put on earth like nuts and bolts: each must connect with the only perfect other to make a sort of cosmic screw. You would not believe the messes Americans get into pursuing their fantasy ideal. Why, the very first American letter I received in my professional capacity was from a woman who had shot three holes in her husband. Why? Because she no longer loved him. This, you will agree, is a fairly extreme expression of disenchantment. Up to then, I had seen only British letters and the most awful thing any Englishwoman had done to her man was read Germaine Greer aloud to him in bed.

'Dear Hapless of Hoboken, surely you knew when you married your handsome long-distance truck driver you would have to spend many nights alone. I'm afraid you must accept your part of the bargain. As for the other problem you mention in your letter, couldn't you ask your husband nicely if he'd mind buying his own silk panties?'

And this, if I do say so myself, brings us rather neatly to *sex*. 'Good old sex,' you're thinking, aren't you? 'Where would we be without it?'

Let me tell you, from where I sit, we'd be a lot better off. In my opinion, binary fission would be an altogether neater and friendlier way for us to procreate. Think of it. Have you ever heard an amoeba go into a song and dance about sexual jealousy? I doubt it. Everything in nature does it better than we. Do carp complain about premature ejaculation? Has there ever been a feathered flasher? Do you know any poodle feeling the need to come out of the closet? Does a lion read *Mayfair*? Does a kangaroo save herself for her wedding night? Who has met a cockroach into leather? Do apes need agony aunts? No. No. No. And certainly not. Yet, in front of me at this moment are letters ostensibly from human beings, and each of them was inspired by one of the above problems; one of them, by all but one of them. Here too, Americans take the biscuit. You name it and some lass in Salt Lake City regrets doing it, or can't stop doing it, or is dying to do it. The British, on the other hand, often have the good sense to wonder whether any of it is really worth doing at all.

'Dear Depressed of Carlisle, I am sorry to hear about your inability to have "organisms". I wonder if it would help to learn how to spell them? If your failure to make it continues, maybe you would like to make something else, instead? A soufflé, for instance. Many women find this equally satisfying and easier to achieve.'

By and large, it seems that English women manage their sex lives with more dignity and control than their sisters over the water. To be absolutely fair, I must grant that many Americans have special disadvantages in life. Some of them, for example, live in Detroit. One American woman who wrote to me complaining that she was frigid had my earnest and worried sympathy until I looked at the postmark on her envelope. I'll bet you never knew there was a town in Georgia called 'Climax'.

Well, good-looking, that's my story and I hope you're satisfied. I'm in the love-trade. Love pays my rent and love puts my little boy through school. (Did I tell you I had a little boy? We'll save that for another time, right, Johnny?) If ever you need me, just whistle. Or better still, drop me a line.

Irma Kurtz 8.2.1984

'I said, "And that's another thing I can't stand – the way he slurps his tea".'

'We've decided against divorce. Neither of us wants custody of the dog.'

'See what I mean? No sense of humour.'

SINGLE-MINDED
HANDELSMAN goes it alone

*'I wish I was single again, again,
I wish I was single again,
For when I was single,
My pockets did jingle,
I wish I was single again.
Present company excepted, of course.'*

*'After that? Well, Prince Charming and
Sleeping Beauty stayed together a
little while for the sake of the kids,
then got a divorce and lived
happily ever after.'*

*'Marry if you must, Gwendolyn, but in
twenty-five years you'll find yourself
washing socks for some pompous ass.'*

'You mean you haven't **got** a wife? You seemed so frustrated and lecherous and miserable, I just naturally assumed you had one.'

'You're still waiting for the right woman to come along? Good God, man, if we all waited for the right woman . . .'

'Yes, I feel very sorry for you single people. It must be awful, going home every night and having nobody to fight with.'

'Do you ever get this nostalgic longing to be lonely and unfulfilled?'

'Well, Frederick, you always wanted to be single again, and now you are.'

PURITAN BACKLASH

Very soon the pendulum is likely to swing away from permissiveness. PUNCH is horrified to provide some extracts from a new wave encyclopedia which show the completeness of the reaction.

Charles II: One of the kindest of British monarchs. No trouble was too great to bestow on even such humble subjects as an orange girl at the theatre. Not all the objects of his interest were of lowly birth and his court was, indeed, noted for its duchesses.

Chastity, Girdle of: Award given to nuns for exceptional purity.

Chatterley: The Chatterley family are the centre of a society novel by D. H. Lawrence. Sir Clifford had been wounded in the war and his wife nursed him devotedly on their Nottinghamshire estate. Lady Chatterley was much beloved by the servants, especially the gamekeeper, Mellors, who would wheel the invalid round the countryside and always did what he could to make up to his mistress for her rather lonely life. A real character, he liked to pick wildflowers for Lady Chatterley to use for decoration and did a great deal to make time pass quickly for her. It was a similar relationship to that of Mr Pickwick and Sam Weller, though Mellors was less gay and amusing, if deeper.

Cleopatra: Patriotic and beautiful queen of Egypt. She married first Julius Caesar and then Mark Antony. When he was defeated in battle and fell on his sword, she felt that a wife's place was by her husband's side, in the next world as in this, and, very reprehensibly, followed his example and committed suicide.

Decameron: Book of tales by Boccaccio, supposed to be told by a group of friends escaping from the plague in Florence. They deal with pirates, trickery and practical jokes. The emphasis is on good manners.

Desdemona: In Shakespeare's tragedy, Othello, a general at Venice, is wrongly persuaded by an evil subordinate, Iago, that his wife, Desdemona, is betraying his plans to the enemy and executes her himself. The plot is supposed to have been revealed when she dropped a handkerchief, prepared by Iago, with a plan of the Venetian forts embroidered on it.

Dilke, Sir Charles: Victorian politician who fell from power because he refused to give evidence against a friend.

Eden: On being created in the Garden of Eden, Adam's first act was to sew himself a long robe, with underdrawers, from fig leaves. Immediately on her arrival, Eve did likewise. She was just beginning to sew for the animals, when the expulsion from Paradise occurred and henceforward the beasts went naked.

Gloucester: Cathedral city. Site of famous limerick:
> There was a Young Lady of Gloucester
> Whose parents both feared they had lost her.
> They found on the grass
> A ring made of brass
> From the nose of a bull that had tossed her.

Goat, The: Nickname of the wartime premier Lloyd George. So-called by politicians because of his surefooted agility in handling tricky problems.

Hamilton, Lady: Nelson's second wife, the widow of an Ambassador and scholar. Emma Hamilton played a leading part in the Admiral's career, giving him encouragement in many ways and providing the great sailor with the domestic life he needed. She frequently accompanied him to sea and was at his side when he died with the words, 'Kiss me, Emma.'

Héloise and Abélard: Héloise was the pretty niece of a Canon of Paris. She fell in love with her tutor, the brilliant young philosopher Abélard, and he with her. Because it was not considered right for the clergy to marry, they had to remain just good friends. Unhappily the Canon became jealous of the friendship and hired ruffians who tried Abélard's Christian charity severely. However, they did not impair his intellectual brilliance and all turned out for the best, with both of the friends at the head of religious institutions, Abélard a famous author and Héloise one of his most loyal readers.

Hill, Fanny: Heroine of an eighteenth-century novel. Reflected in her artless prattle we see the life of the period close to, its commerce, houses, tables and beds. Fanny had a great love of fun and she is the ancestress of all the lively girls we meet in the pages of Scott, Jane Austen and Thackeray. Generous, enthusiastic and accomplished, she shows the century at its most attractive.

Juan, Don: Spanish grandee and traveller. Many well-known plays and operas have been written about this lively character. He married the daughter of the Governor of Ulloa. When his father-in-law died, a statue of him was erected. On Don Juan's Silver Wedding anniversary, the guests assembled at a great banquet. What was their surprise to hear a knocking and see the statue enter and sit down at the feast: the Governor's affection had extended beyond the grave!

Nell, Eskimo: Heroine of ballad celebrating her exploits cf. *Barbara Frietchie, Clementine, The Lady of Shalott.*

Rabelais: French comic novelist and leading figure in history of medicine and science. His work is largely concerned with eating and drinking.

Spanish Fly: The drug cantharis, said in legend to unite lovers.

Stopes, Dr Marie: Pioneer of action to preserve world food resources.

Ward, Stephen: Osteopath.

Wife-swapping: Old English game in which players exchange their wives, who have to cook a meal for their new 'husbands'. Often the game ends with all returning happily to their lawful mates.

Wilde, Oscar: Wit, poet and dramatist. Towards the end of his life he fell foul of the tyrannical Marquess of Queensberry whose son, Lord Alfred Douglas, Wilde had tried to protect from his bullying father. The Marquess made many unkind remarks about Wilde, who had to sue him for libel to stop his cruel tongue.

Unhappily, Wilde's enemies, including some politicians jealous of his popularity, took revenge by accusing him of stealing from a number of young men whom he had befriended. Wilde was convicted and sent to prison, where he wrote a poem which made it famous. Indeed, without Wilde's ballad would anybody ever have heard of Reading Gaol? So some good came from the sad episode after all.

Zeus: Chief of the Greek Gods. He enjoyed playing pranks on girls, using his magic powers to disguise himself as a bull or a swan or a shower of gold. However, sooner or later the maidens usually found him out.

R. G. G. Price 7.1.1970

WOULDN'T TOUCH IT WITH A BARGE POLE

Of course the *real* disease has yet to be identified but I predict it will get much, much worse. This is just the tip of the iceberg. Ninety per cent of it is under water, leaching its vile aromatic immoralities into the murky waters of our, our, that's the trouble with metaphors, once you start them off, as it were unto a swallow which, flitting into a hall from the outer darkness, wherein men are feasting and singing, like unto a great ox which seeth not the axeman's blade which, like a thundery storm, poised to descend, um, anyway, there you are. The point is that there are going to be more articles about AIDS, if American experience is anything to go by.

Two years ago, only three journalists in America were known writers of AIDS pieces. The exact number of carriers is unknown, but statistics suggest that, for every journalist who actually writes an AIDS piece, up to six others may be harbouring ideas for AIDS pieces.

The exact point at which the carrier becomes

'active' is relatively easy to pinpoint. Early symptoms include drinking, laughing and sitting around sharpening pencils. Later on, the sufferer may go to the pub and make jokes about the subject, but this is rarely a prolonged stage. The first true symptoms include inexplicable gloom, the inability to articulate the words 'shirt-lifter' and a tendency to sit in the dark doodling viral forms on Kleenex.

I am often asked 'When should one start to avoid a journalist who one suspects may be harbouring an AIDS article?' This is a difficult question. The overriding concern must be to avoid exposure. The most common form of transmission is through media *of any sort*, but it must be clearly understood that this is a mind-borne disease, and contact with *any* of the victim's mental processes must be eschewed until we know for sure that there is no risk. Even the most seemingly-innocuous social contact can carry a hidden risk, and the most non-committal inquiries, such as 'Hi! How ya doin'?' can precipitate the transmission of infected thought droplets.

High-risk groups should definitely be avoided if at all possible. These include ANY journalist who has, within the past five years, been a medical correspondent. Please note that even apparently normal journalists may have at some time or another written medical articles; unless you are absolutely sure, stay clear. If you *cannot* avoid such contacts, at least practise SAFE TALK. It is all very well to use 'modern' methods of thought control, such as drink or television, but these do not offer full protection. Old-fashioned rubber or wax plugs, inserted BEFORE SOCIAL INTERCOURSE and not removed until AFTER THE CLIMAX of the conversation (which can be recognised by the presumptive carrier saying glumly, 'Of course it could wipe out mankind, you know. We could be in for the Big One, this time') will prevent most of the dangerous mental processes entering into the partner's thoughtstream. Despite all these precautions, can you still become infected? The answer must, I fear, be 'Yes'. You will not necessarily be aware that you are a carrier, however, nor is it easy to identify the source. Again, it is necessary to state the obvious: THIS PLAGUE IS NOT CONFINED TO THE OBVIOUS GROUPS. That friendly clergyman in the village may be carrying in his head a letter

"Happy, darling?"

to *The Times*; your local schoolmaster may be a part-time St John's Ambulanceman, and may *even as we speak* be contemplating a brief monograph in the Parish Magazine . . . the Parish Magazine published by the *very same vicar* who is contemplating a fling with *The Times*. You can see how it spreads.

Nobody is immune. Take the tragic case of the aptly-named 'Willie' Whitelaw, a man of distinction in his career, of public prominence, widely respected. Yet even he had a fatal flaw: he haunted the promiscuous and over-heated atmosphere of Parliament, perhaps the most immoral and flagrant of all London's talking-shops, where infected thoughts were exchanged without heed for the consequences. The disease as always took time to incubate; yet only recently it burst forth in its most virulent form. The result is public scorn and a ruined life.

The bitter truth is that nobody is safe, from the humblest sub-editor to the greatest foreign correspondent. Television pundits, with their lax morals and constant seeking after cheap thrills, are most at risk, yet even staid, almost fusty, people can fall victim. You might think,

'Yes, but I am all right; I work for the *Daily Telegraph* and have remained faithful to the same ideology all my life; there is no risk for *me*,' but can you be *sure*?

To sum up, then:

1) Avoid contact with core carriers, medical correspondents, television journalists and similar groups. They are ALMOST CERTAINLY carrying AIDS articles and some may even have been confirmed as published.

2) Do not indulge in casual conversation with anyone unless you are *sure* that they are not harbouring ideas.

3) Use old-fashioned protective methods BEFORE CONVERSATION BEGINS. Once the subject has been entered, it is TOO LATE.

4) Now wash your hands.

No, really, it's all very well making jokes, but this is all serious. I'm only sending it up because what else can you do? I mean, this could be the end of . . . OH MY GOD. I HAVE GOT IT. I AM CARRYING AN AIDS ARTICLE, OH GOD. EXCUSE ME . . .

Michael Bywater 19.11.1986